COMPARATIVE POLITICAL INQUIRY

A Methodological Survey

THE DORSEY SERIES IN POLITICAL SCIENCE

Comparative Political Inquiry

A Methodological Survey

LAWRENCE C. MAYER

Assistant Professor of Government
Texas Tech University

1972

The Dorsey Press   *Homewood, Illinois   60430*
IRWIN-DORSEY LIMITED   *Georgetown, Ontario*

First Printing, March 1972

Library of Congress Catalog Card No. 75–187062

Printed in the United States of America

To MARILYN—Who encouraged and helped
To MAURY—Who delightfully distracted
and
To MOM and DAD—Who inspired

Preface

In this book I attempt to present a critical survey of the major substantive and analytical work in the field of comparative politics. Because so much of the activity in comparative politics since World War II has the ostensible goal of being "scientific," I am deriving the standards for such a critical approach from a summary and interpretation of the scientific method and an examination of how applicable this method is to the study of political variables.

The justification for a restatement of the principles of the scientific method, in view of the increasing proliferation of methodology books,[1] begins with my perhaps presumptuous belief that these principles can be made more intelligible to most undergraduates. Furthermore, they should be stated concisely so that the student can extract what is necessary for his development as a political scientist without becoming a full-fledged philosopher of science. Most existing works are addressed to a very sophisticated audience and presume a prior familiarity with the terminology of the philosophy of science. Moreover this is, to my knowledge, the first attempt to integrate these principles into a survey of the major substantive and analytical work in comparative politics.

The outline of the methodology of science which comprises Part I is intended to provide a relatively precise and consistent set of standards for evaluating the literature which is surveyed in Parts II and III. Inasmuch as the principles of methodology of modern comparative politics are not

---

[1] The principal examples are Abraham Kaplan, *The Conduct of Inquiry* (San Francisco: Chandler Publishing Co., 1964); Eugene Meehan, *The Theory and Method of Political Analysis* (Homewood, Ill.: The Dorsey Press, 1965); Eugene Meehan, *Contemporary Political Thought: A Critical Study* (Homewood, Ill.: The Dorsey Press, 1967); Richard Rudner, *Philosophy of Social Science* (Englewood Cliffs, N.J.: Prentice-Hall, 1966); Alan C. Isaak, *Scope and Methods of Political Science* (Homewood, Ill.: The Dorsey Press, 1969); and George Graham, *Methodological Foundations for Political Analysis* (Waltham, Mass.: Xerox College Publishing, 1971).

fundamentally distinct from those of political science as a whole, Part I is, to a large extent, generally applicable to the entire field of political science. The survey of the literature, beginning in Part II, introduces the field of comparative politics as distinct from general political science. I have attempted, wherever possible, to use examples from comparative politics in Part I and thus to anticipate some of the problems of comparative politics. Nevertheless, it should be kept in mind that Part I, as its title implies, is a summary of methodology.

This foundation is necessary, in my judgment, because many or most students approach the field of comparative analysis without a great deal of methodological competence. Yet it is difficult to discuss the literature of that field intelligently without a thorough understanding of the methodological assumptions which underline the directions the field has taken in recent years.

For the student who already has acquired such a methodological competence, or for the instructor who considers a discussion of methodology, as such, extraneous to a course on comparative politics, the text is designed to make it possible to begin with Chapter 6. The references back to Part I which are found throughout Parts II and III will enable the reader who elects such a course of action to take account of those aspects of Part I which are either unfamiliar or, to some extent, unique.

Chapter 6 introduces the field of comparative analysis as such and also introduces Part II. Some may find it useful to read it in advance of Part I as well as subsequent to it. The material in this book is, however, written to be read in the order in which it is presented.

After Part I, the book proceeds with the critical survey of major approaches and selected substantive problem areas in which some of the best known or most significant writing has been done. The aim here is not to be exhaustive but rather to give the student an overall picture of the current state of knowledge in the field. A previous familiarity with the literature is not assumed by this text. However, a concurrent reading of some of the literature surveyed would be desirable for the serious student.

One difficulty that I have encountered in teaching methodology is that the various aspects of it are so integrated that to understand the importance and ramifications of one aspect is difficult without an acquaintance with the other aspects. Thus, a full understanding of the requirement for precision in the definition of scientific concepts is difficult without an understanding of how laws are tested, and this criterion of testability cannot be fully comprehended without a knowledge of what is meant by explanation; yet explanation cannot be grasped without an understanding of what is meant by concepts, laws, and so on.

Thus, some things will be mentioned to help make a point, although a full understanding of them will not be possible until complete discussion of them follows several other points being made. This is an unfortunate consequence of the integrated nature of the subject matter. For example, models and conceptual frameworks are mentioned in Chapter 1 but not fully explained until Chapters 4 and 6. The student should not let patience succumb to frustration but wait until all the information is in. At that point the pieces should fall into place.

Obviously, some arbitrary decisions have to be made with respect to the order of presentation. For instance, I decided to move from the more specific aspects of methodology, such as concept formation, to the more general, such as laws and theory. Explanation is discussed between concepts and laws, since I believe that laws (or generalizations) are best understood in terms of their role in scientific explanation. Theory in the strict sense of the term is not a requisite for some levels of explanation. Yet theory cannot be understood in terms of its purposes unless the nature and requirements of explanation are first specified.

Individual instructors, however, may choose to alter the order of reading.

I wrote Part I with the assumption that there is a discernible methodology which may be identified as scientific, and, furthermore, that this methodology is applicable and relevant to the study of social and political phenomena. I will attempt to justify this assumption. The scientific method to which I refer is the one discussed by such formally oriented philosophers of science as Nagel and Hempel rather than the less formal approaches of writers such as Toulmin and Braithwaite.[2] What I am suggesting is that the epistemological differences between the social sciences on the one hand and the physical and biological sciences on the other are differences in degree, not differences in kind. The former type of discipline is able to predict more accurately, and explain more completely, than the latter. However, even the natural scientists are unable fully to explain the occurrence of all observations that are relevant to them or to predict all relevant events with 100 percent accuracy. It is not the standard for knowledge that distinguishes the social sciences; it is the size of the gaps in the knowledge of these disciplines.

The survey of approaches in Part II assumes that these approaches are similarly constructed to facilitate the construction of empirically testable theory, a major goal of the scientific methodology discussed in Part I. The literature surveyed in Part III constitutes an attempt to apply the method-

---

[2] Ernest Nagel, *The Structure of Science* (New York: Harcourt Brace & World, 1961); Carl Hempel, *The Philosophy of Natural Science* (Englewood Cliffs, N.J.: Prentice-Hall, 1966); Carl Hempel, "Fundamentals of Concept Formation in Empirical Science," *International Encyclopedia of Unified Science,* Vol. II, No. 7 (Chicago: University of Chicago Press, 1952); Carl Hempel, "Aspects of Scientific Explanation," in his *Aspects of Scientific Explanation and Other Essays in the Philosophy of Science* (New York: The Free Press, 1965), pp. 331–496; Stephen Toulmin, *The Philosophy of Science, An Introduction* (New York: Harper Torchbooks, 1960); and R. B. Braithwaite, *Scientific Explanation* (New York: Harper & Row, 1960).

ology discussed in Part I and the approaches surveyed in Part II to substantive problems. The overriding focus of Part II and Part III is the question of the extent to which the existing literature has contributed to the explanation and prediction of political phenomena.

It should be obvious that the book proceeds from the analytical and abstract to the increasingly substantive and concrete. There are certain inherent disadvantages in this approach. Specifically, a student often approaches a course in comparative politics expecting to be fed a body of substantive facts about major foreign powers. Such a student can be alienated or frustrated by being immediately led into abstract methodology. This is a risk which must be run, however, because a methodological critique of the literature is impossible unless the applicable methodological standards are first specified.

I have tried to minimize this difficulty by using as many examples as possible to relate abstract principles to specific problems of research. In addition, I try to define specialized terms and concepts likely to be unfamiliar to the reasonably literate student. The glossary at the end of the book is designed to aid students in coping with specialized vocabulary. Words are defined there as they are used in the book.

One further word of caution or clarification should be added. Part I is not intended to be a complete text on epistemology; it is intended to state, simply and free from extraneous conceptual problems, the basic principles necessary for critically analyzing the literature surveyed. Clearly, much more can be included in a complete course in epistemology or methods.

It is impossible fully to acknowledge all of the individuals who have guided my intellectual training and development. In a book of this scope, I owe all of them a tremendous debt of gratitude. Yet two must be singled out. First is Professor James R. Soukup, now chairman of the political science department at S.U.N.Y. at Fredonia. A rare combination of competent scholar, exciting teacher and concerned human being, he was able to convey to me both an intellectual excitement and a tolerable comprehension of the analytical aspects of comparative politics. Without his encouragement throughout my graduate student career, this book clearly would have been impossible. I wish to thank also Professor William S. Livingston of the University of Texas, for his encouragement and valuable advice. Both of these men effectively combined the roles of friend and mentor.

Several colleagues at Texas Tech University read and discussed with me large portions of the manuscript. I have profited from their astute and challenging critiques. They were: Gordon G. Henderson, Abdi Abdushah, Roland E. Smith, and William Oden. Professor Abdushah was particularly encouraging and inspiring to me. When he died suddenly and prematurely this year, the discipline lost a promising scholar, and all who knew him lost a good friend.

I am very grateful for a grant from the organized research committee of Texas Tech University without which this project would have been greatly delayed.

This book would not have been possible without the competent and reliable help of Mrs. Sarah Roberson, Miss Pat Ratliff, Miss Gay Phipps, Mrs. Twyla Sims, and my wife, Marilyn, who translated my barely legible handwriting into typed drafts. I am especially indebted to Miss Pat Campbell who typed the final draft.

The help and encouragement I have received from all members of my family must be acknowledged, although it is not possible to discharge my indebtedness to them.

It should be unnecessary by this time to take the time-honored step of formally assuming responsibility for the failings of the book. It should be obvious that whatever faults exist are mine alone.

February 1972   L.C.M.

Contents

xiii

Part I
Epistemology

1

The Empirical
Base of Science

If one were to characterize much of the work in comparative politics since World War II, one would have to say that the field is marked by a conscious effort to become more scientific. Perhaps more so than in any field of political science, specialists in comparative politics have been methodologically self-conscious. This is indicated by the voluminous amount of analytical writing concerned with the framing of approaches or the discussion of methodological problems. Moreover, the justification of much of the substantive research has been in terms of scientific criteria or in terms of the contribution of that research to the current state of knowledge on that question.

This book will argue that it is no mere coincidence that much of the leadership of the effort to put the science in political science has come from the field of comparative politics, assuming for the moment that a set of methodological criteria can be identified as scientific. An important aspect of such a methodology is the building of empirically testable generalizations with predictive power. The comparative method is particularly well suited to the construction of such generalizations. A generalization's explanatory power is directly related to its scope (the variety of contingent circumstances to which it applies) as will be shown below.

Comparative politics, in the sense that this term is used in this book, refers to inquiry whose scope extends beyond the borders of any single nation state on a cross-national or cross-cultural scope. Comparative politics thus refers to the development of cross-nationally valid scientific generalizations. It is a method rather than an object of study. Therefore, comparative politics in this modern sense is to be distinguished from the more traditional conception of comparative politics, the description of foreign governments. This distinction will be expanded upon below, especially in Chapter 6. The logic of the comparative method may in principle be applied also on a temporal dimension. That is, generalizations should be sought that are applicable not only to different systems but to different points in time for each given system. In practice, data from the past is often difficult to obtain, however. To the extent that studies from other subfields of political science become involved in cross-cultural comparisons, they also become examples of comparative political analysis. To the extent that studies of foreign government may be characterized as intensive descriptions of one political system, they are not included in what this book means by comparative political analysis. This is not meant to cast pejorative judgments on such country studies; they are simply outside the scope of this book.

Although much of the analytic work in the comparative field, as well as in political science in general, has ostensibly been written for the purpose of furthering the development of the field into a science, this work has often been done with either an unclear or even indefensible conception of what a scientific discipline consists. Much the same could be said with respect to much of the substantive work. Consequently, any evaluation of what is being done in the field would do well to base itself on a clear statement of what is meant by a science and precisely what characteristics distinguish scientific scholarship from nonscientific writing.

In the judgment of the present writer, there has been far too facile an acceptance and adoption of approaches and models without a critical awareness of their limitations with respect to the kinds of questions to which they are applicable or, more basically, of the amount and kind of explanation they are capable of providing. Furthermore, the work will attempt to argue that the popularity of newly acquired skills in statistical analysis and electronic data processing has led to an unhealthy preoccupation with methodological tools at the expense of analysis. The result has been an uncritical use of mathematical or other methods to process problems to which the methods are not really applicable. Sometimes this overplaced reliance on mathematical tools or methods results in the misinterpretation of the obtained results, particularly in the form of overgeneralizing from one's data.[1] This tendency has been characterized by a failure to recognize that the value of both approaches and methods is instrumental, and that their uncritical use does not constitute a good in and of itself. Accordingly, this survey of the literature of comparative politics is based upon the methodological standards of science. What follows is an attempt to render those standards unambiguous.

---

[1] Abraham Kaplan has described this tendency brilliantly as "the mystique of quantity" and "the law of the instrument," namely the tendency to view techniques which have instrumental value as ends in themselves. *The Conduct of Inquiry* (San Francisco: Chandler Publishing Co., 1964), p. 172.

There are three basic elements to that area of concern in political science which has loosely been labeled *methodology*. All three are to be distinguished from what has been called *scope,* which would be a delineation of what the fields of study and their objects in political science consist.

Courses in methodology generally include a study of one or more of the following: research methods such as statistics or survey research, approaches or models, and epistemology. This last area, constituting the most widely accepted use of the term methodology, deals with the nature and limits of knowledge in the discipline. The philosophy of science constitutes a type of epistemology.

Methodology should be distinguished from methods. The term methods refers to research tools and techniques. Statistics consists not only of mathematical procedures and techniques but of a system of quantitative reasoning leading to the specification of error probability when engaged in inductive inference. Probability and inductive inference are discussed later in the book. An understanding and awareness of the principles of epistemology affords the researcher a standard for what constitutes a legitimate and useful research project. Therefore, it is clear that a knowledge of the epistemological foundations of a discipline constitutes the core of any concern with the nature of political inquiry and ought to be a prerequisite to any consideration of methods, approaches, or substance.

It has been argued by proponents of the traditional ways of studying politics and government that the principles of epistemology ought to vary with the objects of study. Some fields of study, it is asserted, are inappropriate for the application of the rigorous epistemological standards of natural science. Whether political science in general and comparative politics in particular constitute fields of study which are susceptible to the application of the epistemological rules of natural science is therefore a question which must be explored in some detail.

Such an exploration might well begin by taking note of the bases for the apparently powerful appeal of the methodology of the natural sciences. The strongest element in this appeal is the positive achievements to which scientists can proudly point, a record of achievement which the social sciences, unhappily, do not share. For example, it is apparent that chemists now know a great deal more about their subject matter than did Lavoisier or Priestly and knowledge in physics has progressed beyond the achievements of Newton. On the other hand, it cannot be said that political theorists today know more about the nature of justice than did Plato some four thousand years ago. While we in political science do know more today than previously about certain matters within the scope of our discipline, that is true in precisely those areas in which we have tried to apply the methodology and even the techniques of the hard sciences. For progress in knowledge is only possible when the word knowledge is used in its scientific sense. Only then does knowledge become cumulative;[2] that is, the work of each succeeding scholar can be built on what has gone before. The cumulative nature of scientific knowledge might best be conceptualized in terms of the incremental building of an accepted body of knowledge.

What then is the nature of scientific knowledge that differentiates it from nonscientific knowledge and makes it possible for it to be cumulative? At the very minimum, scientific knowledge is empirical; that is, it is about observable facts or events.

Systems of pure logic, such as mathematics, are often thought of as science. Without denying that mathematics is a branch of science, it is a tool for achieving the purposes of science: explanation and prediction. Systems of logically related symbols, such as mathematics, cannot contribute to the explanation of observable phenomena unless some of these symbols are given empirical content.[3] The occurrence of specific events, such as the French cabinet losing a vote of confidence, would constitute an example of what is meant here by observable. The precise relation between such observables and scientifically meaningful statements is a rather complex one which will be considered below under the heading of concept formation. However, let it suffice to say for now that an empirical base distinguishes scientific statements from nonscientific statements, which may conveniently be referred to as metaphysical or logical statements. The precise nature of an empirical statement and the reasons why statements should be so formulated can be more effectively described after students have become acquainted with the nature of conceptualization.

Empirically based statements have two major advantages over metaphysical statements. First, only statements which are based on events or states of affairs in the real world can tell us something about that world. This will become apparent from the discussion of scientific explanation. Second, the empirical base of scientific statements minimizes subjectivity.[4] That is, by framing propositions in such terms that they would be accepted by anyone who views the evidence, the biases of the different observers are neutralized. If a number of people, who disagreed among themselves as to who was the best candidate in an election, could view all the ballots, they would still come to the same conclusion as to which candidate actually received the most votes despite their divergent preferences. On the other hand, even if all the observers could observe all of the actions and read all of the policy statements of each candidate, the observers might still fail to agree on the best candidate. The reason is, of course, that the resolution of this

2 Cf. James B. Conant, *On Understanding Science* (New York: Mentor Books, 1958) for the argument that cumulative knowledge constitutes the main criterion for distinguishing science from nonscience.

3 Kaplan, op. cit., pp. 6–7.

4 Kaplan, op. cit., p. 35.

latter question does not depend solely on observable facts but also on the subjective preferences of the observers.

Similarly, it has been found that Germans disagree on whether Adolph Hitler was one of their greatest statesmen. The reason for this lack of agreement is that the criteria of greatness are to a large extent subjective and a function of one's value priorities. However, both Nazis and anti-Nazis agree that the allied armies seized control of Europe in 1945. Although winning a war is not a directly observable event, it is definable in terms of observable indicators, so that the question of the outcome of a war can be agreed upon by all regardless of their preferences.

Because the empirical base of scientific propositions provides an accepted criterion for the resolution of questions to the satisfaction of anyone who views the evidence and understands its relevance, it is possible for all scholars in a scientific discipline to operate on the basis of tentative agreement on what is known and to go on from there. It is not necessary for each scholar to start from scratch as if nothing had been previously resolved, as one does in normative philosophy. This is one of the factors in the cumulative character of scientific knowledge.

The second factor in the cumulative character of scientific knowledge is the existence of a common framework, a common *model* of these aspects of the world in which they are interested or, as Thomas Kuhn puts it, a common *paradigm.*[5] This means that researchers are asking related or comparable questions about their subject matter, a practice that is a great asset in the incremental building of a body of knowledge. This practice is an asset because it facilitates the dissemination of what is already known among scholars in the discipline.

This search for a common framework will be explored in greater detail in Chapters 4 and 6. The role of such frameworks in the discipline should become clearer at that point in the book.

Meanwhile, a brief illustration may begin to clarify that role at this point. Obviously, when a researcher looks at a political system, there is an almost infinite number of different things to look for. To make his task manageable, he must have some way of organizing all of the available facts in advance so that he knows what types of facts and what kinds of relationships between facts to look for. Chapter 6 will explain how framework models or paradigms perform this task.

A research project on the contribution of French political parties (or lack thereof) to the political stability of that country could add to the knowledge of the effect of parties on stability generally. It would not complement a study about the logical consistency of the French legal code. In

---

[5] Thomas Kuhn, *The Structure of Scientific Revolutions* (Chicago: University of Chicago Press, 1962).

this way, only studies done with a common framework add to cumulative knowledge.

CONCEPTS AND OPERATIONAL DEFINITIONS

What actually is observed in political science is physical activity or the lack thereof. Language gives meaning to such activity and defines this activity in terms of patterns of behavior and interaction by actors in their political roles. Role is a concept referring to the environmental frame of reference that determines an actor's behavior.[6]

A concept is a construct of the mind, an idea, if you will. Thus, when a professor is interacting with his wife, he is playing the role of husband and lover and is expected to behave differently toward her than he would toward his female students when he assumes the professorial role. The concept of role involves a pattern of expectations with regard to the behavioral (observable) response to a given set of stimuli (a pretty female). Hence the movement to make political theory empirically oriented has been loosely labeled the behavioral movement.

The propositions that we form in the discipline, however, are generally not about such directly observed action but about concepts which use such action as their empirical referents or indicators, thus assigning meaning to these formerly isolated actions.

An empirical referent is an observable phenomenon (or phenomena) that constitutes the definition of a concept. A high per capita income or the percentage of the population employed in nonagricultural economic activities constitute possibly empirical referents to the concept of a developed or mature society. An empirical referent or indicator thus becomes an unambiguous cue as to whether the concept is assumed to be present. When a concept is defined in terms of such observable indicators (or tests or "operations" to obtain such indicators) we say the concept is *operationalized.*

In this way, an operationalized concept is a mental construct that assigns meaning to the raw observed activity that constitutes its definition.

INDIRECT INDICATORS

A concept may be assigned a meaning in the world of essential ideas but still be rendered empirical by the use of indirect indicators. These are indicators that indicate the presence of the concept but do not constitute its definition per se. For example, Ted Gurr has postulated frustration as the

---

[6] See Heinz Eulau, *The Behavioral Persuasion in Politics* (New York: Random House, 1964), pp. 39-46, for a discussion of the use of the concepts of role in political science.

major cause of civil violence.[7] Frustration is a mental state that is difficult to measure directly. (Interview techniques, discussed in Chapters 9 and 10 may constitute a possible direct measurement of such mental states; however, they are expensive and difficult to conduct on a cross-national basis.) Gurr therefore assigns measures of economic deprivation and political repression as indirect measures of the mental state, frustration. It is important to note that there is an unestablished inference that economic deprivation and political repression cause frustration. Gurr does not imply, however, that economic deprivation and political repression are the same thing as frustration. They merely serve as cues to its presence.

A certain ingenuity in specifying indirect indicators to concepts difficult to operationalize can greatly enhance our ability to apply the canons of scientific methodology to hitherto nonempirical subject matter. It must be remembered, however, that the conclusions thus obtained are dependent on the validity of the unsubstantiated inference that the indicators are related to the concept. This is a question of validity that assumes concepts can have a real or "essential" meaning apart from their empirical referents, an assumption upon which reasonable men disagree. For example, is there such a thing as true intelligence that is different from whatever it is that a Stanford-Binet test measures?

VARIABLES AND THE PRECISE USE OF INDICATORS

When a concept can manifest itself in either more than one quantitative magnitude or qualitative type, it is known as a variable. Variable is sometimes used interchangeably with factor. The latter term refers to a concept that affects something else. It may or may not be a variable, depending on whether it can appear in a variety of magnitudes or types.

Thus, a behavioralist, who forms propositions based upon concepts which have empirical referents, is to be distinguished from a behaviorist who generalizes directly from raw human behavior. Examples of behaviorism may be found in psychology[8] among those who feel that knowledge about human behavior is limited to directly observed associations between stimuli and responses, S $\longrightarrow$ R, in the Pavlovian fashion, and that inferred propo-

---

[7] Ted Gurr, "Sources of Rebellion in Western Societies," *The Annals of the American Academy of Political and Social Science,* Vol. 391 (September 1970), pp. 128–44, and "A Comparative Survey of Civil Strife," in Hugh Graham and Gurr (eds.), *Violence in America: Historical and Comparative Perspectives* (New York: Praeger, 1969), chap. 17.

[8] The classic example of this is J. B. Watson, *Behaviorism,* 2nd ed. (New York: Norton Publishing Company, 1930). See also his "Psychology as a Behaviorist Views It," *Psychological Review,* Vol. 20, (1913), pp. 158–77. See also Charles E. Osgood, "Behavior Theory and the Social Sciences," in Roland Young (ed.), *Approaches to the Study of Politics* (Evanston, Ill.: Northwestern University Press, 1958), pp. 217–44.

sitions about the modifying influence of dispositional sets of the organism on the observed responses, S———→ O———→ R, are not scientifically valid because they cannot be directly observed. Simply put, all political scientists today recognize that organisms (people) differ one from the other and are predisposed toward given patterns of action. Such predispositions are products of the innumerable variables in any individual's experience. Thus, different individuals (organisms) may respond differently to the same immediate stimuli. In this way, the simplistic stimulus-response relationship is modified by the predispositions or psychic states of the organism. But crude empiricists would allegedly point out that since we cannot observe such predispositions of people, we should exclude such variables from our analysis.

In political science, the widespread use of concepts modifies the empirical basis of our propositions and makes it less direct than the empirical basis of strict behaviorism. Thus, we frame propositions about conservatives, stable democracy, ideological or legalistic political styles, and political socialization. Obviously, these cannot be directly observed in the sense one can say, "I see a table." Hence, reasonable men may disagree as to whether they have encountered a conservative even though they had the same information about the individual in question. The meaning of such indirectly observed concepts is a matter of definition unless one chooses to assume that a true or essential meaning of concepts does exist in the world of ideas, an assumption characteristic of Platonic ontology but meaningless for the purposes of scientific inquiry. Thus, concepts are considered empirical if they are defined in terms of an unambiguous class of observable characteristics.

An example might help clarify this point. Ted Gurr and Charles Ruttenberg attempted to posit a series of such indicators for a violent political system.[9] Their indicators are as follows: the number of participants per 100,000 population, the geographical area affected by the most violent event of the year, the number of casualties per 1,000 participants reported as a direct consequence of civil violence, and the amount of property damage "relative to the scope of action indicated by the preceding basic measure."

Clearly, the first three indicators are unambiguous provided threshold levels are specified. If it is specified in advance that any political system having more than x number of participants in violent actions per 1,000,000 population will be called violent, then there is no room for argument as to which system is violent. (This is assuming data collection is agreed upon as reliable and that participation in a violent action is itself an unambiguous concept.) Yet the third indicator, as stated here, may leave some room for

---

[9] Ted Gurr & Charles Ruttenberg, *The Conditions of Civil Violence* (Princeton, N.J.: Princeton University Center of International Studies Research Monograph No. 28, April 1967), pp. 31–32. Cited in Richard L. Merritt, *Systematic Approaches to Comparative Politics* (Chicago: Rand McNally & Co., 1970), pp. 32–33.

discussion until the concept "scope of action" is rendered less ambiguous and until the relationship between such scope and the amount of property damage is more precisely specified.

Once these indicators are rendered unambiguous, however, a violent political system becomes a matter of definition and there is no room for argument as to which system is "really" violent. Thus, there is no essentially correct definition of a concept; there is no logical limit to the choice of what may be included in the class of empirical referents which serve to define a concept. There are, of course, practical considerations which may serve to suggest such limits. Clearly, concepts come to have imprecise meanings which are widely understood and accepted and to define a concept outside of these imprecise limits would create confusion. For example, the adoption of the term democracy by a number of noncompetitive political systems to describe themselves[10] has created a certain amount of confusion among western students who had previously thought of the concept as being limited to regimes permitting open competition between elites at more or less regular elections. While there is no logical barrier to include closed systems within the concept, no useful scientific purpose is served in doing so inasmuch as scientific concepts are supposed to facilitate the communication of knowledge among scholars.

One proffered definition of *constitutional democracy* may be found in a recent essay by Barry Farrell. He specifies the following attributes:

competitive regular elections, legalized two or multi-party organizations aimed at offering alternative governmental leadership, a high degree of toleration for autonomous groups in politics and acceptance of constitutional restraints on governmental power.[11]

This example, while attempting to make democracy a matter of definition, contains certain ambiguities which preclude it from being fully operational as stated. While the first two indicators appear to be precise enough (what one means by "regular" elections could be a source of confusion, however), a serious question remains as to how much toleration constitutes "a high degree" and furthermore how the degree of toleration is measured. A question also remains as to the criteria for determining how much acceptance of constitutional restraints on governmental power exists. With the lack of such criteria for measurement, it would prove difficult if not impossible to establish threshold levels for such acceptance (below which constitutional democracy would not exist).

---

[10] For example, Sukarno's Indonesia was called "guided democracy," the USSR has described its system as "democratic centralism," and various other communist dictatorships have been called "peoples' democracies."

[11] Barry Farrell, "Foreign Policies of Open and Closed Systems," in Farrell (ed.), *Approaches to Comparative and International Politics* (Evanston, Ill.: Northwestern University Press, 1966), p. 168.

Thus, there are no essentially correct meanings to concepts in any scientific enterprise. (The meaning of a concept is whatever we define it to be.)

Another example might illustrate the potential confusion here. Herbert McClosky, in a well-known article, attempted to relate people who held conservative political attitudes to certain personality traits and to intelligence levels.[12] McClosky first had to specify an unambiguous category of individuals who would be included within the concept of conservative *for the purposes of his article*. His definition of conservative was not intended to finalize the meaning of the concept for all time. Another scholar doing a different study might find it convenient to define the concept differently. The meaning of the concept liberal, for example, has certainly changed from the mid-19th century to the present day due to a greatly changed economic and social milieu. The term previously referred to opposition to governmental restraints on individual choice and action. Now liberal commonly refers to those who advocate positive governmental action to remove social and economic impediments to the realization of human potential. The attempt to finalize the meaning of a concept and consequently not to allow for new circumstances or new observations which may make it useful to change or expand the meaning of a concept was what Abraham Kaplan meant when he warned against the "premature closure" of meaning.[13]

McClosky defined conservative by extracting from the literature of the leading self-styled exponents of conservative thought from a variety of political and cultural contexts those attitudes which seem to be common among them. He then constructed a questionnaire designed to measure the intensity with which these attitudes are held.[14] This intensity was quantified by assigning points to the various levels of agreement with each statement on the questionnaire. An arbitrary but precise numerical cutoff point then established the unambiguous class of "conservatives" that McClosky needed when the questionnaire was administered to a group of students.

The questionnaire was designed largely with reference to American issues and applied to an American sample. To render the questionnaire applicable to other cultural and political contexts, considerable revision would be required.

The results of the study showed a high strength of association between conservatism and various personality disorders as defined by standardized personality tests and low I.Q. as defined by standardized intelligence test. Inasmuch as these results do not flatter self-styled conservatives, such people frequently react to the article with the claim that those people so categorized by McClosky were not "really" conservative.

---

[12] Herbert McClosky, "Conservatism and Personality," *The American Political Science Review*, Vol. 52 (March 1958), pp. 27–45.

[13] Kaplan, op. cit., pp. 70–71.

[14] The questionnaire consisted of a 12-item scale which had been condensed from a 43-item pool by a process of applying the original pool to some 1,200 respondents.

The point is that such an objection is invalid. There is no essential definition of conservative. McClosky categorized a group who held attitudes that most people find it convenient to label conservative;[15] however, there is no logical reason why one could not call them "zonks." McClosky showed that people who hold specified attitudes tend to get specified results on specified tests. He merely gave widely understood names to the categories of data to facilitate the communication of his findings. Students of comparative politics would be interested in the problem of whether the concept of conservatism refers to the same set of attitudes in other political and social systems.

This is not meant to imply that there are no criteria for the value of scientific concepts—concepts may be evaluated in terms of whether or not they can be related to other concepts. As we shall see below, one of the other hallmarks of scientific methodology is the effort to generalize. Thus, there is no logical reason why all political scientists with blond hair cannot be categorized and labeled with any name that one chooses to give them. However, it is unlikely that this group would display any consistent behavior pattern in such a way that this concept could be related to any other relevant concept. There is no way in which blond political scientists differ systematically from other political scientists except for the fact that they have blond hair. Therefore, such a concept would not be useful in the construction of scientific generalizations.

McClosky's definition of conservative is a good example of an operational definition—a definition that specifies the observable indicators of the presence of that concept. Thus, McClosky's definition of a conservative specified that the term conservative referred to anyone who scored over a certain magnitude on a given test. That test score was an observable indicator and when conservatism is so defined, all observers should agree on which subjects are included in the concept.

Similarly, intelligence or genius may be defined in terms of a given score on a Stanford-Binet test. As long as it is recognized that such a test measures acquired skills more than innate intelligence, such a definition is useful for establishing a class of individuals to generalize about (for example, geniuses so defined tend to earn a higher lifetime income than nongeniuses).

Operational definitions are a standard way of adding precision to concepts and laws. You cannot test a statement in the form of "all democracies are X" unless you specify beforehand which countries are considered to be democracies. Otherwise, deviant cases can conveniently be excluded from the concept. For example, if someone were to say, "Here is a democracy that is not X," it would be possible to reply that that country is not really a democracy.

---

[15] The instrument which categorized these people was validated (a demonstration that the test measured what it purported to measure) by asking a group of students of political philosophy what they would call people who held these attitudes. The overwhelming answer was "conservative."

Not all concepts in either the social or natural sciences are operationally defined. Some concepts derive their meaning solely from the analytic structure of which they are an integral part and are themselves not even indirectly observable. The term analytic structure is here taken to include theory in the scientific sense of the word (see below) at various stages of development as well as analytic models which, although often referred to as theory by the poorly initiated, lack some of the essential characteristics of scientific theory. Simplistically, we are talking here about systems of ideas and the logical relationships between them rather than sets of observable phenomena. All of this will be discussed more fully in Chapters 4 and 7.

David Easton's and Talcott Parsons' systems analyses, for example,[16] utilize concepts such as boundary exchange inputs, outputs, or feedback loops, which would be impossible to define except as integral parts of the systemic formulation. It will be argued below that the fact that all of the concepts have systemic or theoretic meaning and none has operational or empirical meaning constitutes one of the most serious limitations on the scientific utility of systems analysis as presently formulated for the social sciences. The natural sciences also make use of theoretic concepts. For example, molecular energy would lack meaning outside of the kinetic theory of matter.[17]

HOLISM AND REDUCTIONISM

Another aspect of concept formation involves the basic unit of analysis that comprises the concept. This issue takes the form of debate over the subject matter of the social sciences between the proponents of holism and those of reductionism. Briefly stated, the issue revolves around whether the unit of analysis in social science consists of social groups or of the individuals and/or elements that comprise such groups. The latter view, labeled reductionism, holds that collective terms are analyzable in terms of the pattern of behavior or psychological characteristics of actors in their po-

---

[16] These are two important examples of analytical writing which cannot be fully explained at this point. (Systems analysis is summarized, discussed, and evaluated in Chapter 8.) David Easton's seminal article is "An Approach to the Analysis of Political Systems" *World Politics,* Vol. 9, No. 3, (April 1957), pp. 383–400. His most complete formulation may be found in *A Systems Analysis of Political Life* (New York: John Wiley & Sons, 1966), the last of a trilogy of books. Parsons' works are too numerous to cite and he fluctuates between a micro or reductionist "action theory" and a macro or systems approach. The best example of the latter is probably "On the Concept of Political Power," *Proceedings of the American Philosophical Society,* Vol. 107 (June 1963). See also William Mitchell, *Sociological Analysis and Politics* (Englewood Cliffs, N.J.: Prentice-Hall, 1967) for a thorough summary of Parsons' influence on political science. Mitchell writes from the point of view of a disciple rather than from the perspective of a critic.

[17] See Carl G. Hempel, *The Philosophy of Natural Science* (Englewood Cliffs, N.J.: Prentice-Hall, 1966), p. 73.

litical roles. As one exponent of reductionism asserts, ". . . the social scientist can continue searching for explanations of a social phenomenon until he has reduced it to psychological terms."[18] By this position we cannot say that a party or group did something; rather, because of motives susceptible to psychological analysis, a given individual or set of individuals who belonged to that group did something. In its most extreme formulation, the individualist position would hold that a social group has no essential existence beyond the sum total of individuals that comprise it and, furthermore, one could predict the occurrence of social events by knowing the complete psychological makeup of each of the actors involved in it. It should be noted that the various approaches which involve the use of psychological data or theory to develop lawlike propositions about the behavior of political actors or groups must assume the reductionist position to some considerable extent.

The holist position avers that a social group is more than the sum of its parts. The reason for this is that the interaction among the individuals becomes a variable which affects both individual and group behavior. Thus, a normally calm, rational, dispassionate man may act quite irrationally when he becomes a member of a lynch mob. This position is not usually intended to deny the influence of great men. It does aver that the choices such men make are influenced by their milieu. As Ernest Gellner points out, reductionists seem to "preclude a priori the possibility of human disposition being the dependent variable."[19] Thus, according to the holist, it can never be possible to completely analyze the psychological or chemical state of a living organism because those states are constantly being acted upon by the environment. Adolph Hitler, born and reared in another time and place, probably would not have had a career paralleling his historical one. The frustrations, hates, and visions that induced him to action were in part a product of the society and era in which he lived.

Most literature in comparative government is written from a holistic point of view. Comparative government, in its more modern manifestations, has been heavily influenced by sociology, which is by nature holistic. However, as we shall see below, due to the seminal work of men like Fred Greenstein,[20] psychological analysis as a means of constructing political explanation is beginning to gain some respectability among reputable scholars.

[18] J. W. N. Watkins, "Ideal Types and Historical Explanation," *British Journal for the Philosophy of Science,* Vol. 3 (1952), reprinted in H. Feigel and May Brodbeck (eds.), *Readings in the Philosophy of Science* (New York: Appleton-Century-Crofts, 1953), pp. 723–43.

[19] Ernest Gellner, "Holism versus Individualism" in May Brodbeck (ed.), *Readings in the Philosophy of Social Science* (New York: Macmillan Co., 1968), pp. 254–68.

[20] Fred Greenstein, *Personality and Politics* (Chicago: Markham Publishing Company, 1969).

TYPOLOGIES AND CLASSIFICATION

The process of concept formation constitutes a means by which a vast heterogeneous array of isolated facts or data may be organized and labeled so as to explicate their relevance for political analysis. This process of aggregation and labeling simplifies reality (the directly observed facts) within the bounds of manageability. The criterion for manageable simplicity is that the data are so structured that patterns among and relationships between concepts may be discerned.

Another method of simplifying reality to the standards of manageability imposed by the generalizing imperatives of the scientific method is the construction of typologies or classification schemes (sometimes referred to in the literature, with unnecessary obfuscation, as taxonomies).[21] Thus, classification and concept formation fulfill the same purpose for the scientific method.

This method involves the grouping of individual empirical phenomena into distinct categories according to some criterion or criteria. Phenomena which have thus been identified as similar, though not identical, with respect to a given characteristic may be related as a group to other phenomena, thus obviating the necessity of relating each of the former group cases individually to the latter phenomena.

Classification is not only useful but, as Nagel puts it, an "indispensible stage in the development of systematic knowledge." He points out that modern physics and chemistry came into being only after the preliminary classification of their data.[22]

The terms *classification scheme* or *taxonomy* have sometimes been distinguished from the term *typology*,[23] a distinction which needs to be clarified. The categories of a typology are concepts which are arbitrarily defined by a researcher in terms of selected *qualitative* variables. The categories of a classification scheme, on the other hand, are defined in terms of *quantitative* variables. An example of a typology would be Riggs' division of social systems into manifestations of "agraria and industria."[24] An example of a classification scheme might be a grouping of political systems according to such quantifiable criteria as literacy rate, gross national product, or degree of urbanization. Since so many of the variables used in comparative

---

[21] *Taxonomy* is sometimes used to refer to the theory of classification procedures rather than to classification itself. Cf. Carl Hempel, "Fundamentals of Taxonomy," in Hempel, *Aspects of Scientific Explanation and Other Essays in the Philosophy of Science* (New York: The Free Press, 1965), p. 137n.

[22] Ernest Nagel, *The Structure of Science* (New York: Harcourt, Brace and World, 1961), p. 31.

[23] Howard Scarrow, *Comparative Political Analysis, An Introduction* (New York: Harper & Row, 1969) p. 11.

[24] Fred Riggs, "Agraria and Industria," in William Siffen (ed.), *Toward the Comparative Study of Public Administration* (Bloomington, Ind.: Indiana University Press, 1957), pp. 23–110.

politics are qualitative, typologies are more common than classifications. Moreover, until recently, there has been a relative paucity of quantitative data on foreign political systems available to the American scholar.

This situation has, to some extent, been improved by the development of data banks such as the Inter-University Consortium for Political Research. Here data such as those from Bruce Russett and others, *World Handbook of Political and Social Indicators,* from Banks's and Textor's *Cross Polity Survey,* from Almond and Verba's *Five Nation Study,* and from various other collections, are stored in computers and can be reproduced on machine-readable decks (card stacks) or tapes. These decks and tapes are made widely available to universities. Banks and Textor, for example, have classified 115 political systems according to 57 characteristics.[25] Examples of these characteristics include population density, area, gross national product, freedom of the press, type of party system, ideological orientation, and sectionalism. Clearly, both qualitative and quantitative variables have been used.

A well-known typology in comparative politics is Gabriel Almond's classification of political system types into four categories: Anglo-American political systems, preindustrial political systems; totalitarian political systems, and continental European political systems.[26]

The utility of such classifications or typologies for producing scientifically valid explanation can best be evaluated after some of the criteria for useful classification have been delineated.

The first such criterion is that the categories of a classification scheme or typology should be exhaustive; that is, there should be a category for every possible case. Conversely, there should be cases to fit each category. To illustrate this with an absurd example, a typology of nations into democratic and nondemocratic would not be very useful if the criteria for inclusion in the democratic category were such as to exclude every nation. The purpose of a classification (hereafter used to include both classifications and typologies) is to group cases according to specified similarities and differences. Generally, if all or most of the cases were grouped in a single category, too many relevant differences between the cases would probably be excluded from consideration. Moreover, statistical manipulation of data is distorted whenever there are too few cases in a given cell or category.

The criteria for the classification of each case may be arbitrary but they should be precise. The requirement of precision serves to clarify the boundaries between categories so as to remove doubt as to which category a given case belongs. There is no essential or logical necessity that the boundaries

---

[25] Arthur Banks and Robert Textor, *A Cross Polity Survey,* (Cambridge, Mass.: M.I.T. Press, 1963).

[26] Gabriel Almond, "Comparative Political Systems," *Journal of Politics,* Vol. 18 (August 1956), pp. 391–409.

should be drawn at one point rather than another, however. A scholar may define freedom of the press any way he chooses so long as it is clear which countries would be classified as having a high degree of such freedom and which countries fit in the other categories. This is a matter of the construction of operational definitions discussed above. Qualitative criteria may also be precise if they are defined in terms of observable indicators.

Finally, all categories should be defined in terms of the same criteria. For example, a good typology would not define one type in terms of economic indicators and another in terms of political indicators.

Almond's typology referred to above may be criticized on these grounds and has been ably so criticized by Arthur Kalleberg.[27] Kalleberg points out that the Anglo-American and continental European types are based on geographical criteria, the preindustrial type on economic criteria, and the totalitarian type on social criteria. Almond does discuss rule structure with each class but apparently not as part of the definition. There are no common criteria utilized to render the analyses of the role structures comparative.

Moreover, the criteria are not precisely specified in such a way that there could be no question as to which category a given political system belongs. While the class Anglo-American implies a geographic class (North America, the United Kingdom, and perhaps the other older dominions), Almond says they are identified by a secular and homogeneous culture. However, he does not suggest empirical indicators of the presence or absence of such a culture. Some diversities are inevitable in any modern culture. What level or distribution of such diversities would render a culture nonhomogeneous?[28] Other attributes include a "highly differentiated role structure" and a "high degree of stability." Unless one can say precisely how much differentiation constitutes "a highly differentiated role structure" and how much stability constitutes "a high degree of stability" in some measurable sense, one is unable to objectively state whether a given system possesses these attributes. This is not to deny that some or all of Almond's criteria could possibly be operationalized. Until such a task is achieved, however, Almond has here taken only the initial step toward a contribution to empirical research.

Finally, it must be noted that Almond's scheme is not exhaustive. There are no cells or classes, for instance, for the Scandinavian democracies. Thus, any propositions ultimately derived from this classification scheme will necessarily systematically omit some potentially relevant cases without any logical reasons for doing so.

The utility of classifications such as Banks's and Textor's is also a func-

---

[27] Arthur Kalleberg, "The Logic of Comparison, A Methodological Note on the Comparative Study of Political Systems," *World Politics,* Vol. 19, No. 1 (January 1966), pp. 69–82.

[28] See Lawrence Mayer, "Federalism and Party Behavior in Australia and Canada," *Western Political Quarterly,* Vol. 23, No. 4, (December 1970), pp. 795–807, for a brief discussion and a tentative definition of cultural homogeneity.

tion of whether the criteria for assigning cases to one or the other category along a given dimension (high freedom of the press versus restricted freedom of the press, for example) are related to other relevant variables. In other words, can the indicators for operationally defining a category be related to other indicators of operationally defined concepts? The answer to the question can ultimately only emanate from extensive use of this particular set of data. The question of whether the indicators that are used are logically promising leads to an examination of how the categories in each qualitative classification are defined, an examination that is beyond the scope of this book. The purpose here has been to give the student criteria for the critical evaluation of these and other classification schemes.

CONCLUSION

Clearly, concepts themselves do not add to our knowledge about observed political phenomena, if by such knowledge is meant answers to questions about the how and why of observed patterns of behavior and the interaction of actors in their political roles. The task of providing such answers is referred to as explanation. Explanation in turn depends on the use of laws and theory. The manner in which laws and theory utilize concepts for the purpose of explanation constitutes the subject of the following chapters. This analysis begins with a delineation of the nature of explanation itself and the extent to which the classical forms (or paradigms) of explanation must be modified when dealing with political science.

Explanation and Predictions

The basic purpose underlying any scientific endeavor is to explain. The ability to explain and predict events within a given field of study is a necessary (but not sufficient) precondition for the ability to control the occurrence of such events. Because of relatively well developed ability to explain and predict physical phenomena, we can exercise a great deal of control over our physical environment. However, our relatively less well developed ability to explain and predict social phenomena occurrences is thus directly correlated with our ability to control them.

Observable facts or empirically defined concepts cannot explain anything unless they are integrated in a generalization or law. Therefore, all science seeks to establish propositions of general scope. The relationship between laws and explanation will remain unclear, however, until the nature of both are thoroughly described and defined.

Simply stated, an explanation of an empirical event or state of affairs seeks to answer the question, "Why did that event or state of affairs occur rather than any other?" To explain Negro voting essentially means to say why blacks voted the way they did rather than any other possible way. This is to be distinguished from the clarification of a definition which is often given the term explanation. For example one might say, "Explain what that word means." This is what Kaplan calls *semantic explanation*.[1]

The former "why" question about a social or political "fact" is answered by subsuming or integrating that fact in a more general proposition, by relating the fact, in other words, to another fact or concept. The more general

---

[1] Abraham Kaplan, *The Conduct of Inquiry* (San Francisco: Chandler Publishing Company, 1964) p. 327.

proposition (or covering law, as Hempel calls it) entails the fact to be explained.

THE DEDUCTIVE PARADIGM IN POLITICAL SCIENCE

It has been persuasively argued by Brodbeck[2] that the logical form of all explanations is essentially the same; the fact to be explained is deduced from a general proposition or law. Meehan argues that the deductive model is inappropriate for political science since all of our explanations are probabilistic.[3] The deductive model means that we infer the particular fact to be explained from a generalization; that is, we move from the general to the particular. The essence of the disagreement lies in the fact that Meehan takes the deductive model to mean that we infer the *necessary* occurrence of the fact from the generalization while Brodbeck interprets it to mean we can infer its probable occurrence. In either case, however, we are moving from the general to particulars, which is the form of deductive reasoning.

If we had a universal generalization (without any exceptions) of the form *all x* are *y,* then we could deduce that any individual case of class *x* will necessarily be *y*. If we could say all Jews are liberals (operationally defined), then we could infer the *necessity* of Mr. Goldberg being a liberal and behaving accordingly. Unfortunately for methodological purposes, there are deviant cases (Milton Friedman, for example) and we can only say *most* Jews are liberal. We are still deducing this probability, however, not inducing it.

Thus, Meehan is quite correct when he asserts that universal laws, which we do not have, are a prerequisite for a deduction of the necessary occurrence of a given event. Evidently, Meehan would assert that the derivation of the probable occurrence of a given event from an incomplete generalization is not deduction. However, deduction and induction are dichotomous alternatives; you either reason from the particular to the general (induction) or from the general to the particular (deduction). It may be argued that both the inference of the necessary occurrence of a fact from a generalization, or its probable occurrence, constitute a movement from the general to the particular, and the difference is one of precision rather than one of form. Deduction requires a precise statement of the empirical implications of the premises, not certainty or universality of the premises themselves.[4]

---

2 May Brodbeck, "Explanation, Prediction and Imperfect Knowledge," in Brodbeck (ed.), *Readings in the Philosophy of Social Science* (New York: Macmillan Co., 1968) pp. 363ff.

3 Eugene Meehan, *Contemporary Political Thought, A Critical Study* (Homewood, Ill.: The Dorsey Press, 1967), p. 96, and *The Theory and Method of Political Analysis* (Homewood, Ill.: The Dorsey Press, 1965), pp. 100ff.

4 Brodbeck, op. cit., pp. 373–76. Cf. Ernest Nagel, *The Structure of Science* (New York: Harcourt, Brace & World, 1962), pp. 18–23, for the converse argument that

One may choose not to call inferring the probability of an event from a law deduction but it does not fit any known definition of induction.[5]

In the foregoing example, the question, "Why is Mr. Goldberg liberal?" is answered by the known generalization "The overwhelming majority of Jews are liberal."[6] In other words, we are inferring that there is something about Jewishness that causes the likelihood of being liberal. Thus, the fact has been deduced or derived from a generalization or subsumed within a generalization and explained.

The foregoing distinction between the subsumption of a fact within a generalization and the derivation of a fact from a generalization constitutes another way of delineating Kaplan's distinction between the "pattern model" of explanation and the "deductive model."[7] However, as Kaplan himself suggests, this is an analytical distinction made by philosophers of science and should not be taken to infer an actual distinction about how social or natural scientists actually operate.[8] In both cases, what is to be explained and not known is related to a relationship or a system of relationships that is known.

COMPLETE VERSUS INCOMPLETE EXPLANATION

A distinction which was implied by Meehan's logical separation of deductive and probabilistic explanation is the distinction between being able to derive and predict the *necessary* occurrence of an event or social fact and the ability to derive or predict its probable occurrence.[9]

The ability to predict the necessary occurrence of an event depends on having a complete explanation of the event. A complete explanation involves the specification of all of the factors which were to any extent, directly or indirectly, involved in bringing the event about and the extent of the involvement of each.

---

deduction requires that the necessary occurrence of a given event must be implied by a universal law. Nagel argues from the point of view of a pure scientist.

[5] Arthur Goldberg, "Politics as a Science," in Nelson Polsby, Robert Dentler, and Paul A. Smith (eds.), *Politics and Social Life* (Boston: Houghton-Mifflin Co., 1963) adopts the term *deduction* to mean the inference that something must be and adopts a new word, *retroduction,* to refer to the inference from a premise of a probable event (p. 31).

[6] See Lawrence Fuchs, *The Political Behavior of American Jews* (Glencoe, Ill.: The Free Press, 1956).

[7] Kaplan, op cit., p. 332.

[8] See his distinction between "logic in use" (how scientists actually seek knowledge) and "reconstructed logic" (how philosophers of science say the scientist seeks knowledge). Ibid., pp. 3–6.

[9] Cf. Carl Hempel, "Deductive Nomological versus Statistical Explanation," in Herbert Feigel and Grover Maxwell (eds.), *Minnesota Studies in the Philosophy of Science,* Vol. 2 (Minneapolis: University of Minnesota Press, 1962) for a full exposition of this distinction.

Explanation, clearly, is identical to prediction insofar as formal logic is concerned. Some philosophers have tried to suggest an analytical distinction between them by suggesting that it is possible to do one without the other. Kaplan, for instance, offers an example of an automobile accident which was explained in retrospect by defective brakes, an accident which, however, could not have been predicted before its occurrence.[10] In Kaplan's example, the inability to predict the accident, which could in retrospect be explained, stems not from logical distinction between the ability to explain and predict but from the fact that the knowledge of the defective brakes, available in retrospect, was not available *prior* to the event.

While the specific event could not have been predicted with certainty even with prior knowledge of the defective brakes, a higher probability of its occurrence could have been derived from such knowledge in advance of the event. If one knew the percentage of all cars with defective brakes that become involved in accidents in relation to the number of miles driven, a precise statement of the mathematical probability of an accident could be given. But the very fact that all cars with defective brakes are not involved in accidents suggests that the brakes were not the sole cause of the accident, that defective brakes will result in accidents only when other factors (out of a class of factors) happen to be present. We only know one of many factors which brought about the event in question; thus, we have an incomplete explanation. Because we only know part of the "causes" of the event, we could only have predicted its probability. If we knew all of the causal variables, we could have predicted the necessary occurrence of the event.

Thus, to explain something completely is to subsume it under a general law which infers all of its antecedent causes. Such general laws take the form of all x and $y;$ thus, they are universal statements and without exception. It is inferred that x is a sufficient condition for the occurrence of y. The letter x here designates a class of phenomena of which particular instances may be observed. We know from this general statement that any and all instances of class x have the characteristic y. Therefore, from the general statement, all x and y, we can derive the statement if x then y, or, more fully stated, if a phenomenon belongs to the class of phenomena designated as x, then this particular phenomenon has the characteristic y.

If, to use the above example, it were possible to say that *all* Jews are liberal, we could then say, if Jewish, then liberal. Jewishness would then correspond to x in the above scheme. Mr. Goldberg would be a particular instance of class x. We would then be able to say, if Jewish, then liberal, inferring that being Jewish was in itself a sufficient precondition for being liberal. The statement would not imply that Jewishness is a necessary condi-

---

[10] Kaplan, op. cit., p. 348.

tion, however, in that it would not logically exclude the possibility that other causes of liberalism may also exist; non-Jews may also be liberal. Since we would know Mr. Goldberg is an instance of class *X,* Jewish people, we would also know he is liberal. We would know that his religion is a sufficient cause of his political disposition and, by knowing his religion, we could predict his political disposition with certainty.

We cannot of course say that all Jews are liberal. We can only say most Jews are liberal (or perhaps, at least a given percentage of Jews are liberal). Thus, we are inferring the Jewishness is not a sufficient condition for a liberal disposition; it is not the sole cause of any particular Jew's liberal propensities. We only can say that Jewishness results in a liberal political disposition in combination with or in the presence of other as yet unknown variables. Consequently, we can only deduce the probability that any given Jew is liberal. Of course, the more that we learn the nature of some of the aforementioned unknown variables and their effect on the fact to be explained (hereafter referred to by its more technical term, the explicandum), the more we correspondingly increase our ability for accurate prediction. At the present, the goal of prediction in political science must be framed in terms of increasingly high probabilities.

Clearly, as the number and variety of observed specific cases of a phenomenon increases, the number of known variables that can affect the likelihood of the phenomenon's occurrence will also increase. For the sake of clarity, let us consider a highly simplified example, the phenomenon of stable democracy, operationally defined.[11] Logically, it is possible to infer from a comparison of the Anglo-American democracies on the one hand and Italy and Latin American democracies on the other that stable democracy is a function of some definable economic indicators (gross national product or per capita income, for example). Confidence in this proposition would increase with each additional case of a stable democracy that possessed such economic characteristics. However, when one examines a deviant case, such as prewar Germany, which possessed said characteristics but had not attained stable democratic government, one must conclude that economic prosperity alone is insufficient to cause that form of government. By ascertaining the way the deviant case differs from the stable democracies with economic prosperity, one may be able to uncover additional necessary preconditions for stable democracy. One may now be able to suggest that economic prosperity leads to stable democracy only in the presence of additional specified circumstances, such as a particular cultural context containing particular patterns or norms of authority.[12] A prediction that a country which possessed the first characteristic would have a stable democ-

---

[11] An example of such a definition may be found in Seymour Lipset, *Political Man* (New York: Doubleday Anchor Books, 1963), pp. 30–31.

[12] Cf. Harry Eckstein, "A Theory of Stable Democracy," in his *Division and Cohesion in Democracy* (Princeton: Princeton University Press, 1966), pp. 225–287.

racy would have a given rather low probability of being correct, but a prediction that a nation which possessed both characteristics would have a stable democracy would have a higher probability of being correct.[13] As stable democracy is observed in an increasing variety of contexts, it becomes increasingly possible to sort out those variables which are uniformly associated with stable democracy and those which are peculiar to certain contexts, to inferentially distinguish spurious (coincidental) associations from causal associations.

INCOMPLETE EXPLANATION AND EXPLANATION SKETCHES

Due to the lack of laboratory conditions in the social sciences, all explanations are likely to be incomplete. Yet, the completeness of an explanation is a relative term. The more of the totality of factors that were involved in bringing about the event to be explained that are accounted for, the more complete the explanation. Completeness of explanation is a goal toward which we strive but which we never reach.

An understanding of this notion of incomplete explanation is necessary to have an appreciation of the applicability of scientific methodology to political inquiry. The major hurdle to such applicability is not the unattainability of laboratory conditions for social research but rather a lack of precise empirical indicators for our hitherto amorphous concepts. One should not foreclose the possibility that increased ingenuity in specifying such indicators might go a long way toward remedying this situation. Indirect indicators can play a large role here, as shown in Chapter 1, especially with regard to dispositional concepts (referring to states of the mind).

Even an incomplete explanation implies a precise statement of the empirical implications of the premises or covering laws. Covering law is a term referring to a generalization that subsumes the fact to be explained and logically implies the expected occurrence of that fact. Such implications (or entailments) of the covering laws may refer to the probability of the occurrence of an event rather than its necessary occurrence.

When the observable expectations deduced from a covering law cannot be precisely specified (generally due to the use of imprecisely defined concepts in the covering law), the proposition generates explanatory appeal but not explanatory power in the sense that those terms are used on page 44. Much of the literature in comparative politics consists of such "explanation sketches"[14] rather than scientific explanations capable of enhancing

---

[13] The probability would be equal to the number of cases reflecting the relationship between the characteristic and stable democracy divided by the total number of countries possessing the characteristic, stable or otherwise.

[14] This term was coined by Carl Hempel, "The Function of General Laws in History," in Hempel, *Aspects of Scientific Explanation and Other Essays in the Philosophy of Science* (New York: The Free Press, 1965), p. 238.

the ability to predict. Yet, the prevalence of such quasiscientific explanation sketches, producing only explanatory appeal and generated by imprecise covering laws, should not be taken as an indication of the inapplicability of the scientific method in comparative political analysis. In the event the concepts in such imprecise covering laws are rendered empirical, such propositions could indicate the direction of fruitful inquiry.

The efforts of men like Lucien Pye, for example, are primarily directed toward the construction of such explanation sketches. Pye's work on Burma, discussed in Chapter 8, has the heuristic or suggestive function of pointing out some dispositional variables that might logically account for some observed characteristics of non-Western political systems.

Thus, explanation sketches might be argued to provide one attainable intermediate step toward the goal of explanatory power. The fact that such efforts fall short of directly generating explanatory power does not necessarily mean that they are not instrumental to that ultimate goal. It becomes increasingly possible to become aware of more of the relevant variables. It is one thing to know A has resulted in B thus far. It is more accurate to know that A only results in B in the presence of C when more cases are observed. The qualifications on oversimplified causal propositions may be derived from the discovery of deviant cases.

When Ferdinand A. Hermans proposed that elections by proportional representation caused instability,[15] he overlooked the deviant cases of Norway and Sweden, among others. By including these cases, Hermans's proposition may be refined to say that proportional representation results in a high probability of instability in the presence of an already fragmented political culture. A prediction of instability based upon the election system alone would have a lower probability of being correct than one based upon both the institutional and the cultural variables.

THE PROBLEM OF CAUSALITY

Causation is usually used to mean that some phenomenon is an effective agent in bringing about some event or state of affairs or that the explicandum (the fact or event to be explained) has a *functional dependence* on the explicans (the concepts which putatively account for the explicandum). In other words, some essential quality of the explicans gives effect to the explicandum.

A variable whose magnitude or type is a function of (wholly or partially caused by) another variable is called a dependent variable with relation to that other variable. Technically speaking, the magnitude or type of an independent variable is, as the name implies, completely independent or

---

15 Ferdinand A. Hermans, *Europe Under Democracy or Anarchy* (South Bend, Ind.: University of Notre Dame Press, 1940).

autonomous of all other variables. In practice, we give the name independent variable to the causal variable in the particular relationship to which we are referring.

In this sense, independent variable and explicans on the one hand and dependent variable and explicandum on the other are practically interchangeable. Professor Nagel lists the conditions for the *necessary* conclusion that a given relationship is causal as follows: (1) the relationship is invariable; (2) the explicans is both a necessary and sufficient condition for the explicandum although the practice is rather than list the sufficient conditions, to list the event that completes the sufficient conditions; (3) the relationship is between phenomena that are spacially contiguous; and (4) the explicandum follows the explicans in an invariable temporal sequence and the relation is asymmetrical (A results in B but B does not result in A).[16] If these conditions are not met, one may still conclude that the relationship *may* be caused or that the explicans may *partially* cause the explicandum. In such circumstances causation is inferred.

As the above examples imply, causation is inferred, not proven in science. David Hume has told us that propositions about causality are derived from experience; that is, by observing the repeated conjunction of observable phenomena, we infer that similar phenomena will continue to occur in conjunction in the future.[17] However, there is no logical reason why this should be so. What can actually be observed is either the repeated association or the correlation of phenomena. Association simply refers to the fact that two phenomena tend to occur together. Correlation refers to the propensity of one variable to change at a proportional rate to changes in the magnitude of another variable. When two variables or phenomena have a high frequency of joint occurrence, the fact is frequently used as supporting evidence for the inference that one variable is at least a partial cause of the other. To logically infer that a phenomenon is a sufficient precondition of another, the pattern of association between them would have to be invariable.

To continue with the same example, the proposition that all or most Jews are liberal is a statement of contingency or association. The great contribution of David Hume was that he made us realize that propositions about causation (e.g., that there is something about Jewishness that causes its adherents to be liberal) must be logically inferred and are not a direct consequent of observation. Thus, such causal propositions cannot be scientifically proven.

Clearly, the ability to infer causation is enhanced from a general familiarity with the subject matter. In the above example, we know that Jews have

---

16 Nagel, op. cit., p. 74.

17 David Hume, *An Inquiry Concerning Human Understanding* (1748), reprinted in Ernest Nagel and Richard Brandt (eds.), *Meaning and Knowledge, Systematic Readings in Epistemology* (New York: Harcourt, Brace & World, 1965), pp. 323–30.

suffered discrimination, feel themselves to be something of a pariah people, and often possess an internationalist predisposition, perhaps stemming from their sense of community with their fellow Jews in other countries. Moreover, we know that the theological bases of the religion do not specify a rigid set of beliefs or truths, a lack of dogma which could encourage that philosophical relativism, that sense of contingency with regard to propositions, which would be a prerequisite for susceptibility to new ideas. Therefore, we have *logical* bases for saying the essential properties of Jewishness could *cause* liberalism. This provides additional grounds for inferring causation from empirical contingency (association). However, the proposition about causation is in large part logically based and only partially empirically based.

Fig 2–1 constitutes an example of a table illustrating an association between two dichotomous variables. It presents hypothetical data on the relationship between interparty competitiveness (as measured by Banks and Textor)[18] and literacy rates. The numbers indicate the number of countries falling within each cell. For simplicity the variables have been dichotomized into discrete high and low cells. The data suggest that countries with a high degree of such competitiveness tend to also be the countries with a high literacy rate, although this is not invariably the case.

Two things should immediately be noted about Figure 2–1. The data themselves do not distinguish the independent and the dependent variable; according to the strict canons of logic, one could as easily infer that party competitiveness caused a high literacy rate as vice versa. Only an independent (from this data) familiarity with the subject matter would enable one to distinguish cause and effect. Secondly, inasmuch as some cases fall in the upper right-hand and lower left-hand cells, it must be inferred that

FIGURE 2–1

LITERACY RATE

		High	Low
COMPETITIVENESS	High	30 A	2 B
	Low	15 C	40 D

---

[18] Arthur Banks and Robert Textor, *A Cross Polity Survey*, (Cambridge, Mass.: M.I.T. Press, 1963).

high literacy itself is neither a necessary nor a sufficient cause of party competitiveness.

The cases in cell B suggest that it is possible to have high competitiveness without high literacy, but the unspecified preconditions for such a relationship rarely are present. The cases in cell C suggest that since a high literacy rate does not invariably result in high competitiveness, other unspecified variables must also be necessary for this relationship.

The point of the foregoing illustration is that measures of association do not constitute proof of causation. They do not even establish a temporal sequence for the occurrence of the phenomena in question. Such measures merely furnish empirical support (or the lack thereof) for the inference of causation based upon familiarity with the subject matter. There is an additional problem in the inference of causation from association implied by Professor Nagel's fourth condition for such an inference. Causal relations are asymmetrical (A causes B but B does not cause A). However, it is likely than many strong associations are a function of reciprocal relationships.

When it is inferred that a two-party system causes stable democracy from the invariable relationship between that party system and that type of political system, the possibility that two-party systems may be a consequence of stable political conditions is being ignored. In short, unless a temporal sequence can be definitely established, it may be (1) that the effect is being mistaken for the cause and vice versa or (2) more likely, that both phenomena in question encourage one another in reciprocal fashion.

FIGURE 2-2

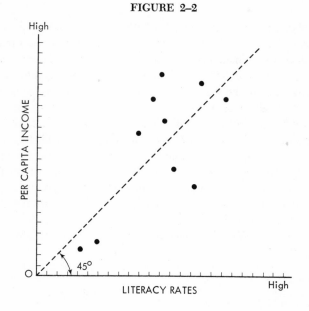

The foregoing problems of causal inference also apply to correlation. This statistical technique results in the widely used "Pearsonian r," the magnitude of which may vary from 0 to 1.

Figure 2–2 illustrates a graph showing the correlation between the various magnitudes of two continuous variables. The data on the relationship between literacy rates and per capita income in several nations are hypothetical. The dots represent the individual nations to which a value from each variable may be attributed.

If the magnitude of the independent variables were a necessary and a sufficient condition for the magnitude of the dependent variables (the independent variables were the sole cause of the dependent variables), all of the cases would fall on a straight line forming a 45° angle with each axis of the graph. The measurement of linear correlation is based on the variation in magnitudes of the two variables about their means (actually the squared variation). The resulting figure for the coefficient of correlation indicates the extent of the variation in the dependent variable that is explained by the independent variable.[19]

Clearly, this is another example of a statistical relationship from which causation must be inferred. One may find a positive correlation over a period of time between life expectancy and the per capita consumption of alcohol; however, few people would conclude that alcoholism prolongs life.[20] The question of whether the variation in the values of the independent variable can be construed to partially explain the variation in the values of the dependent variable is as much a function of a prior knowledge of the properties of the two variables as the magnitude of the correlation coefficient.

Thus, a choice is encountered of whether to conclude that whatever strength of correlation or association that is observed and measured is the result of chance or coincidence or whether the observed contingency or correlation is due to an underlying causal relationship between the variables. Statistics cannot tell us how to choose. Statistics can provide us with the probability that a given measure of contingency could have occurred by chance in an infinite number of trials. The choice that is made depends on whether one would rather take a chance on rejecting a true hypothesis or accepting a false hypothesis. One may be less willing to risk a wrong decision when it involves the hypothesis that the public sale of a new drug will not result in death or harm to its users than when the hypothesis involves a relatively unexplored field of knowledge and when a mistake does not involve any significant human suffering.

The necessity of such decision making is a result of a probabilistic body

---

[19] Herbert Blalock, *Social Statistics* (New York: McGraw-Hill Book Co., 1960), pp. 274–82 and 295–99, esp. 296–97.

[20] John H. Mueller and Karl F. Schuessler, *Statistical Reasoning in Sociology* (Boston: Houghton-Mifflin Co., 1961), p. 325.

of knowledge in a field where it is unlikely to ever be possible to assert with finality that the nature and effect of all relevant variables are known. It is because of this lack of certainty about unexamined variables that predictions in political science are (and will almost certainly always be) probabilistic rather than deterministic.

It is possible to argue that a substantial number of generalizations or laws in the natural sciences are also probabilistic. The difference between the natural sciences and the behavioral sciences is that in the former disciplines the probabilities of a correct prediction or a correct decision on the acceptance or rejection of hypotheses are much higher because a much higher percentage of the relevant variables are known. Exceptions have in fact been discovered to a number of laws and even major theories in the physical sciences. Galileo's law about the relation between time and distance in free fall and Kepler's law about the relation between the period of revolution of a planet and its distance from the sun hold only approximately.[21] Newton's laws of motion leave some phenomena unexplained; these are accounted for by relativity theory. Even the latter is unable to logically subsume certain observed movements of heavenly bodies.

Hempel argues that there is a fundamental difference between deductive nomological explanations, in which the premises or explicans logically infer the necessity of the fact to be explained (the explicandum), and probabilistic explanations, in which the explicans merely infers that the explicandum is highly likely but allows for its non-occurrence.[22] The difference, he asserts, is that the claim of universality by the premises of the deductive nomological paradigm of explanation constitutes a different form from the less presumptuous claim of probabilistic statements. The distinction threatens to reduce itself to a matter of semantics; however, it should be noted that the *claim* of universality for a premise does not logically exclude the possibility that a deviant case may turn up in the future. A probabilistic statement, one may conclude, is simply a more frank and perhaps realistic assertion of the finite character of supporting evidence for any proposition. Insofar as a logical difference exists, one may say that in the probabilistic propositions deviant cases have already been found while no deviant case has been observed for a universal statement thus far.[23]

An additional problem in making propositions about causation is that such propositions logically infer a distinction between independent and dependent variables. However, in political science, absolutely independent variables are unknown. One may also elect to reduce the analysis to the cause of the cause ad infinitum. To use the Hermans example cited above,

---

[21] Carl Hempel, *The Philosophy of Natural Science* (Englewood Cliffs, N.J.: Prentice-Hall, 1960), p. 55.

[22] Ibid., p. 66.

[23] Karl Popper, *The Logic of Scientific Discovery* (New York: Harper Torchbooks, 1959), p. 315.

it was asserted that an instability resulted from a fragmentation of the party system which in turn was a direct consequent of a particular type of election system. The regress is arbitrarily halted at this point by a failure to raise the question of why this type of election system, propositional representation, is adopted by a given country rather than a single member district plurality system. The answer to that question may lead to an analysis of cultural variables which, presumably, were also caused.

CONCLUSION

The structure of all explanation is logically the same. The explicanda are subsumed in a more general relationship from which they could be deduced. Explanations are incomplete if all the causal variables and the impact on the explicanda are not known. Explanation and prediction have the same logical form; the power to do one necessitates the power to do the other. However, the ability to predict the necessary occurrence of an event is a function of having a complete explanation, something which is very rare in any discipline and virtually nonexistent in comparative politics. The basic distinction between the natural sciences and political science is that explanations in the former are relatively more complete than in the latter, and predictions of given events can thus be made with a higher probability of correctness.

Propositions about causation must generally be inferred rather than proven in any discipline. This is particularly true in political science, where propositions involve the contingent association of a very limited number of the variables relevant to a given problem. Hence, causal inferences have relatively less empirical support in political science than in the natural sciences, where the associations are more nearly invariable. This is a function of the natural sciences possessing much more complete explanations than does political science.

Laws and Generalizations

Science involves a search for regularities and patterns in the way phenomena are related to one another. It was pointed out in the previous chapter that the explanation of phenomena involves the subsumption of those phenomena in a statement about how they are related to other phenomena. Such a statement about the relationship between empirical phenomena is referred to in science as a law or generalization.

THE LOGIC OF INDUCTIVE INFERENCE

The term law is often reserved for statements about invariable relationships in the form of *all x* are *y* or *all* two-party systems are stable. If this interpretation is adopted, there are very few laws in political science; the relationships thus far discerned by political scientists are almost always contingent rather than invariable and probabilistic rather than deterministic. Whether one wishes to reserve the term law for deterministic relationships or to use the terms law and generalization interchangeably is simply a matter of semantic preference. Of course, even statements about invariable relationships in the natural sciences as well as in political science are tentative. Such statements are invariable as far as we know, but the possibility that a deviant case may be found can never be logically excluded.

This is what Karl Popper meant by "the problem of induction." As he put it, no matter how many white swans you have seen without encountering a swan of a different color, you still cannot say with certainty that all swans are white. At some undiscovered place or at some future time a black swan may still turn up.[1]

This does not mean that once phenomena are observed that are logically incompatible with a generalization (or theory), that generalization loses

---

[1] Karl Popper, *The Logic of Scientific Discovery* (New York: Harper Torchbooks, 1954), p. 27.

its scientific utility. The wide range of phenomena that are subsumed under Newton's laws of motion are still in large part explained by those laws despite the fact that some observed events in the physical universe cannot be subsumed under those laws. To put the point in a political context, it is still useful to know that overy ninety percent of the American Jews are liberal despite the existence of a few Milton Friedmans.

The logical consequence of the problem of induction is that there is no such thing as an eternal truth in science in the theological sense of that term. Perhaps it is no accident that organized religion more often loses its hold on people who have been highly educated in a scientific discipline than on those who have not; certainly the imperatives of the scientific method lead to an epistemological relativism. The problem of induction discussed below refers to the tentative nature of all scientific propositions. This means that a proposition can never conclusively be proven to be eternally true. If deviant cases have never been found thus far in the case of a deterministic proposition, or if few enough deviant cases have been observed *thus far* in the case of a probabilistic proposition, the proposition is tentatively accepted. However, if incompatible evidence is found, the good scientist will discard his original proposition or revise it to fit the new evidence. The difference between theology and science may be observed here by noting that the orthodox Christian doctrines were not revised to accommodate the discovery of the Dead Sea Scrolls.[2] Religious truths are true for all times regardless of whatever evidence may be discovered; scientific propositions cannot be. Scientists sometimes do in fact reject incompatible data to preserve semisacred propositions. The persecution of Galileo and the resistance of the adherents to the Ptolmeic theory of the universe to Copernican theory constitute classic examples of such practices. This, however, is simply not science.

THE CRITERION OF TESTABILITY

If the truth of a scientific proposition can never be proven, what then is the essential nature of a scientific statement that distinguishes it from other statements? What is the precise relationship of a scientific statement to empirical data that makes such a statement scientific?

Clearly, it is inadequate to merely say that a scientific statement must be empirically testable. This could be construed to mean, for example, that the statement must correspond to some empirical evidence. An example of this type of distortion of scientific methodology will be discussed below under the heading "the tentative nature of scientific conclusions," illustrating the fact that no finite number of observations which are compatible with a proposition will prove its truth.

---

[2] See Hugh J. Schonfield, *Secrets of the Dead Sea Scrolls* (London: Valentine Mitchell Co., 1957).

The criterion for testability is that a statement be stated in such a way that it could be proven false. More specifically, such a statement must precisely delineate a category of empirical data which are incompatible with the statement and which, if observed, would cause the statement to be rejected or revised. Thus, for every empirical statement there must be a category of data which could not be explained away, if observed, thereby saving the hypothesis. Accordingly, statements with unspecified ceteris paribus (other things being equal) qualifiers are incapable of being falsified.

A few examples should help clarify the foregoing. Clearly, a proposition about a universal or invariable relationship would be falsified by the appearance of a single deviant case. Thus, if Hermans intended his now famous proposition that proportional representation causes instability[3] to imply that proportional representation is a necessary and sufficient condition for instability, the case of Norway would require the rejection of Hermans's thesis. If, on the other hand, Hermans meant that the existence of proportional representation makes instability more likely to occur, but that this consequence will occur only in the presence of other *unspecified* circumstances, Hermans could retain his thesis despite any number of deviant cases by claiming that the other unspecified conditions were not right.

Of course, it is unreasonable to expect Hermans to specify all of the factors that could affect a nation's stability. However, he must specify some precise, unambiguous result of his premise. Perhaps he could say that a given proportion of those nations which adopt proportional representation will be unstable on the grounds that if that election system were a partial cause of instability, the occurrence of mitigating circumstances which would produce stability despite proportional representation should not exceed a given frequency according to the accepted laws of statistical probability. Unless Hermans's premise could specify that one consequence will be observed (for example, a given frequency of instability in the presence of proportional representation) rather than any other possible observation, he has not explained even partially why we see one thing rather than the other. Moreover, he has not afforded us any logical basis for expecting that when proportional representation is adopted, any particular political consequences are more likely to ensue than if a different electoral system were adopted.

The widely used illustration of Freud's Oedipus Complex provides another excellent example of the same principle. Freud asserts that human males naturally possess a sexual desire for their mothers. However, the social taboos against incest are so strong that this desire is often severely repressed, often to the point of a boy manifesting a greater affinity for his father as a means of overcompensation. Consequently, if a boy is observed to have a strong affinity for his mother, Freud could say that repression

---

[3] Ferdinand A. Hermans, *Europe Under Democracy or Anarchy* (Notre Dame, Ind.: University of Notre Dame Press, 1951).

was weak in that case and the Oedipus Complex was manifesting itself. If the boy was closer to his father, Freud could say that repression is in operation. Thus, any conceivable set of observations could be construed as compatible with that aspect of Freudian theory known as the Oedipus Complex. Consequently, the theory does not explain why a boy loves one parent more than the other.

A proposition must therefore discriminate between data that are compatible with it and data which are not in order to possess explanatory power. Insofar as the category of data that is incompatible with the proposition is larger, the proposition offers a relatively more complete explanation. That is, a proposition which rules out more potential observations has a higher degree of falsifiability.[4]

Ideally, a proposition should specify the necessary and sufficient conditions under which a phenomenon will occur. When the phenomenon fails to occur under the specified circumstances, or when it occurs in the absence of the specified circumstances, the proposition should, according to the canons of the deductive-deterministic model of scientific epistemology,[5] be rejected. But when the proposition withstands empirical testing, it has provided a complete explanation of why that phenomenon rather than any other has occurred insofar as any scientific explanation can be called complete. Such a proposition would be falsified by one or more deviant cases; hence, it would imply a larger class of falsifying data than would a probabilistic proposition which could only be falsified by the observance of some specified percentage of deviant cases.

The difficulties encountered by the tolerance of deviant cases are aptly illustrated by two well-known works in the field, Maurice Duverger's *Political Parties* and Seymour Lipset's article "Some Social Requisites of Democracy."[6] Unless the conditions under which deviant cases will be tolerated are unambiguously specified, the distinction between what is compatible with a proposition and what is not will be blurred. Under such conditions, the proposition is not testable and is incapable of providing an explanation. The tolerance of an unspecified category of deviant cases allows the retention of a proposition no matter what evidence is found. Accordingly, the phrasing of a hypothesis in such a manner is frequently called "the saving the hypothesis fallacy."

Duverger claims that "the simple-majority, single ballot system *favours the two party system. . . . An *almost* complete correlation is observable be-

---

[4] Popper, op. cit., pp. 112–13.

[5] This model consists of the deduction of the necessary occurrence of specific events as in Newtonian mechanics. This is the classic model generally adhered to by philosophy of science purists.

[6] Maurice Duverger, *Political Parties,* trans. Barbara and Robert North (New York: Wiley Science Editions, 1963) and Seymour M. Lipset, "Some Social Requisites of Democracy: Economic Development and Political Legitimacy," *The American Political Science Review,* Vol. 53, No. 1 (March 1959), pp. 69–105.

tween [them] . . . . The exceptions are very rare and can generally be explained as the result of special conditions."[7] (Italics mine.) Several deviant cases are then accounted for by conditions which are unique to those social and historical contexts. The special conditions which could account for deviant cases are never grouped in an unambiguous category. Furthermore, Duverger does not suggest any minimum frequency with which it can be assumed that the unspecified special conditions would be absent and the hypothesis would hold true.

We are left with the proposition that a particular election system makes a two-party system more likely. But we are not told *how much* more likely. Therefore, the proposition is logically compatible with any number of deviant cases and does not satisfactorily account for the existence of a two-party system in some countries with the aforementioned election system and a multi-party system in others.

Even if the proposition were stated in a universal nomological form (*all* countries which have that election system *must* have a two-party system), this would not account for the adoption of that particular election system. It could logically be argued that the election system and the two-party system are both consequents of other unspecified conditions.[8] Hence, even if Duverger's "sociological law" were of a universal nomological form, it still would not prove a causal relationship.

Seymour Lipset also provides a clear example of a nonfalsifiable proposition. Lipset is asserting that social variables, such as income, education, and religion, are related to the ability of political democracy to take root. Specifically, he suggests that conditions of high per capita income and education and a de-politicization of religion will tend to support political democracy.

However, Lipset cautions that "unique events may account for either the persistence or the failure of democracy in any particular society."[9] Hence, there is no logical reason why a high degree of association between these variables would actually be observed. Democracy could exist despite conditions which are, ceteris paribus, adverse to that form of government.

Therefore, as presently stated, Lipset's proposition is logically consistent with any combination of these social variables and political formats in any

---

[7] Ibid., p. 217. Obviously the term *two-party system* would have to be rigorously defined to cope with the problem of minor parties. Although two political forces alternate in control of the national governments in both Australia and Canada, for example, there are more than two significant political parties in each country. Thus, it is possible to construct a defensible definition of a two-party system so as to either include or exclude either or both of these nations. See also the discussion of Duverger's thesis in Chapter 10, and Aaron Wildavsky, "A Methodological Critique of Duverger's 'Political Parties,'" *Journal of Politics,* Vol. 21, No. 2 (May 1959), pp. 303–18.

[8] Leslie Lipson, "The Two Party System in British Politics," *The American Political Science Review,* Vol. 47, No. 2 (June 1953), pp. 337–58, presents this very argument and even attempts to specify the other conditions.

[9] Lipset, op. cit., p. 72.

number of observed nation states. Thus, it does not explain why democracy exists in one place but not someplace else, and it does not afford us a known probability of predicting either the emergence or the maintenance of any particular political format in a given social setting. Lipset says that "the existence of deviant cases (such as Germany which succumbed to dictatorship in spite of an advanced educational system) cannot be the sole basis for rejecting the hypothesis."[10] What Lipset is saying is that the above-mentioned economic and social variables provide an incomplete explanation for the existence of democracy. Democracy, he would say, is *more likely* to exist in a country with a high per capita level of education than in one with a low level, other things being equal. In order to provide such an explanation, however, Lipset would have to specify what *would* provide the basis for rejecting the hypothesis. If not one deviant case, then how many deviant cases or what percentage of deviant cases out of the total number observed would provide the basis for rejection? In other words, if the proposition does not imply some specific empirical implications (for example, that among the countries with a mean level of per capita education above a certain figure at least some two thirds or more will be democratic), then the ceteris paribus is without bounds and the proposition does not tell us why any given country is democratic or not.

The specification of a set of probabilistic empirical implications from a proposition assumes a statistically normal distribution of the other unspecified but relevant variables, so that the specified variables will bring about an unambiguous result with some precisely stated minimal frequency. The existence or nonexistence of Lipset's "unique events" which could cause democracy to fail despite a high level of education should balance one another out to some extent in a large enough number of cases. Clearly, if a high level of education never resulted in a democracy, it would not be very helpful to say that the unique events are always present. This is tantamount to saying x causes y in circumstances which never occur.

LAWS AS RELATIONSHIPS

The mere fact that a proposition is testable according to the canons laid down in the preceding section is not in itself sufficient to justify the classification of a proposition as a scientific generalization. The ultimate purpose of such generalizations, to explain and predict, must be borne in mind.

Take, for example, the statement "it is going to rain this afternoon." Clearly, this is a testable statement. One merely has to define the time period known as this afternoon and observe if measurable precipitation occurs. Yet, the statement does not to any extent attempt to explain why it will rain

---

[10] Ibid., p. 70.

or to answer any other how or why question. Such a statement lacks explanatory and predictive power and is without scientific importance.

As the preceding chapter pointed out, explanation involves subsuming the fact to be explained (explicandum) in a more general proposition or set of propositions that are accepted as true (in the tentative scientific sense of truth). While the commonly held notion that explanation consists in relating the unfamiliar to the familiar has been shown to be untenable in numerous cases,[11] explanation does consist of the relationship between the explicanda and their premises (or explicans).

Thus, to say that a given political system will (or will not) be stable is clearly testable providing the concept of stability is precisely defined. But only a statement relating the fact of stability to some other variable (such as the congruence of authority patterns in the governmental institutions with the authority patterns of the society in which it operates)[12] will offer even a tentative answer to the question of why some democracies are more stable than others.

Relationships may take several forms, as noted in Chapter 2. They may be causal, they may be contingent (where two or more variables either tend to or invariably occur together), or they may be covariational (as indicated by measures of correlation discussed in Chapter 2). The latter two forms of relationship may be observed; causal relationships must be inferred as shown above.

THE TENTATIVE NATURE OF SCIENTIFIC CONCLUSIONS

One of the most difficult points about science for laymen to grasp is that there is no truth in science in the sense of eternal absolutes. That sense of the word must be reserved for the realm of beliefs, such as in theology. Alfred J. Ayer even argues that there is no point in asking whether a given proposition is true or false. His reasoning appears to be that the issue of truth is simply not relevant to the purpose of scientific propositions—the explanation and prediction of empirically defined phenomena. Thus, the assertion of truth in the metaphysical sense of the term implies an assertion of essential reality in the Platonic sense. The truth issue in this sense is neither possible nor necessary to resolve in scientific inquiry.[13]

---

[11] Ernest Nagel, *The Structure of Science* (New York: Harcourt, Brace & World, 1961), pp. 45–46.

[12] This is the thesis of Harry Eckstein, "A Theory of Stable Democracy," (Princeton: Princeton University Press Monograph No. 10, 1961), reprinted as an appendix to his *Division and Cohesion in Democracy* (Princeton: Princeton University Press, 1966), pp. 234ff.

[13] Alfred Jules Ayer, *Language, Truth and Logic* (New York: Dover Publications, 1952), pp. 88ff.

An empirical proposition specifies either by implication or explication what data, if observed, would cause its rejection. The proposition is accepted as long as that data is not observed; however, the possibility that such data may be observed at some as yet unencountered time or place cannot be excluded. The very notion of testability implies that the rejection of the proposition be considered as a possibility.

The criteria for the selection of data to fit the proposition must rest upon other grounds than whether or not the data are compatible with the proposition. This may seem so obvious as to be absurd; yet, data are so often selected in this manner as to make this self-evident statement worth explicating. One often finds this technique of defending propositions used with regard to the stereotyping of minority groups, for example. People, in defending an untenable statement to the effect that all Negroes are genetically possessed with certain pejorative characteristics such as stupidity or laziness, will often cite a few concrete examples as "proof" of their proposition. They offer no logical reason, however, for the exclusion of any intelligent, industrious Negroes as relevant data.

Thus, in testing a proposition, the researcher establishes some logically justifiable criteria for what data will be considered relevant and analyzes that data so selected to see if it is in fact compatible with the proposition as stated. Hermans, in the example cited above, might have had some difficulty justifying his failure to consider Norway and Sweden when he was presenting data to justify his proposition that proportional representation leads to the multiplication of parties, the rise of powerful extremist parties, and political instability. The fact that he cites pre-Gaullist France, prewar Italy, and Weimar Germany as examples does not prove his case. What makes them more relevant than Scandinavia other than the fact that they "fit" his conclusions?

Scientific propositions are, in a real sense, logical constructs which fit the data of which we are aware, constructs which must be revised to fit new data that are incompatible with the original construct. Of course, such revision can consist of specifically limiting the scope of the proposition to those data which it fits. For example, if a proposition to the effect that all political systems had a given characteristic were to be found to be inapplicable outside the western world, one might restate the proposition to assert that all Western European political systems possessed that characteristic and find the new proposition still useful in its more circumscribed scope. To put the point as lucidly as I can, propositions should be constructed or revised to fit the data rather than the data selected to fit the proposition.

THE NEED FOR PRECISION

One of the most frequently encountered complaints of traditionally oriented political scientists is that the so-called behavioralists unnecessarily spend a great deal of time attempting to specify the meaning of amorphous concepts, time which could more profitably be devoted to the analysis of more pressing and less trivial concerns. It is alleged that the numerous books and articles discussing precisely what we mean by a traditional political system, a developing political system, and a developed political system constitute a fruitless waste of energy. Such traditionalists argue that it is self-evident that the United States, the older Commonwealth, and Western Europe constitute developed nations, while most of the nations of sub-Sahara Africa, Latin America, and Asia are relatively underdeveloped. Accepting this as a self-evident postulate enables scholars to proceed with more fruitful analysis without any further waste of time and energy.

It is not, however, merely an exercise in pedantics to devote attention to the precise definition of concepts. Such precision is a necessary part of making propositions testable. The category of potential data that is logically incompatible with the proposition must be unambiguous. To be able to say definitely which cases of a concept are compatible with a proposition and which cases are not, one must first specify those cases that are included in the concept itself. If this is not done, it will always be possible to explain away any deviant cases and save a hypothesis with the assertion that the deviant cases lie outside the scope of the proposition. The proposition that all stable democracies have a high literacy rate cannot be falsified as long as it is possible to say of a deviant case (a nation that is apparently a stable democracy with a low literacy rate) that it is not what is meant here by a stable democracy. One must establish precise criteria for which nations are to be called stable democracies independent of their literacy rate, the data to which they are being related. Failure to establish this nonambiguous class of falsifying data could result in a selection, if not a definition, of a class of items in terms of the characteristic with which that class is alleged to be associated. It is always possible to define a concept so as to exclude the deviant cases that appear. Certainly, if one is determined to do so, one could select some data to support almost any proposition.

Hence, empirical testing must be systematic in the sense that there must be a consistent criterion for which data will be examined. With regard to the proposition "Stable democracies have high literacy rates," the ideal situation would be to include all stable democracies in the analysis. If the universe of cases to which the proposition refers is so large that to examine every case would be impractical or impossible, care must be exercised to draw a representative sample for analysis. There should be some justification for excluding relevant cases from the analysis other than their lack of compatibility with the hypothesis.

THE SCOPE OF SCIENTIFIC PROPOSITIONS

The goals of explanation and prediction underlie the construction of scientific generalizations. Prediction refers to unexamined or not observed data. Professor Nagel has therefore suggested that a generalization, to have scientific utility, must generalize beyond the known evidence for it.[14] Thus, a proposition to the effect that all members of the current British Prime Minister's cabinet are Labourites would fulfill two basic requirements for the status of scientific generalizations. In the first place, the proposition is clearly testable. In fact, one deviant case would falsify it. The statement appears to take the form of what philosophers of science call a nomological universal (all *x* are *y*). Secondly, the proposition states a relationship. In this case, it relates position in the government to party affiliation. However, the scope of the proposition is restricted to a particular group of men and, as stated, does not imply anything beyond those 25 or so individuals that provide the direct evidence for the proposition. As such, it does not predict any unobserved phenomena such as the composition of future cabinets. As for explanation, the proposition does not suggest that there is a recurring relationship between the phenomena of party affiliation and position in the government; consequently, it does not offer any logical reason for inferring that their juxtaposition in this instance is anything but coincidental. Of course, if the position taken in Chapter 2 about the logical identity of explanation and prediction is valid, it would follow that a proposition that is utterly unable to predict would be equally unable to explain. This expectation seems to be borne out in this instance.

An all *x* are *y* proposition of such limited scope is commonly referred to as a restricted universal. Such propositions are not what is meant by scientific generalizations. A scientific generalization posits recurring relationships between phenomena beyond those which can be directly observed. This is why inference plays such a necessary role in building scientific propositions. These propositions describe phenomena or relationships that are not directly observed. Inductive inference assumes the patterns that have been observed will hold true for the unobserved future.[15] Deductive inference tells what observations can logically be expected in advance of observation. Both deduction and induction are techniques for arriving at justifiable propositions about that which has not been observed, propositions which further the process of explanation and prediction.

It should be clear by now that the number and variety of cases that can logically be subsumed in a proposition and hence explained are directly proportional to its scope. It would therefore be advantageous for the goal of a science of politics—that of *explaining* (in the sense of that term developed in Chapter 2) as much of the behavior of actors in their political roles as possible—to develop generalizations of the widest possible scope consistent with the standards of scientific rigor. This search for empirically justifiable propositions of the widest possible applicability clearly involves

14 Nagel, op. cit., p. 63.

15 Hans Reichenbach, "The Problem of Induction and Justification of the Principle of Induction," in Ernest Nagel and Richard Brandt (eds.), *Systematic Readings in Epistemology* (New York: Harcourt, Brace & World, 1965), pp. 334–35.

a search for discernable patterns among the widest variety of social and political contexts.

This is perhaps the primary justification for the comparative analysis of numerous political systems. This is one reason why the field of comparative analysis has been a leader in the attempt to construct empirically justifiable explanation in political science. A specialist in American government does have a distinct advantage with respect to the adherence to standards of scientific rigor in that he has a great amount and variety of reliable empirical data readily available. However, generalizations with explanatory and predictive power about phenomena not confined to the American context cannot be drawn from the American context alone. Propositions about such matters as political stability, the reason for a two-party system, or the cultural prerequisites for specified political consequences must be tested in as wide a variety of cases where the phenomena occur as possible. Failure to do this results in propositions heavily influenced by an ethnocentric point of view. For example, beginning students in American government courses often assert that the separation of powers constitutes a structural requisite for the maintenance of democracy. Such an assertion could only be made in ignorance of the fact that all of the Western European democracies are based upon the parliamentary system involving a fusion of legislative and executive powers. Any proposition about the requisites of democracy can only be empirically tested on the basis of a justifiable sample of all of the known democracies.

The scope of generalizations in cross-cultural analysis is limited by the fact that many social phenomena relevant to the explicandum (the phenomenon to be explained) are the product of conditions that are unique to a particular social context or are the product of a unique historical development.[16] Obviously, the histories of no two countries are identical, and these differences between societies will affect certain relationships being analyzed. For example, as shown above, the existence of a two-party system is alleged to be the consequent of one or two clearly delineated factors which recur in numerous societies. However, any nation's party system is to some extent a product of geographical and cultural characteristics and historical events that are peculiar to that nation alone.

Thus, propositions have to limit themselves to the similarities or patterns between societies and ignore the inevitable differences. Such differences are dealt with by the ever present but often implicit ceteris paribus qualifier referred to above.

THE FORMULATION OF LAWS

The persistence of the inductive model for the scientific method illustrates a common misconception about how generalizations are formulated. This

---

[16] Nagel, op. cit., p. 453.

model suggests that models are derived from random observations as patterns among these observations apparently manifest themselves. As an observer travels about just happening to see a number of swans, he suddenly comes to the realization that all of the swans he has seen are all of the same color. He therefore infers that all swans are of that color.

Aside from the problem of induction already discussed, this model has another serious deficiency. Reality is too complex for patterns to automatically manifest themselves. There are simply too many possible alternative objects of observation; hence, a selection must be made. One must know what to look for before observation is undertaken.

Hypotheses or generalizations are therefore extracted from experience in a much less direct manner than with regard to any formal rules of inductive inference. Experience contributes to that general familiarity with the subject matter referred to in the previous chapter which, together with a process of what might be called creative intuition, provides the researcher a basis for an expectation of what may be related to what and in what manner. This process of creative intuition closely corresponds to what laymen refer to as an educated guess. This is essentially what Albert Einstein meant when he said physical theories were " 'free products' of the human imagination."[17] To put it another way, generalizations are not really derived directly from experience but rather from human logic based partially upon experience and then tested against experience.

THE EXPLANATORY POWER OF GENERALIZATIONS

It has been asserted that the purpose of scientific generalizations is the explanation and prediction of political behavior. The explanatory power of a generalization may be distinguished from its explanatory appeal.[18]

The concept of explanatory power relies on the distinction between the ability to predict an event before its subsumption in a generalization and the ability to predict the event after its subsumption. If the subsumption of an event in a generalization substantially increases the ability to predict the event, the generalization has great explanatory power. Rapoport illustrates this with two examples. The laws (and theory) of celestial mechanics sub-

---

[17] Stephen Toulmin, *The Philosophy of Science, An Introduction* (New York: Harper & Row Torchbooks, 1955), p. 43.

[18] This distinction was most effectively made by Anatol Rapoport, "Explanatory Power and Explanatory Appeal of Theories" (unpublished paper prepared for a conference on Explanatory Theory in Political Science, sponsored by The Department of Government, University of Texas at Austin, February 1968). The discussion of this distinction in the ensuing paragraphs relies heavily on this paper. The paper referred to theories; however, since most of our explanation is at the generalization rather than the theory stage. Rapoport's arguments are applied to the former phenomenon. Thus, in the following discussion, theory, generalizations, and laws are not clearly distinguished inasmuch as Rapoport's concepts of explanatory power and explanatory appeal can apply equally well to any of them.

stantially increase one's ability to predict a solar eclipse over a wild guess. The random probability that an eclipse will occur at any given time is, of course, infinitesimal. Such predictions, when made with the benefit of the appropriate astronomical laws, are quite accurate. However, the theory of water divining does not substantially increase the ability to predict where water may be found over mere chance. Explanatory power is thus an objective concept insofar as the distinction between the probability of an accurate prediction of an event before its subsumption in a law or theory and the probability of an accurate prediction after such a subsumption can be measured.

The concept of explanatory appeal, on the other hand, is strictly a subjective phenomenon. A generalization with explanatory appeal engenders satisfaction that an event has been understood. Actually, Rapoport refers to the explanatory appeal of a theory in terms of its "integrative potential," the extent to which a wide variety of apparently disparate events are "seen in the light of the theory to be related."[19] But a generalization can provide a satisfying explanation even though its integrative potential is low, a satisfaction that may be the result of an unjustifiably inferred causation. (The previous chapter should have amply clarified the fact that the standards of justification for the inference of causation are imprecise. Such justification must be derived from a familiarity with the essential properties of the relevant variables).

Kaplan provides an example of such satisfying but unjustified (he calls them "runic") explanations.[20] Germany's problems just prior to World War II were said to be caused by the Jews. Kaplan's anecdote illustrates the runic nature of this explanation, an explanation that apparently satisfied many German citizens. When this explanation was proffered by a Nazi to a Jew, the Jew agreed that the troubles were due to the Jews and the bicycle riders. "Why the bicycle riders?" the Nazi demanded.

"Why the Jews?" came the reply.

Such runic explanations in comparative politics are supported by the widespread acceptance of myths. Oversimplified national character stereotypes constitute one important type of debatable premise, sometimes rooted in a partial truth, which lend support to appealing but spurious explanations. Other such debatable premises involve assumptions about the nature of man, the universe, or the deity.

Obviously, in the social and behavioral sciences, the explanatory power of generalizations is much lower than of those of the natural sciences in that the predictive power generated by propositions in the social sciences

---

[19] Ibid., p. 5.

[20] Abraham Kaplan, *The Conduct of Inquiry* (San Francisco: Chandler Publishing Company, 1964), pp. 330–31. See also Karl Hempel, *The Philosophy of Natural Science* (Englewood Cliffs, N.J.: Prentice-Hall, 1966), p. 48. Hempel says laws which provide such explanation fail to meet the standards of "explanatory relevance."

affords a rather low probability of accuracy. The probability of accurate prediction, as we have seen in the preceding chapter, is a direct function of the other-things-being-equal (ceteris paribus) qualifier. The size of this qualifier is very large in most of the generalizations of comparative politics. This is understandable in view of the fact that a widespread and systematic attempt to generalize in the field did not take place until after World War II. In short, probabilistic explanations and predictions are said to be of a lower level than deterministic explanations or predictions (of the type deduced from unrestricted universal laws of the form *all x* are *y*). An ongoing process of cumulative comparative analysis, however, should yield knowledge about the identity and relative effect of an increasing percentage of the variables that are relevant for the explanation of given political phenomena. This would progressively reduce the scope of the ceteris paribus clause attached to the explanatory propositions in comparative politics and thereby increase their explanatory power.

CONCLUSIONS

An answer to the question raised in Chapter 1, "What then is the nature of scientific knowledge that distinguishes it from nonscientific knowledge?" may now be attempted. A scientific statement consists of a statement about a recurring relationship between empirically based concepts or observable facts that implies or specifies a precise category of conceivable observations that would be logically incompatible with it. Knowledge of what relationships and in which form can be empirically justified in this manner offers man some measure of control over that aspect of his environment. To the extent that one knows that certain variables make a given political state of affairs more probable, one can possibly manipulate those variables so as to increase or decrease that probability to suit one's purposes. Thus, scientific knowledge is instrumental; if the scientist's assumptions about a relationship enables man to bring about a certain desired result or to predict events, that proposition would be useful from a scientific point of view and the question of its essential truth would be irrelevant. Laws by their very nature are tentative. They specify the consequences of conditions which may or may not appear in an if. . . , then. . . form.[21] Whether these consequences are specified in a tendency, probabilistic, or deterministic manner is irrelevant; the form of all laws is the same.

The term law in its more restricted sense cannot usefully be applied to comparative politics where such unrestricted universal propositions scarcely exist. However, comparative political analysis is a useful means of generating empirical generalizations, a name given here to the probabilistic version of what the philosophy of science purists refer to as laws. The adequate

---

[21] Nagel, op. cit., p. 470.

justification of scientific statements requires that either all the known cases containing the phenomena to be explained be included in the analysis or a justifiable sample of such cases. Consequently, propositions about phenomena that occur in more than one country cannot be adequately tested except through cross-national comparative analysis.

In a real sense, the proposing and testing of any relationship necessarily involves comparison at some level. If generalizations refer to recurring patterns, then the very process of constructing an empirical generalization involves the comparison of cases, selected according to some justifiable criterion of relevance, to ascertain the similarities among them. In this sense, the scientific study of political behavior inexorably involves comparative analysis. Comparative politics, in this sense, rather than be considered as a subfield of the discipline, may be thought of as synonymous with political science itself insofar as the latter aspires to be a scientific discipline. Nothing in political science can logically be excluded as irrelevant to comparative political analysis in this broader sense of that term. Comparative analysis can only be justified as a distinct subfield of political science if it is restricted to the study of foreign governments, a restriction not adhered to by most scholars in the field.

4

Theory

If a field of inquiry is to have the coherence necessary to merit the appellation of a discipline, something is required to relate the propositions of that field of inquiry to one another. Vaguely speaking, this is where theory comes in. As in every other field of inquiry which aspires to the status of a discipline, theory has occupied a major role in political science since its beginnings. Unfortunately, however, few terms have been used with so many different and incompatible meanings as has theory in political science.[1] Moreover, the term *theory* has been used interchangeably with several other concepts in the discipline, thereby adding to the confusion. This confusion and misuse of the concept theory will be repeatedly illustrated in the survey of the literature beginning in Part II. This allegation that the concept is misused is based, of course, upon the assumption that there is a widely accepted and clearly defined meaning of the concept theory in the lexicon of the philosophy of a science, an understanding which is also widely shared among practitioners in the natural sciences.

DEFINITIONAL

Theory, in the scientific sense of the concept, is understood to refer to a system of logically related, empirically testable, lawlike propositions.[2] Theory, in this sense, thus is based upon both the empirically observable world and upon deductive logic. Theory is not purely empirical in the sense of "the facts speaking for themselves"; there is a large element of human creativity involved in theory construction. However, scientific theory must

---

[1] Anatol Rapoport, "Various Meanings of Theory," *American Political Science Review,* Vol. 52 (December 1958), pp. 972–88.

[2] Ibid, p. 973. "A Theory is a collection of theorems . . . . but the theorems have to be translatable into assertions about the tangible world." See also, for example, Abraham Kaplan, *The Conduct of Inquiry* (San Francisco: Chandler Publishing Company, 1964), p. 295, and May Brodbeck, "Models, Meaning and Theories" in Brodbeck (ed.), *Readings in the Philosophy of the Social Sciences* (New York: Macmillan Co., 1968), p. 583.

be logically compatible with the observable facts that are within its scope. In this sense, theory cannot be held in contradistinction to practice or practicality; theory is, indirectly at least, about practice. In short, an empirical or scientific theory explicitly or implicitly rules out a precise category of potential observations. When observations are made which cannot be subsumed under or integrated within an existing theory, the imperatives of scientific methodology require that that theory be either discarded, revised, expanded, or circumscribed in its scope to remove such incompatibilities.

When David Easton wrote his classic book, *The Political System,*[3] he was calling for a new role for theory in the discipline of political science. Easton was here one of the early prophets of the so-called behavioral revolution in noting that political science has been unique among disciplines in that research and the discovery of political facts had no impact on what has been known as political theory.[4] What political scientists have called political theory is of course political philosophy. Specifically, it has aspired to consist of the discussion of such nonempirical and hence nonresolvable questions as the nature of the good state, of justice, of the extent of duty, of obedience to authority, or of the right of revolution. In fact, books and courses labeled as political theory have tended to consist of a chronological survey of what various allegedly "great thinkers" said about such questions, usually beginning with Plato.

Political theory has also included logically coherent, speculative thought systems which attempted to postulate sets of very broad outcomes based upon debatable sets of axioms or premises, or to postulate a series of relationships so sweeping as to defy testing. In this sense, theory becomes interchangeable with ideology. However, scientific truth status is claimed for these thought systems. The various deterministic thought systems, such as those of Marx, Hegel, and Toynbee, constitute examples of this use of the term theory.[5] They have in common the attempt to delineate a pattern in a set of impersonal forces (economic, political, ideological, etc.) together with the unsubstantiated inference that such a pattern is inevitable and will continue in the future. In short, certain such impersonal forces determine the course of history *irrespective of the will of man* to alter this course, hence the name determinism. In its most extreme form such a philosophy becomes a denial of free will.

Stage theory, in the literature on political development, constitutes an example of this type of "theory" in the comparative politics field. Like

---

[3] David Easton, *The Political System* (New York: Alfred A. Knopf, 1951).

[4] See Harry Eckstein, "Comparative Politics, Past and Present," in Harry Eckstein and David Apter, *Comparative Politics, A Reader* (New York: The Free Press of Glencoe, 1963), p. 1–33, for a comprehensive survey of this strange dichotomy between theory and research.

[5] See Karl Popper, *The Open Society and Its Enemies,* 2 vols. (New York: Harper Torchbooks, 1966) for a scathing attack on the deterministic philosophical systems. Popper refers to such writing as historicism.

Marx and Hegel, stage theorists postulate a series of stages through which all political systems must evolve. Kenneth Organski and Walt Whitman Rostow are among the leading proponents of such philosophical systems.[6] Organski postulates that all systems evolve through four stages: political unification, industrialization, national welfare, and abundance. Such theorists usually infuse their historical analysis with thinly disguised value preferences presenting a desired state of affairs as "scientifically" inevitable. With Marx it was the classless society; with Toynbee, it was a nostalgia for the *Pax Christiana* of the Middle Ages; with Organski and Rostow, it is western industrial democracy. Such philosophical thought systems tend to select empirical examples haphazardly to support their assertion without any criterion of relevance; hence, such philosophical systems are not logically capable of being falsified. They do not precisely exclude any potential observations. One of the interesting occupations in the study of contemporary Marxists is to observe how they rationalize all sorts of events as compatible with Marxism, events that seem utterly contradictory to the logic and predictions of the writings of Marx himself. Examples of this are the failure of capitalism to collapse, the failure of the class structure to polarize, the inclusion of the peasants as the backbone of most non-Western revolutionary movements, and the increasingly bourgeois orientation of the industrial labor force as defenders of the status quo. (Witness the current "hard hat" movement.)

Easton and Eckstein, along with countless others, called for a political theory that would be about how the political world actually is rather than, as they alleged to be the principal concern of traditional political philosophy, how the political world ought to be. The term generally used to refer to theory that is concerned with what is rather than with what ought to be is empirical theory. Traditional political philosophy is therefore widely referred to as normative theory.

One who is committed to empirical theory is, according to this dichotomy, accepted as "doing science." The difficulty is with the loose use of the term *empirical*. Empirical, in this sense, simply means being concerned with how political systems actually operate rather than with how they ought to operate; criteria of testability are often largely ignored when constructing allegedly empirical theory. The point is that simply proposing that something actually does occur in a certain way is not a scientific statement unless it can conceivably be falsified. Accordingly, theory built upon such propositions is not scientific theory. As pointed out in the first chapter, the requirements of being empirical according to the methodology of science are that concepts are precisely defined in terms of empirical indicators.

---

[6] Kenneth Organski, *The Stages of Political Development* (New York: Alfred A. Knopf, 1965) and Walt Whitman Rostow, *The Stages of Economic Growth* (London: Cambridge University Press, 1960).

THE CONCEPT OF SYSTEM

A distinction can thus be made between a system that is theory and a system that is not. It is first necessary to define what is meant by a system. A system consists of a set of *logically related* elements and the relationships or interactions between them. Such elements are distinguished from all elements not included in the system by some criterion or criteria of relevance. Therefore, there is a logically implied concept of boundaries. Boundaries refer here to the criteria that distinguish those elements included in the system from the elements not in the system.

The concept of a political system is one of the most frequently used manifestations of the concept of system in the discipline of political science. In designating what is included in this system, the initial task would be to define what is meant by political. Numerous attempts to define this concept have been made, many of them incompatible with one another. This widespread lack of consensus as to the precise meaning of what is perhaps the most fundamental concept in our discipline is one indication of the primitive state in which political science, as an aspiring science, currently finds itself. The definition of what is to be included in the concept *political,* once decided upon, would provide the criterion of relevance for deciding which elements are to be included in the political system. When David Easton, for example, defined political as "the authoritative allocation of values for a society,"[7] his criteria for what would be included within the political system became the elements that were directly involved in the process of authoritative decision making. Those elements which may influence those processes but do not formally or directly participate in them, such as institutions involved in the transmission of demands to the authoritative decision makers, are presumably not part of the system itself. Rather they are conceived of as part of the environment that interacts with the system. It is also possible to define the concept more broadly to include within the concept of a political system those elements that only affect or influence the process of authoritative decision making. The decision as to where to draw the boundaries of a system is based on the needs of a particular research project, not upon any rules of formal logic. It should be obvious that the concept of a political system is broader than the traditional focus on governments or nation states in that the concept can legitimately include those variables which are not part of the legal decision-making process, yet, which vitally affect that process.

A system is an analytical concept, as the foregoing should have made clear. There is not necessarily any empirical content to the elements of the system. That is, the elements of an analytical system are not necessarily

---

[7] Easton, op. cit., p. 129.

operationalized by precisely defining them in terms of empirical indicators. However, the elements of a theory must be so defined that statements about the logical relationships between them become testable lawlike propositions.

In this way, a system of logically related but, as stated, untestable propositions or concepts cannot have direct scientific utility. Such systems can be utilized to generate testable propositions which, because of the logical coherence of the original system, can be integrated into theory. This can be done by assigning empirical content to the elements of the analytical system.

MODELS

When an analytical system is devised or constructed so that the logical relationships between its elements correspond in logical form to the relationships between a set of elements in the observable world, such a construction is generally called a model. The technical term which refers to this correspondence between the model and that aspect of reality the model ostensibly represents is isomorphism. The correspondence is one of structure or form rather than one necessarily of content. By this I mean that key elements of the model have not been defined in terms of observable reality. Rather the isomorphism lies in the logical relationships between the elements of the model and the corresponding relationships in the empirical world. In a model of a simple communication system, for example, the input receptors are connected to selective information screens which filter messages on the bases of bias or prior perceptions. There are no such physical screens in the message network of a real political system, of course, nor are there necessarily formal, specialized receptors. However, the logical relationship between whatever set of institutions collects information for the real political system and whatever mechanisms filter out messages on the basis of prior perception is the same as the logical relationship between the corresponding symbols in the model. Models thus represent reality imperfectly.

Models are, moreover, to some extent a simplification of reality. Being a type of system, the elements of the model are selected from reality according to some consistent criterion of relevance. Easton's political system, which is a model of real political systems, focuses on the relationship between inputs and outputs and leaves the political system itself pretty much unspecified. Thus, when Easton defines the political system as that system which performs "the authoritative allocation of values," he is saying that phenomena which are directly involved in the performance of that function are part of the political system. His definition becomes his "criterion of relevance." Unfortunately, it is not always obvious whether an element is directly involved in this authoritative decision-making process or merely affects this process. In the latter case, the element becomes part of the environment which is the source of inputs to the system. Hence, the boundaries of the system are somewhat ambiguous.

Deutsch's model of a communication system focuses on the message transmission process, which of course does not in reality operate in isolation from all other processes.[8] Models, by simplifying reality, thus distort reality. By selecting a set of elements from reality and analyzing them as if they interacted in isolation from all other elements, the model builder is necessarily omitting some perhaps marginally relevant elements, elements that may have some effect on the outcomes in which he is interested. In this way, the distortion of reality inherent in models can lessen the predictive power of the research based on the model.

On the other hand, were models a perfect mirror of reality in every respect, there would be no point in model building. Models are useful precisely because they simplify reality. This process of simplification makes a complex reality manageable to man. Such a simplification is made necessary by man's limited biological capacities, as an observer and analyst, to absorb or to perceive a large number of elements and relationships.

Model building is, in a sense, one of the social scientist's ways of dealing with his inability to duplicate the natural scientist's laboratory conditions. The natural scientist is often able to physically isolate certain elements or variables for analysis in his laboratory; the social scientist cannot. A model does enable the social scientist to artificially isolate a set of elements for analysis, but the deliberate omission of other potentially relevant elements renders probabilistic any predictions about reality derived from a model.

This simplification of reality constitutes an important reason why model building is useful to the social scientists. A second reason is that the structural correspondence of relationships between elements in the model to relationships between a set of observable phenomena enables the model to be suggestive of what relationships logically ought to exist in the real world. When such suggested relationships survive a process of empirical testing, the model has generated lawlike empirical propositions. This is known as the heuristic (or suggestive) function of models.

Third, since the logical relationships and rules of interaction among the elements are already formally specified in the model, the task of logically integrating the lawlike propositions generated from the model into theory is facilitated. The relationships between several propositions generated from the same model are already suggested by corresponding relationships in the model. Since theory consists of a set of formally related, empirically testable lawlike propositions, the task of theory building is thereby assisted.

Fourth, models, because of their rigorous logical structure, aid in the organization of a heterogeneous and often amorphous conglomerate of

---

[8] Karl Deutsch, *The Nerves of Government* (New York: The Free Press, 1953) or "Communications and Decision Making Systems" in James Charlesworth (ed.), *Contemporary Political Analysis* (New York: The Free Press, 1967), pp. 273–316.

data. For the same reason, models can be useful in revealing gaps in the data and, consequently, in our knowledge.

One might sum up the utility of models by saying they are heuristic or suggestive of the directions future research on a given topic might most usefully take.

MODELS, SYSTEMS, AND THEORIES: SOME DISTINCTIONS

A system becomes a model when two conditions are satisfied: (1) when the logical relationships between, and the laws of interaction among, its elements are unambiguously specified, and (2) when these relationships and laws are logically similar to a corresponding set of relationships and rules of interaction among a set of elements in the real world. This specification of relationships between the elements of a system is known as the formalization of a system. Such a formalized system is sometimes referred to as a calculus. Models, however, cannot be called theory in the scientific sense of the word theory until precise rules of correspondence are formulated between the elements of the formalized system and a set of observable facts.[9]

The mere omission of certain marginally relevant variables does not automatically mean a system is a model rather than a theory.[10] Market or price economics is a theory which focuses on selected variables. For example, it discounts human motivations other than the maximization of one's economic utilities. The predictive power of the economic "laws" generated by such theory is rendered probabilistic by whatever impact the omitted variables will have on the outcomes in question. Again, for an analytical system to acquire the status of a theory, the elements of the *formalized* system must be assigned *empirical content,* a distinction many behavioral scientists do not seem to clearly recognize. Apart from the careless application of the term theory to many models or even less formalized systems, many of which shall be discussed in Part II, some scholars specifically deny the existence or the utility of such a distinction. Robert Dubin is one of the most blatant examples.[11] Dubin's attempt to bury the distinction serves only the purpose of confusion, however. This distinction is not a mere exer-

9 See Ernest Nagel, *The Structure of Science* (New York: Harcourt, Brace & World, 1961), p. 140.

10 Brodbeck, op. cit., p. 586.

11 Robert Dubin, *Theory Building* (New York: The Free Press, 1969) p. 8. Dubin mistakenly asserts that models and theories are indistinguishable in their power to generate "predictions about the real world," p. 9. In all fairness, it must be pointed out that Dubin distinguished between the *real* formation of a model and the testing of propositions derived from it, at which point empirical indicators must be specified so as to make these propositions testable. A real question exists, however, as to whether a model constructed of non-operationalized units is capable of generating testable propositions. Dubin uses Freudian theory as an example of a useful theory without empirical content (p. 187). But, as noted earlier, Freudian theory has failed to generate any testable propositions.

cise in pedantics among philosophers of science which has no relevance for practical "working scientists," as Dubin strongly implies. Because models lack empirical content, they are unable to directly generate explanation or prediction about the observable world. Only theories and laws with their rules of correspondence with the observable world can do this. Models can lead to predictive and explanatory power only insofar as they can generate laws and theories with empirical referents. The contribution of models to prediction and explanation of empirical data is therefore less direct than that of theory. The foregoing is not intended to imply that Dubin in his otherwise commendable book does not recognize that there is a distinction between "theoretical models" with empirical content and those without. By confusing the terminology, however, Dubin does not make sufficiently clear that only the models whose units are defined with sufficient precision so that they can be given empirical content can be of any utility in explaining and predicting observable phenomena.

GAME THEORY AS A FORMALIZED MODEL

An example of a formalized system whose elements lack empirical content is Euclidean plane geometry. Given the axioms of this system, the theorems are necessarily true by deductive logic. However, the basic elements of the system—rigid, two-dimensional figures—do not correspond to anything in the real world.

An example from political science is game theory. Game theory is a formal arithmetic model of the interaction of actors striving to maximize their utilities. Given certain assumptions, such as rationality and perfect information, the numerical outcomes of the possible combinations of choices can be deduced from the system. However, as the name implies, game theory is a kind of game involving the manipulation of numbers. Until those numbers can be assigned empirical content (precise rules of correspondence with utilities in the real world), game theory can yield neither empirical laws nor predictive power with respect to that real world.

Figure 4–1 gives an example of how game theory works. The most rigorous form of game theory and the easiest to manipulate is the two-person, zero-sum game. Zero sum refers to a finite quantity of utilities so that whatever is gained by one player is lost in identical quantity by the other. If A gains 2, B loses 2. The pluses refer to the gains of A and the losses of B. The minuses refer to the gains of B and the losses of A. Thus, in the first quadrant A gains 5 and B loses 5.

Game theory is generally played according to what is called the *minimax* strategy. This means that the players try to minimize their maximum possible losses. Another possible strategy, maximizing one's possible gain may not be consistent with this. The choice of one action that could possibly lead to his greatest gain could also lead to his maximum loss, depending on the choice of the other actor. If actor A makes choice 1, he could gain 5 if B

FIGURE 4–1

ACTOR A

		Choice 1	Choice 2
ACTOR B	Choice 1	+5	–4
	Choice 2	–6	+4 ← Saddle Point

also takes choice 1. However, if B takes choice 2, A would stand to lose 6. On the other hand, if A takes choice 2, the worst he could do is lose 4. However, the best he could do with choice 2 is gain 4. With the assumption of perfect information and rationality, A must assume B will take the choice that yields the best outcome for B. This would be choice 2 since B could only lose a maximum of 4 while choice 1 could cost him 5. Thus, A must assume he would lose 6 if he took choice 1. This is why the minimax strategy is the "most rational." Since both players are rational and they possess full information about one another's strategy and about all the possible outcomes, players A and B will each make choice 2 and the outcome will be quadrant 4. This outcome, which represents the rational minimal outcome for both players, is known in game theory jargon as "the saddle point."

The actual applications of game theory will be considered in Chapter 7, among them variations on the basic two-person, zero-sum game. For now, suffice it to say that unless the numbers are translated into observable phenomena, game theory cannot tell us anything about the real world. Numbers are symbols and it is necessary to specify what the symbols stand for in order to assign empirical content to an arithmetic model. As stated here, game theory remains a rational calculus, not a theory.

THE UTILITY OF THEORY

Theory itself is a step further removed from the empirical base of science than the system of empirical generalizations that comprise it. The laws which make up a theory are to some extent affected by the process of interaction.[12] In this sense, theory is an abstraction. Nonetheless, scientific theory is based on empirical referents, albeit somewhat indirectly (through laws), and therefore can play a significant role in the process of explanations and prediction of empirical phenomena. Perhaps the crucial function of scientific

---

[12] Kaplan, op. cit., p. 297.

theory is to push the frontiers of knowledge ahead. By systematizing and organizing existing knowledge in a logical system, theory can be suggestive of other laws that, given what is known, logically ought to be true. Thus like a model, theory has a heuristic function.

In this sense, theory helps identify the questions worth asking. These questions are those which would expand or fill the gaps in existing theory. Such a function would make the pursuit of knowledge cumulative, as discussed in Chapter 1. Consequently, as Holt and Richardson assert, a well developed theory would identify those questions the answers to which would contribute to a body of scientific knowledge.[13] Such questions must be kept distinct, they argue, from questions which are socially "relevant," such as the solution to America's Southeast Asia dilemma or the solution to America's racial problems.

Of course, whatever the merits of confining oneself to theoretically relevant questions at the expense of socially relevant questions, there are practical forces which make it difficult for a professional political scientist to make such a commitment to pure science. Society is most willing to support research which is most relevant to its problems regardless of the theoretic relevance of the research. Empirical research, which can become quite costly, can only proceed with the support of society. This involves that aspect of academic politics known as "grantsmanship," and partially accounts for the research supportive of the military-industrial complex that leftist students so vociferously deplore.

In addition to the heuristic function that theory shares with models, theory can play a direct role in the process of explanation. In the first place, as a fact is explained by subsuming it in a more general law (or theory), laws are explained by subsuming them in theories, as was shown in Chapter 2. Second, theory provides an additional means of verification, supplementing empirical observation. Chapter 3 raised the problem of spurious correlations or associations. What these amounted to were generalizations which squared with the available data but were nevertheless rejected as expressing relationships between variables which were not intrinsically related. If such generalizations are consistent with known data, a question is raised regarding the basis for their rejection. The answer to this question is that these generalizations are logically incompatible with a corpus of knowledge or theory that is widely accepted. If a proposition is found to be consistent with available data, that constitutes verification at one level of confidence. If, in addition, that proposition is logically consistent with all other related propositions that are widely accepted, the proposition may be said to be verified at a higher level of confidence.

To view the point from another perspective, if a proposition which squares with the available data is inconsistent with a widely accepted corpus

---

[13] See Robert Holt & John Richardson, "Competing Paradigms in Comparative Politics" in Robert Holt and John Turner (eds.), *The Methodology of Comparative Research* (New York: The Free Press, 1970), p. 25.

of theory, one would be more likely to suspect a bad sample of data used in testing the proposition than to immediately reject the theory. Theory, once established, tends to be viewed with much greater confidence than any given law (almost to the point of dogmatic rigidity).[14] There is perhaps a logical justification for such methodological conservatism. A theory rests on a system of *verified* laws, presumably tested against a variety of data; hence, theory rests upon a broader empirical base than any given law. Of course, any genuine advances in knowledge must contend with this methodological conservatism. This resistance of the scientific community to accept new findings incompatible with its accepted corpus of theory constitutes the thesis of Kuhn's important book.

Theory therefore presents a paradox regarding the extension of the frontiers of knowledge.[15] On the one hand, theory serves to point the way to new avenues of research, as shown above; on the other hand, it provides resistance to findings inconsistent with accepted theory. Despite this resistance, theory is clearly the most efficient vehicle for providing the coherence to a discipline that permits the cumulative extension of knowledge. This cumulative construction of knowledge was suggested at the beginning of Chapter 1 as a distinguishing characteristic of most disciplines regarded as scientific.

Of course, when the outcomes logically implied by a theory are not precisely specified, as is the case in several of the models and conceptual frameworks in political science for which the title of theory is claimed, competing theories may account for the known data that is relevant for the theories.[16] This requirement of precision is part of the requirement of testability. As the previous chapter on scientific generalizations suggested, the social sciences face a dilemma with respect to the requirements for precision which, on the one hand, may result in a stifling of imagination and a preoccupation with trivia. On the other hand, there has been, as Robert Merton suggests, an unfortunate tendency in sociology and in its intellectual heir, political science, to "theorize" with little regard to the ultimate goal of explaining and predicting to a probabilistic extent specific outcomes in the empirical world.

THE INSTRUMENTAL CONCEPTION OF THEORY

Theory is sometimes viewed purely from the standpoint of its utility in building a body of scientific knowledge. Proponents of this view argue

---

[14] See Thomas Kuhn, *The Structure of Scientific Revolutions* (Chicago: University of Chicago Press, 1962).

[15] This paradox is hinted at by Fred M. Frohock, *The Nature of Political Inquiry* (Homewood, Ill.: The Dorsey Press, 1967), p. 107.

[16] Robert K. Merton, *Social Theory and Social Structure* (New York: The Free Press, 1957), pp. 98–99.

that it is irrelevant whether a theory is really true or not; the only relevant question is whether it adds to explanatory and predictive power over observable phenomena. This is what Nagel refers to as "the instrumentalist view of theory."[17] As Nagel points out, this view denies the existence of theoretic concepts which, as we saw in Chapter 1, derive their meaning solely from their role in theory. Thus, "it is irrelevant to ask whether atoms really exist. . . . The meaning of such terms is exhausted by the role they play in guiding inquiry."[18]

This instrumental view of theory is not unrelated to the tentative nature of all scientific knowledge explored in the previous chapter. If all theories are capable of being falsified, none of them can be labeled true in the essentialist sense of an ultimate and final truth. Actually, it is this tentative property of scientific theory that leads to expansion of the frontiers of scientific knowledge. It is only when one or more deviant cases are found that theory is revised or rewritten and an awareness of new relationships is acquired. By contrast, theological "knowledge" is static; it cannot be said that more is known than previously about any given religious dogma. Scientific theory, unlike ideologies (in the sense of a closed comprehensible thought system capable of generating answers to a wide variety of questions), is always an open system capable of adjusting to any inputs in the sense of new unanticipated data. Theory must be revised or constructed to fit the data, not vice versa. This gives rise to something of a paradox with respect to which comes first, theory or data. Theory provides criteria of relevance for problems, hypotheses, and, consequently, data collection. Thus, as Maurice Duverger observed, one cannot do effective research without good theory but effective research is also a prerequisite to good theory.[19]

A possible escape from this dilemma is the construction of analytical models prior to, and as a foundation for, research. In order for such models to be useful in generating theory at whatever degree of generability, they would have to be precisely defined and capable of being operationalized. It would be recognized that such models would be highly tentative and set up with the expectation that they would need considerable revision in the light of subsequent research. Models, in this sense, may be regarded as a kind of a priori theory.

THE TESTABILITY OF THEORY

It should be clear by now that the crucial difference between a theory and a formal model is that the former logically implies some specific observable phenomenon or phenomena. All parts of a theory are not neces-

---

[17] Nagel, op. cit., p. 129.
[18] Ibid., p. 140.
[19] Maurice Duverger, *Political Parties,* trans. Barbara and Robert North (New York: Wiley Science Editions, 1963), p. xiii.

sarily so testable; some portions will be taken as axiomatic and the only evidence for their "truth" will be the empirical verification of those testable propositions to which they are logically related.[20] For example, if some of the events predicted by Karl Marx's philosophical system (which is treated as if it were a scientific theory but which is nothing of the sort) came to pass (for example, a global war or the collapse of capitalism), this still would not prove the truth of Marx's premises.

Moreover, the logically predicted outcomes of a scientific theory usually hold true only in the presence of certain auxiliary premises or additional conditions, some of which rarely obtain.[21] For example Newton's laws of motion do not take friction into account; consequently, they scarcely ever hold true in the observable world. This is simply another version of the ceteris paribus aspect of predictions. In many areas, others things almost never are equal.

Thus, a theory must contain, in addition to those internal rules relating units of a theory to one another, rules relating units of a theory to the real world.[22] To operationalize Veblen's "theory of the leisure class," certain principles would have to be stated about how the concept of "conspicuous consumption" is manifested in specific behavior patterns.

THEORY IN COMPARATIVE POLITICAL ANALYSIS

It may be apparent that this chapter on theory is more devoid of examples from political science than the previous chapter. The reason for this is that very little theory, in the scientific sense of the word, exists in the discipline. As has already been implied, much of that which is called theory consists of models, systems, or merely general orientations toward research. Such general orientations indicate sets of variables to be considered but often do not even specify the relationships between such variables.[23]

There are a number of possible explanations for this paucity of theory. One is the lack of consensus as to the relevant or important problems for study. Related to this is a lack of widespread acceptance of, not to mention research within, any given approach or model. Political science is in a state where the leading scholars are more devoted to the process of constructing competing paradigms or research frameworks than in actual substantive research. Part 2 will demonstrate the proliferation of possible approaches to cross-national research. The consequence of this lack of con-

---

[20] This evidence does not logically prove the axioms; it merely provides some support for accepting them. While the axioms serve as premises which logically imply the outcomes, the converse is not logically necessary. Brodbeck, "Theory Construction," loc. cit., pp. 457–58.

[21] Rapoport, op. cit., p. 988.

[22] Nagel, op. cit., pp. 97–105, refers to these rules relating theory to data as "rules of correspondence." Carl Hempel, *The Philosophy of Natural Science* (Englewood Cliffs, N.J.: Prentice-Hall, 1966), p. 74, calls them "bridge principles."

[23] Merton, op. cit., p. 142.

sensus on these two matters is that those relationships or empirical generalizations that are discovered are so unrelated to one another or formulated in such a manner as to be incapable of being integrated in more general theoretic systems. It is as if there were no glory in merely applying some already developed research paradigm to a specific care or problem; rather, academic prominence seems to lie in developing a new research paradigm and calling for others to apply it (if they can). Research paradigm is here used to refer to models, systems, concepts, and approaches that constitute a framework for research in the sense that Thomas Kuhn refers to a common paradigm in science.[24]

Of course, this lack of consensus on a research paradigm precludes cumulative or additive research. New relationships that are discovered can only supplement other known generalizations if the new generalizations are somehow logically related to the old. It may be said that the importance of widely accepted research paradigms justifies the effort and attention that has been given by political scientists to the construction of such paradigms at the expense of doing substantive research. Such substantive research can only lead to theory, in the scientific sense of the word, when done within the framework of common paradigms.

It should be noted that the plural was used to refer to research paradigms. There is no logical or scientific reason why there must be only one such paradigm in a given discipline. There seems to be a misconception among the "general theorists" of the Parsonian tradition that all knowledge in a discipline worthy of the appellation science must be integrated in a single theoretic system. This is not true even for physics. Einstein's relativity theory exists in the same discipline with Newtonian mechanics. What has been argued here is that several of the research paradigms must eventually acquire wide enough acceptance to generate a variety of substantive research applications within their logical scope. Concretely, for systems analysis, for example, to have utility, scholars will have to operationalize some of its logically derived propositions and apply them to a variety of empirical cases. Of course, it is in being able to provide this empirical variety of possible applications that cross-national comparative analysis has a scientific edge over other subfields of the discipline.

It is entirely conceivable that one research paradigm may be useful in answering only a certain class of questions, while another research paradigm may be suited to another limited class of problems. Similarly, the theory that results from such paradigms can be useful even if such theory is more limited in scope than a general theory of politics.[25] Such theory is much more feasible in the foreseeable future, particularly in a discipline where the objects of possible research are as richly diversified as in political science.

The paucity of theory in political science is also partly a consequent of

---

[24] Kuhn, op. cit.

[25] This is what Merton, op. cit., means in his advocacy of "theories of the middle range."

the paucity of reliable empirical data on a wide variety of important subjects. This is particularly true in cross-national comparative analysis where data collection has not been extensive and the data available has been less reliable. To some extent, the availability and reliability of data has been inversely proportional to the extent of economic and political development of nations. Consequently, the problem of acquiring reliable data is more acute in foreign nations than in the United States, and the problem is particularly acute in the study of the non-Western or developing political systems. It has been a major thesis of this chapter that the development of scientific theory cannot proceed divorced from data collection in an a priori fashion, but rather data collection and theory building must affect one another in a reciprocal fashion. If this is true, the paucity of reliable data is certainly an impediment to the development of empirical theory.

Related to and perhaps in a sense a cause of the paucity of data is the difficulty social scientists have in operationalizing some of their key concepts. It is impossible to develop theory with specific implications about observable outcomes unless the units of the propositions which comprise the logical system can be defined in terms of precise empirical indicators. This was discussed at length in Chapter 1. Clearly there is a notable lack of agreement among political scientists on the operational meaning of many key concepts such as power, democracy, or even a political system.[26]

TYPES OF THEORY IN COMPARATIVE POLITICS

Abraham Kaplan distinguishes "hierarchical" theory from "concatenated" theory.[27] The former is a vigorous deductive system in which the component generalizations are all logically interrelated and from which any of the component generalizations can be deduced. The latter consists of a set of empirical generalizations that possess a common focus; however, the logical relationships between such generalizations are not specified. Lipset's analysis of the prerequisites of democracy constitutes an example of this type of theory. This "theory" consists of a set of propositions specifying a number of factors that make democracy more likely to occur, such as economic prosperity, high literacy rates, etc. The importance of these factors relative to one another is not specified, however. Otherwise put, the factors are imprecisely related to a common focus, democracy, but they are not related to one another. The propositions which make up the set cannot be deduced from it; hence, this "concatenated" or factor theory is theory only in a loose sense of the term.

---

26 See Harry Eckstein, "The Concept Political System, A Review and Revision" (unpublished paper prepared for delivery to the 1963 annual meeting of the American Political Science Association, New York, September 4–8, 1963), pp. 2–4.

27 Kaplan, op. cit., pp. 298ff. Cf. also Eugene Meehan, *The Theory and Method of Political Analysis* (Homewood: Dorsey Press, 1965), p. 133.

Figure 4–2 schematically illustrates the structure of factor theory, using as an example a representation of stable democracy. It is similar to the work of Lipset except he did not consider all of the above variables. Note that the effect of each factor on the probability of stable democracy is indicated in such a theory (by the unidirectional arrows). However, in order to create a hypothetico-deductive theory, arrows would also have to point from stable democracy to each factor indicating a reciprocal relationship. More-

FIGURE 4–2

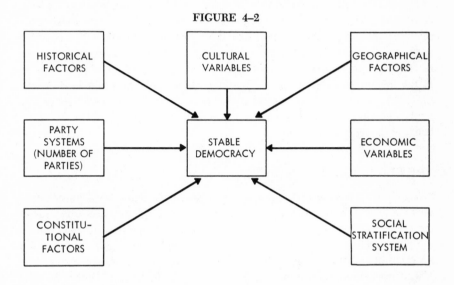

over, each factor would have to be reciprocally related to every other factor. Insofar as any theory is being constructed with regard to political development, it also tends to take on the structure of concatenated or factor theories, as will be shown in Chapter 12. There are no deductive theories in political science as yet. An example of such a theoretic system from the natural sciences would be Newton's theory of gravity, from which many laws could be logically deduced (for example, many laws of planetary motion, Galileo's law of acceleration in free fall).

Many social scientists, particularly in political science and in sociology, identify all logical constructs as theory. This is particularly true of those who engage in the construction of models of whole political or social systems, such as Parsons, Easton, or Riggs. Because such models or logical constructs have not been operationalized (in the sense of defining their key elements in terms of empirical indicators), Joseph LaPalombara has caustically labeled the construction of such exercises in pure logic "the New Scholasticism."[28] Because these logical constructs are not precisely

---

[28] Joseph LaPalombara, "Parsimony and Empiricism in Comparative Politics," in Holt & Turner, op. cit., pp. 126–27.

linked to the world of observation, they cannot contribute to the explanation and prediction of events in that world. (They are even precluded from contributing to incomplete explanation and probabilistic prediction.) For this reason, such constructs are not theory in the commonly accepted scientific sense of that term despite the fact that they are often so misnamed. The distinction between scientific (or empirical) theory and models or other analytic constructs has already been fully discussed. Of course, the fact that a model is not operational as it stands does not necessarily preclude the possibility of its being operationalized. However, there is a dilemma that is perhaps inherent in the situation. The effort to construct models and theory to lead to the explanation of the greatest possible variety of empirical phenomena has resulted in construction of such logical systems at the highest possible level of generality. It will be shown in Part 2 that the elements of a logical system constructed at such a level of generality tend to be vague and difficult (if not impossible) to operationalize precisely because they are so general.

THE CRITERION OF SIMPLICITY

It is widely asserted among scholars (but rarely understood among laymen) that simple theories are preferable to complex theories. The reason for this is best understood when the concept of simplicity itself is clarified. Simplicity refers to a relative absence of qualifiers or conditionals to the applicability of the theory. That is, a simple theory has fewer restrictions placed upon the circumstances under which it is applicable. Otherwise put, the ceteris paribus qualifier is narrower in a simple theory than in a complex one. Complex theories need to account for more variables than simple theories. For example, a relatively complete theory of stable democracy would have to deal at a minimum with party systems, a great variety of cultural variables, economic variables, geographic and demographic variables, and a host of other institutional variables. Compare this with Newton's theory of gravitation. Newton's theory does not have to deal with a large number of variables because it holds true regardless of the state of all other variables. Precisely because it holds in all circumstances, many more propositions can be deduced from it than from a more complex theory, such as a theory of stable democracy.

A simple theory has a greater degree of falsifiability[29] in that there are fewer qualifiers as to what classes of observations are incompatible with it. There are fewer variables involved in a simpler theory than in a relatively more complex theory, because the expected outcomes of a simple theory hold true regardless of the state of all but a few variables. The expected outcomes of a complex theory not only depend on the state of many variables

---

[29] Karl Popper, *The Logic of Scientific Discovery* (New York: Harper & Row Torchbooks, 1959), p. 142.

but also on the complex patterns of interaction among them. Because a simple theory is expected to hold true in a greater variety of contexts, there are many more conceivable states of affairs that would falsify it. For example, Newton's theory of gravity is expected to hold true universally; consequently, any deviant case would falsify it. In contrast Lipset's attempt to build a theory of stable democracy leaves room for explaining away any number of deviant cases, as was seen in the preceding chapter. This is because Lipset must place so many qualifiers on all suggested relationships (as between gross national product and stable democracy).

Because simple theories apply to a wider variety of contingencies, they have more *deductive fertility*. This simply means that more events and propositions can be deduced from or subsumed under such theories.

SUMMARY AND CONCLUSIONS

Theory is the mechanism that provides the integration of facts and laws into a coherent discipline. The behavioral sciences are unique among sciences in that they lack such an integrating theory, in the accepted scientific sense of the term. Theory, in this sense, refers to a deductively related system of propositions which logically implies some precisely specified observable outcomes or events. This paucity of theory is partly due to the paucity of reliable data on many subjects or from many geographical locations. It is also due in part to a lack of widely accepted and widely utilized paradigms or conceptual frameworks.

Because it is impossible to construct good theory *a priori* from sound empirical research and because theory is a major determinant of what constitutes relevant empirical research, an apparent vicious circle is created. Scholars in political science have been trying to resolve this dilemma by the construction of analytic models or conceptual frameworks which, while not directly providing scientific explanation and prediction, can provide that integration of knowledge and research necessary to the development of scientific theory.

In addition to providing criteria for what constitutes significant research and supporting directions for such research by indicating gaps in existing knowledge, theory provides another level of verification for empirical propositions. If a proposition is consistent with known data, on the one hand, but inconsistent with existing theory, on the other, it is always the proposition rather than the theory which becomes suspect. The reason is that theories, being systems of propositions, have been tested in a greater variety of instances than any single proposition. This is a means of recognizing spurious correlations and associations, a term referring to phenomena which manifest a joint occurrence or parallel rate of change purely by chance rather than because of an intrinsic relationship between the phenomena.

Because theory does rule out a specific body of potential empirical phenomena, it may be distinguished from models. Models are purely analytical constructs whose elements have not been assigned precise empirical content. In other words, the elements of a model have not been operationalized. Because of the falsifiability of scientific theory, it may also have been distinguished from such speculative thought systems as Marxism, Toynbeeism, etc., referred to generically as historicism.

Increasingly, general empirical theory is the widely professed goal of those who would make comparative government more scientific, perhaps the ultimate goal. The literature will be surveyed from the point of view of the question of the genuine contribution of each published effort to this goal, based upon the conception of empirical theory set forth in this chapter.

Before this survey can proceed—the task of the remainder of the book— it remains to dispose of the question of whether political or even human phenomena are susceptible to treatment by the scientific method. Although many respected members of the discipline consider this heretofore intense methodological struggle now largely resolved in favor of the "young Turks" of the profession, the so-called behavioralists,[30] there remain significant pockets of hard-core resistance. The task of the remaining chapter of Part 1 is primarily to respond to those who deny that the scientific method is applicable to the study of politics.

---

[30] See, for example, Robert Dahl, "The Behavioral Approach in Political Science: Epitaph for a Monument to a Successful Protest," *American Political Science Review,* Vol. 55 (December 1961), pp. 763–72.

5

Values and the
Traditionalist Protest

It has already been noted that faith in the scientific method, as defined in the preceding chapters, and the belief in its applicability to the search for all forms of knowledge is far from universally shared. The belief in the universal applicability of such a methodology to all knowledge has been an underlying assumption of this book. Knowledge is used here in the scientific sense of the term, a meaning which excludes intensely felt beliefs. "In your heart you know he's right" would not be an example of knowledge in the scientific sense of the term. This distinction between knowledge and beliefs has been hinted at earlier in the book; now that the essentials of the scientific method have been delineated in the preceding four chapters, this distinction can be specified. Knowledge refers to propositions that are testable in principle and consistent with all relevant data of which men are aware. Conclusions that are reached solely by mental processes and without reference to precisely defined observable data constitute beliefs. The failure to keep this distinction in mind underlies much of the reluctance of some political scientists to accept the utility of the scientific method for the study of politics.

It is to be contended here that those who polemicize against the scientific study of politics do so from a highly imperfect understanding of what the scientific method consists. Particularly, the antibehavioral critics tend to attribute "strawman" positions to political scientists who express the aspiration of applying the scientific method to their discipline, positions which no "behavioralist" has, to my knowledge, actually espoused and which many behavioralists have specifically disavowed. Such strawman characterizations of the behavioralists' position are, of course, positions which are ridiculously easy to devastate intellectually.

It should not be necessary to point out that the foregoing is intended to constitute an answer to the charge that the application of the scientific

67

method to the study of political phenomena is either not feasible or not desirable or both. As such, it is not intended to cast any pejorative implications with respect to the merit or utility of other modes of political research. Clearly, there is a need for the consideration of values in various ways as well as a need for more descriptions. The paucity of data about the non-Western world, already noted, testifies to this latter need. Thus, this chapter will be defensive in intent, not offensive. It is not intended as an attack on traditionalism but is rather intended to make a case for the position that the traditional and behavioral modes of research are complementary.

A further caution must be noted. The defense of the feasibility of the application of the scientific method on behavioral research contained herein should not be interpreted as an argument that the behavioral approach is not without serious limitations. A careful reading of Part II should make it clear that this study is not only well aware of such limits but contains serious reservations about the state of "scientific" research in comparative politics today.

VALUES, OBJECTIVITY, AND SCIENCE

It appears that the most frequently levied charge against the behavioralists is that they seek to establish an objective, value-free discipline while in reality it is impossible for any student of human affairs to free himself of his values.[1] The argument runs that behavioralists unavoidably and inexorably allow values to influence their judgments in subtle ways, while claiming scientific objectivity, a case of deceptively false labeling. This critique is applied most frequently and, in the view of this writer, most justifiably, to those systems analysts of the Parsonian school who focus on the question of how to maintain or restore the system's state of equilibrium.[2] Behavioralists seek to study, it is charged, how to achieve pluralist democracy and, in the very process of making that selection, become thinly disguised apologists for that system. Furthermore, without values or, as A. D. Lindsay calls them, "operative ideals,"[3] the work of political science lacks direction or a sense of purpose. There is no point

---

[1] For example: Sheldon Wolin, "Political Theory as a Vocation," *The American Political Science Review*, Vol. 43, No. 4 (December 1969), p. 1064; Christian Bay, "Politics and Pseudo-politics," *American Political Science Review*, Vol. 59, No. 1 (March 1965), p. 39; Leo Strauss, "An Epilogue" in Herbert J. Storing (ed.), *Essays on the Scientific Study of Politics* (New York: Holt, Rinehart and Winston, 1962), pp. 324–25; and Eric Voeglin, *The New Science of Politics* (Chicago: University of Chicago Press, 1952).

[2] For example, James Petrus, "Ideology and United States Political Scientists," in Charles A. McCloy and John Playford, (eds.), *Apolitical Politics, A Critique of Behavioralism* (New York: Thomas Y. Crowell Co., 1967), p. 76.

[3] A. D. Lindsay, *The Modern Democratic State* (New York: Oxford Galaxy Editions, 1943), chap. 1 and especially pp. 37–38.

in scientifically determining how to achieve a given state of affairs unless one has established, by nonscientific processes, a set of priorities about which states of affairs one seeks to bring about. In short, one must choose the topics of one's research in the light of certain ends in view. Political theory, in this view, must concern itself with such questions as the nature of the just policy, for without answers to these questions the discipline will remain in a state of anomie.

The charge, however, that many or most devotees of the scientific study of politics either advocate the complete removal of values from political science or assert that it is possible for the student of political phenomena to divorce his research from his values seems difficult to substantiate. Modern political scientists tend not only to confess to having value positions which underlie and affect their work; some of them go to great pains to clearly explicate those values.[4] Popper has argued that this is more than one can say for some of the great names in classical theory, such as Plato or Hegel, who constructed elaborate rationales for stratified social structures ruled by narrow oligarchies in the thinly disguised form of a search for the just or moral polity.[5]

What the behavioralists seek, in the tradition of David Hume, is to distinguish those propositions which are truly expressions of individual value priorities from those propositions which can be tested empirically. The charge that it is not possible to separate facts and values is based on the misconception that the behavioralists claim the existence of propositions whose formulation has in no way been influenced by values. The position of the behavioralists is much more modest. They simply aver that some propositions are empirically falsifiable while others are not. Thus disagreements about the truth or accuracy of the former category of statements can be tentatively resolved in terms of some objective criteria, while such disagreements about the latter category of propositions are never resolvable by objective criteria. The objectivity here refers to the fact that any number of people who see the empirical evidence must necessarily come to the same conclusion regardless of their values. This was discussed in some detail in Chapter 1.

Antibehavioralists often deplore the tendency of modern political scientists to focus on how individuals or nongovernmental groups seek to realize their parochial demands at the expense of a search for the "common good" or the good of the polity. Leo Strauss epitomizes this school in his explicit assertion that such a good can be known.[6] Modern political scientists reject this assumption that there is an essential national or community interest

---

[4] For example, see Seymour Lipset, *Political Man* (New York: Doubleday Anchor Editions, 1963), pp. xxi–xxii.

[5] Karl Popper, *The Open Society and Its Enemies*, 2 vols. (New York: Harper Torchbooks, 1966) persuasively presents a detailed analysis of these and other greats of the classical tradition from this point of view.

[6] Strauss, op. cit., pp. 322–23.

which is distinct from some combination of particular interests which make up that community. The classicists in the Straussian tradition have never made clear who is to articulate or define this community or national good. They seem to be utterly unaffected by Mannheim's caveat that all social judgments are "relational" to that judge's position in the socioeconomic system.[7] In short, as the classicists themselves constantly remind us, no one can make a social or political judgment utterly unaffected by his socio-economic interests. Mannheim's solution is that the best test of community interest is an open society in which particular interests are forced to compromise in order to win adoption as public policy, a society in which the various biases cancel one another out. Strauss, who was mesmerized by what Karl Popper has called "the Spell of Plato,"[8] has never answered that age-old question of those wise guardians of the community interests, Who guards the guardians? Divesting them of their property, as Plato would have it, does not insure total freedom from old biases, as Americans have seen time and again in the case of former business executives who place their security holdings in escrow to enter government service. For that matter, it seems to many that Plato dismissed with a verbal quibble the powerful argument of Thrasymachus that justice is what the powerful say it is or might makes right.

Be that as it may, scholars in the classical tradition have yet to demonstrate the possibility of delineating the interests of the community as such, totally uninfluenced by particular values. Until such time as classical scholars successfully demonstrate this ability, the argument against the political scientists' concern with the formulation and processing of actual demands advanced by individuals and groups seems hollow indeed.

Finally, even if it were conceded that behaviorally oriented political scientists ought to be more careful and explicit in articulating their biases, it is hard to see how this constitutes an argument against empirical research itself. Rather the argument seems to constitute a suggestion for the improvement of empirical research.

THE UNIQUENESS OF EACH MAN

One of the most frequently offered and most fundamental attacks on the attempt to utilize the scientific method in the study of politics is the argument that each human being is unique and therefore it is impossible to generalize about his behavior. This attack, if valid, would in fact consti-

---

[7] Karl Mannheim, *Ideology and Utopia* (New York: Harcourt, Brace & World Harvest Editions, 1936), pp. 78–79. See also pp. 102 and 106. Mannheim explains this as follows: "All points of view in politics are but partial points of view because historical totality is too comprehensive to be grasped by anyone of the individual points of view which emerge out of it," (p. 151).

[8] Popper, op. cit., Vol. 1.

tute a denial of the assumption developed in the foregoing chapters—that it is possible to apply the same methodological principles to political science that guide research in the hard sciences. For, as the earlier chapter pointed out, the ability to formulate generalizations about classes of phenomena lies at the heart of the scientific method.[9]

It is asserted that it is impossible to generalize about, and consequently to predict, the behavior of man because each human being is influenced by a very complex set of variables which are of an unmanageable quantity and unique to each person. The way a person was weaned, his relationships with each other individual that crosses his path in the course of his life, and various accidental states of his environment, are among the countless variables that are partial determinants of that person's behavior. The sheer quantity of these variables makes a complete explanation and prediction of human behavior practically impossible. The possible combinations and permutations of these variables approach infinity in number, thereby virtually assuring the uniqueness of each human being.

The basic misunderstanding underlying this line of attack concerns the nature of scientific propositions. To generalize means to specify a common property in a group of phenomena. Phenomena may have some properties in common without being identical in all respects. Sometimes the critiques imply that the myriad of knowable differences among people logically precludes the ability to make a general statement about them. Clearly, there are general statements which can be made about people despite the obvious differences between them. All living human beings have a beating heart, for example.

However, there is a second misconception about science implied by the foregoing traditionalist critique, one that is more crucial for political science. The claim that not all the variables which may affect human behavior in a given situation can be known, as a rationale for the abandonment of the attempt to explain and predict such behavior, implies that if explanation is not complete and prediction not completely certain, they are useless. Thus, if one cannot say that all countries with a high degree of rigid ideological commitment are unstable, it is of no use whatsoever to be able to say that most or even the overwhelming majority of such countries are unstable. If the uniqueness-of-man argument is advanced to point out the inherent limitations on the scientific study of any human behavior, the validity of this argument cannot be denied. If it is advanced to justify a total rejection of the scientific study of politics, however, it suggests a lack of familiarity with the nature and utility of probability theory. (Incomplete explanation and probabilistic prediction have been fully discussed in Chapter 2.)

---

[9] See my discussion of "the scope of scientific propositions" in Chapter 3, pp. 41–43.

THE UNIQUENESS OF CULTURES AND EVENTS

Related to the uniqueness-of-man argument is the uniqueness-of-cultures-and-events attack[10]—one cannot explain the French Revolution by the use of general laws, this argument would run, because there can be only one French Revolution. At no other time and at no other place will all of the countless factors that brought about the event known as the French Revolution come together in quite the same way. One can never account for the fact that the right leader was in the right place at the right time. Thus, Professor Kim is correct in his complaint that one can never make a prediction in the form of "a revolution of this nature will occur in that place at that time"; there are simply too many relevant variables which can only be known in retrospect. Moreover, explanations of revolutions given in retrospect are necessarily incomplete for the same reason. The great-man thesis, advocated by some historians, is part of the uniqueness-of-events thesis. If Karl Marx had not lived, would someone else have invented Marxism? In order to completely reject the thesis that historical events are brought about by unique individuals who just happened along at the right time and place, one would have to answer the above question in the affirmative. Historical determinism, the thesis that events are brought about by complexes of impersonal forces regardless of the will of individuals, is the direct antithesis of the great-man argument.

The error here is to regard these two positions as mutually exclusive dichotomies rather than polar extremes on a continuum. What appears to be the most defensible position, a position suggested by the discussion of incomplete explanation and probabilistic prediction, does not completely adopt or reject either polar position. Clearly, the will of individuals can, to some extent, alter events, but some limits on their discretion or ability to do so are imposed by events beyond their control. The Russian Revolution of 1917 would not have taken the course it did had there been no Lenin; however, Lenin could not have shaped the course of the Revolution to his will had the gap between the material well-being of the nobility and of the masses in Russia been much narrower. As Professor Kim admits, there are things which all revolutions have in common[11] about which it is possible, in theory, to formulate testable generalizations. Professor Kim's argument that it is impossible to make deterministic predictions or complete explanations of culturally affected events does not constitute a refutation of the applicability of the scientific method to the study of such events. Sciences,

---

[10] See K. W. Kim, "The Limit of Behavioral Explanation in Politics," in McCoy and Playford, op. cit., pp. 44–47.

[11] See, for example, Crane Brinton, *The Anatomy of a Revolution* (Englewood Cliffs, N. J.: Prentice-Hall, 1952) for a classic study of what revolutions have in common.

both natural and social, have learned to exist with probabilistic predictions and incomplete explanation. Surely it is possible to delineate the conditions under which it is more likely that a man like Lenin would succeed should he happen along.

THE POSITIVIST STRAW MAN

Perhaps the most unfair attack on the scientific study of politics is the frequent equating of it with logical positivism or strict behaviorism.[12] Logical positivism is that philosophical school (exemplified in the writings of such men as David Hume, Auguste Comte, and Ernest Mach) that holds that the only knowledge is that based solely upon sensory stimuli. The positivists, reacting to the metaphysical assertions of the Middle Ages, completely denied the role of understanding, intuition, or similar mental activity in the attainment of knowledge. Simply put, one cannot know what one cannot see (touch, hear, etc.). The earlier proponents of the school, such as Francis Bacon, also limited knowledge to that which can be obtained by crude induction, a position that is not subscribed to by any modern "philosopher of science," as we have seen in Chapter 1.[13]

In terms of the study of human behavior, this leads to the crude behaviorism discussed above. It is interesting how often critics of behavioralists refer to the objects of their scorn as behaviorists. The falsity of this characterization has been made clear in the discussion above,[14] which indicates that the old stimulus-response approach has been replaced by the more sophisticated stimulus-organism-response approach. This change implies a recognition of the fact that nonobservable properties of actors will affect the way they respond to given stimuli.

There is no reason why, as is sometimes charged, the behavioral approach necessarily implies reductionism[15] (the position that the individual is the only legitimate unit of analysis) with all the problems that entails (as shown in Chapter 1). Insofar as the behavioral approach is a term used interchangeably with the scientific method, aggregate rather than psychological data is the norm,[16] and the former is used almost exclusively in comparative politics. The use of social groups as the basic unit of analysis simply renders predictions more probabilistic and explanation more incomplete because of the individual differences such an approach excludes.

---

[12] Strauss, op. cit., p. 312.

[13] See pp. 9–10.

[14] See p. 69. See also David Easton, "The Current Meaning of Behavioralism," in James C. Charlesworth (ed.), *Contemporary Political Analysis* (New York: The Free Press, 1967), p. 12.

[15] Kim, op. cit., p. 39.

[16] See Emile Durkheim, "Social Facts" in May Brodbeck (ed.), *Readings in the Philosophy of the Social Sciences* (New York: Macmillan-Co.).

There is nothing unscientific about such holism, however, as shown above.[17]

Modern political scientists clearly are not positivists. The role of values in determining the focus of research has already been discussed in this chapter. The role of "creative intuition" in the formulation of hypotheses has been discussed earlier. Both of those functions of nonempirical mental activity are freely admitted by modern political scientists.[18] There is a difference between the insistence that a proposition must specify the facts with which it is compatible and the facts with which it is not and the assertion that knowledge consists solely in generalizing inductively about that which is directly ascertained from one's sensory experience. There is nothing unscientific about rationally or logically constructing hypotheses or even models and conceptual schemes as long as they are testable or can lead to testable propositions.

Thus, modern political scientists do not, as charged, teach the "equality of all values by denying there are things intrinsically high and others which are intrinsically low. . . ."[19] They merely assert that one cannot resolve the question of which things are high and which are low; therefore, they state their beliefs about such questions and allow the reader to evaluate their findings in the light of these beliefs. Strauss charges that scientific knowledge denies the status of knowledge to "pre-scientific" knowledge, by which he presumably means revealed religious truths or intuitive judgment.[20] What Strauss apparently objects to is a rejection of the natural law tradition, the tradition of "self-evident" truths. The modernist would welcome insights of a prescientific nature as a source of direction to his research; however, he would not retain those which are incompatible with the evidence and would have to reject those which cannot be made testable as worthless *for the purposes of scientific explanation*. It is unnecessary to decide whether nonempirical propositions have any intrinsic value. It is only necessary to show that they are not scientific in any widely accepted sense of that term.

The argument between Strauss and the behaviorally oriented political scientists on this point might be summarized in this way. Behavioralists do not deny a role of nonempirical activity in the discipline. They merely say that the limits of what can be *known* do not extend to assertions that cannot be empirically tested. When Strauss claims that it has never been

---

[17] Heinz Eulau, "Segments of Political Science. Most Susceptible to Behavioristic Treatment" in James Charlesworth (ed.), *Contemporary Political Analysis* (New York: The Free Press, 1967), pp. 46–49.

[18] Robert Dahl, *Modern Political Analysis* (Englewood Cliffs, N. J.: Prentice-Hall, 1965), p. 105.

[19] Strauss, op. cit., p. 326.

[20] Leo Strauss, "What is Political Philosophy," *Journal of Politics,* Vol. 19, No. 3 (August 1957), pp. 352ff. The example he gives, the knowledge that human beings are different from other beings, is an empirical proposition, given an operational definition of different. Thus, his example is scientifically tenable.

proven that the resolution of value conflicts is insoluble,[21] he appears to be shifting the burden of proof. The fact remains that such problems are at present and have always been insoluble. It seems that Strauss is applying the term knowledge to assertions about which reasonable men can and do disagree.

THE POST-MODERN CRITIQUE OF BEHAVIORALISM—RELEVANCE

There is, of course, some merit to the claim that a concern with what is to the exclusion of what ought to be or even what might be will result in a bias in favor of the status quo. In fact, there is an incipient revolution within the field of political science that is critical of the behavioral approach because it is not "relevant" to the solution of the pressing political and social problems of the day, for example, poverty, racism, and war. This critique of behavioralism should be distinguished from the traditionalist attack. The latter denies the feasibility of the application of the scientific method to the field. The former questions whether the work done by the behavioralist is useful or important.

The solution to these pressing problems, it is argued, requires a concern with how to change society, thus, with what society might be rather than what society is. Admittedly, this seems to require vision and imagination more than mathematical manipulations. When one is not satisfied with the state of our society or with the policies of governments with respect to these problems, it seems perfectly logical to assert that political scientists, being the most qualified thinkers on social and political problems, ought to address themselves to such problems. When one has reached this conclusion, an impatience at the direction of so much effort towards the collection and processing of empirical data on apparently minute and trivial concerns becomes understandable. To put this point of view bluntly, Who cares if this party system maintains a higher degree of cohesion on legislative roll-call voting than that party system or whether a system type should be designated as modernizing, transitional, prismatic, or developing, when there is an "immoral" war in Southeast Asia that must be stopped and when fifteen percent of our population cannot afford an adequate diet?

When it is argued that political scientists, of all people, must devote themselves to these more pressing problems, there is an underlying assumption that they do so with a special competence. It is difficult to see logically why the intuitive judgments of political scientists as to the "morality" of the Vietnam war are any more righteous than those of any layman. The special competence of political scientists to deal with political issues is

---

[21] Ibid., p. 351.

based upon an assumption of professional knowledge about the probable consequences of choosing each one of the various alternatives of public policy. This means knowledge in the form of "if a government does this, such and such a state of affairs will probably follow, while if they do that, this other state of affairs will follow." For example, it is logically conceivable that political scientists might be able to say something about the probability of maintaining a noncommunist government in South Vietnam and what the domestic and military costs of such a result are likely to be. Such advice would have to be based at a minimum on a knowledge of the historical development of the area and the conflict, the distribution of attitudes and demands among politically active people in the area, and a theoretical knowledge of the relationships between ideology, psychology, and behavior. Political scientists would not have any special competence, however, in determining if those results would be worth the price.

It is therefore clear that for political scientists to be able to claim special competence in advising on matters of social and political policy, they must first develop a body of widely accepted propositions. The acceptance of such propositions has to be based on their empirical foundation so that, as discussed in Chapter 1, any two observers viewing the same evidence would have to reach the same conclusion regardless of their values.

The point is that by ignoring the methodological criteria proposed in the foregoing chapters, the political scientist places himself on the level of the layman. It is no accident that while no layman would argue with the diagnosis of an M.D., laymen have not felt disposed to uncritical acceptance of the prescriptions of political scientists. The popularity of Vice President Agnew's anti-intellectual stance is a recent example of this. This stems in no small way from the fact that political scientists had, for many years, ignored these methodological criteria. This amounted to an abandonment of the most effective defense of their findings from attacks by the uninitiated. It is not enough to say that the solution to a problem is important or desirable. It is necessary to be sure, as Holt and Richardson put it, that "a solution exists."[22] This assurance is provided by working within the criteria of this scientific method.

The charge that political scientists often engage in seeking a solution to trivial problems to the exclusion of "more important" concerns is not wholly without merit. The danger is that researchers who ascribe to high standards of scientific rigor will select problems according to the availability of empirical data susceptible to measurement and mathematical manipulation rather than according to the problem's social, political, or theoretic importance. Some political scientists would rather solve a trivial problem by rigorously following the criteria of the scientific method than to tackle an

---

[22] Robert Holt and John Richardson, "Competing Paradigms in Comparative Politics," in Holt and John E. Turner, *The Methodology of Comparative Research* (New York: The Free Press, 1970), p. 26.

important problem without the benefit of empirical data. The dilemma is a real one. It may be argued that by building a body of reliable knowledge on what appear to be trivial problems now, the discipline can by a cumulative process develop a body of knowledge on problems of greater concern. However, aside from the fact that this would at best be a very long process, a line of progression from trivia to important problems in empirical research is by no means obviously ineluctable.

One might also reply to the admonition that political scientists should address themselves to problems more relevant to the needs of contemporary society with the question of who decides what is relevant and by what criteria. There are those who would deny, for example, that there is a problem in the distribution of values in the United States. The designation of a problem as relevant or pressing is, to a large extent, a function of one's values and intuitive processes.

FREE WILL AND THE INFERENCE OF CAUSATION

It is sometimes argued that one cannot ascribe causation to human behavior because man is free to choose his behavior patterns. The implication is that this choice among alternative courses of behavior is made completely autonomous of any factors external to that person's will. Of course, if valid, this argument would undercut much of the goal of the modern political scientist which, as discussed earlier, seeks the inference, if not the proof, of causation. The assumption, however, that choice is made totally uninfluenced by factors external to human will is debatable at best. The converse assertion, that choice is limited by external variables and further that specific choices are made more probable, if not determined by such contextual variables can best be supported by example.

Clearly, the number of alternatives available to a given issue are finite. The goals or intentions of given decision makers are frequently frustrated by events beyond the control of such decision makers despite the fact that they "choose" such goals. If the state of Israel is able to maintain a given degree of military strength, the elimination of that state may not be a choice available to Arab leaders, regardless of how much they desire it. This points up a difference between will, in the sense of desire, and choice between alternative courses of action. The latter is clearly circumscribed by variables many of which theoretically can be known; the former is not so circumscribed.

Although any given individual is free to choose the unexpected, a substantial proportion of choices are what would be expected from a knowledge of the context in which each choice was made. This context would include the chooser's perception or knowledge of the probable consequences of each alternative and the order or value priorities of the chooser. Both types of data can be empirically determined. For example, if President

Sadat expected to win a war with Israel, he would be more likely to provoke one. The assertion of such an expectation would have to be balanced against an assessment of the actual relative military strength of the two countries. In short, is this a genuine or rational expectation? A national leader may, in a fit of insanity start a war he was clearly sure to decisively lose; however, predictions against such courses of action would be reliable in most instances.

The freewill argument, like the uniqueness-of-man argument, is therefore negated by the aggregate nature of social data. Any given individual is free to choose the unexpected, but predictions of the expected choice, given the circumstances, will be correct with enough frequency in the long run to make them useful. The circumstances which make a rationally unexpected choice more likely may also be an empirical problem (such as the psychic state of the chooser). The aggregate nature of data is, of course, more pronounced in cross-national comparative research; hence, in this area the uniqueness-of-man and freewill arguments would have even less force. Random deviations from the expected tend to cancel one another out in a large number of individual cases.

In summation, individuals are free to choose but the choice they make is usually determined by contextual variables which can be empirically known. This knowledge of such variables and their relation to the issue at hand enables social scientists to predict human behavior with a frequency of success considerably above chance. This power, while imperfect, is still useful.

It is therefore possible to infer that action was caused in the sense that variables external to the actor narrowed the alternatives available to the actor, given a set of value priorities and a degree of rationality on his part.

VALUES IN COMPARATIVE ANALYSIS

When this chapter argued that empirical statements could be separated from nonempirical statements, it did not intend to imply that comparative politics could or should be value free. Clearly, there are valued present or future states of affairs which are implicit in almost all research. Hermans' work, cited in Chapters 2 and 3, Eckstein's monograph, cited in Chapter 2, and Lipset's work, cited in Chapter 3, clearly were written to clarify the means of preserving or achieving stable democracy. Many of the works in the field of development implicity or explicit ask the question of how a non-Western system might achieve the production capacity of a modern Western nation state. These values give direction to the research referred to above. Clearly, therefore, it is desirable for political researchers to seek to know their own values insofar as they may affect the results of their work and explicate them so that the reader may read the research results taking account of such bias.

The danger is that political scientists may erroneously assume either the universality of their values or their necessary realization. This danger is particularly acute in the area of political development, where some conceptions of development appear to adopt the Anglo-American democracies as the epitome of what non-Western states want to become, should become, or inevitably will become with greater or lesser facility.

The realm of values may itself be the subject of systematic research. As will be shown in the discussion of political culture in a later chapter, the values that people perceive that they hold are clearly a factor influencing their political behavior and, as such, are relevant to the study of such behavior. Whether or not people perceive that they hold given values constitutes an empirical fact as does the ordinal ranking of such values. Such data may be obtained with a high degree of reliability through survey research. Several studies are now underway in the area of cross-national survey-research,[23] adding to the Almond and Verba classic five-nation study and other completed projects.

An additional aspect of values that is susceptible to empirical research is the specification of the consequences of various preferences. Preferences imply alternative courses of action, the consequences of which may be investigated by the methodology outlined in the preceding three chapters.

Many Americans, for example, seem to prefer a fragmentation of decision-making authority to the concentration of such authority. However, such fragmentation results in a decrease in the capacity of the system to process the demands that it faces.

The alleged incompatibility between values and the scientific method is based upon a conception of values as ultimate goals or purposes that are simply posited in a manner unaffected by empirical considerations, a conception not universally shared. There is a school of philosophical thought which rejects the notion of absolute, ultimate values as absurd.[24] Values, in this view, are not valued for their own sake but as a means to some further end. Everything that is valued must be valued in terms of something. People do justify their values. For example, withdrawal from Vietnam (or more military pressure) is "good" because it hastens peace, which is "good" because it preserves life. But even life is valued for what it can bring rather than for its own sake. This view would have the continuum of values as endless without any final or absolute value.

Clarence Ayres refers to the continuum as a "life process" or a "knowing and doing process." Dewey calls it a "means-ends continuum." Ayres suggests that all human existence can be identified as a process of extending knowledge and building "tools" which afford man greater control over his

---

[23] See Frederick W. Frey, "Cross-Cultural Research in Political Science" in Holt and Turner, op. cit., pp. 185–87, for an annotated list of such projects.

[24] This school is epitomized by institutional economists such as Thorstein Veblen and Clarence Ayres and by the philosopher John Dewey. For the single most comprehensive, yet lucid exposition of this position, see Clarence Ayres, *Toward a Reasonable Society* (Austin: University of Texas Press, 1961).

environment and the consequent extension of human life itself. Since this life process is the only existence that man knows, Ayres argues that values must be established in terms of it.[25] Without this process, there would be no human life and hence no values. Thus, an absolute taboo against sexual activity would be for Ayres an absurd value because it would lead to an end of human existence and an end to all valuation. How, he would ask, can something be good that cannot exist? "Moral significance arises only within the system of human activities."[26]

For Dewey, all ends are means to further ends. If all values are considered as means, clearly the question of whether they are an optimal means becomes, to a large extent, an empirical question.

If someone posited the value that all human pleasure is evil, a philosopher at this school would retort "evil in terms of what standard?" Mannheim, for example, suggests that an ethical value is "false" if the reality of the situation precludes compliance.[27] Thus, a moral code, such as that of early Puritans, which denied the reality of strong human drives would by this standard be considered false or perhaps unrealistic.

This is not totally unrelated to the position of Eugene Meehan, who claims that human choice implies some standard for choosing. Meehan suggests that these standards are derived from the consequences of each choice,[28] consequences which can be determined by empirical methodological procedures. What Meehan does not clearly provide is an unambiguous standard for evaluating the aforementioned consequences. However, he suggests that "ethical standards must be applicable to specific [empirical] situations."[29] It would be nonsense, in this view, to postulate ethical principles that assume a mythical state of affairs. This could not be a value in Meehan's sense of the term because it is not an available choice.

In summation, there exists a significant group of scholars who reject the widely held assumption that values are simply posited or intuited by transcendental mental processes. Rather, they suggest that a standard exists for the justification of evaluating, that standard being the pattern of human life as it is known. Anything outside this realm of human experience is neither good nor bad but simply meaningless.

CONCLUSION

Most of the attacks on the feasibility of applying the scientific method to the study of politics are based upon a faulty conception of science. This

---

[25] Ibid., p. 122.

[26] Ibid., p. 117.

[27] Mannheim, op. cit., p. 95.

[28] Eugene Meehan, *Value Judgment and Social Science* (Homewood, Ill.: The Dorsey Press, 1969), p. 40.

[29] Ibid., p. 139.

conception assumes that any science worthy of the name possesses the ability to generate complete explanation and deterministic prediction of specific events, such as the ability to predict that a revolution will occur in this country and at that time.

Inasmuch as one can never be certain that all variables have been accounted for in any discipline, complete explanation in the strict sense of the term is not a characteristic of science. (We have noted earlier that gaps exist in the knowledge of physics.) Chapter 2 pointed out that probabilistic explanation and incomplete explanation are prefectly compatible with the imperatives of the scientific method. It is the failure to understand the nature of probabilistic prediction and incomplete explanation that underlies much of the traditionalist attack.

The argument that because one cannot take account of every relevant variable he should not try to ascertain as many relationships relevant to his field of research as possible is something like throwing out the proverbial baby with the bath water. It amounts to saying that if political sicence cannot predict with absolute certainty, it should not try to predict at all.

The argument that it is logically feasible to apply the scientific method to political science is one thing. The argument that political scientists have been at all successful in doing so is quite another matter. It is to this latter question, particularly with reference to the field of cross-national comparison, that the remainder of the book addresses itself.

Part II

Approaches

6

The Comparative Method
and Paradigm Construction

One of the changes in political science since the advent of the behavioral revolution that is most apparent (and often most disconcerting) to the observer who is introduced to the state of the discipline suddenly is the vast proportion of the literature which says little or nothing about the substance of politics. This nonsubstantive (henceforth referred to as analytical) literature focuses on the search for ways to study politics rather than on the study of politics itself. As part of the survey of existing analytical writing in Part 2, this chapter will explore the reasons for this relatively recent interest in frameworks for analysis at the expense of what has traditionally been the focus of comparative government, the description of the legal institutions of foreign governments, especially those of Great Britain, France, Germany, and the Soviet Union.[1] Further, this chapter will explore the connection between this proliferation of analytic literature, the method of comparison, and the interest in the application of the scientific method discussed in Part II.

The proliferation of analytic literature has been deplored as an unnecessary distraction from the legitimate focus of comparative politics. It is difficult for the uninitiated to comprehend the contribution of a lengthy discussion of, for example, how broadly the concept political system can most usefully be defined or of the functions performed in all societies when we ought to be concerned about how Britain and France govern themselves.

---

[1] It is interesting that even the most recent and conceptually modern textbooks on European politics focus exclusively on these four countries even though it would be more logical to include other Western European nations and to group the Soviet Union with a different class of systems. See for example, Harvey Rothman, *European Society and Politics* (Indianapolis: Bobbs-Merrill, Inc., 1970) and Roy Macridis and Robert Ward, *Modern Political Systems, Europe,* 2d ed. (Englewood Cliffs, N. J.: Prentice-Hall, 1968). An admirable exception, now somewhat dated, is Herbert Spiro, *Government by Constitution* (New York: Random House, 1959).

Aside from the issue of what contribution such outright description of Western European government can add to the already existing mountain of such description, this chapter will show that the precise formulation of frameworks for analysis is a prerequisite for the optimal use of the comparative method. The initial task of this chapter is to discuss the nature of the comparative method, which is at the foundation of this book, and its connection to the proliferation of analytical literature.

COMPARISON AND THE SPECIFICATION
OF UNITS OF ANALYSIS

It has already been suggested that one might justifiably think of comparative analysis as coterminous with the *scientific* study of politics as this latter methodology was outlined in Part 1. The scientific method, we have seen, involves the construction of empirically falsifiable generalizations relating classes of political phenomena to one another. A proposition stating a relationship between two or more specific phenomena is not what is meant here by a scientific statement.[2] Thus, it is of no scientific utility to point out that political stability has been associated with the constitutional structure of the United States. However, it may be of scientific interest to point out that political stability has invariably been associated with a group of nations that all share some constitutional arrangement, that is, a class of political systems. Clearly, assertions about classes of phenomena must be based upon the observation of a variety of specific instances or manifestations of the political phenomena included in the class.

The very formulation of a class of political phenomena implies a specification of what a group of such phenomena, different from one another in some respects, has in common. This involves the process of comparison. Although The United Kingdom, Third and Fourth Republic France, contemporary Italy, and all of the Scandinavian nations are very different from one another, they are all included as members in that class of political phenomena known as parliamentary democracy. Despite a vast array of institutional distinctions among them (for example, the number of parties, the presence or absence of the power of dissolution, the status of the chief of state), they do have specific institutional arrangements in common, namely, the formal responsibility of the head of government to a democratically elected legislature. This distinction between the similarities and the differences among the group can only be ascertained by comparison.

If it were then possible to ascertain another distinct property that all the countries in this class share, this would constitute a generalization in the scientific sense of the term. For example, all countries which share the aforementioned institutional property (that is, all parliamentary democ-

---

[2] See above, pp. 41–43.

racies) also share another property (such as stability or instability). Of course, care must be exercised that the two properties being related are not defined in terms of one another or the proposition becomes tautological (true by definition). The statement that all parliamentary democracies have a head of government responsible to a democratically elected legislature would constitute an example of such a tautology because having such a responsible head of government is part of the definition of parliamentary democracy.

HOLDING RELEVANT VARIABLES CONSTANT

Comparison is also of particular utility in dealing with one of the major problems of social science, that of holding constant.[3] This involves the problem of the other-things-being-equal (ceteris paribus) clause, discussed in Part I, that is always present in social science propositions. Briefly, a statement about the way two classes of phenomena are related to one another implies the presumption that no variables unmentioned by the statement will significantly affect the relationship included in the statement. When one says, for example, that two-party systems are stable, the statement, being cast in a universal (all x are y) form, presumes that two-party systems will always be stable regardless of differences (for example, cultural, historical) between the political systems in question. If two-party systems turn out to be stable only in certain cultural contexts but not in others, the inference may be drawn that other things are not equal and that the heretofore omitted cultural variables do indeed significantly affect the relationship between party systems and stability.

In the social sciences, every phenomenon or variable, involving as it does human behavior, is affected by so many factors that no proposition can include every variable that may in some way affect the stated relationship. These omitted factors constitute the ceteris paribus clause of the proposition.

In the natural sciences, it is often possible to isolate two variables in a laboratory from all other variables in order to determine the relationship between them. This is not possible in political science. One obviously cannot extract a set of institutions from the culture in which they operate or equalize the childhood influence on a set of political actors. If it is not possible to equalize other things, the next best thing is to account for them insofar as possible. This is where the advantage of comparative analysis becomes apparent.

If a relationship holds in one cultural context or class of such contexts but not in another, additional variables that are relevant to that relation-

---

[3]Robert E. Holt and John Turner, *The Methodology of Comparative Research* (New York: The Free Press, 1970), pp. 11–13.

ship are accounted for, and the proposition should be restated so as to limit the scope of the relationship only to those cultural contexts in which it does apply. It is only when the relationship has been tested in a variety of cultural contexts that one can justifiably infer that the relationship holds true regardless of the state of cultural variables. To put the point as succinctly as possible, since one cannot isolate the variables one wishes to study from all other variables that may influence the study, one should try to determine the nature and extent of the influence of external variables insofar as possible. This does not mean that the precise effect of each external variable needs to be specified. Such a demand would make research impossible. This does mean that one attempts to determine the extent to which other things (in the aggregate) are not equal and in what kinds of circumstances the relationship under study does not hold.

For example, if one finds that a posited relationship between political instability and multi-party parliamentary democracy does not hold in a highly secularized, pragmatic culture, one has still not demonstrated the precise relationship between that cultural state of affairs and stability. A question remains as to whether that cultural context only promotes stability in that type of political system or in any type. Also, one might ask if such a culture appears to be independently related to that outcome (a stable parliamentary democracy) or if a third factor appears to have caused both stability and a secular culture. (It should be kept in mind that all of the hypothetical examples used in this book would have to deal with the problem of operationalizing their concepts before becoming testable, a problem which in some cases might prove to be insurmountable. The examples are meant to be illustrative, not necessarily suggestive of actual relationships).

It follows that if proposed relationships must be tested in a variety of contexts to find out the extent to which other things are or are not equal, the comparative approach must be utilized. Only comparative analysis considers a variety of social, cultural, political, and ecological contexts as included within its discipline. A student of American government only cannot transcend the American context. On the other hand, the subject matter of American government is not irrelevant to the student of comparative politics in the modern sense of that term. For modern comparative politics is the process of actually comparing classes of political phenomena defined without regard to their geographical location. (It will be recalled that the older conception of comparative government was the study of foreign governments, a conception that would effectively eliminate American data from the discipline.)

It also follows that it would be desirable to test a proposition in as wide a variety of contexts as possible. It should be noted that such contextual differences may occur in one geographical location at different points in time as well as between geographically defined contexts. The logic of comparative analysis would apply to studies encompassing such a variety of relevant contexts on a temporal dimension (or longitudinal dimension as such comparisons are sometimes called). However, comparative politics as a field is primarily concerned with cross-national comparison.

It is highly probable that many of the sacred propositions of traditional political science are culture bound, if not to the Anglo-American democracies, then to the Western industrial nations. One may suspect, for instance, that the assumption of political scientists of Woodrow Wilson's time that all people both understand and highly value civil liberties in the same way does not apply when one begins to investigate African and Asiatic political systems. Thus, an expectation based upon this assumption that the "oppressed" subjects of authoritarian systems will rally to opponents of their governments is likely not to be realized. (A number of the recent failures of American foreign policy, such as the Bay of Pigs fiasco, might be considered as cases in point.)

There have been a number of generalizations about the requisites of stable democracy that political scientists of a generation ago reached by comparing two of their pet subjects, Fourth Republic France (unstable) and Britain (stable). A number of these were discovered not to apply when tested in a wider variety of contexts. The politicization of religion, particularly with a strong Catholic population has been suggested as incompatible with stable democracy.[4] While this may appear true looking at England, without a religious party, and France, where the center parties (the M.R.P. and the Radicals) have been unable to govern due largely to the clerical issue, it is also true that a number of Western nations have remained remarkably stable despite the existence of significant religious parties (for example, Austria, Netherlands, Norway). Of course, the case of the Republic of Ireland belies the contention that Catholicism is necessarily incompatible with stable democracy.

For example, if one desired to inductively determine the cause of instability in parliamentary democracies, one might observe two relatively unstable parliamentary democracies, such as France and Italy, to see what they have in common. One might observe that they both have narrow streets or some other irrelevant property. Patterns in such complex and theoretically relevant variables as the degree of cultural fragmentation or cultural ideologism can usually only be discerned by scholars who search for precisely those patterns. Thus, an a priori expectation of what is related to what sems imperative to select and to order one's possible observations.

It would seem that a proposition about the requisites of stable democracy would have to specify what all members of that class of nations have in common and what is not present in any nation outside that class (that

---

[4] Even so modern a "political sociologist" as Seymour Lipset has made this suggestion, principally on logical grounds. His claim is that the claim to know truth, inherent in Catholic dogma, is incompatible with the tolerance of dissent imperative to the democratic process. See his *Political Man* (New York: Doubleday Anchor Editions, 1963), p. 72n.

is, an unstable democracy). This would seem to be more of an inductive process[5] which would appear to belie the case made for the deductive nature of explanation made in Chapter 2 and more especially for the deductive nature of hypothesis formation made in Chapter 3. However, it would be more accurate to say that deduction and induction work in a complementary fashion. While it is true that the validation of propositions may be done inductively, seeing if the pattern holds on a case to case basis, it also remains true that without first deductively determining what patterns to look for, it would be impossible to sort out the myriad of observable "facts" into any sort of coherent pattern.

Classical literature on political change, from Woodrow Wilson's *The State* (1895) and the turn of the century works of Max Weber to Gabriel Almond's relatively modern first formulation in *The Politics of the Developing Areas* (1961), has either implicitly or explicitly assumed a unilinear and inevitable direction of change from a primitive non-Western society to an industrial democracy patterned after Western Europe and the Anglo-American nations. While the issue is far from resolved, the subsequent research has suggested that the data do not clearly support such an assumption (of the ineluctable westernization of all political systems).[6] This issue is thoroughly explored below in Chapter 11. It appears that the assumption of the inevitable westernization of political systems was largely derived from an observation of the development of Western systems. A more variegated source of data should not have led to such an ethnocentric set of assumptions about the direction of political change.

It should be clear from the foregoing examples that the comparative method seeks to pose the question of what makes one class of countries different from another class of countries.[7] To simply pose the question of what makes France different from Britain does not fulfill the function of holding significant variables constant. If one asks what differences exist within the class of stable Catholic countries, one has succeeded in at least holding that religious variable constant.

Another utilization of the comparative method which has obviously more limited possibilities is to compare two nations which are alike in nearly

---

[5] See John Stuart Mill, "How We Compare," in Roy Macridis and Bernard Brown (eds.), *Comparative Politics, Notes and Readings,* 3d ed. (Homewood, Ill.: The Dorsey Press, 1968), pp. 25–29, for an older view that the comparative method and the inductive process are virtually coterminous. It must be kept in mind that it was written in 1834. At this time, the Age of Reason reaction to the Medieval epistemology was still being felt. Such medieval practices consisted of a priori deduction from great philosophical systems, in the mode of Thomistic philosophy, without regard for the compatibility of the outcomes with empirical data.

[6] For example, Fred J. Riggs, *Administration in Developing Countries, The Theory of the Prismatic Society* (Boston: Houghton-Mifflin Co., 1964). See also Alfred Diamant, "Is There a Non-Western Political Process," *Journal of Politics,* Vol. 11, No. 1 (February 1959), pp. 123–27.

[7] David M. Wood, "Comparative Government and Politics," in Stephen L. Wasby, *Political Science, The Discipline and its Dimension* (New York: Charles Scribner's Sons, 1970), p. 488n.

all respects except those in which one is interested. Thus, the variables which are common to both countries are held constant. An example of this may be found in this author's study of the effect of the presence (or absence) of geographically defined diversities on party behavior.[8] By drawing data from Australia and Canada, two members of the older Commonwealth, the author was, to a large extent, able to hold constant the variables of cultural heritage (British) and political structure (two-party,[9] federal, cabinet government). Australia and Canada did significantly differ from one another in the amount of economic and cultural regionalism and in the extent to which electoral support of parties was regionally defined.[10] The article was on much firmer ground in attributing this geographical distribution of party support to the economic and cultural regionalism in Canada because other potentially revelant variables were held constant. Robert Alford attempts to control a study of four nations by the same method in *Party and Society*. By confining his study of the sources of class voting to the Anglo-American democracies, Alford attempts to hold many relevant variables constant, variables he claims all of these nations have in common.[11]

COMPARISON AND LEVELS OF ANALYSIS

It should be apparent that this book views comparative politics not merely as the study of foreign governments but rather as the systematic effort to develop scientific generalizations (and eventually theory) whose applicability is not confined to particular social and political contexts. In this sense, comparative analysis may be thought of as distinguishing the explicans (or putative causes) of political phenomena we wish to explain that are common to all systems from those that are particular to a given class of systems or to single systems. This is essentially what is meant by the level of analysis.[12] It refers to this holistic-reductionistic dichotomy with respect

[8] Lawrence Mayer, "Federalism and Party Behavior in Australia and Canada," *Western Political Quarterly,* Vol. 23, No. 4 (December 1970), pp. 795–807.

[9] By defining two-party systems as those systems in which control of the role of government alternated at more or less regular intervals between two political forces, the author constructed "an almost operational" definition of that concept which enabled him to include Australia (where the Liberal and Country parties also act in coalition against Labour) and Canada (where the N.D.P., Social Credit, or R.P.F. never control the government) as members of that class of party systems. Since these party systems behaved, for the purpose of the study, more like two-party systems of the Anglo-American variety than like Continental multiparty systems, it was useful to so define the concept. This is another example of the pragmatic approach to empirical concept formation discussed in Chapter 1.

[10] A less significant difference in party cohesion on legislative roll-call votes was also noted. Ibid.

[11] Robert Alford, *Party and Society* (Chicago: Rand McNally & Co., 1963), chap. 1.

[12] This discussion of levels of analysis is in large part suggested by Adam Przeworski and Henry Teune, *The Logic of Comparative Social Inquiry* (New York: John Wiley & Sons, 1970), especially chaps. 2 and 3.

to the generality of units of analysis discussed in Chapter 1. One may seek an explicans in the properties of individuals or groups contained within systems, on one level, or seek the explicans in the properties inherent in systems themselves, on another level.

Systems (used interchangeably with the concept "nation state") may be thought of as repositories of unspecified social, economic, cultural, and political variables. They may be similarly thought of as aggregated individual or within-system level properties. These variables often constitute those "other things" that are never equal in the ceteris paribus clause that attaches itself to all social science generalizations that relate one class of individual or group properties as the putative cause of another such class.

For example, Almond and Verba, in their famous survey of attitudes in five nations, discussed in Chapter 9, found that the United States and Great Britain differed to a significant extent from Italy and Mexico with respect to a number of attitudinal dimensions, such as a sense of one's obligation to participate in politics, a sense of one's competence to do so, and a sense of pride in a nation's political institutions or regime. It was also found, however, that these variables were, to a significant extent, a linear function of the educational level of the respondent. In other words, educated Italians were not significantly different with respect to these variables from equivalently educated Englishmen. Thus, a question is suggested as follows: If the mean educational level of the four countries were standardized, would the countries still differ with respect to the other variables? If the answer is yes, we must assume that there is something about being an Englishman or an American that makes any given person in these two countries more likely to possess high levels of the aforementioned properties than citizens of other countries. These characteristics of Englishmen and Americans should hold true irrespective of variations among Englishmen and Americans with respect to such individual characteristics as years of formal education. This something may be found in the institutional structure, geography, history, or any other property unique to those particular systems.

Thus, one could not say that one's sense of civic competence varies directly with formal education irrespective of whether one is an Italian, Mexican, Englishman, or American. Less highly educated Americans and Englishmen score higher on this variable than do Italians and Mexicans at an equivalent level of education. Therefore, education can account for only part of this variation in the variable "sense of civic competence." We have to look at those repositories of other variables designated by the proper names of particular systems to account for the remainder of the variation. Otherwise stated, we can explain part of the variation in the sense of civic competence at the individual level (that is, education) but must explain the rest of the variation at the system level. It may be argued that one of the primary tasks of comparative political analysis is to establish the level at which explanation must be sought.

This would leave us with a generalization in the form of "Education is a determinant of the degree of the sense of civic competence except in the United States and Great Britain." (In these two countries that sense is high regardless of the educational level of the respondent.) As long as the generalization contains the proper names of systems, however, it is not generally applicable and does not generate predictive power. It was shown in Chapter 3 that in order to generate predictive power, generalizations must refer to phenomena beyond those that constitute its direct justification. Such generalizations cannot be limited to a finite number of cases.[13] Science generates a predictive power when it increases one's accuracy in extrapolating from what can be directly observed to what cannot be so observed.

It follows that the goal of replacing proper nouns, referring to particular phenomena, with more general concepts is an imperative in the process of building scientific theory. This leads back to the specification-of-general-units-of-analysis function of comparison discussed earlier in this chapter. Thus, rather than simply naming the Anglo-American democracies as exceptions to the applicability of a generalization relating two classes of individual-level properties, it would be preferable to isolate those properties common to Anglo-American democracies that might logically account for the observed exceptions to the generalization. Then, it should be possible to hypothesize that in any country possessing such characteristics (including countries not observed in that respect), the generaliaztion will not hold true.

THE SCOPE OF COMPARATIVE POLITICS

It should be noted that the examples given here have been confined to what has been called macro-politics, that is, propositions which utilize whole political systems as their units of analysis. Cross-national comparison has, in fact, been a subfield of the discipline which, along with international relations, conceived of whole political systems as actors. One surveyor of the field has even gone as far as to suggest that macro-analysis on this level is the hallmark of comparative politics. Comparison of lesser units of the field is part of that discipline known as comparative politics only insofar as such focus on lesser units is an asset in explaining differences between whole systems.[14] Some might argue, however, that this is an unnecessarily narrow conception of the scope of the discipline. While it must be granted that most studies in the field are, in fact, directed toward explaining differences between whole systems or that studies focusing on narrower units of analysis (such as political culture or party systems) utilize such narrow

---

[13] Cf. Carl Hempel, "Aspects of Scientific Explanation," in Hempel, *Aspects of Scientific Explanation and Other Essays in the Philosophy of Science* (New York: The Free Press, 1965), p. 358.

[14] Wood, op. cit., p. 496.

units for macro-explanation, there is no logical reason why this must necessarily be so. As a matter of fact, subfields of the discipline are developing rapidly which do focus on narrower units of analysis as objects of explanation rather than as mere tools of explanation. The field of comparative administration is one such field.

Studies such as the one by Alford which attempts to explain the differences in the amount of class voting in four nations or the one by this author which attempts to assess the consequences of geographically defined diversities on party behavior in a tightly defined class of nations would, by the narrow definition, be excluded from comparative politics. Yet, if they are not comparative, it is hard to know how to classify them. Stein Rokkan has done research in Scandinavia on the relationship between the range of party alternative and voter turnout[15] which also obviously deals with units more narrow than whole systems clearly within the field of comparative politics.

A study concerned with nations outside the United States would be classified as comparative in the traditional sense of the term. Insofar as the propositions resulting from research are intended to apply to more than one nation, that study becomes comparative in the modern sense of the term.

Thus, there is a disadvantage in conceiving of comparative politics as merely the study of foreign government. This, the traditional conception of the discipline, would eliminate much data from the United States which would be useful in explaining the recurrence of certain political phenomena. The narrow macro-analysis conception of the field, discussed above, would eliminate many objects of explanation that the method of cross-national comparison would be useful in explaining. It would therefore seem advantageous to simply think of the subfield of comparative politics as encompassing any study which attempts to generalize about similarities and differences with respect to politically relevant phenomena between two or more nation states. This conception of the discipline has the advantage of separating what is most widely regarded as coming within its purview from that which is not so regarded. It also emphasizes multinational studies which utilize the comparative method outlined in this chapter. Thus, a study of one foreign (to Americans) country which made no attempt at cross-national comparison would not, contrary to the traditional conception, be regarded as germane to the discipline unless it was clearly designed to lead to such comparison. Also excluded from the concept of comparative politics by the definition proposed here would be comparisons between subunits of one nation state, even though the comparative method was utilized, unless such resulting propositions were intended to be expanded

---

15 Stein Rokkan and H. Valen, "Parties, Elections and Political Behavior in the Northern Countries: A Review of Recent Research" in O. Stamming (ed.), *Politische Forshung* (Kohn-Opladen, Germany: West deutscher Verlag, 1960), pp. 120–25.

to a cross-national applicability. Comparisons between American state legislatures would fall in this excluded category, for example. However, the logic of the comparative method would still apply to such studies. The only reason for such exclusion is to delimit the field to studies which are generally thought of as within its jurisdiction. Otherwise, comparative politics becomes synonymous with political science itself.

Clearly, comparison as a method is inherent in the scientific method. For science, we have seen, involves the establishment of empirically testable propositions about the relationships between concepts or classes of data. Such propositions about relationships imply statements about the similarities and differences between the concepts or classes of data. When one says two phenomena are related, that is another way of saying the phenomena have something in common. Of course, there must be differences between the phenomena as well, else there would be an identity rather than a relationship. Relationships, therefore, imply similarities and differences, which are precisely what are determined by comparison.

In this sense, political science in the modern sense of that term becomes synonymous with comparative politics. Certainly data from none of the other subfields (for example, public administration, public law, and American politics) can be summarily excluded from the task of building a body of empirically testable propositions about politics. One cannot be an expert on public law, political parties, or bureaucracies to the exclusion of data from other phenomena if expertise includes the ability to formulate explanatory generalizations, because political phenomena are so interrelated. For example, the character of the French administrative system has been linked to the instability of the French party system[16] or to the French political culture.[17] Clearly, its character cannot be explained in isolation from other variables.

PARADIGMS AS COMMON CATEGORIES OF ANALYSIS

The effort in comparative politics to build empirical generalizations applicable to the widest possible variety of cases leads naturally to the search for paradigms which are similarly broadly applicable. *Paradigm,* a widely used term with an imprecise meaning, refers here to conceptual frameworks or models at various stages of formalization which serve to provide a set of categories for the collection and organization of data. The term has been used elsewhere interchangeably with the term *model*

---

[16] Alfred Diamant, "The French Administrative System—The Republic Passes but the Administration Remains," in William E. Siffin (ed.), *Toward The Comparative Study of Public Administration* (Bloomington: Indiana University Press, 1959), pp. 182–218.

[17] Michael Crozier, *The Bureaucratic Phenomenon* (Chicago: University of Chicago Press, 1964).

or with the Weberian concept of "ideal type," an epitome or archetypal hypothetical example of a class of phenomena. Both of these terms are discussed in Chapter 7.

The development of these aforementioned categories for the collection and organization of data is necessary for fruitful comparative analysis for two reasons. First, wtihout the common categories, the uniqueness of political systems would make data from several of them difficult to compare. From the very first chapter, on concept formation, it became clear that data do not speak for themselves. It is an oft-stated cliché that facts alone have no meaning. The meaning attributed to such raw data is often affected by, if not derived from, their cultural contexts. The different meanings so acquired by sets of data from their different cultural contexts would deprive such sets of data of that common conceptual basis needed to formulate general propositions relating them.

An example might be illustrative. A comparison of two constitutions with respect to their protection of certain freedoms might be misleading if the countries came from two different cultural contexts as, for instance, the United States and the Soviet Union. For, as pointed out earlier, the meanings we attribute to such basic concepts as freedom and civil liberties are far from universally shared; therefore, similar or even identical legal wordings could take on different meanings.

Similarly, to compare the supreme national representative bodies in the United States, Great Britain, and the Soviet Union would be difficult. The only attribute these bodies share is the fact that they are supreme representative bodies. The American Congress is to some extent a deliberate body in the sense of making a choice between authoritative policy alternatives. The British House of Commons' function is not a deliberative one in that sense of the term. Rather its functions are limited to those of political communication (the articulation and discussion but not the resolution of public issues), of legitimating authoritative decisions of the cabinet and the higher civil service, and of providing broad limits to the discretion of the cabinet. The Supreme Soviet is in no sense a deliberative body. It does not even attempt to limit the discretion of the actual Soviet decision makers. The function of the Supreme Soviet lies rather in the legitimation of, the mobilization of support for, and the dissemination of decisions reached elsewhere. (The Russian Constitution stipulates the function of the Supreme Soviet as the duty "to hear and approve reports".) Thus, while these institutions fit in a common class by virtue of the fact that they are all representative bodies, they seem to have nothing else in common. Thus, the class of which these bodies are members cannot be related to any other class of phenomena. In this sense, they are not comparable; one cannot establish a scientific generalization about them in the sense in which we have used that term.

Thus, it becomes necessary to construct categories of analysis that are not culture bound but rather are applicable to a broad variety of political systems regardless of the cultural differences among such systems. Traditional units of analysis, the formal, legal institutions of the state, do not meet this requirement.

PARADIGMS AS CRITERIA OF RELEVANCE

There is an even more serious problem about the traditional categories of analysis, that is, the legal institutions of government (e.g., legislatures, executives, bureaucracies). These institutions fit into their various cultures in very different ways in the sense of the roles they play or the functions they perform. These institutions are not universal even in a formal sense. The farther from Western cultures one ventures (in an analytical rather than a geographical sense), the likelier it becomes that one will encounter societies in which parallel institutions are not even formally present. It is conceivable that some primitive political systems may not possess any institution which even structurally resembles a Western-type legislature.

Another reason for the formation of these categories of analysis is that the very quantity and variety of data make it mandatory to have some criteria for the selection of data. It has already been pointed out that the number of possible "facts" about a nation that one could choose to observe approaches infinity. Unless this number could be drastically reduced by some sort of selection process, the analysis of any nation would be an unmanageable task. There would simply be more variables to consider than the human mind could comprehend. The paradigms developed in comparative politics, many of which are surveyed in Part II, are designed to provide, among other things, criteria of relevance for the selection of data. That is to say, these paradigms are intended to provide standards for distinguishing those facts which will be included in the analysis and those facts which will be excluded or ignored.

If these criteria of relevance are stated with precision and a lack of ambiguity, the task of conducting a research project will be greatly facilitated. The precision and lack of ambiguity of such criteria is a function of how clearly the concepts and elements of the paradigm are related to observable facts. This is another way of saying that there must be precise "rules of correspondence" between the elements of the paradigm and observable reality or that the concepts or elements of the paradigm must be operational (or susceptible of being rendered so).

For example, we will see that the systems analysis paradigm deals with concepts such as boundary exchanges between systems and their environment or other systems. Unless the concept of boundary exchange is translated in precise terms to concrete behavior patterns or other observable phenomena, the concept does not offer a workable clue for deciding which kind of facts to look for. Unless one knows unambiguously whether a given action constitutes a boundary exchange or affects such an exchange, the concept has not provided a clear criterion for deciding if that action is germane to a study conducted under the systems paradigm.

PARADIGMS AND THE ORGANIZATION OF DATA

In addition to providing criteria for the selection of data, paradigms may, to variable extents, offer frameworks for the organization of data. Insofar as the categories of data or concepts of a paradigm are logically interrelated, the paradigm can be suggestive of what kinds of relationships to look for in the real world. This property of paradigms is therefore a function of the degree of formalization of the paradigm discussed above. This means the extent to which the logical relationships between the elements of the paradigm are precisely specified. Paradigms vary greatly with respect to the degree to which they are formalized. Unfortunately, we will see that there is some tendency for this degree of formalization to vary in inverse proportion to the empirical content of the paradigm. That is to say, the more rigorously the logical relationships between the elements of a paradigm are specified, the less likely it becomes that these elements will be defined in terms of observable indicators. This was exemplified by the example of game theory discussed in Chapter 4. Highly formalized paradigms tend to take on the characteristics of an abstract calculus rather than those of a model isomorphic to aspects of observable reality.

There is a logical reason for this unfortunate tendency. Observable reality tends to be too complex for man, given his limited capacities, to be able to specify relationships between aspects of that reality with any great degree of precision. It is only when a paradigm is highly abstracted from reality and correspondingly simplified that it becomes possible to specify its relationships with mathematical precision.

PARADIGMS AND THE DISSEMINATION AND COMMUNICATION OF KNOWLEDGE

In Chapter 1 it was suggested that one of the distinguishing hallmarks of a scientific discipline is that in such a discipline knowledge is increased incrementally over time. Each generation of scholars should be able to explain (in the scientific sense of that term) more than the previous generation. This increase in explanatory power refers to the quantity of facts explained and to the completeness of available explanations. It was suggested that paradigms facilitate making knowledge cumulative.

Cumulative knowledge builds on what has gone before. By constructing or revising propositions and theory to account for deviant cases that a previous proposition and theory had left unexplained, a discipline acquires a body of knowledge which can account for more events than at any previous time. Moreover, more relevant variables are accounted for in available explanations.

The cumulative building of a body of knowledge means that scholars do not start from scratch. Existing theory or knowledge provides clues as to what solvable gaps exist in the knowledge and as to where to look for solutions to such puzzles (e.g., what kinds of variables are most likely to be relevant). This was suggested in Chapter 4 on the functions of theory and again in Chapter 5 in the discussion of the social relevance of behavioral research. The dictum that researchers should not start from scratch requires that the existing body of knowledge be widely disseminated in a manner which transcends differences in the way concepts are understood.

It was pointed out in Chapter 1, however, that the meaning of concepts is often, to a large extent, derived from the analytical structure (theory or paradigm) of which they are a part. To illustrate, the precise meaning of selective recall screens, memory banks, and input receptors are not acquired independently from Karl Deutch's cybernetic paradigm in which such terms are found.[18] Thus, knowledge can only cumulate when research efforts are directed at the further articulation of previously used paradigms. Paradigm *articulation* refers to the discovery and empirical testing of relationships between the elements of the paradigm.

It should not be necessary to state that a discipline need not develop a universal paradigm for all research. While only research done within the framework of a common paradigm can be cumulative in the strict sense, research need not relate to all previous work in the discipline. For example, it is conceivable that knowledge about cultural variables which affect the likelihood of successful stable parliamentary democracy can, to a point, be built autonomously from knowledge about how all political systems adapt to external stress. Clearly, the foci of competing paradigms will eventually overlap if they are progressively articulated. The question of how systems react to stress may have to account for cultural variables at some point. This may involve an eventual consolidation of several competing paradigms at a more advanced stage in the discipline's development. At the present primitive stage of development, however, there is certainly room for several frameworks within which knowledge may be usefully pursued.

THE EVALUATION OF PARADIGMS

Paradigm selection then becomes, to some extent, a function of the question being asked. A body of concepts, techniques, and even suggested relationships is being developed with respect to research on politically rele-

---

[18] Karl Deutsch, *The Nerves of Government* (New York: The Free Press, 1953).

vant personality types. Clearly, a paradigm selected from this area would be more useful to a researcher who was interested in a possible relationship between modal personality types and a certain class of political system than a paradigm which relied exclusively on macro concepts (taking the whole political or social system as the smallest unit of analysis).

The literature on scientific methodology surveyed in Part 1, does suggest, however, some criteria for paradigm evaluation that are independent of the interests of the researcher. These criteria might be profitably summarized in advance of the critical survey of popular paradigms in the chapters that follow. These criteria are based, of course, on the imperatives of the scientific method discussed in Part I and on those of the comparative approach summarized in the present chapter.

(1) The concepts or elements of a paradigm must either be defined in terms of empirical indicators or be susceptible of being so defined. Unless this criterion is adhered to, a paradigm will be incapable of generating empirically testable propositions.

(2) A paradigm should be applicable to a wide variety of cultural and political contexts. This is a function of the role of the comparative method in holding constant or accounting for the effect of as many relevant variables as possible. Unfortunately, the requirement for wide applicability seems to be in conflict with the first criterion, the operational definition or empirical content of the concepts of a paradigm. Criteria (1) and (2) seem to be fulfilled in inverse proportion to one another. It is easy to visualize the reason for this. Since empirical indicators are derived from and often peculiar to particular social and political contexts or narrow classes of such contexts, any concept precisely defined in terms of such parochial indicators is likely to have limited applicability. The dilemma is a serious one.

(3) The relationships between the elements of the paradigm should be specified as rigorously as possible. When the elements are related only in a loose manner, the paradigm does not suggest empirically testable relationships to be investigated.

(4) The paradigm should include enough relevant variables to suggest hypotheses that will withstand some empirical testing, yet it should be kept simple enough to be manageable. This again involves treading a tightrope between conflicting standards.

(5) The axioms, givens, or assumptions of the paradigm should have enough prima facie validity to enable the paradigm to yield propositions that will withstand empirical testing. For example, the propositions derived from a model that assumes human rationality will be false to the extent that men behave irrationally. This is not to say that an assumption which is not universally valid renders a paradigm useless. It may be that men behave rationally enough of the time to render propositions based upon this assumption useful though not perfect vehicles for prediction.

(6) A paradigm should provide clear criteria of relevance for the col-

lection of data. This implies that if the paradigm takes on the attributes of a system or model, the boundaries should be unambiguous. This requirement is not unrelated to the requirement of the precise definition of terms or concepts or to the requirement of the specification of relationships between the elements of the paradigm. Simply put, a good paradigm will provide unambiguous clues to tell the researcher what facts (or classes of facts) and what relationships to look for.

Armed with the above criteria of evaluation, the next step is to survey major existing paradigms in the field.

7

Models and
Quasi Models in
Comparative Politics

This book takes a somewhat more restricted view of what is meant by a model than is taken by many political scientists. *Model* is a term often used interchangeably with what is referred to in this book as a paradigm, a set of concepts around which data may be organized and which is applicable to a variety of cases or contexts. Paradigms, thus defined, may have any degree of formalization or lack thereof. Paradigm is a broader concept including models, ideal types, and conceptual frameworks or approaches.[1] A model, it will be recalled, was defined in Chapter 4 as a highly formalized system, that is, a set of elements in which the interrelations among such elements are precisely specified. There is an additional criterion for the class of constructs referred to here as models, a criterion which distinguishes models from any formalized system. This criterion specifies that those particular relationships must correspond in structure or form with a set of relationships in that part of the real world which the model is supposed to represent.

This notion of structural correspondence is a difficult and abstract one.[2] It can best be clarified through the use of examples; therefore, this chapter

---

[1] See Arthur Kalleberg, "The Logic of Comparison: A Methodological Note on the Comparative Study of Political Science," *World Politics,* XIX (Jan. 1966), p. 72, for an attempt to distinguish conceptual frameworks from approaches. The former term refers "to a set of more *interrelated* definitions." (Italics mine.) Approaches are merely "expressions symbolizing alternative foci of scholarly interest." Examples of the latter would include decision making, power, or political culture.

[2] For a well-known discussion of structural isomorphism, see May Broadbeck, "Models, Meaning and Theory" in Llewellyn Gross (ed.), *Symposium on Sociological Theory* (New York: Harper & Row, 1959), pp. 373–403.

will refer to this notion in the course of discussions of existing models in comparative politics. For the present, a familiar example may be helpful, that of a physical model.

A model airplane is a representation of that type of full-size airplane. It is, however, not identical to the full-size version or else it would not be a model. The parts of the model, however, take on the same shape as those corresponding parts of the full-size airplane. More significantly, these parts bear the same structural relationship to one another as do the corresponding parts of the larger version. If the wings of the larger airplane are two thirds the way down the fuselage from the stabilizer to the nose, so will the wings of the model be similarly two thirds down its fuselage. The parts of the model and of the airplane are not identical: they are constructed from different materials, for one thing, and fastened together by different means, for another. But they do bear the same structural relationship to one another. Thus, structural correspondence may be distinguished from substantive correspondence. When the elements of the model substantively correspond to elements of reality, then it becomes possible to deduce empirical propositions from it. The model has then become a theory.

It should be clarified that a usage of the word *model* prevalent among laymen, a normative conception of the word, is unrelated to the usage of the term in the lexicon of scientific methodology. When Hitler referred to Denmark as "his model protectorate," he meant that the Danes exemplified a standard of behavior patterns that he wished his other subject peoples would emulate. *Model* in this sense refers to an ideal or actual normative standard by which to judge other members of that class. This normative conception of the term *model* is unrelated to the conception of scientific model developed here.

The elements of a model, in the sense that the term is used here, lack empirical content. That is, they do not correspond to directly observable events or patterns of behavior. Rather they are non-operationalized logical or analytical constructs. Their very abstraction from the complex domain of empirical reality facilitates the determination of logical relationships between them. The empirical validity of these relationships can only be determined when the key elements of the model are defined in terms of empirical indicators. When rules of correspondence between the elements of the model and empirical reality are so specified, the model becomes a theory. This point cannot be emphasized too strongly. Models, as pointed out in Chapter 4, usually involve a set of axioms or givens. It was pointed out in Chapter 6 that the accuracy of the predictions about reality generated by a model depend, to a certain extent, on the validity of these axioms. Although valid axioms do not in themselves guarantee accurate predictions about empirical reality, they are a necessary precondition for accurate predictions. Predictions will be rendered inaccurate to the extent that the axioms of the model are invalid.

This chapter will show that formalized models in the social sciences nearly always involve an expressed or implied axiom of rational behavior. This assumption has been widely criticized since it is not difficult to point out instances of irrational behavior. Yet, an assumption of rationality is necessary if the model is going to generate propositions with predictive power. Only rational behavior is predictable. Irrational behavior is by definition haphazard and therefore not predictable. The question, therefore, is whether human behavior is rational to a great enough extent to render useful probabilistic predictions possible.

In the following survey of existing attempts at model building, it should be possible to discover whether the propositions which are logically true by virtue of the model also correspond to empirical reality. To whatever extent this correspondence between logical truth and empirical validity is observed, the axioms of the model can be presumed to be valid. In other words, if a model based upon the assumptions of rational behavior generated a high percentage of successful propositions, then apparently people behaved rationally to that extent.

WEBERIAN IDEAL TYPES

Models, in the sense that term is used here, are distinguished from what Max Weber meant by an "ideal type." The Weberian constructs consist of hypothetical examples which are the most characteristic of a class of phenomena and which actual examples of that class in the observable world resemble to varying extents. The major ideal types in the Weberian literature are of bureaucracy and of legitimate authority types. These latter are rational authority, traditional authority, and charismatic authority. These idea types are not unrelated, as we shall see below.

In a sense, ideal types may be viewed as polar types on a continuum. For example, bureaucracy may be conceived of as a form of organization to which actual organizations partially conform. This organizational form is defined in terms of the following characteristics: a hierarchical structure, members subject to authority only with respect to their official roles, selection of candidates on basis of demonstrated competence, compensation of officials by fixed salaries, a system of promotion based upon seniority and performance, and a system which functions according to a comprehensive, consistent system of abstract and impersonal rules.[3] Actual bureaucracies will conform to this description to varying degrees. Those which closely fit the description, such as the public bureaucracies of France and Germany, are labeled "classical" bureaucracies. The ideal type provides the standard for such an evaluation.

---

[3] Digested and paraphrased from Max Weber, *The Theory of Social and Economic Organization,* trans. and ed. by Talcott Parsons (New York: The Free Press, 1964), pp. 329–34. See also H. H. Gerth and C. Wright Mills (eds.), *From Max Weber: Essays in Sociology* (New York: Oxford Galaxy Books, 1958), pp. 196–98.

Such an ideal type is not precisely what is meant by a model. The logical relationships between the properties or elements of the ideal are not always specified. In fact, they are occasionally incompatible with one another. For example, the property of hierarchy implies control by the supervisor of his subordinates; however, a comprehensive system of impersonal rules would eliminate direct authority relationships. Everyone would, by the latter characteristic, be equal under the rules. The Weberian formulations are therefore less formalized than models in the strict sense of that term.

Ideal types, like other analytical formulations, suggest questions that it might be useful to pose and in this way provide standards of selecting and organizing data. The Weberian ideal type of bureaucracy is alleged to be "capable of attaining the highest degree of efficiency and in this sense formally the most rational known *means* of carrying out imperative control over human beings. It is superior to any other form in precision, in stability, in the stringency of its discipline and in its reliability."[4] (Italics mine.) This asserts that this organizational form is the most rationally efficient means of attaining given social ends. Therefore, it would follow that real world organizations are more or less efficient to the extent that their characteristics correspond to those of the ideal type. Given such a set of assumptions, it would be useful to investigate the extent to which a given nation's administrative sector is organized according to the principles of hierarchy, etc., in order to reach conclusions about its efficiency in applying national policy. In this way, the concept of hierarchy becomes a useful category around which to organize facts about administrative organizations in a variety of political systems.

This claim of efficiency does seem to inject a normative standard into the ideal type despite disclaimers to the contrary.[5] It seems inescapable to conclude that since his ideal type represents the most rational and efficient means of organization, Weber would encourage real world organizations to strive to emulate his ideal type. The ideal type may, in this sense, be compared to Plato's republic. They both become standards for normatively evaluating real world cases.

The claim of efficiency can probably be given some justification on logical grounds despite certain logical inconsistencies in the ideal type. (These inconsistencies were referred to above.) However, it is doubtful whether this claim of efficiency can be empirically tested. How, for example, can one measure efficiency? Such measurement would be necessary in order to establish lower limits of efficiency below which any suitably "rationalized" organization could not perform without falsifying the proposition. Also unanswered is the question of the precise relationship between degrees of correspondence of actual organizations to the ideal types, on the one hand, and degrees of efficiency, on the other. The inescapable introduction of the

---

[4] Weber, trans. Parsons, op. cit., p. 337.
[5] Weber, trans. Gerth and Mills, op. cit., p. 59.

concept of degrees would seem to hopelessly complicate the relationship beyond the bounds of testability.

The claim of efficiency is also based upon the assumption that political and social ends can be clearly separated from means of achieving them. In short, the efficiency of Weber's ideal type is based upon the assumption that politics is separate from administration. This means, in effect, that bureaucrats do not make decisions which significantly allocate the values of society but rather merely apply such decisions. It is easy to demonstrate that this assumption is false. As a matter of fact, an increasing tendency exists in both the Western and non-Western world for more and more decision making to be centered in the administrative process. In the non-Western world this has been a function of the weakness of other institutions; the administrative sector has often been the most, if not the only, effective institution in such systems.[6] In the Western world, the administration, by virtue of its characteristics of recruitment according to demonstrated competence and specialization of function, is by definition uniquely qualified to handle the complex decisions of a technologically mature society. In both cases, the result is the increasing participation of the administrative sector in the actual decision-making process.

When it is apparent that the bureaucracy is engaged in decision making as well as decision application, the Weberian claim of efficiency must be viewed from a different perspective. While it may be true that this form of organization logically appears to be the most technically efficient means of reaching given societal goals, it is not obvious that bureaucratic organization is an effective instrument for deciding among alternatives of public policy. This decision-making role in which bureaucracy now finds itself involves a process of adaptation, a process of formulating appropriate responses to inputs that are ceaselessly changing in both nature and volume. Such an adaptive role requires innovative behavior patterns, patterns which, we have seen, the bureaucratic form of organization does not encourage.

This somewhat extended discussion of the discrepancies between the Weberian ideal type of bureaucracy and the actual operation of bureaucratic organization is intended to clarify basic weaknesses in Weberian ideal types. These Weberian constructs imply standards for engineering their real world counterparts. Supposedly, the more like an ideal type bureaucracy a real world organization becomes, the better an organization it will be. However, since the ideal type implies normative goals (for example, rational effi-

---

[6] See Fred Riggs, *Administration in Developing Countries, The Theory of the Prismatic Society* (Boston: Houghton-Mifflin Co., 1964), pp. 222ff. This argument can also be applied to certain unstable "western" nations, most notably France. See Alfred Diamant, "The French Administrative System—The Republic Passes but the Administration Remains," in William J. Siffin (ed.), *Toward the Comparative Study of Public Administration* (Bloomington: University of Indiana Press, 1957), pp. 182–218, and Micheal Crozier, *The Bureaucratic Phenomenon* (Chicago: University of Chicago Press, 1964), especially pp. 237–69.

ciency), it offers but one of several possible alternative criteria for judging a real world case. For example, flexibility and adaptability may be a justifiable goal that is not consistent with rational efficiency. Moreover, these constructs are based on certain assumptions without which the entire normative argument collapses. In the case of the rationalized bureaucracy, the claim of efficiency cannot be sustained to the extent that the assumption of a clear separation of politics and administration is shown to be invalid. With these unsustainable claims, such an ideal type is unable to generate propositions that will withstand empirical testing. The futile efforts of American public administration experts to rationalize and thereby render more efficient several growing non-Western civil service systems constitute illustrations of this point.

Moreover, it is not easy to see much heuristic (suggestive) value in ideal type construction. These ideal types are primarily lists of characteristics rather than formalized constructs. Rather than constituting a system of logically related elements, we have seen that the ideal type of bureaucracy contains elements some of which are logically inconsistent with one another. Since the ideal types do not directly stipulate relationships, they are incapable of generating scientific propositions which, as Chapter 3 shows, are, at a minimum, statements about relationships.

They do, however, perform the functions characteristic of typologies in that the classes in such typologies may be related to other phenomena. It is conceivable that cases which most closely resemble one "pure type" of authority may also tend to possess another characteristic (such as a particular class structure or a type of economy); thus, a relationship would be established between that authority type and that characteristic. For example, legal rational authority in the Weberian schema is virtually identical with the bureaucratic form of organization and is asserted to be associated with modernity. Thus, economic development and industrialization are in this scheme inexorably associated with a movement from traditional or charismatic authority types to the rational legal type. Both charismatic and traditional forms of authority are shown to be incompatible with a modern form of economic order.[7] However, even if it is granted that the pre-modern authority types are dysfunctional for an industrial society, this is far from an adequate demonstration that these authority types will necessarily be replaced by a form of authority more functional for an industrial society. Such an assertion of inevitability is not logically different from the determinism of a Marx or Hegel. The fallacy of such pro-Western determinism has already been discussed and will be mentioned again with respect to the concept of development.

---

[7] Weber, trans. Parsons, op. cit., pp. 354ff and p. 362. See the discussion of his famous concept, "The Routinization of Charisma," pp. 363ff. This is a thesis of the inevitable rationalization of charismatic authority because of its dysfunctional aspects.

The difficulty in deriving valid relationships from Weberian ideal types seems to lie in the fact that they do not constitute abstractions of reality which are, in some respects, isomorphic to reality. Rather, they are constructs which do not have any necessary degree of correspondence to empirical reality. In form, Weberian ideal types are more like Platonic essences[8] than scientific models. As such, they are more suited to function as normative standards than as instruments for prediction of observable events.

ANTHONY DOWNS' ECONOMIC THEORY OF DEMOCRACY

A much more rigorous construction with much more precise empirical implications is Anthony Downs's *An Economic Theory of Democracy.*[9] Not only does this formulation possess all of the characteristics of a scientific model; it is arguable that it, in fact, constitutes a narrow guage theory. Such an argument would have to be based on the testability of the propositions derived from the theoretic construct.[10]

The elements or variables in Downs's theoretic construct include the following: voting behavior, party behavior, party ideology, information about the utilities of each possible outcome for each actor in the system, and the distribution of public opinion in the system. Unlike classical game theory, Downs does not make the unrealistic assumption of perfect information about precisely measured utilities for each of the nearly infinite variety of possible outcomes. Rather, Downs goes to great lengths to cope with the problem of uncertainty, the lack of such information.

As can be seen from the above list of variables, Downs's theoretic construct is, in a real sense, more of a theory (or model) of parties in a democracy than about democracy itself. The relationship of parties to public opinion and voting behavior has been thought to constitute the very essence of a modern democratic system;[11] nevertheless, some may argue that a complete theory of democracy would have to include variables that are omitted from this theoretic construct (for example, political structure, political culture).

As with so many social science models (particularly those derived from or related to the theory of games), Downs bases his model on an assumption

---

[8] Platonic essences are ideal forms of classes of objects which may or may not resemble observable representations of such objects. For example, reality is not this table or that table that one sees, feels, etc. Rather, reality lies in the idea of "tableness," an ideal which has no direct manifestation in the observable world.

[9] Anthony Downs, *An Economic Theory of Democracy* (New York: Harper & Row, 1957).

[10] This is a catch-all term which is meant to refer to both theories and models when it is not convenient to distinguish the two.

[11] For example, Joseph Schumpeter, *Capitalism, Socialism and Democracy,* 3d ed. (New York: Harper & Row, 1949), pp. 235–83, especially pp. 269–72, has given one of the classic definitions of democracy as the competition between two or more elites at more or less regular and open elections.

of rationality for all parties concerned. Such an assumption is necessary to any model of political behavior because, as noted earlier, only rational behavior is predictable. Irrational behavior is by definition erratic and, after all, one of the purposes in social science in model building is to increase predictive power about human behavior. Rationality in Downs's construct refers to the most efficient (in the sense of getting the most output for the smallest input) means of attaining certain specified ends, the maximization of political utilities for the electorate and the maximization of votes for parties. It may be, however, that it would be "rational" not to seek the most effective means of attaining such ends. Rather, it may be that there are compelling personal reasons for ordering these ends lower on a priority scale with competing goals. However, such considerations would greatly complicate the model and Downs explicitly omits them. It will be recalled that this is perfectly consistent with the criteria of model building set down in Chapter 4, that of the simplification of reality to within the bounds of manageability. Second, there is the problem of distinguishing irrational behavior from lack of information. This dilemma weakens the model, as Downs admits. One partial solution is the fact that the error of a rational man tends to be systematic and tends to be self-correcting. This solution is partial, however, and Downs simply points out that imperfect models are better than no models at all.

Downs assumes that the goal of parties is to maximize votes[12] rather than to articulate an ideology or achieve a policy goal. To the extent that ideology or program takes precedent over electoral success, the parties are presumed to behave irrationally. This pragmatic "self-interest" axiom states that parties seek to win rather than to perform a social function. Downs, drawing upon classical market theory, suggests that the "social function" of creating and implementing policy will be an incidental by-product of the parties' pursuit of their rational political self-interest. This becomes a version of Adam Smith's "invisible hand" applied to politics.

Downs actually constructs two models: one in which information is certain and free and another in which it is not. One of the more interesting aspects of the book is the extent to which the injection of the variable of uncertainty and scarce information alters expected outcomes or behavior patterns. From the former model, Downs derives expectations of the government's (read: winning party's) actions based upon these variables: expected votes, opposition strategies, and individual utilities. It is not the actual utility payments to each individual flowing from each alternative decision that the government takes into account. Such elaborate calculations clearly would be impossible. Rather they must calculate on the basis of how they

---

[12] This conflicts with the "size principle" of William Riker, *The Theory of Political Coalitions* (New Haven: Yale University Press, 1962) to be discussed below. Once Riker's "size principle" is modified by the reality of uncertain information, the conflict with Downs with respect to vote maximization is no longer so apparent.

expect the voters, in the aggregate, to perceive the effect of government decisions on their own utilities. If a majority of voters perceive that a given policy option will maximize their utilities, any party that wants to win For example, Downs asserts that government readings of voter perceptions that is crucial for determining governmental behavior. The behavior of individual voters is influenced not only by expectations and assessments of governmental performance. Such behavior is also influenced by the variable of how each voter expects others to vote. These expectations may or may not be based on sound information.

Thus, it is easy to see how uncertainty can be introduced into this model. For example, Downs asserts that government readings of voter perceptions will be most influenced by those who have the most information. Furthermore, the net gain in added (marginal) utilities earned by making the rationally best choice must be calculated by subtracting the cost of the information needed to make such a rational decision from the gross gain in marginal utilities. If the cost of such information exceeds the marginal utilities derived from making the rational decision, it may, paradoxically, be rational to be irrational. That is, it may be rational not to bother to acquire the information necessary to determine which choice will maximize utilities. The variable of ideology is introduced here as a "cost saving device" to facilitate choice without the trouble and expense of acquiring information. In short, when dealing with actual behavioral expectations, the concept of what is rational is defined in terms of the existence of uncertainty.

The real merit of Downs' theoretic construct is that a variety of allegedly testable propositions have been deductively derived from it.[13] They can be so derived because the theoretical construct is to some extent a logically formalized system. A question may be raised as to whether the propositions are testable as stated. (Whether they can be made testable without altering their meaning is another question.)

Many of the propositions are formulated as tendency statements. For example, note the following: "Democratic governments *tend* to redistribute income from the rich to the poor. . . ." "Democratic governments *tend* to favor producers more than consumers. . . ."[13a] (Italics mine.) Clearly, such tendency statements are difficult to falsify because they do not specify how many deviant instances must occur before such propositions are rejected. Only statistically significant relationships in the opposite direction (as democratic governments favoring consumers) could refute such propositions. Threshold levels, of course, could be specified, but at our present state of knowledge they would have to be purely arbitrary.

Other propositions deal with unmanageable variables. For example, Proposition 1 states: "Party members have as their chief motivation the

---

[13] Downs' concluding chapter consists of nothing more than a list of 25 such propositions.

[13a] Downs, op. cit., p. 297.

desire to obtain the intrinsic rewards of holding office; therefore, they formulate policies as a means to holding office rather than seeking office in order to carry out preconceived policies." The concept of intention is a very difficult one to manage. Intentions can only be inferred from behavior and such inference involves the danger of what Blalock calls "the fallacy of affirming the consequent."[14] Applied to this problem, the fallacy would operate in the following manner. Knowledge about intentions (or any mental state) is desired but only behavior can be observable. Intentions are therefore inferred from behavior. If a given mental state existed, certain behavior patterns will result. If one observes the behavior patterns, one assumes they are caused by that mental state. However, this behavioral outcome (or consequent) does not prove the existence of a cause (mental state) unless it can be proven that no other cause could have brought that behavioral outcome about. Actually, the proposition is not clearly distinguished from the assumption that parties seek to maximize their votes.

Because so many interesting propositions have been deductively derived from Downs's model, it becomes a powerful explanatory tool. The statement that they are deductively derived means that the propositions are *logically true* given the assumptions of the model. The *empirical truth* of the propositions is another question. If the propositions are logically true but not empirically true, then doubt is cast on one or more of the axioms or givens of the model. For example, irrational behavior (defined as in the model in terms of the existence of uncertainty) would result in the empirical rejection of one or more propositions inasmuch as such rationality is an axiom of the model. Such a conflict between what is logically true and what is empirically true may be taken as an indication of the limited validity of such an axiom.

Downs's model, despite its often imprecise empirical implications, is perhaps the closest construct available in the discipline to the type of hierarchical deductive system that Chapter 4 designated as theory. The propositions are logically true given the axioms and the specified relationships between the elements of the system. Given actions or events are logically implied by the propositions. Thus, facts are logically subsumed in propositions which are in turn logically subsumed in a theoretic construct or logical system. This is what is meant by explanation, as was fully discussed in Chapter 2.

It is beyond the scope of this book to describe all of the many propositions and insights to be found in this most illuminating work. However, lest one conclude that the limited validity of the rationality axiom renders the model of little use, it would be useful to note a couple of examples of propositions, logically derived from Downs's model, that are also empirically valid. One which seems clearly true (although perhaps untestable in a rigorous

---

[14] Hubert M. Blalock, *Social Statistics* (New York: McGraw-Hill, 1960), pp. 92–93.

quantifiable sense) is that in a two-party system, party policies tend to be more vague and to resemble one another more than in a multiparty system (Propositions 2 and 3). Logically, such policies tend to be vague, given the goal of electoral success and the assumption of rationality, because parties must strive to aggregate a greater variety of interests and opinions in a two-party system in order to maximize their votes. The logical reasons for the convergence of party programs in a two-party system lie, first, in the necessity for both parties to appeal to those sentiments shared by a majority of the electorate and, second, in the fact that such parties can usually take their extreme wings for granted. Thus, they can only expand their electoral support by competing for the uncommitted center.

A second proposition which appears to possess empirical validity is that extreme voters will support their more moderate parties except when they become future oriented. In such instances, extreme voters may desert their party in the hope of forcing it to make more concessions to the party's extreme wing in future elections. Downs might have added that such instances appear more likely to occur in cases where the difference between the dominant wings of the two parties is minimized and the gap between the dominant and extreme wings of a party is widened. This appears to be what happened when members of the American new left deserted Hubert Humphrey's presidential candidacy in 1968. Of course, the conditions of such future orientation are not only not clearly specified by Downs; it is not clear that they could be specified in any precise way.

For a third example, there is a logical reason why governments tend to favor producers over consumers. The utilities that can be derived by a producer of a product greatly exceed those which can be realized by a consumer; consequently, the former will expend more scarce resources (for example, information) to influence policy than will the latter. Because producers have more at stake on any given issue, they are more likely than consumers to organize. As Ralph Nader will attest, producers are in fact more likely to get their way. (The methodological weakness of such a tendency statement has already been noted.)

The point is that there are events or facts in the contemporary political life of nations which could be subsumed under propositions derived from Downs's model and thus *explained*. Apparently, those axioms of limited validity are valid enough of the time to permit a high degree of correspondence between propositions which are logically true by virtue of the model and propositions which are empirically true. This suggests that the explanatory potential of the model is considerable. For this potential to be realized, however, the propositions will have to be rendered more precisely testable and the model adjusted where necessary.

Downs's model is clearly germane to comparative politics. It deals with a variety of types of party systems and electorates and thus has implications that go beyond any single nation. Its *scope* appears to be limited, however, to Western democracies. This is not a pejorative observation. Its very limited scope may be the most important characteristic of the model with respect to its ability to generate propositions about the real world with greater precision than most other available models. This ability leads to the conclusion that Downs's effort is one of the most promising exercises in model building that has occurred in the discipline to date.

WILLIAM RIKER AND THE APPLICATION OF GAME THEORY

Inasmuch as the theory of games is a rigorous, highly formalized model, it has had limited application to the field of comparative political analysis. As was pointed out in Chapter 4, the conditions under which game theory can function in its pure form rarely occur in the real political world. Among the highly limiting axioms of game theory are the assumption of rationality, the zero-sum condition,[15] the two-person condition, and perfect information. It was shown in the discussion of Downs's formulation that useful models can be built on axioms of limited validity, such as rationality and certainty. William Riker's theory of political coalitions is an attempt to construct such a model based upon the theory of games. One limited type of circumstance in which a zero-sum condition appears to hold is in the competition for elective office in a two-party arrangement. (Riker conveniently chooses struggles for the American presidency for several of his illustrative examples.) Another would be the struggle for survival in a bipolar world. Total wars would have a winner-take-all character. Riker, however, simply suggests that common advantages in a situation may be ignored for the sake of the zero-sum model.[16]

Riker's condition of rationality is defined in a way that is not only more precise than definitions found elsewhere[17] but in a way that is quite consonant with his zero-sum interpretation of political events. Riker says that, given alternative courses of action which are known to lead to differing payoffs, a rational man will choose the highest payoff. In short, the rational man desires to win rather than lose.[18]

Since Riker is talking about coalitions, the two-person condition is not adhered to in this study. Coalitions involve the interaction of at least three persons (two winners and one loser). This is called an N-person game.

---

[15] As explained in Chapter 4, this refers to a condition of a finite number of utilities so that whatever is won by one party must be lost by another.

[16] Riker, op. cit., p. 29.

[17] Riker dwells on the difficulty with the concept of power in rejecting commonplace notions of rationality. A more common conception of rationality, it seems to me, equates it with efficiency (as with Weber). Yet, the concept of efficiency is as difficult to manage as the concept of power.

[18] Riker, op. cit., pp. 22–23. Riker draws an analogy between a political representative and a legal guardian of an economic trust ("fiduciary agent"). Both are under strong pressures to act rationally for the benefit of their clientele.

The major proposition derived by Riker from the foregoing set of axioms is what he calls the *size principle*. This means that in conflict situations, participants seek "to create coalitions just as large as they believe will ensure winning and no larger." Riker himself notes that this concept of a minimum winning coalition conflicts with the assumption of Downs that parties seek to maximize their votes. The logic underlying the size principle consists principally in the costs of building a winning coalition and in the amount of utilities which can pass from the losers to the winners for winning. To entice participants into joining one's coalition rather than joining another or remaining neutral, payments must be made to them. Such payments would have to be subtracted from the profits or winnings of the winning coalition. Simply put, when the winning coalition becomes larger, there are more participants among whom the winnings must be divided. Consequently, each share is smaller. Also, to the extent that a zero-sum situation exists, the utilities extracted by the winners must be extracted from the losers. Consequently, when there are few losers, there is little to win.

The size principle can be mathematically demonstrated to be logically true, and such a demonstration is in fact performed in an appendix. For the empirical truth of the principle, Riker offers a series of illustrations of the breakup of grand coalitions rather than a systematic testing of the proposition. Perhaps the most familiar of such illustrations is the breakup of the allied coalition after World War II. The First World War and the Napoleonic wars are two other total war examples offered.[19] Several examples are also offered from American domestic politics. However, Riker does not justify the omission of several apparently viable grand coalitions, such as the alliance of the Socialist and Catholic parties in Austria. Presumably, such deviant cases would constitute examples of nonrational behavior; however, such an interpretation would be a classic example of the saving-the-hypothesis fallacy discussed above and would render the size principle not testable (unless, of course, one could define irrational behavior independently of deviation from the size principle). Nevertheless, Riker does rigorously deduce from a set of axioms a principle which appears to subsume and explain a great many political events. Other illustrations immediately come to mind, such as the short life span of the C.D.U./C.S.U.-S.P.D. alliance in the Federal Republic of Germany. (It would be helpful, incidentally, to have some precise indication of how long a coalition would have to survive to be considered a deviant case. For example, Riker offers the breakup of the Indian Congress party's massive majority as an illustration of the size principle. Yet, the fact remains that the Congress party remained overwhelmingly dominant for a significant length of time. Thus, it could also be offered as an illustration of a deviant case.)

A corollary principle is the *information effect*. This refers to the assertion that "the greater degree of imperfection or incompleteness of information,

---

19 Ibid., pp. 66ff.

the larger will be the coalitions that coalition-makers seek to form. . . ."[20] The logic of this is that unless the threshold degree of strength between winning and losing is precisely known, the participants will want to allow for a margin of error in order to ensure that they at least win. In a zero-sum social situation, there is nothing to be gained by losing. The difficulty is that this corollary renders the size principle completely untestable. Since there is no known way of precisely measuring the amount of information available, it is possible to say of any coalition that is above minimum winning size, "That is the result of too much uncertainty." Therefore, Riker's theoretic construct cannot explain why this coalition is of minimal winning size and that coalition is larger than minimal winning size.

A further difficulty is that Riker does not make it clear whether (ignoring the information problem) any increase in coalition strength over bare minimum will be considered a deviant case and, if not, how much above the minimum size would be permitted. As indicated in the concluding pages of Chapter 6, the fact that the propositions generated by a paradigm are not testable as stated does not constitute a fatal criticism unless such propositions cannot be made so testable. A principle which is not testable because of the imprecision of its empirical implications can often be rendered testable by two operations. First, it is necessary to define these implications in terms of observable indicators. Second, one may arbitrarily, if necessary, specify precise thresholds which unambiguously distinguish between data which are compatible with the principle and data which are not. It is not possible to say here whether Riker's size principle is in this class of propositions which can be rendered testable. The answer to this question depends largely on whether the completeness-of-information variable is ever rendered susceptible to precise measurement.

It must be concluded, therefore, that there appears to be some correspondence between the size principle derived from the model and actual behavior; however, inasmuch as the size principle is not strictly testable, the precise degree of such correspondence cannot be ascertained.

Riker has produced some evidence elsewhere, though, that people in a social conflict situation do behave rationally to maximize their utilities.[21] Using a three-person game involving college students playing for monetary rewards, Riker and Zavoina persuasively demonstrate the overwhelming preponderance of rational behavior in coalition formation. Such evidence is, of course, not conclusive, but strongly supportive of the assumption that people behave rationally most of the time.

Both Riker's and Downs's models, even if rational behavior can be assumed, have uncertain predictive power due to the inevitability of some

---

[20] Ibid., pp. 88ff.

[21] William Riker & William James Zavoina, "Rational Behavior in Politics: Evidence from a Three Person Game," *American Political Science Review,* Vol. 44, No. 1 (March 1970), pp. 48–61. Maximization of quantitative reward was discounted by the probability of winning in the selection of coalition partners.

uncertainty (lack of information). Complete information is necessary for rational behavior. One cannot make a rational choice unless one knows in advance the outcomes of each of the alternatives that he faces. Rationality could be defined so as to include behavior based upon misinformation, behavior which would be rational if the information were true. However, erroneous perceptions are not known to occur systematically; consequently, such a definition of rationality would not lead to testable propositions with precise predictive power. The degree of completeness cannot, it was shown, be specified. This seems to be an inherent difficulty with models based upon the assumption of rationality.

Riker deductively derives a number of other expectations from the model. The concept of side payments (payments made by the organizers and leaders of coalitions to attract potential followers) combined with uncertainty by leaders is shown to lead to an inexorable disequilibrium in the model. This can lead to the expectation that coalitions will be perpetually shifting. However, as in the final chapter, "The Role of the United States in World Affairs," Riker introduces various mitigating circumstances that can affect the rate and extent of coalition shifts. Thus, we are not left with a means of deriving a set of expectations about the precise duration of any given coalition or the extent of any expected political change.

Of course, Professor Riker would undoubtedly recognize the fact that the expected outcomes generated by his model are not precisely testable as stated. To point out that more research needs to be done on the model is not intended to detract from the value of his model as a first step in generating a theory about a defined range of political behavior. Nevertheless, at the risk of being unnecessarily repetitive, scientific theory must imply some precise class of outcomes. A useful model should lead to such theory. It remains to be seen if models of political behavior based upon the axiom of rationality can overcome their inherent difficulties and generate such theory. Certainly Professor Riker has come closer to demonstrating the relevance of game theory, the most rigorous of available formalized models, to comparative politics than has anyone else.

A RATIONAL DECISION-MAKING MODEL

The possibilities of rational behavior in political decision making are explored in an imprecisely formulated model of decision making by Charles Lindblom and Robert Dahl.[22] Basically, this model explores the possibilities for rationality in decision making, the techniques for rational decision making, and the structural and biological impediments to rational decision

---

[22] Robert Dahl and Charles Lindblom, *Politics, Economics and Welfare* (New York: Harper Torchbooks, 1953). See also Charles Lindblom, "The Science of Muddling Through," *Public Administration Review*, Vol. 29, No. 2 (Spring 1959), pp. 79–88, for a concise formulation of some of the basic arguments.

making. Rationality is defined in terms of efficiency. The authors state that "an action is rational to the extent that it is 'correctly' designed to maximize goal achievement given the goal in question and the real world as it exists." Thus, unlike Riker, Dahl and Lindblom explicitly exclude from this definition the concept of perceptual rationality.[23] By the standard of perceptual rationality, behavior is rational according to that picture of the real world perceived by the actors. It is called rational behavior even if that perceived picture of the real world is erroneous in an objective sense. Objective rationality, on the other hand, is the standard of what is the most efficient means to achieve given ends given the objective state of the real world regardless of the perceptions (or misperceptions) of the actor in question. As stated above, defining rationality as the perceptual variety leads to enormous problems in measurement and testing as well as to enormous opportunities for saving a hypothesis of rational behavior despite any number of apparently deviant cases.

The authors make a clear and persuasive argument for what may be called *incrementalism*, the abandonment of the technique of posing choices in terms of alternative weltanshauungen (closed, comprehensive ideologies, such as the various isms)[24] in favor of piecemeal, step-by-small-step tinkering to produce small changes in the existing order of things. Lindblom refers to this as the distinction between the *root* and the *branch* methods. The argument may be briefly summarized as follows: The human mind could not possibly comprehend all of the possible alternatives of any given policy decision, let alone the consequences of each alternative. Moreover, one cannot predict the consequences of an alternative that is very different from the system state one has known. (We are very uncertain about, for example, how a stateless or classless society or a totally unregulated national economy would operate. Nothing quite like them has ever been tried.) By limiting the alternatives considered to small changes in existing reality, one accomplishes several things. First, one reduces the number of alternatives to be considered to a more manageable number. Second, one considers only alternatives whose consequences are, to a significant extent, predictable. One can more accurately predict the consequences of small changes in existing reality than of the adoption of a new socioeconomic order. We

---

[23] Dahl and Lindblom, op. cit., pp. 38–39.

[24] The abandonment of the consideration of the various isms as irrelevant to today's issues is a fairly widespread phenomenon among serious scholars. This is popularly referred to as the decline-of-ideology thesis. This thesis and its critics is discussed in Chapter 10. Only a few highly traditionally oriented (and in this writer's view, highly naive) writers still expend energy on the fruitless debate between such comprehensive total ideologies as capitalism, socialism, etc. For a classic example of such polemics on the relative merits of irrelevant ideological positions, see William Ebenstein, *Today's Isms,* 5th ed. (Englewood Cliffs, N.J.: Prentice-Hall, 1967). Other classical polemical defenses of one ism or another include F. A. Hayek, *The Road to Serfdom* (Chicago: University of Chicago Press, 1944) and Norman Thomaas, *Socialism Reexamined* (New York: Norton, 1963).

can fairly accurately predict the consequences of small adjustments in the availability of capital engineered by monetary and fiscal policy within the framework of our current mixed economy. We are to a much smaller extent able to predict the consequences of the total elimination of private property. We do not know the extent to which incentives other than economic dues could motivate people to productive effort. Thus, the latter alternative should be removed from consideration. Of course, when the consequences of various alternatives cannot be accurately predicted, one cannot rationally choose among those alternatives (in the objective sense). Objective rationality involves relatively accurate and complete information. Third, one can use the experience of various small and therefore reversible decisions to readjust one's preference orderings. It is difficult to choose among conflicting goals in advance of having experienced them or having had some relevant experiences.

Incrementalism is presented as one technique for the maximization of rationality in decision making. While it is the focus of Lindblom's article, it is but one of numerous such techniques presented in the Dahl and Lindblom book. In this longer effort, the authors discuss numerous political and economic mechanisms that allegedly facilitate the process of calculation and control. These are presented as purely instrumental means which are calculated to achieve a set of seven goals or values.[25] While there is some discussion of the compatibility of some techniques with others, the elements of this "model" are not interrelated in any precise sense. While the authors discuss how these techniques or processes are related to the efficient and rational attainment of their posited goals, they make no real effort to deduce any empirically testable propositions from their formulation. Thus, while they offer some intuitive or logical explanations for states of affairs, in the sense of suggesting logical reasons for the existence of such states, they do not attempt scientific explanation in the sense of that term developed in Chapter 2. Clearly, the authors did not intend to do so.

For example, they offer logical reasons why direct command is one of the least frequently used (and least effective) techniques of control.[26] These reasons are derivable from certain assumptions or axioms about human motivation implicitly developed in the consideration of seven basic goals. Presumably, then, one could deduce an expectation that command will be supplemented by a variety of other techniques in all decision-making systems (that are rational). However, in order to render such an expectation testable, one would have to specify precisely how marginal command as a technique is likely to be.

What Dahl and Lindblom have accomplished is to suggest a set of techniques that are likely to result in more efficient rational calculation and

---

[25] This constitutes one more example of the fact that modern political scientists rarely, if ever, suggest either the possibility or desirability of remaining value free.

[26] Dahl & Lindblom, op. cit., pp. 106–109.

control and to offer logical reasons for the postulated instrumental efficiency of techniques. In doing so, they have postulated some relationships between these techniques. What they have said appears to be applicable to a variety of political and cultural contexts (although far from universally so). In this sense, their work could be a useful framework for comparative research. While it is impossible to deny the value of such an effort as a first step in building a set of empirical propositions about decision making, much more needs to be done before any unambiguous empirical expectations can be deduced from the formulation discussed here.

POLITICAL STYLE

A more systematic model of the decision-making process was formulated by Herbert Spiro,[27] a model which had been previously applied (albeit in a less systematic fashion) to European politics.[28] Spiro's model revolves around the processing of issues. This involves four variables: the formulation of issues (identification of the real problem), the deliberation of issues (consideration of alternatives in the light of available resources), the resolution of issues (reaching a decision), and solution (the application of the decision). Other elements in the model include a two-by-two classification scheme of types of issues. One set of dichotomous categories consists of the temporal distinction between fundamental and circumstantial issues. The former refers to issues which are basic to the system; the latter refers to issues which are products of a particular time or situation. The second set consists of the distinction between procedural and substantive issues. Procedure deals with the rules by which decisions are reached; substance deals with the content of the decisions. Issues are also classified with regard to their general content—Spiro calls this a classification of problems. These problem types are constitutional, economic, power, and cultural. They correspond to a fourfold classification of system goals: stability, flexibility, efficiency, and effectiveness. These classifications are all interrelated, as shown in Figure 7–1, a composite of several figures taken from the article. For example, issues involving questions of a system's constitution or culture are likely to be fundamental or basic to that system. Similarly, the type of problem is related to a particular phase in the flow of policy. Cultural values and the nature of the constitution affect the way an issue is formulated (or identified).

The concept of political style is derived from the fact that political systems differ with respect to the emphasis given to one or more phases of the policy process and/or to one or more types of issues and problems. For

---

[27] Herbert Spiro, "Comparative Politics: A Comprehensive Approach," *The American Political Science Review,* Vol. 56., No. 3 (September 1962), pp. 577–95.

[28] Herbert Spiro, *Government by Constitution* (New York: Random House Paperbound, 1959).

FIGURE 7-1

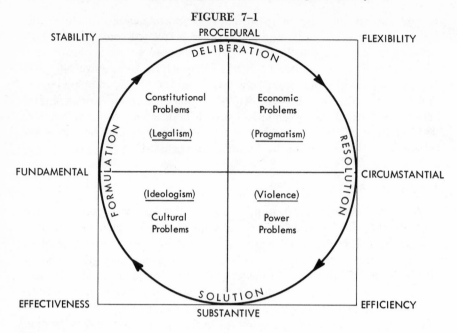

example, a system that emphasizes the formulation and deliberation of constitutional issues to the neglect of the resolution and solution of such issues and to the neglect of the consideration of economic, power, and cultural problems is said to be legalistic. Obviously, such a system would not be processing its real problems. France and Germany, Spiro asserts, are high in fundamental legalism in that they keep the nature of their constitution very much in the political arena.[29] To this extent, they ignore power problems and political realities; there is a propensity in these nations to attempt to delegate political disputes to the "impersonal" authority of the law. It is perhaps noteworthy that Crozier makes the same observation about France, namely, an avoidance of power problems in favor of a preference for impersonal rules.[30] This propensity prevents these systems from reaching a viable solution to their real problems in terms of the existing power realities of that time and place. Other "pure" political styles include pragmatism, violence, and ideologism, which are related to the other variables as shown in Figure 7-1. Of course, Spiro recognizes that pure types do not exist in actuality; rather, actual nations exhibit combinations of styles. However, they do emphasize certain styles and deemphasize others, occa-

---

[29] Ibid., pp. 213ff.

[30] Michael Crozier, *The Bureaucratic Phenomenon* (Chicago: University of Chicago Press, 1964), Part 4. Spiro, "Comparative Politics," op. cit., pp. 581, suggests that while the Fourth Republic was legalistic and ideological, the Fifth Republic has been "preoccupied with resolution and solution" to the neglect of formulation and deliberation of issues. Presumably this latter style would be pragmatic and violent.

sionally to the detriment of the flow of policy. One may read into Spiro's writings a scarcely concealed preference for pragmatism as that style most conducive to processing real problems and issues.[31]

Spiro has introduced a concept—political style—which appears to lead to explanations of differentials between political systems with respect to stability and success in processing issues. (These outcomes, of course, are themselves not related.) These explanations, while incomplete and imprecise, appear to be intellectually satisfying. That is, these explanations correspond to, and more clearly articulate, some vague impressions that have long been held about the differences between certain political systems. This is one of the most attractive features of the efforts of Professor Spiro. He addresses himself to concrete questions about actual political systems— for example, Why are some constitutional democracies, such as Great Britain and Sweden, more stable and successful than others, such as Italy and France? This appears to be more useful than the construction of a model at such a high level of generality and abstraction that no such application is readily apparent. After all, the ultimate goal of systematic comparative political analysis is the explanation and prediction of relevant problems about actual political systems, such as the success and stability of actual constitutional democracies. The construction of intellectually elegant models is only instrumental to this goal; yet, with some model builders, who admit their lack of concern with the empirical content or relevance of their model, the instrument becomes an end in itself. Talcott Parsons, discussed below, will be shown to constitute a classic example of those model builders unconcerned about the empirical content of their formulations.

Spiro's discussion of ideologism,[32] one of his four political styles, clearly illustrates the manner in which his scheme can be used in the attempt to explain differences among political systems. Simply put, he shows how preoccupation with the relative merits of closed, comprehensive thought systems, such as Marxism, Catholicism, and, to a lesser extent, 19th century liberalism, results in a system ignoring its real problems. French deputies in the "house without windows" in the Fourth Republic engaged in considering the relative merits of such ideologies; thus, they never came to grips with such problems as the Indochina War, the unrest in Algeria, or the stagnating French economy. Adopting as a basic axiom that the output of a system (the solution to problems) must to some extent counterbalance inputs (the issues or disagreements about optimum solutions to such prob-

---

[31] "Processing" issues refers in his writing to the entire policy-flow process: the formulation, deliberation, resolution, and solution of issues. Spiro's distinction between pure pragmatism—meaning total absence of principle—and "purposive interests"— pragmatic bargaining based upon loosely held principle—should be noted. See his *Government by Constitution*, op. cit., pp. 178–82.

[32] Spiro, *Government by Constitution*, op. cit., chap. 14.

lems), Spiro concludes that a successful system must process its real issues. From his plausible assumption that ideologism detracts from the attempt to process such real issues, Spiro can generalize that ideological systems will be less successful (and presumably less stable). A level of ideologism beyond some threshold level would, by this analysis, lead to the failure and break-down of the system. Spiro even suggests reasons for differences in the degree of ideologism among political systems. His proposition is to the effect that systems which exclude significant corporate groups or idea lead-ers from the political process are likely to be more ideological. Such groups, having no responsibility for actual government, tend to state their goals in exaggerated and unworkable forms. For example, labor parties which gain sole control of the government, or threaten to do so, in Western democracies have always modified or abandoned their socialist ideological baggage. Thus, Spiro has devised an interrelated set of concepts from which he can deduce propositions which subsume and thus explain important political "facts" (for example, the instability of Third and Fourth Republic France).

There are, however, serious methodological difficulties with Spiro's works which stem from his failure to specify precise empirical indicators for his key concepts. Presumably, ideologism and pragmatism are polar ends at a continuum, and given systems approach one or the other polar extreme by degrees. Yet, there are no criteria for measuring the degree of ideologism in any given system. Without this ability to measure the degree of ideologism, it is impossible to specify threshold levels of ideologism beyond which sys-tems will fail. It is even impossible to specify the probability of failure for any given system on this basis because it is not possible to unambiguously state just how ideological a given system is on some quantified ratio scale. One cannot even posit that one system is relatively more likely to persist or fail than another because it is not possible to state without contradiction that this political system is more ideological than that system. Reasonable men could disagree, for example, on whether Third Republic France was more or less ideological than Weimar Germany.

Moreover, it is not obvious that the concepts of political style are capa-ble of being rendered operational. Until one can specify without ambiguity what the real issues of society are, it will be very difficult to delineate an un-ambiguous category of issues or statements that can be justifiably classed as ideological. In Chapter 1 the difficulty that Gurr and Ruttenberg have had in operationally defining civil violence was noted.[33] This difficulty does not bode well for the prospects of operationally defining a violent political style. It appears that the concepts of political style really refer to some sort of psychological predisposition to behave in certain poorly defined patterns on the part of some undefined aggregate within a system. Aside from these last two aspects of imprecise definitions, the study of psycho-

---

[33] See p. 10.

logical predispositions is highly resistant to systematic empirical inquiry.

The basic axiom that a system must process its issues or fail is also fraught with methodological difficulties.[34] Clearly, it is not meant that a system must process every issue. If this is the case, what percentage of issues must be processed? Spiro is on stronger grounds here than is Easton in the model discussed below in that he speaks of the "relative success of political systems." Thus, if a system fails to process a number of issues and still continues to exist, it cannot be assumed that issues are equal in importance; the failure to resolve certain kinds of issues might have more catastrophic consequences than the failure to resolve others. Yet, what objective criteria exist for assigning weights to various issues? Reasonable men might even disagree as to whether a given issue is in fact resolved. While, if not the authors of the Constitution of the United States, certainly the victors in the American Civil War thought that they had resolved the issue of State "sovereignty" once and for all. Yet, to this day it appears that many "unreconstructed" southerners have not received this message. Much the same thing might be said of the clerical issue and the monarchical question in France. The French Revolution did not remove the Church from possessing an influence on French political life as many Jacobins of that time supposed, and it did not prevent the existence of a small but significant group of monarchists until well into the 20th century.

Many of the paradigms in comparative politics, especially those that revolve around the concept of a political system, attempt to postulate the prerequisites for the viability of such systems. Conversely, this gives rise to the necessity of being able to pinpoint those indicators or events that constitute the failure of a political system. Unless one can pinpoint such failures, the proposition that a system will fail in the absence of specified conditions is not testable. One can always take a case that is held up as inconsistent with the proposition and raise a question of whether that is really a case of system failure. Yet, the ability to precisely specify what constitutes the failure of a political system is not an easy thing to achieve.

For example, Spiro suggests that fundamentally legalistic and ideological systems are unlikely candidates for a viable democracy. Yet, while Spiro himself argues that the Third Republic France was both legalistic on fundamental issues and ideological, the regime did last nearly 70 years. Reasonable men might differ as to whether or not this is a sufficient time span to constitute an example of a viable democracy and therefore a deviant case (assuming that the question of France's political style was resolved to everyone's satisfaction). Spiro was actually not so precise as to say that a regime that had a fundamentally legalistic and ideological style would fail; he merely implied that such a system was more likely to fail than other

---

[34] Cf. Seymour Lipset, op. cit., who discusses the political consequences of failure to resolve issue conflicts sequentially (one at a time), pp. 70ff.

kinds of systems. He did not say how much more likely. Therefore, he does not provide us with a basis for making any precise predictions about given systems (including probabilistic predictions). How many or what percentage of observed legalistic and ideological democratic systems must fail within what span of time before Spiro would say that there is no essential relation between political style and the viability of democratic systems?

SYSTEMS ANALYSIS AS A MODEL

Insofar as he addressed himself to the question of the prerequisites for the viability of a political system, Spiro was engaged in a form of analysis generally called *systems analysis*. Systems analysis, therefore, includes a variety of specific paradigms all of which have in common the concept of a political system that interacts with its environment (which may partially consist of other systems). The basic underlying concern of systems paradigms is to ascertain the necessary and/or sufficient forms of this interaction for maintaining the system in an adequate state. Thus, it is the form of the interaction between the system and its environment that primarily interests the systems analyst, not the nature of the system iself. (The next chapter will show that functionalism is intimately related to, if not a special form of, systems analysis. However, inasmuch as functionalism is possibly the dominant paradigm in comparative politics, it will be accorded a chapter by itself.) Moreover, it is possible to distinguish paradigms which simply presume the existence of a political system from those based upon the interaction of a system with its environment. This latter paradigm, system analysis, constitutes a particular application of the broader concept of a political system and corresponds to what Oran Young calls *input-output* analysis.[35]

To conceive of a system interacting with its environment, one must analytically separate the political system from that environment. This involves the specification of analytic boundaries, the imaginary line separating the elements of a system from all external elements. A boundary, in this sense, is not a physical entity, such as the geographic frontiers of a nation state. Rather, it is an analytic concept which refers to the distinction between that which is included in the system and that which is not. The criteria for what is included in the system becomes a matter of definition; however, any definition, arbitrary though it may be, should specify those boundaries in a precise and unambiguous fashion. This means that there should be no room for confusion as to what is included within the political system and what is not. Unless one can precisely define the political system, one is logically unable to make precise, testable statements about the state of the

---

[35] Oran Young, *Systems of Political Science* (Englewood Cliffs, N.J.: Prentice-Hall, 1968), pp. 37–48.

system, its maintenance, or its adequate functioning, as is explained below.

The nature of a system's interaction with its environment consists of the adaptation of the system to changes or disturbances in the environment in order to preserve an equilibrium. All versions of systems analysis involve the conceptualization of the system receiving inputs of some form from the environment and processing them into outputs which are fed back into the environment. Thus, the system is open; it is not self-contained.

Systems analysis may be characterized as a model in that it postulates a set of relationships between concepts which possess a one-to-one correspondence with a set of relationships between corresponding entities in the real world. The relationship between the environment and the system consists of the balance (or lack thereof) between the inputs, on the one hand, and the outputs, on the other. The concepts which comprise the model have imprecise empirical content; the elements of the system itself or the environment are never precisely specified. Yet, presumably, the logical relationships between these imprecise concepts can generate expectations about relationships between corresponding elements in the observable world. This is what is meant by structural correspondence. If this alleged correspondence exists, then propositions about the real world will have been deductively derived from the systems paradigm. Thus far, the paradigm appears to meet the criteria of a model laid down in Chapter 4. The elements of a model are not expected to have precise empirical content. If they did, the construct would be a full-fledged theory rather than a model.

The underlying axiom of systems analysis (sometimes made explicit while other times left implicit) is that if the stress caused by inputs from the environment pass a certain threshold level, the system will break down (the boundaries will collapse). The corollary axiom is that such stress tends to build up when inputs are not offset by outputs which, when fed back into the environment, mitigate the stress from subsequent inputs. In the less pretentious terms of Professor Spiro's paradigm, one might say that in order to survive a system must process its issues and an efficient system will maintain a high ratio of outputs to inputs.[36] Thus, one might conceivably argue that the Weimar Republic broke down because it failed to process such issues (or generate such output) as runaway inflation and national pride injured from the loss of World War I. When such issues are resolved or the demands repressed, the consequence of these decisions or outputs are transmitted back to the society (feedback), presumably resulting in an amelioration of stress from subsequent demands in both a quantitative and a qualitative sense.

To derive testable propositions from these axioms, one would have to find a way to measure stress both quantitatively and qualitatively as well as to precisely specify the class of observable indicators or events that de-

---

[36] Spiro, "Comparative Politics," op. cit., p. 578.

fine the concept of system breakdown. Reasonable men might disagree as to whether a change in regime constitutes an example of the breakdown of the political system or simply the adaptation to stress generated by a host of unprocessed demands, as in the case of the adoption of a new constitution by peaceful, legitimate means in France in 1958. One cannot tell if the system is breaking down unless there is no question as to what is meant by the system. This is what is meant by the boundary problem.

It is even more difficult to see how stress could be measured. An event that resulted in stress in one political and social context might be supportive of a system in another context. The extent to which the consequence of an event constitutes some degree of stress for a system is a function of how that event is interpreted in that socio-cultural context and of the capacities of a system to respond to demands and control tensions.[37] Such differential capacities appear to be difficult if not impossible to operationalize at the present state of methodological and substantive knowledge.

These principles and criticism can best be made clear by an examination of the paradigm of one of the leading exponents of system theory among political scientists, David Easton. Easton began with a relatively simple model;[38] however, as he attempted to demonstrate its potential application to real and important political phenomena, the model increased in complexity with the addition of numerous elements or variables and relationships.[39]

The basic framework focuses on the exchanges between a highly abstracted concept, the political system, and the environment or context in which that system is situated. In this respect, the approach owes an enormous intellectual debt to the sociologist Talcott Parsons. Parsons's work is difficult to characterize within the scope of this book in that it encompasses more than one intellectual tradition and includes an enormous number of printed works. Nevertheless, it seems both possible and useful to precede the discussion of Easton with a brief consideration of influences that Parsons has had in paradigm construction in comparative politics.

Parsons began his intellectual career with an action-oriented approach. That is, Parsons attempted to delineate the alternative contextual frames of reference facing an individual actor in his social role. This simply means alternative orientations that influence behavioral propensities one way or

---

[37] The concepts of systematic capabilities as an important variable to consider are most clearly articulated by Gabriel Almond and G. Bingham Powell, *Comparative Politics; A Developmental Approach* (Boston: Little, Brown & Co., 1966), pp. 190–212.

[38] The simpliest outline of the model may be found in David Easton, "An Approach to the Analysis of Politics System," *World Politics,* Vol. 9, No. 3 (April 1957), pp. 383–400.

[39] The most complete and complex development of the model is found in Easton, *A Systems Analysis of Political Life* (New York: John Wiley & Sons, 1968).

another. Action may be distinguished from behavior in that action is a more narrow term that includes choice and will, while behavior may include the mechanistic response characteristic of lower animals in addition to what Parsons calls action. This leads to delineation of his *pattern variables,* five dichotomous choices, one side of which must be chosen by an actor before he can act or "before the situation has a determinate meaning for him."[40] These pattern variables are as follows: *universalism-particularism,* referring to the choice between treating objects as members of an undifferentiated class or with reference to their unique properties; *ascription-achievement,* referring to the choice between the allocation of values on the basis of unearned status or performance (membership in the British House of Lords is acquired by ascription while election to the House of Commons is an achievement); *diffuseness-specificity,* referring to the level of generality or abstraction of the objects of orientation (as the distinction between orientation toward one's society as contrasted with orientation toward specified outputs of one's government); *self-orientation–collectivity orientation,* referring to the choice between maximizing the interest of one's self or of some larger group to which one belongs whenever the interest of the two are in conflict; and, *affectivity–affective neutrality,* referring to the "problem of whether or not evaluation is to take place in a given situation."[41]

These patterns are apparently intended to exhaust the possibilities for human choice and, thus, to provide a framework of categories in which all cases of social behavior are classified. These concepts have had a significant influence on the literature on political development, as we shall see in Chapter 12, especially on the attempt to distinguish Western from non-Western political systems.[42] In each dichotomous pair, one orientation is implied to be more characteristic of a modern Western industrial society than the other.

Enormous methodological problems would present themselves immediately if one tried to utilize this scheme for research purposes. The scheme is at best one of classifying human orientations. It does not suggest precise relationships between the categories; thus, the scheme is logically incapable of generating propositions about relevant relationships in the real world. Second, the number of possible combinations and permutations of orien-

---

[40] Talcott Parsons and Edward Shils (eds.), *Toward a General Theory of Action* (New York: Harper Torchbooks, 1951), pp. 48 and 78.

[41] Ibid., p. 78. See the distinction between immediate "gratification of impulse v. discipline," p. 80.

[42] For example, see Fred Riggs, "Agraria and Industria," in William Siffin (ed.), *Toward the Comparative Study of Public Administration* (Bloomington, Ind.: Indiana University Press, 1957), pp. 23–110; F. X. Sutton, "Social Theory and Comparative Politics," in Harry Eckstein and David Apter (eds.), *Comparative Politics, A Reader* (New York: The Free Press, 1963), pp. 67–81; and Lucien Pye, "The Non Western Political Process," in Eckstein and Apter, op. cit., pp. 657–64.

tations has been calculated to total 1,048,586.[43] If the concepts in the scheme were susceptible of being operationalized, the problems of calculation might prove unmanageable. Third, the concepts are so imprecisely defined that it would be extremely difficult to assign concrete social actions to specific categories in this classification scheme. For example, acts which are justified by their perpetrators as in the collective interest are often labeled by others as selfish in motivation and dysfunctional in terms of their social consequences. Thus, the categories lack precise empirical content, with all of the methodological difficulties that this problem entails. Specifically, because the categories are not defined in terms of actual behavior patterns, there can be no concrete expectations of such precisely defined patterns of behavior being derived from the categories. Finally, the scheme is extremely vulnerable to criticism on the logical grounds that the inference of psychological orientations (read: predispositions) from observable behavior is hazardous at best. This is especially true when the classification of orientations is defined at such a high level of abstraction. The influence of the action framework seems to be more obvious in the case of functional analysis (following chapter) than in the case of systems analysis.

The Parsonian influence on what is called systems analysis is not obvious from this action theory orientation outlined above. The influence becomes more apparent from Parsons's concern with the social system. While in his action theory the actor is the unit of analysis, in his systems approach the social system is the unit of analysis. The former approach appears to be at the micro level of analysis. That is, it appears to be reduced to its lowest common denominator, the role of the actor. In the latter approach, however, the system, an entity which is more than the sum of actors that comprise it, becomes the unit of analysis. Supposedly, his systems theory is "emergent" from his action theory; that is, the former can be derived from the latter.[44] However, the logic of this derivation is nowhere made clear. A systems framework ostensibly "emerges" from the interaction of roles specified in the action framework. Yet, the action framework concerns itself with orientations of an isolated actor in his social role. Thus, the framework has nothing to say about the consequences of interaction. Once the systems framework is outline, it becomes possible to ask questions about how the system, as an undissected entity, behaves without analyzing the components of the system. In this framework, like that of Easton, the system becomes a blank box.

---

[43] Robert Dubin, "Parsons Actor: Continuities in Social Theory," *American Sociological Review*, Vol. 20 (August 1960), pp. 457–66. Cf. Eugene Meehan, *Contemporary Political Thought: A Critical Study* (Homewood, Ill.: The Dorsey Press, 1967), who claims there are 3,000 permutations to a single act in the Parsonian action scheme.

[44] Edward Devereux, "Parsons' Sociological Theory" in Max Black (ed.), *The Social Theories of Talcott Parsons* (Englewood Cliffs, N.J.: Prentice-Hall, 1961), p. 26.

The key contributions of Parsons's systems approach seem to lie in the concepts of system boundaries, boundary exchanges, and equilibrium.[45] It has been noted that the specification of boundaries is a matter of definition. Parsons defines a social system very broadly; a political scientist will tend to define a political system, which to Parsons is a subdivision of the social system, more narrowly. The researcher defines the system to suit his own purposes. The breadth of the definition will depend on which variables he wishes to include.

Once the boundaries are specified, it is possible to conceive of the system as interacting with that which is not within the system. This is conceptualized by Parsons as interactions between various systems or subsystems, such as between the political system and the economic system. Political scientists such as Easton have tended to lump that which is external to the system under the heading *the environment.*

The focus of inquiry for Parsons, a focus which has been adopted in somewhat modified form by Easton and other political scientists, is the question of how the system maintains the existing pattern of interactions among the elements of the system in the fact of external disturbances. Basically, this *pattern maintenance,* as Parsons calls it, is achieved through the maintenance of an equilibrium or balance between inputs and outputs.

Thus, for both Parsons and Easton, the system is engaged in a pattern of relationships with that which is external to the system. This pattern consists of the transmission of what we will call concepts from the environment to the system and vice versa across the boundaries of the system. Compare the schematic presentations of Parsons's and Easton's paradigms in Figure 7–2, noting thier similarity. Actually, Parsons conceptualized rather distinct sets of dual interchanges without any serious attempt to integrate them. In this respect, Parsons's system paradigm lacks the formalization of a model.

For Easton, the inputs of the environment consist of demands (for some more or less concrete governmental output) and supports. These penetrate the boundaries of the system despite the "gatekeeping" functions of some filtering agents, such as parties and groups. These gatekeeping institutions combine similar demands and eliminate extreme or unreasonable demands so as to keep the flow of demands manageable for the decision-making institutions of the political system. Supports may be either for the society (the set of political institutions comprising the current regime) or for the output of the political system. The first type of support is, of course, much more stable than the last type. The outputs of the system consist of the decisions which authoritatively allocate the values of the society. The basic proposition of the Eastonian paradigm is that these three variables—de-

---

[45] See Talcott Parsons, Kaspar Naegele, and Jesse Pitts, *Theories of Society,* 2 vols. (New York: The Free Press, 1961), vol. 1, p. 36.

FIGURE 7-2

PARSON'S SCHEME

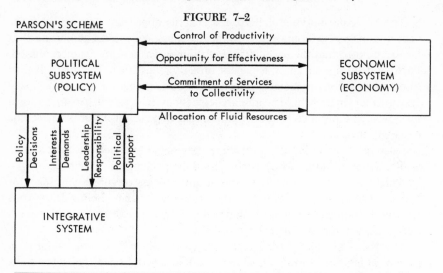

EASTON'S SCHEME

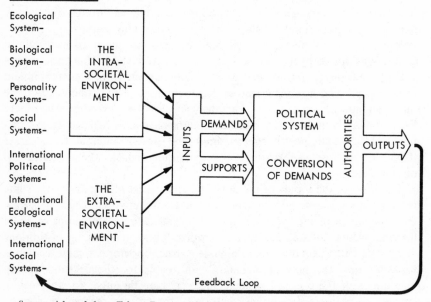

Source: Adapted from Talcott Parsons, "On the Concept of Political Power," *Proceedings of the American Philosophical Society,* Vol. 107 (June 1963), p. 260.

mands, supports, and outputs—maintain a dynamic equilibrium. That is, the system tends to maintain a balance among the three variables despite changing magnitudes of each of them. Supports, especially general support for the regime as distinguished from support for outputs, can reduce the stress caused by demands and thus reduce the need to react to demands. Insofar as the interaction of demands and supports leaves a residual of stress (insofar as demands > supports), this residual stress must be counterbalanced by favorable outputs. In other words, when the level of generalized support is not sufficient to make the articulate sectors of society willing to defer concrete demands, the system must either meet these demands through authoritative output (for example, legislation, administrative fiat, court decision, etc.) or take steps to suppress those who are making such demands. If the output of the government does not thus counterbalance inputs, the system will break down.

Thus, the primary concern in the input-output system paradigm is with the maintenance of the system. Indeed, Parsons lists the four functions that any ongoing system must perform as adaptation, goal attainment, integration, and pattern maintenance. Adaptation refers to the ability of the system to react to stress by changing its capacities. In short, adaptation is instrumental to goal attainment. It is easy to see how the concept of adaptation has influenced Almond's and Powell's concept of systemic capabilities.[46] Goal attainment refers to collective goals. Integration refers to the subsumption of the individual in the collectivity. Pattern maintenance is not fundamentally distinct from that current American slogan "law and order." Thus, Parsons, given his basic concern with the needs of the collectivity rather than the needs of the individual[47] and his concern with the maintenance of existing patterns of interaction, has left himself vulnerable to a barrage of criticism from scholars interested in rapid and significant social change.[48] Easton and others who have adopted or heavily borrowed from the Parsonian paradigm for political analysis have felt a need to grapple with similar accusations of having a conservative, static, or status quo bias.

The systems paradigm offers a number of advantages to a discipline seeking to build a body of increasingly general empirical theory. In the first place, it is sufficiently general to allow the inclusion of a large proportion of relevant variables for the explanation of political output. Thus, Easton can include elements which would not ordinarily be considered as elements of the political system per se but which have an effect on political output. In this way, his explanations should have the potential of being relatively more complete than a legal, institutional analysis. In the second

[46] Gabriel Almond & G. Bingham Powell, *Comparative Politics, A Developmental Approach* (Boston: Little, Brown and Co., 1961), chap. 8.

[47] For example, see Talcott Parsons, *The Social System* (New York: The Free Press, 1951), p. 29. See Wililam Mitchell, *Sociological Analysis and Politics, The Theories of Talcott Parsons* (Englewood Cliffs, N.J.: Prentice-Hall, 1967), pp. 63–64, for a sympathetic treatment of this aspect of Parsons. Cf. Eugene Meehan, *Contemporary Political Thought, A Critical Study* (Homewood, Ill.: The Dorsey Press, 1967), p. 125, for a vigorous attack on Parsons with respect to this orientation.

[48] Robin Williams, "The Sociological Theory of Talcott Parsons," in Black, op. cit., p. 71, and Meehan, op. cit., pp. 125–27 persuasively argue along these lines.

place, because Easton does not precisely specify the elements or relationships occurring within his black box (as the empty rectangle he uses to diagram the political system is sometimes called), the political system can refer to any format of governmental structure: democratic or authoritarian, primitive or modern, federal or unitary, presidential or parliamentary, or whatever. Easton has conceptualized his relationships at the greatest possible level of abstraction; thus, they can apply to the greatest variety of actual polities. In the third place, Easton has postulated a number of relationships which ostensibly correspond to relationships in the real world. To the extent that it does postulate such isomorphic relationships, the paradigm has the potential of deductively generating propositions relating elements of the real world.

The dilemma posed in Chapter 6 becomes quite apparent in the case of systems analysis. In the best tradition of classical Greek tragedy, the very strength of the paradigm is also the fatal flaw. The fact that the paradigm is formulated at such a level of generality and abstraction from the real world to be universally (in the geographic sense) applicable also renders the crucial concepts of the paradigm incapable of being operationalized. The consequence of this inability to operationalize basic concepts is that the propositions derived from the model are untestable. For example, it may be deduced that unless the stress generated by demands which penetrate a political system from the environment is not counterbalanced by diffuse support and/or political outputs, such stress will cause the system to break down. Yet, in order to test such a proposition, one would need to have some means of measuring the amount of stress generated by demands and to have precisely specified threshold levels of stress which pinpoint the exact minimal magnitude of stress that will cause a given system to break down. These requirements seem to call for further explanation and justification.

In order to falsify the proposition that some amount of stress will cause a system to break down, one would have to first answer the question of how much stress will cause such a breakdown. The measurement difficulties in answering such a question have already been noted. If this question is not answered beforehand, one could always say of an allegedly deviant case that there is not quite enough stress, rather than be forced to concede that there is no necessary relationship between the stress from demands and system maintenance. Obviously, in order to specify the minimal amount of stress that will result in system breakdown, one must be able to measure stress. In addition to the enormous difficulties in specifying quantifiable indicators for specific demands, one is faced with the enormous logical difficulties of specifying precise relative weights among demands. In other words, does one type or class of unsatisfied demands generate more or less disruptive stress on a political system than another type? Yet, it does not seem unfair to suggest that the crucial propositions about politics derived from Easton's paradigm are based upon this proposition of an equilibrium between inputs and outputs. In short, the nontestable nature of the proposition about the equilibrium between inputs and outputs results in a lack of any concrete expectations that can be derived from the paradigm. For instance, one cannot deduce that unless this system satisfies these demands within this time span, it will break down (or it has some stipulated probability of breaking down).

Furthermore, the entire paradigm is beset by the fundamental methodological difficulty of being unable to unambiguously distinguish an ongoing system from one that is breaking down, a difficulty which, we shall see, also besets functional analysis. The difficulty here is distinguishing system change (or adaptation) from system breakdown. (Query: Could they be logically indistinguishable?) If system breakdown is simply conceived of as more than some specified amount of system change, then one is compelled to specify what constitutes the permissible levels of system change. Clearly, all systems are changing to some degree, but it would not be useful to conceptualize system breakdown as a continual process. Such a conceptualization would place all systems in the same category, while one of the purposes of concept formation is to distinguish a group of phenomena from other phenomena.

Easton is not oblivious to the enormous complexity of his model and the enormous difficulty of operationalizing his basic concepts. With regard to the variable of demands, for instance, he discusses a number of dimensions that must be considered in order to operationalize the concept. The stress caused by demands is not only a function of the volume of demands but of their scope, their explicitness, their compatibility with community goals, their complexity, and the time lag between input and output.[49] Volume is, in principle, measurable despite the obstacles to such an undertaking. It is difficult to say as much for the other dimensions of demands.

One does not need to minimize the value of the creative insights of Professor Easton in contributing to an intuitive understanding of important relationships in order to conclude that relationships posited at Easton's level of generality are simply not empirical propositions in the sense of that term used in this book. It would certainly be less than fair to leave the implication that Professor Easton is not entirely cognizant of the importance of the boundary problem. Furthermore, his work would not have attained the professional status that it has attained had he dismissed the problem of distinguishing system change from system breakdown with the relatively simpler solution of equating system breakdown with the total disappearance of the "authoritative allocation of values" or minimal public order. Easton equally rejects the temptation to equate system maintenance

---

[49] Easton, *A Systems Analysis of Political Life* (New York: John Wiley & Sons, 1965), pp. 57–69.

with the total absence of change.[50] He introduces the concept of *persistence* as distinct from the rigid *maintenance* of the status quo. However, his solution fails to enable us to clearly distinguish a system that is persisting from one that is not. This distinction appears to revolve around a perception of continuity with the past. Yet, to take his example, it is unclear why he can find such continuity with the Tudor period in Great Britain, yet not with the Celtic kingdoms. Where would the line be drawn and with what justification? Specifically, is there any way to measure the strength of such continuity? Easton's axiom now seems to be as follows: systems will react to normal variations in the amount of stress by changing or adapting their capacities to handle such stress. But, when the quantitative volume or qualitative intensity of stress exceeds a certain point, the system will not be able to adapt to such stress while remaining within a range of permissible change. In short, systems can change up to a point while still persisting. Beyond that point, they have by definition broken down.

Easton clearly acknowledges the need to specify threshold levels of stress upon a system beyond which the system cannot persist and threshold levels of change beyond which it is said that a system has failed to persist. He offers in the way of solution to the latter problem the concept of *critical variables* as a kind of sine qua non for system persistence.[51] For example, there are many permissible variations in structural arrangements consistent with saying that a democratic system is persisting. However, it would be difficult to continue to call a system a democracy if it abandoned freedom of speech, which thus becomes a critical variable. The difficulty, which Easton recognized, is that this variable is a matter of degree. Easton does not offer us any means of measuring such degrees or standards for specifying threshold levels, if we could. Much the same can be said with respect to levels and types of stress. Admittedly also, the amount of stress resulting from a given phenomena or disturbance is a function of the social, economic, and political context in which the stress occurs.[52] Therefore, if it is said that Easton's basic proposition is false because here is a system subject to great stress that did not break down, Easton could always reply that the disturbance was not severe enough, in that context, to exceed the permissible (but unspecified) threshold. Thus, he could always save the hypothesis.

In the sense that scientific comparative politics must be systematic, systems analysis may indeed constitute a paradigm within which all scientific research in the discipline must be conducted. By systematic it is meant that science needs to specify recurring patterns of interactions among a set of variables or elements analytically abstracted from the totality of elements that might be considered according to some consistently applied

---

[50] David Easton, *A Framework for Political Analysis* (Englewood Cliffs, N.J.: Prentice-Hall, 1965), pp. 82–84.
[51] Ibid., pp. 92ff.
[52] Ibid., pp. 97.

criterion of relevance.[53] This corresponds to the very definition of the concept of a system discussed in Chapter 4. However, if systems analysis is more narrowly construed to refer to the input-output paradigm developed by Professor Easton, the contribution of the paradigm to the development of a body of scientific knowledge appears at this writing to be much less promising. For the reasons already elaborated on at great length, it appears that a paradigm formulated at that level of generality is unlikely to generate testable propositions; hence, it cannot produce explanations in the scientific sense of that term as developed in Chapter 2.

Despite demonstrating a superficial awareness of the problem of operationalizing concepts, as described above, and liberally sprinkling his writings with the term *empirical theory,* Professor Easton does not appear to be primarily concerned with the empirical content of his paradigm. He does not actually specify or suggest precise indicators of any of his key concepts. Easton's position, derived from Parsons's, seems to be that the a priori development of a theoretic construct must precede empirical research. Unless research proposals, he would argue, are deduced from a common paradigm or theoretic construct, such research is likely to result in isolated, meaningless fact gathering. Easton rather looks toward the development of coherent body of knowledge manifested in a *general* theory of politics. This appears to imply that all political facts and knowledge should be integrated in a single theoretic structure. We have seen in Part 1 that if that is based upon desire to emulate the natural sciences, it is based upon a misconception of the nature of such disciplines. No discipline, including physics, integrates *all* its knowledge in a single theory. Furthermore, there are conflicting theories which are used to explain a phenomenon—for example, light.

If Easton wishes to emphasize the basic deductive nature of scientific explanation, he is quite correct in this conception of science, as was shown in Chapter 2. However, although it is proper to seek to integrate scientific knowledge in theoretic structures that are deductive in form, the correspondence between propositions (and hence the theory of which they are a part) and empirical data must constantly be ascertained by procedures that are basically inductive. Unless paradigms are constructed with a view toward their susceptibility of being operationalized, it is not likely that they will produce a scientific explanation of any concrete observations.

The foregoing analysis of the Eastonian paradigm indicates that his basic concepts are not operational; hence, his basic propositions are as yet untestable. It would be perhaps premature to foreclose the possibility of their being rendered operational. Yet, in view of the level of generality at which the paradigm is pitched, it is difficult to be optimistic about this possibility.

---

[53] Herbert Spiro, "An Evaluation of Systems Theory," in James Charlesworth, ed., *Contemporary Political Analysis* (New York: The Free Press, 1967), p. 164.

The contribution of men like Easton and Parsons in pointing the direction for the social sciences remains unchallenged. The fact that they were among the major catalysts to the trend in the discipline toward building theory that corresponds to the real world (albeit in an imprecise way) has earned them the respect of their colleagues. Yet, it seems imperative to separate this catalytic contribution with regard to the orientation of their disciplines from the current scientific potential of the actual paradigms they devised.

CYBERNETICS

The term *cybernetics* refers to communication theory. Communication theory has been developed into a type of systems paradigm by Karl Deutsch. The crucial distinction between Deutsch's paradigm and that of Easton is that the concept of message units or informative bits in Deutsch's system replaces the less precise concepts of demands and supports in the Eastonian paradigm. This is crucial for the development of scientific knowledge, as such knowledge has been conceived in this book, in that information can, in principle, be counted and measured.[54] The difficulty of operationalizing the concepts of Easton's paradigm has been discussed above.

Basically, Deutsch's paradigm involves the input-system-output-feedback approach explained above with respect to Easton. In this sense, it suggests a pattern of relationships and takes on the character of a model. These relationships usually depend on abstract, verbal contact; even overt physical events have their effect on the system in abstract, verbal form.[55] The leader does not see an invasion of his country; he is told about it. Thus, much of political analysis can in fact be subsumed within the cybernetic paradigm. The basic axiom is that the system is self-regulating in the sense that it can learn from inputs which reflect the system's previous outputs. By virtue of what the system has learned, it will adjust its subsequent outputs to the inputs it receives, thereby modifying the system's environment and the subsequent inputs that environment will produce. Thus, Deutsch is careful to avoid the charge levied against equilibrium analysis of a status quo bias, a charge based on a particular conception of equilibrium.[56] This conception is that a system reacts to disturbances by returning to its previous state. This is what was meant above by static equilibrium.

Deutsch's paradigm appears to be somewhat more complex and sophisticated than Easton's in that he goes further toward filling in the black box. As long as the political (or any other kind of) system is conceptualized as an empty rectangle, it is impossible to generate expectations about the effect of

---

[54] Karl Deutsch, *The Nerves of Government* (New York: The Free Press Paperbacks, 1953), p. 149.

[55] Robert C. North, "The Analytical Prospects of Communication Theory," in Charlesworth, op. cit., pp. 309.

[56] Deutsch, op. cit., pp. 88–93.

the nature of the system on the outputs. The paradigm becomes, in effect, one of stimulus-response. This, as shown in Chapter 1, is equivalent to crude behaviorism with all of the methodological problems of that paradigm. Clearly, the nature of the form of government, the culture, the history of a political system, and other internal factors are variables which affect output in addition to stimuli from the environment.

Easton, in all fairness, introduces the concept of *withinputs* to cope with this difficulty.[57] This concept refers to demands and supports that originate from within the political system rather than in the environment. Particularly in his third book[58] Easton begins to introduce systemic variables that would affect differential system reactions to given stimuli. It is noteworthy that these are precisely the variables that are usually perceived as peculiar to a cybernetic approach. For example, he hypothesizes that the quantity of channels for the transmission of demands (read: information) affects the time lag between the articulation of such demands and the response of the system. The fewer the channels, the greater the lag. For this reason, it is unfair to criticize Easton on the basis of his second book.[59] His third book is much closer to the promise of a cybernetic model. To the extent that Easton's fully articulated paradigm approaches a cybernetic model, it shows increased promise of generating partial but useful explanations of observable political phenomena. Potentially, the channels of communication collectively constitute a quantitative concept. However, such concepts are also in part qualitative. One must be able to identify channels of communication before one can count them. Furthermore, all such channels may not be of equal importance. Do parties, for example, have a greater impact than other groups or vice versa? The complexity of the problem results in outcomes that the simplistic hypothesis *more channels, less lag* would not predict. A fragmentation of the party system may result in more lag as demonstrated by Fourth Republic France and Weimar Germany. This is because the qualitative aspects of the channels and the distortion they cause must be accounted for. Yet, it is difficult to measure effectiveness and distortion, variables which appear to be qualitative in nature.

One important variable included within Deutsch's system, and also mentioned briefly in Easton's latest formulation, is that of memory units which can store information, perceptions, myths, or values. These messages can be added to messages received from outside the system, changing the nature of the inputs that the decision-making process acts upon. The inputs to a cybernetic system are also modified by analytical screening mechanisms which filter out some messages while permitting others to reach the decision-making apparatus. For example, messages are screened or filtered by the

---

[57] Easton, *A Systems Analysis of Political Life,* op. cit., pp. 55–56, and *A Framework for Political Analysis,* op. cit., p. 114.

[58] Easton, *A Systems Analysis of Political Life,* op. cit.

[59] Easton, *A Framework for Political Analysis,* op. cit.

mechanism of *selective attention*. The point is that Deutsch has specified a number of potential sources of withinputs or of differential output reaction among systems to identical stimuli. It remains to inquire whether Deutsch has assigned sufficient empirical content to the elements of his model to enable one to derive predictions about specified empirical outcomes. In other words, do concepts such as channels of communication or selective attentions screens correspond to things one sees in actual political systems so as to increase one's power to predict or explain what given systems do?

Deutsch's selective attention screen seems to be a mechanism of individual psychology rather than one of social systems. This raises the question of whether the communication system of an individual is merely a microcosm of the communication system of a social system and, if not, whether Deutsch's paradigm distinguishes the two. The answer to both questions appears to this writer to be negative.

Deutsch's scheme clearly can be applied to some empirical political phenomena. These applications seem, in a commonsense fashion, to correspond to experience. For one example, students of international relations have referred to Deutsch's work in measuring the communications flow between nations.[60] For another example, Deutsch suggests that effective communication must be on two dimensions—the vertical dimension between the upper and lower strata of the system (leaders and followers) and the horizontal dimension among the members of one stratum. The highest level (that is, the generals) are too far removed from the doers of the system (that is, the enlisted men) to mobilize them, and the lower levels (that is, the lieutenants) are too numerous to effectively communicate among themselves. Thus, one would expect most military coups d'etat to be led by middle levels of the military hierarchy (that is, the colonels).[61] Cases like Nasser and Naguib in Egypt, Papadopolis in Greece, Castillo Armas (1954) and Peralta (1963) in Guatemala appear to reinforce this interesting insight. Yet, generals did organize the most recent coups in Brazil (1964), Columbia (1957), Peru (1962 and 1968) and Venezuela (1958). On the other hand, colonels also participated which, it may be argued, takes care of the vertical communication problem. One may also ask about the relevance of countries, such as El Salvador, Guatemala, and Honduras, in which the top command structure is normally comprised of colonels. The point is that the proposition appears to be too simplistic for empirical explanation; variables other than communication appear to be involved. It therefore appears to be very difficult to specify precisely what class of events would be considered inconsistent with Deutsch's proposition. The coup which brought Colonel Juan Perón ultimately to power in Argentina (1943), which Deutsch uses as

---

[60] Karl Deutsch, "Toward An Inventory of Basic Trends and Patterns in Comparative and International Politics," *American Political Science Review,* Vol. 54, No. 1 (March 1960), especially pp. 46–56 for an inventory of such work.

[61] Deutsch, *The Nerves of Government,* op. cit., pp. 154–57.

support for his hypothesis, was originally initiated by generals. This illustrates that it is often unclear whether a given case is supportive or deviant.

Paradigms are commonly of greater utility for solving certain types of problems or questions that for others. Deutsch's paradigm has grown out of a long interest in the problems of national integration or nation building,[62] and communications theory seems to be clearly suited to dealing with this research problem. A relatively cohesive nation will have developed a set of communication grids by means of which all of the significant elements of the nation interact. Such an integrated communications network can serve to intensify a member's sense of identification with the whole system through the dissemination of commonly shared symbols, attitudes, and stored sets of messages (memories). In such an integrated communications system there should be no *communications differential* whereby communication is more rapid and effective among members and parts of a subsystem than among members and parts of the political system as a whole.[63] Thus the opposite of national integration—regionalism—would be fostered by communications networks in political or cultural subsystems that are autonomous from the communications network of the whole system.

The autonomy of communication subsystems can be defined in terms of measurable indicators. For example, the extent to which data sources are shared can be indicated by aggregate data that is readily available. The case of the autonomy of the French Canadian subsystem in Canada can serve to illustrate this point. The fact that over 90 percent of the non-French Canadians cannot read or write French while almost two thirds of the French Canadians are not proficient in English provides a strong basis for inferring that sources of information are not widely shared between the two cultures. The bitter debate over the adoption of a new Canadian flag in 1964 illustrates the lack of shared symbols or sense of a shared past (*withinputs* in the lexicon of Easton's system and *memory units* in Deutsch's terminology). Data on such lack of shared perceptions could be obtained through the use of modern survey techniques and reported in terms of percentages of the respective populations. The point is to illustrate how a communications framework could be used to formulate quantified, testable propositions about such amorphous concepts as national integration or regionalism. Thus, Deutsch is not altogether misleading when he says, "Information can be counted and measured. . . ."[64]

While some aspects of his model are subject to measurement, other aspects are not. Deutsch suggests that power can be measured as the extent

---

[62] See for example, Karl Deutsch and William J. Foltz (eds.), *Nation Building* (New York: Atherton Press, 1963), pp. 1–16; Karl Deutsch, *Nationalism and Social Communication* (New York: John Wiley & Sons, 1953); and Karl Deutsch, "Social Mobilization and Political Development," *American Political Science Review,* Vol. 55, No. 3 (September 1961), pp. 493–514.

[63] Deutsch, *The Nerves of Government,* op. cit., p. 205.

[64] Ibid., p. 149.

to which the behavior of the significant other (power is always a relationship involving two or more actors) is modified by the will and activity or the power wielder.[65] However, in practice it is virtually impossible to empirically separate behavior which was affected by a power wielder from behavior which is the result of other causes.[66]

The concepts of Deutsch's model are selected as relevant to a cybernetic model. However, such a selection process necessarily omits many variables relevant for the explanation of actual political events or behavior. Political systems are cybernetic systems but they are also more than that. A model based upon cybernetic variables alone can lead to probabilistic predictions at best. However, since a selection of variables is part of the function of models, probabilistic prediction is, of course, all that can be expected from any model.

Despite the many insights and suggested relationships that one may find in Deutsch's writings, many of them empirically testable,[67] the logical relationships between elements or concepts in his model are not precisely specified. For example, Deutsch does not specify the relative weight of memory inputs in relation to inputs from a system's environment. Moreover, one would need to know more about the operating principles of certain concepts in the model, such as selective attention screens, before one could use such concepts to generate precise expectations about events in the observable world. Thus, Deutsch's model is not as yet fully formalized. Perhaps it is fair to take him at his word when he states in *The Nerves of Government* that his intention is to present "an interim report from an enterprise of thought that is still continuing."[68]

CONCLUSIONS

The question of whether the paradigms surveyed in this chapter constitute models in the strict sense of that term as developed in Chapter 4 and in the introduction to this chapter, is largely a semantic or definitional issue. A more serious and substantive issue is the extent of the contribution of each paradigm to the generation of empirically testable propositions about politically relevant phenomena and ultimately to coherent empirical theories

---

[65] Ibid., p. 247.

[66] See Harrison Wagner, "The Concept of Power and the Study of Politics," in Roderick Bell, David Edwards and R. Harrison Wagner, *Political Power, A Reader in Theory & Research* (New York: The Free Press, 1969), p. 5. See also Roderick Bell, "Political Power: The Problem of Measurement," Ibid., pp. 13–27. Something of a classic analysis of this problem is Robert A. Dahl, "The Concept of Power," *Behavioral Science*, Vol. 2, No. 3 (July 1957), pp. 201–15. A more elementary introduction to this problem is Dahl, *Modern Political Analysis*, 2d ed. (Englewood Cliffs, N.J.: Prentice-Hall, 1970), chap. 3.

[67] See his attempt to develop a set of empirical indicators for the concept of social mobilization in his "Social Mobilization and Political Development," op. cit.

[68] Deutsch, *The Nerves of Government,* op. cit., p. xxv.

about politics. It is crucial to make a distinction between (1) shortcomings of a given model or paradigm which are, according to these utilitarian standards, due to faulty applications of the paradigm or incomplete development of the paradigm and (2) shortcomings which are inherent in the paradigm. The first type of shortcomings is potentially correctable by such techniques as the more precise specification of relationships among the elements of a paradigm of operationalizing the concepts of a paradigm. The second type of difficulties is inexorably part of the nature of the paradigm and the correction of such difficulties is logically precluded without abandoning the paradigm itself.

The formulations of Downs, Riker, and Spiro, as well as the Eastonian and Deutschian versions of input-output analysis, qualify as models in a somewhat loose sense of that word in that there appears to be some attempt in each of these paradigms to suggest a set of relationships among the elements of each paradigm and to suggest how such relationships correspond to relationships among real-world phenomena. The specification of these relationships is not always precise. Except in the formal model of Riker, derived from the theory of games, the formalization of the paradigms surveyed tends to be distinctly incomplete. That is, the relationships among the elements of the respective paradigms are not stated in such a way as to be measurable. This partial formalization is, to a large extent, a consequence of the failure to operationalize the basic concepts of the paradigms.

It has been frequently argued that it is unfair to impose the methodological standards of natural science on the social sciences. We have also seen the more cogent argument that an insistence on measurability inexorably dooms research to a preoccupation with trivia. Arguments about fairness are of course impossible to resolve; hence, they add nothing to the discipline. While the second argument contains more than a germ of truth, it is not obvious that a great many relevant concepts which are not now operational are logically incapable of being rendered operational. Chapter 1 provided a number of illustrations of promising, if only partially successful, attempts to operationalize important but heretofore amorphous concepts. This process of operationalizing concepts is, after all, basically one of specifying precise observable indicators. The models surveyed have not yet reached the stage of specifying indicators.

While the models based upon game theory, political style, and input-output analysis seem to possess some potential for generating empirical propositions, the Weberian ideal type analysis and Dahl and Lindblom's decision-making analysis are not promising in this regard. These latter formations appear to constitute normatively determined constructs of how the real world ought to look rather than abstractions of how it does look. While they can hardly be classified as scientific models as that term is used in this book, it seemed useful to include them as illustrations of a common misuse of the term.

It was suggested that models which attempt to generate precise predictions about human behavior must assume human rationality. It was shown that such an assumption, being only partially valid, can lead at best to probabilistic predictions. However, the rationality assumption was not considered with respect to the macro-analysis models of Easton, Deutsch, and Spiro. The reason that this assumption is not vital to these macro-system approaches is that they do not attempt to generate precise predictions about human behavior. The concepts of these approaches are framed at too high a level of generality for such predictions.

It appears necessary to conclude that model building in comparative politics is presently in a primitive state. There are so few approaches that possess the necessary degree of formalization to qualify as a model that it seemed useful to include a sampling of constructs which have been called models but which did not in actuality possess the characteristics of a scientific model. Once a class of approaches labeled *quasi models* is opened up, consistent criteria for selection for or exclusion from this survey become difficult if not impossible to formulate. Some important and arbitrary omissions are inevitable. Some important constructs which could logically have been included in this chapter are included elsewhere. Any attempt to prevent some overlap between categories when classifying the writings in comparative politics is foredoomed to failure. David Apter has ultilized requisite analysis to construct a typology of political systems (quasi models) in order to deal with the substantive problem of political development (see Chapter 8). In this way, his writings could be included in any of three separate chapters.

It would perhaps be helpful if models in comparative politics were framed with a view toward the explanation of concrete phenomena. It appears that the most promising attempts at model building are those directed at a more manageable range of phenomena. Models, it must be remembered, are only instrumental to the purpose of explanation of empirical phenomena. To strive only for generality or logical elegance at the expense of empirical content or testability is to defeat the purpose of model building. Such a state of affairs would constitute an example of elevating means to the status of ultimate ends.

Functional Analysis

Rather than constituting the name of a single identifiable approach to comparative analysis, *functionalism* is a name given to several rather distinct approaches, each involving somewhat distinct assumptions and relationships. Even the meaning of the terms *function* and *functional requisite* is not entirely uniform in the literature.[1]

This chapter will concern itself with those manifestations of functional analysis that have had the greatest impact on comparative political analysis. These manifestations are classified here under three headings: universal functionalism, empirical functionalism, and requisite analysis. The first and last of these forms are intended to constitute paradigms which are applicable to all political contexts. Empirical functionalism, epitomized by the writings of Robert K. Merton, is less ambitious in its aims. The distinctions between universal functionalism, epitomized by men such as Gabriel Almond and Robert T. Holt, and requisite analysis, epitomized in the writings of David E. Apter, appear to be semantic rather than logical. When referring to all three of the aforementioned types of approaches, the generic term *functional analysis* will be used.

Taken as a whole, functional analysis has probably attained a widespread dissemination and popularity unequaled by any other paradigm in the field. Formulated as one of the first alternatives to the more traditional modes of analysis, this approach quickly acquired widespread popularity among students of African, Asian, and Latin American political systems. This is largely due to the fact that the units of analysis offered by the functionalist

---

[1] Robert K. Merton lists several distinct meanings assigned to the term in social science literature: occupation, the activities assigned to the incumbent of a social status, a dependency relationship of one variable to another, processes "considered in the respect in which they contribute to the maintenance of the organism." Robert K. Merton, *Social Theory and Social Structure,* rev. ed. (New York: The Free Press, 1957), pp. 74–77. Cf. Ernest Nagel, *The Structure of Science* (New York: Harcourt, Brace & World, 1961), pp. 520–35, who lists six meanings of the term function.

or requisite approach seemed to be widely applicable, even to those political systems that did not share standard Western-type governmental structures.

This rapid growth in the popularity of the approach has been met by an equally determined and vociferous critique of the approach. These criticisms have been directed both at the formulation and application of the approach in specific instances and at the inherent logic of the approach itself. This controversy can best be examined in the light of the methodological principles developed in preceding chapters.

THE LOGIC OF UNIVERSAL FUNCTIONALISM

It has already been stated in the last chapter that functional analysis is closely related to systems analysis. Functional analysis may be to some extent distinguished from input-output analysis in that it postulates the specific necessary (and perhaps sufficient) preconditions to maintain a system in a given state. Thus, in addition to merely postulating a pattern of interaction between the system and its environment, a pattern which could manifest itself in an almost infinite variety of ways in given systems, requisite analysis stipulates certain specified conditions which must be present in all systems. In this respect, it appears less general than the systems of Easton and Deutsch despite the fact that most of the practitioners of this approach have claimed universality for the structural or functional requisites postulated.

The postulated requisites for political systems usually take the form of functions; hence, this approach is frequently identified as functionalism. However, some scholars, such as David Apter,[2] have postulated structural requisites, a distinction which is not always entirely clear. Functionalism was actually imported from the disciplines of sociology and anthropology as political scientists, anxious to emulate their apparently more fully developed sister disciplines, uncritically adopted their dominant paradigms.[3] It may appear to some that political scientists overestimated the methodological rigor of their sister disciplines, an error which can perhaps be partially attributed to their awe of the unfamiliar world of systematic, non-normative analysis.

Function, as utilized by leading scholars in political science in the Parsonian general theory school, appears to refer to the contribution of phenomena or patterns of behavior to the maintenance of a system in a given state.[4] Function is thus more specific than effect or consequence. Function

---

[2] David Apter, "A Comparative Method for the Study of Politics," *American Journal of Sociology,* Vol. 64, No. 3 (November 1958), pp. 225–26.

[3] A. James Gregor, "Political Science and the Uses of Functional Analysis," *The American Political Science Review,* Vol. 62, No. 2 (June 1968), p. 426.

[4] Karl Hempel, "The Logic of Functional Analysis," in May Brodbeck (ed.), *Readings in the Philosophy of the Social Sciences* (New York: Macmillan Co., 1968), pp. 186–7.

refers to those objective or observable effects or consequences of phenomena or activities *that are relevant to the persistence or maintenance of the system.* Function in this sense generally connotes a positive contribution toward system maintenance. Negative contributions are frequently referred to as dysfunctions,[5] that is, contributions to the breakdown of a system. In other words, a functionalist would not be interested in all consequences of a political activity such as the psychic satisfaction the actor derives from the activity. The interest of the functionalist would be confined to the contribution of that activity toward the maintenance or breakdown of a system.

In its simplest form, the recurring features of the functional paradigm may now be outlined. While social and political structures vary widely among political and social systems, thus limiting the general applicability of a structural analysis, there are certain functions which are necessary for the maintenance of any society.[6] This means that there are "certain things which must get done" or certain roles which must be filled if the social or political system is "to continue as a going concern."[7] Accordingly, differences among systems with respect to how "adequately" they operate or maintain themselves can be "explained" by differences in the effective performance of these necessary functions. The differences among systems with respect to functional performance appear to be "explained" by their necessity for the adequate maintenance of the systems.[8] Thus, the answer to the question of why the functions are performed appears to be that they are needed. Since the functions are defined as those tasks or phenomena that are needed, the preceding proposition becomes nothing more than a tautology (true by definition). Functionalism, therefore, cannot explain why the functions, which are postulated as necessary to the adequate maintenance of any system, are performed more effectively in one system than in another.

To put the matter differently, an adequately performing system appears to be defined as one that effectively has all the functional requisites performed. Sometimes it appears to be implied that a system will function adequately if some fraction of those requisites are performed or if those tasks are performed with something less than perfect effectiveness. But, unless the functionalist can offer standards for answering questions such as what fractions of the functions must be performed, whether the functions are equal in importance, and to what degree of effectiveness the functions must be performed, the paradigm appears to be incapable of generating a lawlike

---

[5] Robert K. Merton, op. cit., pp. 51ff.

[6] There appears to be some ambiguity as to whether the functions are crucial (in the sense of very important) or indispensable (a sine qua non) in the writing of many functionalists.

[7] D. F. Aberle, et al., "The Functional Requisites of Society," *Ethics,* Vol. 60, No. 2 (January 1950), p. 100.

[8] See the point-by-point outline of the logical structure of functional analysis in Hempel, op. cit., pp. 191, 195, and 197.

proposition. The proposition that the adequate maintenance of a system or some other specified system state depends on the effective performance of a set of functions simply cannot be falsified unless one can first define a precise category of data that would unambiguously constitute an example of the ineffective or unsatisfactory performance of the functions. This demand for a precise category of data that is inconsistent with the above proposition (the proposition that specified functions must be effectively performed if a system is to survive) means that the degree of effectiveness in the performance of functions must be measurable. This ability would enable a researcher to specify unambiguous dividing lines or threshold levels between satisfactory and unsatisfactory performance.

ALMOND'S FIRST FORMULATION

As with other paradigms, it will be easier to discuss this paradigm in terms of the specific form it has been given by specific authors. The classic formulation of functionalism in political science appears in the writings of Gabriel Almond. Almond's thinking on this matter has not been exactly static; therefore, any fair survey of his contribution must take account of changes and development of his paradigm.[9] Almond's initial formulation of the functional paradigm may be found in the introduction to *The Politics of the Developing Areas*.[10] In this seminal essay Almond postulates eight functions which are apparently performed in all systems or at least in all viable systems. Actually, Almond is never really clear on this point. The functions are supposedly concepts which are common to both Western and non-Western systems, therefore useful concepts for drawing comparisons between the two types of systems. Yet, Almond has derived his functions from Western systems.[11] In effect, Almond seems to be saying that here are the functions which are performed in the United States and Great Britain. How are these functions performed in Indonesia and Ghana? To what extent are they performed by similar structures?

One might, therefore, criticize Almond for his rather bold inference that the functions which are performed in Western systems are necessarily part of non-Western systems. This in itself is not a fatal criticism of the paradigm. Assuming that the functions, being, after all, concepts, can be operationally defined, this assertion of the universality of his functions becomes an empirical statement capable of being tested. The real difficulty lies in the specification of the functions themselves.

---

[9] The changes in Almond's thinking and the progressive sophistication of his paradigms are best reflected in a one volume collection of his key analytical writings, arranged chronologically: Gabriel Almond, *Political Development* (Boston: Little, Brown & Co., 1970).

[10] Gabriel Almond and James Coleman (eds.), *The Politics of the Developing Areas* (Princeton: Princeton University Press, 1960), pp. 3–64.

[11] Ibid., p. 16.

Briefly, Almond's eight functions are divided into five input functions and three output functions. Input and output are used in relation to the political system. Easton utilizes these forms in the same sense as was shown above. The input functions consist of the following: (1) political socialization, involving the transmission of a political culture from one generation to the next or the dissemination of a new political culture, (2) political recruitment, involving the selection and training of leaders, (3) interest articulation, involving the identification of demands and their transmission from society to authoritative decision makers, (4) interest aggregation, involving the filtering and consolidation of demands to a manageable load on the political system, and (5) political communication, involving the transmission of messages among the elements of a system and between the system and its environment. The output functions seem self-explanatory: rule making, rule application, and rule adjudication. They closely resemble the traditional separation-of-powers functions except that they have a slightly broader connotation. Rule making, for example, can include both formal and informal processes, of which lawmaking is only a part. It can thus refer not only to processes in non-Western systems that have not acquired the highly developed Western lawmaking institutions but also to executive and bureaucratic rule making in Western systems, rules which are not laws in the strict, formal sense.

The scientific utility of this classification of functions may be challenged on the grounds that it does not conform to the criteria for a sound classification discussed in Chapter 1.[12] Specifically, the boundaries between the categories are imprecise. When a group leader voices the sentiments of his group, he is engaged in political communication, interest articulation, and interest aggregation at the same time. It is one thing to recognize that one structure may perform several functions. But when several functions are performed by the *same act,* the purpose of analytically distinguishing them is not apparent.

It is difficult to see the scientific utility of applying several terms to the same act. Terms, to be scientifically useful, should refer to a precise and distinct set of phenomena.

This difficulty of specifying the boundaries between functional categories is not unique to Almond's functional scheme. Parsons's putative functional requisites,[13] goal attainment, pattern maintenance, adaptation, and integration, face the same difficulty. Integration, for example, may constitute a means of adapting to changes in a system's environment. More fundamentally, the functions of Almond and Parsons are defined at such a high level of generality that it is virtually impossible to translate these func-

---

[12] See pp. 16–19.

[13] Talcott Parsons, Robert Bales, and Edward Shils, *Working Papers in the Theory of Action* (New York: The Free Press of Glencoe, 1953), pp. 177–81.

tions into concrete actions. In short, a precise class of empirical indicators has not been specified for any of the functional requisites posited by either of the two aforementioned authors.

Functionalism focuses on the consequences of activities, institutions, or phenomena in a given system for other elements of that system, consequences that have relevance for the survival of that system. It purports to relate how these activities, institutions, or phenomena contribute to the survival or effectiveness of the whole system (or to its destruction if one wants to include the concept of dysfunction—a negative contribution). If the functionalist paradigm is broadly interpreted as dealing with system *effectiveness* rather than system survival, the paradigm can presumably explain differences among systems with respect to the effectiveness of their operations. One system operates less effectively than another because its functions are performed less effectively.

Two problems immediately manifest themselves. First, such differences among systems are not explained unless the differences among systems with respect to the effective performance of the functions are accounted for. Yet, in functional analysis, the functional requisites are given; the paradigm cannot logically account for their presence or lack thereof. When one says that this system is in trouble because the socialization function is inadequately performed, a question arises as to why it is not adequately performed. This goes back to the old problem in the social sciences of identifying independent variables. One could seek the cause of the cause, ad infinitum.

Even this problem would not be fatal for the paradigm's explanatory potential if performance of given functions could be defined independently of the adequate functioning of a system. In short, are there criteria for making the judgment that this or that function is not adequately performed without knowledge about the state of the system as a whole? Apparently, we can identify such an inadequate functional performance only by the phenomena such a performance is supposed to explain, an inadequately performing system. Thus, the argument runs as follows: Why is the system performing ineffectively? Because the functional requisites are not being adequately performed. How do you know that these requisites are not being adequately performed? Because the system is not performing effectively. The argument is clearly circular.

Moreover, it exemplifies "the fallacy of affirming the consequent,"[14] unless one can safely assume that the stipulated functions are not only necessary but sufficient for the adequate performance of a system. One can neither predict that the inadequate performance of stipulated functions will result in system failure nor infer the inadequate performance of such functions from system failure unless one can rule out the possibility that other

---

[14] See the explanation of the fallacy on p. 111.

functions that have not been thought of can equally result in the effective performance of that system.

Inasmuch as the adequate performance of a function has thus far not been operationally defined autonomously from the adequate functioning of a system, one cannot rule out the possibility that the relationship between function and system state is reciprocal. That is, the performance of the function could be as much a consequence of the state of the system as the system state is a consequence of the function. However, causal relationships, we have seen, must be unidirectional, that is, moving from cause to effect and not vice versa. One reason why one cannot rule out the possibility of a reciprocal relationship in favor of a unidirectional one is that it is impossible to establish a temporal sequence between functional performance and system state. In causal relationships, cause precedes effect.

Finally, a third problem stems from the tendency of functionalists to conceive of a political (or social) system as an undifferentiated unit. When one asks about the system relevant consequences of a set of activities or phenomena, one is implicitly assuming that such activities affect all elements of the system uniformly. Obviously, a set of activities or a phenomenon could be functional for certain elements of a system and dysfunctional for others, or functional at one time and/or place while dysfunctional at another. Religion, as Robert K. Merton points out, can be integrative in some circumstances and very divisive in others.[15]

Thus, the functional paradigm, due to its inherent logic, is incapable of generating scientific explanations. To be sure, it is capable of generating descriptions about relationships that logically seem to exist in a wide variety of, if not in all, political systems. Unless the precise nature of this relationship can be specified, however, explanations of concrete phenomena will not be forthcoming from the paradigm.

ALMOND'S SECOND FORMULATION: COPING WITH CHANGE AS A DYNAMIC PROCESS

It would be grossly unfair to consider and dismiss the work of Almond on the basis of his introduction to *The Politics of the Developing Areas.* Clearly aware of the body criticism the above-mentioned essay received,[16] criticisms which have been discussed above in this chapter, Almond revised his functional paradigm, partially in an effort to meet and deal with some of these criticisms.

---

[15] Robert K. Merton, *On Theoretical Sociology* (New York: The Free Press, 1967), p. 82.

[16] Gabriel Almond, "A Developmental Approach to Political Systems," *World Politics,* Vol. 17, No. 2 (January 1965), pp. 183ff.; Almond and G. Bingham Powell, *Comparative Politics: A Developmental Approach* (Boston: Little, Brown & Co., 1966), pp. 12–13.

Almond is most acutely aware of the alleged status quo bias of earlier functional formulations, particularly as his work and interests have been principally concerned with the problems of political development, hence of system change. Almond further demonstrates some awareness of the need to develop a paradigm that leads to the explanation of system states and system change. However, his earlier functional approach was descriptive rather than explanatory.

Almond left the implication in his first formulation that development was conceived as the increasingly effective performance of the specified functional categories.[17] But, as has already been pointed out, an explanation of the differences among political systems with respect to such functional performance cannot be deduced from the universal functional paradigm as outlined by Almond in *The Politics of the Developing Areas.* Thus, his original functional paradigm was unable to explain change.

Although part of this inability to explain political change is inherent in the logic of the basic functionalist formulation, part of it is also related to a lack of satisfactory indicators that can be used to distinguish non-Western or less developed political systems from Western or relatively modern political systems.[18] Obviously, if we are seeking to explain something like political development, it is first necessary to specify the indicators of development. In other words, the first question is as follows: Political development consists of moving from what to what?

Almond sought to rectify this problem by reconceptualizing the basic distinction between Western and non-Western political systems. The more modern or developed systems are said to have higher capabilities or capacities, which stem from more specialized, functionally specific structures and from a more secularized political culture.[19] Thus, development as a *process* can be defined as *acquisition* of a higher capability through the process of structural differentiation and cultural secularization.

The usefulness of these concepts for explaining development will be discussed in Chapter 12. It may be tentatively suggested at this time, however, that Almond's later indices of development can be used to indicate a process (that is, the *acquisition* of capabilities) as well as a state of being. In this manner, Almond seems to have successfully met the criticism that his paradigm was inherently a static rather than a dynamic one. (A *static* paradigm deals only with states of being; a *dynamic* paradigm can also be used to analyze processes.)

It is relevant here to note that Almond's concepts have no logical dependence on the functional categories introduced earlier and retained in his

---

17 Almond and Coleman, op. cit.
18 Alexander J. Groth, "Structural Functional Analysis and Political Development: Three Problems," *Western Political Quarterly,* Vol. 23, No. 3 (September 1970), pp. 492ff.
19 These rather ambiguous concepts will be thoroughly discussed in Chapter 12.

later formulations. It is clearly possible to define political development in terms of functional differentiation[20] without attempting to specify a priori the functions all societies must perform for survival. It is difficult to see how Almond's reclassification of these functional categories under the headings of *conversion* functions and *adaptation* functions, instead of the former headings of *input* functions and *output* functions, alleviates the logical difficulties inherent in universal functionalism.

It seems fair to say that Almond contributed a major step in the systematic description of a greater variety of political phenomena by introducing his functional paradigm. However, the logical problems of functional analysis afford reason for skepticism regarding the *explanatory* potential of his functionalism regardless of how his functional categories are grouped and classified. The explanatory potential of his later concepts dealing with political development will be evaluated in Chapter 12. They should stand or fall on their own merits, however, independent of the logical problems inherent in universal functionalism.

THE EMPIRICAL FUNCTIONALISM OF MERTON

Another variety of functionalism, referred to in this chapter as empirical functionalism, does not postulate universal requisites. Neither does this use of the concept of function claim to explain the states of whole systems, not to mention all viable systems.

This approach, exemplified by Robert K. Merton, envisions function as the fulfillment of a specific set of demands in a particular political or social system. The question, therefore, is What set of institutions fulfill a particular set of functions or satisfy a specific set of demands in a particular time and place? Rather than making assumptions about characteristics of all social systems, such as the degree of social order that prevails, Merton simply seeks to identify the social mechanisms that produce such characteristics.[21] In this sense, Merton's approach is unabashedly descriptive rather than explanatory.

We have seen that, despite the apparent pretensions of universal functionalism to be capable of generating a general, probabilistic theory of politics,[22] universal functionalism is also descriptive rather than explanatory. It has been argued that this descriptive nature of the paradigm is inherent in the logic of universal functionalism. Merton's paradigm is descriptive for another reason; it is particularly (confined to specific cases).

Chapter 6 touched on the dilemma between the scientific need for generality and the equally important scientific requirement for empirical indi-

---

[20] For example, see Fred Riggs, *Administration in Developing Countries: The Theory of the Prismatic Society* (Boston: Houghton-Mifflin Co., 1964), pp. 19–31 and passim.

[21] Merton, *Social Theory and Social Structure,* op. cit., pp. 49ff.

[22] Almond and Coleman, op. cit.

cators for concepts, two needs which often seem to be incompatible. By opting for empirical relevance, Merton has developed propositions that can apply to particular cases. Explanation, it will be recalled from Chapter 4, involves the subsumption of the event to be explained in a more general proposition relating classes of events. Insofar as Merton's propositions are particularistic ones which do not relate classes of events, they are incapable of explaining anything. Scholars in the Parsonian tradition[23] have concentrated on fulfilling the generality requirement with the result, we have seen, that it is difficult to translate anything they have said into specific expectations about the real world. The very process of defining concepts in terms of real-world indicators limits their applicability to those contexts in which the indicators occur.

Merton demonstrates perhaps more awareness of the dilemma between the conflicting needs of generality and precise empirical content than any other social scientist. To resolve this dilemma, he advocates what he calls "theories of the middle range."[24] By this he means theoretic constructs that are broad enough to involve abstraction and the subsumption of propositions from a variety of specific contexts but narrow enough to permit operationalization of key concepts and empirical testing of some of the propositions. Merton is thus concerned with the development of a paradigm that can subsume a set of specific working propositions, yet a paradigm that is much more narrowly defined than those so-called general theories that aspire to encompass all the phenomena and their disciplines. We saw examples of such general theorists in Talcott Parsons and David Easton in the preceding chapter.

Such middle-range theories, possessing empirical content, cannot be deduced from any Parsonian-type general theory precisely because the latter lacks empirical content. Conversely, such middle-range theories could consistently be subsumed under several competing general theories for the same reason.

An example might help clarify the nature of Merton's functionalism. Perhaps the most famous application of his paradigm consists of "The Latent Functions of the Political Machine."[25] The concept of *latent functions* constitutes one of Merton's most important contributions to functional analysis. It simply refers to consequences of an activity for a system state or for the satisfaction of a need or demand that were not consciously intended by the actor or actors involved in the activity. Consequences of an activity which were consciously intended are referred to as *manifest functions*. The advantage of these two concepts is that they provide for the

---

[23] This refers to that group of disciples of Talcott Parsons, discussed in the preceding chapter, who endeavor to construct a universal model of political or social behavior.

[24] Merton, *On Theoretical Sociology,* op. cit., chap. 2, especially pp. 39–53.

[25] Robert K. Merton, *Social Theory and Social Structure,* op. cit., pp. 71–81.

consideration of all of the consequences of a pattern of activity, not merely those consequences that were consciously and overtly avowed.

In a famous and brilliantly insightful passage, Merton describes how American political machines, traditionally the object of scorn among reform-minded and idealistic intellectuals, actually performed valuable functions for American society. One such function is the mobilization of power. Since formal power is highly fragmented among American governmental structures, it often appeared that no governmental official or agency had sufficient power to act in order to satisfy perceived public needs. An informal or unofficial figure, the political boss, was often able to mobilize sufficient power to accomplish what no public official was able to accomplish because the boss's influence transcended single official public offices or roles. Another set of functions might be summarized under the heading of social welfare. Political machines flourished primarily in the pre–New Deal era when poverty relief, unemployment insurance, care of aged and incapacitated, free legal advice to the poor, etc., were not provided by governmental agencies. Political machines filled the need for those services for their constituents as part of their effort to win and maintain public support. By offering places for needy on the public payroll, and similar devices, machines performed this function without the loss of self-respect that often accompanies outright charity. Machines performed a third latent function for many residents of poor neighborhoods, that of a vehicle for upward social mobility in circumstances in which few other such vehicles existed.

Veblen's concept of conspicuous consumption is offered by Merton as another example of latent functions.[26] The acquisition of expensive goods, such as Cadillac automobiles or imported, vintage wines, is valued not so much for their obvious uses as for their function as a symbol of class status. After all, the superiority of a luxury automobile in performance of the transportation function over the performance of a less expensive automobile is not proportional to the added cost of luxury cars. One can reach most destinations in a Pinto as quickly and safely as in a Continental for about one third the price. The purchase of an expensive item serves the latent function of a sign or badge saying its possessor is a member of the upper class.

This discussion of Merton's concept of latent functions points up a crucial distinction between his approach to functional analysis and the paradigms of such universal functionalists as Almond. Rather than postulating omnipresent functional requisites in an a priori fashion, Merton seeks to empirically ascertain what functions a given institution or pattern of activity performs in a particular social setting.

Precisely because Merton's functional paradigm is easily applied to

---

[26] Thorstein Veblen, *The Theory of the Leisure Class* (New York: Vanguard Press, 1928).

concrete, observable phenomena, it tends to be descriptive rather than explanatory. It does not purport to offer generalizations which are able to account for the existence of a class of observable phenomena. To say that some activity, such as the Hopi Indian rain dances, or some institution, such as a political machine, makes some contribution to the society in which it exists, either in lieu of or in addition to those consequences consciously avowed by the instigators of such activity, does not really account for the existence of such activity or phenomena. There is some hint that the apparent persistence of certain phenomena that have failed to fulfill their avowed purposes can be accounted for by the fact that such phenomena perform latent functions. However, this vague suggestion is nowhere formulated into a testable proposition; consequently, specific phenomena cannot be integrated in such a generalization and therefore explained. One cannot really make a lawlike proposition about institutions that perform latent functions unless one can specify the distinction between manifest and latent functions more rigorously than Merton has done. His distinction is based upon intent or conscious motivation, concepts which are difficult to operationalize.

Because those political scientists who have turned to functionalism have been seeking paradigms with high explanatory potential, Merton's brand of empirical functionalism has not attained widespread popularity in the analytic literature of the discipline. However, it is precisely this use of functionalism that has appeared frequently in substantive analyses of specific countries. When writers discuss the functions that the parties in some system or class of systems perform, they are using a Mertonian rather than an Almondian approach to functional analysis. Rather than attempting to postulate the requisites for all societies autonomously from observation, these substantive writers of the Mertonian school ask what functions these particular observed institutions perform. Their approach is thus inductive while Almond's attempts to develop a set of axioms from which expectations about given systems can be deduced. Despite the fact that Almond does not succeed in developing general explanatory theory, it seems fair to conclude that the aims of his analytic efforts are much more ambitious than those of Merton.

APTER: REQUISITE ANALYSIS AND SOCIAL STRATIFICATION

Another version of functional analysis is offered by David Apter. Apter offers the concept of structural requisites as one of several variables comprising a comprehensive framework for comparative analysis.[27] These variables are laid out along three "dimensions": social stratification, government, and political groups.

---

[27] Apter, op. cit., pp. 221–37.

The dimension of social stratification includes the criteria by which the divisions and groupings of the people in a society are formed. Examples of such criteria or standards could be socio-economic class, ethnic affiliation, geographical residence, or origin. Britain would epitomize a society which is stratified along socio-economic class lines while Canada is stratified along a combination of ethnic, religious, and geographic lines. Apter's variables are economic, political, generational (referring to parentage), and religious. In practice, however, economic criteria are usually inseparably infused with aspects of prestige and even generational variables. The British aristocracy constitutes an example of such a mixture. The feelings of alienation, not to mention the separatist tendencies, among the Catholic, French-Canadian citizens of Quebec, are based upon ethnic, religious, geographical, and even economic variables. The perceived regional loyalties of western Canada, as distinct from loyalty to the Canadian nation as a whole, involve both geographic and economic considerations. Consequently, concepts such as socio-economic class seem to be more readily applicable to given political or social systems than variables such as Apter suggests, variables which may be separated only in an analytic sense. It may very well be, however, that it is difficult to pinpoint the precise criteria along which any given nation is stratified since the variables are so difficult to distinguish in practice.

The bases of social stratification could in principle be useful in trying to explain and predict the bases of political conflict in a society. Societies which appear to be stratified along criteria which are not uniformly distributed in a geographical sense, such as the concentration of French Canadians in Quebec, may find it more difficult replacing regionally defined parochial loyalties with national loyalties. Party systems may be expected to reflect the basis of social stratification. Eckstein has shown that the Norwegian multiparty system reflects the numerous dimensions along which society is stratified.[28] Alford has argued persuasively that societies which are stratified primarily along socio-economic lines tend to develop class-based parties and that issues in such countries are more easily resolved by a process of bargaining and compromise because class-based politics reflects genuine interests, rather than values.[29]

Social stratification also includes the variable of the extent of social mobility, the opportunities for upward movement in the stratification system. This raises questions about the openness of recruitment to political and social elites, the barriers to movement from nonleadership to leadership roles. For example, when the standards for admission to leadership roles involve ascribed characteristics, such as the social status of parents, the possibilities of such advancement are foreclosed to non-elites. When such standards involve demonstrated achievement, as through competitive ex-

---

[28] Harry Eckstein, *Division and Cohesion in Democracy, A Study of Norway* (Princeton: Princeton University Press, 1966).

[29] Robert Alford, *Party and Society* (Chicago: Rand McNally, 1963).

amination, the chances for such advancement are greatly increased.

Apter does not thoroughly exploit the possibilities of the stratification variable. For example, the classic mass-society thesis of Kornhouser is a study in social stratification.[30] Briefly, Kornhouser argues that when non-elites form an undifferentiated and atomized mass, there is no middle level of association between the individual and government. (Interest groups would be one important example of such middle level associations.) Consequently, in such a mass society, the elites become highly vulnerable to the masses, a situation which could result in some form of mob rule. Conversely, the masses become vulnerable to mobilization and domination by elites, a situation which could result in totalitarianism.[31] Obviously, Kornhouser, like so many other political sociologists, is dealing in non-operational concepts. Indicators are not even specified for so basic a distinction as that between a mass society and one in which elites are insulated from the masses by secondary associations. Nevertheless, the degree of atomization of society into a relatively unorganized mass seems to be a variable of theoretic import, one which would logically be subsumed under the social stratification dimension.

Apter's approach moves into the area of requisite analysis when he introduces the dimension of government. He defines the *structural requisites* of a political system as those activities engaged in by all governments regardless of the many forms governments take. Government itself is a structural requisite for all social systems. Apter apparently uses the term structure in the sense of an institution, a recurring pattern of activity or interaction. Structural analysis concerns itself with the organizational or institutionalized limits on choice, thus leading to the analysis of policy.[32] The structural requisites postulated by Apter are "(1) the structure of authoritative decision making, (2) the structure of accountability, (3) the structure of coercion and punishment, (4) the structure of resource determination and allocation, and (5) the structure of political recruitment and role assignment."[33] What is immediately apparent is the somewhat confusing use of terms. It is very difficult to distinguish Apter's use of the term *structure* from what other scholars surveyed in this chapter mean by

---

[30] William Kornhouser, *The Politics of Mass Society* (New York: The Free Press of Glencoe, 1954).

[31] Cf. Joseph R. Gusfield, "Mass Society and Extremist Politics," *American Sociological Review,* Vol. 27, No. 1 (February 1962), pp. 19–30, for a somewhat contradictory argument that mass society may in fact promote a viable democracy while a pluralistic society could in some respects promote extremist politics.

[32] David Apter, *The Politics of Modernization* (Chicago: University of Chicago Press, 1967), p. 16.

[33] Apter, "A Comparative Method For the Study of Politics," op. cit., p. 225. In his book, Apter lists the structural requisites as merely "the structure of authoritative decision making" and "the structure of accountability." The other structural requisites plus a "consent group" are here listed as contingent structures or "analytic substructures" of government, pp. 245–247.

the term *function*. What Apter apparently means by his term *structural requisite* is some form of institutionalization of the performance of what others would designate as a necessary function. Thus, designation of the structure of resource determination and allocation as a structural requisite means that every society must have some structural arrangement which can perform the function of resource determination. The term *functional requisite,* on the other hand, is not used by Apter to refer to necessary functions. Rather, he uses the term to refer to the minimum tools a political system needs in order to perform the functions implied in the list of structural requisites. Apter lists these tools as information and coercion.

Apter further lists what he terms the *contingency functions* of all governments, the functions which serve as *indicators* (rather than determinants) of governmental legitimacy. These contingency functions consist of (1) a "source of social norms," (2) a "link between past and future," (3) the "orderly arranged performance of the roles," and (4) "the definition of membership."[34] The functions are contingent in the sense that they are *not necessary* for the persistence of the system, but they are alleged to be universal. Contingent functions reflect failures in the functional requisites.

While structural analysis for Apter seems to emphasize the institutional determinants of choice or policy, his functional analysis is concerned with the bases of legitimacy for authority. Thus, no political system can persist without some balance of information and coercion which, incidentally, are suggested to be inversely correlated. While Almond and Parsons refer to a functional requisite as the minimum tasks or activities a government must *perform* in order to survive, Apter uses the term functional requisite to refer to something a government must *have* in order to function.

While a government must have enough capacity for coercion to balance any lack of information or knowledge of (1) "the values in a choice situation" and (2) "the limits within which the public will support action,"[35] it must institutionalize the performance of the coercion function. Thus, coercion can be listed as a functional requisite while the structure of coercion is listed as a structural requisite.

While Apter is postulating the requisites of all systems in the manner of the aforementioned functionalists and further postulating that each functional requirement must be institutionalized in an appropriate structural arrangement, he leaves the question of the precise form that the manifestation of such structural arrangements will take an open question to be empirically determined in given cases.

The concept of functional requisite can be an extremely important one in the Apterian paradigm for, in suggesting what is needed to perform the functions that Almond, etc., merely list, Apter is at least suggesting a

---

[34] Apter, *The Politics of Modernization,* op. cit., pp. 240–41.
[35] Ibid., pp. 237–38.

conceptual tool for beginning to account for differences among systems with respect to the performance of the requisite functions.[36] Much work needs to be done with this concept before this potential is realized, however. At a minimum, the postulation of the functional requisites must be made an empirical statement to be tested and refined.

By defining these structural requisites as the conditions which are "vital" to the persistence of the system, Apter has fallen into the trap of trying to distinguish those systems which persist from those which do not, a distinction fraught with all the difficulties discussed in the previous chapter. Moreover, if Apter were successful in making such a distinction, it would not be a terribly useful one. Most of the systems in which political scientists are most interested fall in the one category of persisting systems. Requisite analysis does not help with the explanation of differences among the many systems which do persist. In short, requisite analysis postulates the conditions for the minimum political system;[37] political scientists are interested in real systems that have more than met these minimal requirements.

Apter does make an attempt to relate these requirements to one another. For example, the amount of coercion and punishment that is present in a system is suggested to be inversely related to the extent to which decision makers are accountable. As a preliminary statement of such relationships, Apter's propositions are not made testable. In addition to the fact that variables like accountability have not been rendered operational and hence are incapable of being measured, his propositions are infused with such terms as "normally" and "very often." Apter is thus saying his putative relationships hold true not only not invariably but to an *unspecified* extent. In other words, if his relationships do not hold true 100 percent of the time, he must state what minimum percent of the time the relationships are expected to hold. Without specifying in quantitative terms the extent to which relationships are expected to hold, there can be precisely specified class of no potential observations which is logically incompatible with such propositions. Nevertheless, in suggesting the direction that certain relationships might take, it could be argued that Apter has taken a first step in the direction of the explanation of some phenomena.

Apter not only attempts to relate structural and functional requisites to one another; he suggests some general relationships between such requisites and the normative dimension of political analysis, different types of values. These include consummatory values (ultimate or fundamental ends) and instrumental values (which are merely means to the attainment of more fundamental values). Certain patterns of political structure (that is, of account-

---

[36] By now it should be clear that requisite function, a function which must be performed, is not the same thing as a functional requisite in Apterian terminology, something which is necessary to perform the functions.

[37] Gabriel Almond, "A Developmental Approach to Political Systems," *World Politics,* Vol. 17, No. 2 (January 1965), p. 201.

ability, format, etc.) such as what we would call liberal democracy (in Apterian jargon, *a reconciliation system*) tend to be associated with and supported by certain value patterns (in this case, instrumental). These authority types and value patterns are combined into political models. These models, consisting of abstracted elements which are related to one another, represent classes of political systems in the observable world. By demonstrating the logical suitability of a certain model (his *mobilization system*) for modernization, Apter partially explains the prevalence of that class of political format in actual modernizing societies.

The point is that whatever explanatory utility Apter's work may have appears to be based upon the fact that he has gone far beyond the conventional functional paradigm and is, in fact, quite autonomous from whatever use he has made of the elements of that paradigm.

REASONS FOR THE POPULARITY OF FUNCTIONALISM

In view of the many logical and operational difficulties raised about the conventional functional paradigm, it may be legitimately asked at this point why the appeal of functional analysis has apparently been so widespread, particularly among scholars widely recognized as among the most competent in their discipline. The answer to this must take into account the conceptual state of the discipline in the period that immediately preceded the advocacy of functionalism by men such as Almond, Apter, Holt, and Richardson.

Relative to the predominant propensity to concentrate on the formal, legal structures of government, especially those peculiar to Western industrial political systems, the appeal of functional analysis is easy to understand.

In the first place, function offers a concept that is much more widely applicable than the previous units of analysis—ethno-centrically defined constitutions, laws, and governmental structures. Such formal, legal structures are usually unique to a particular political system or relatively small group of such systems. Certain functions, on the other hand, are putatively common to all political systems regardless of institutional differences among them. The advantages, including the widest possible variety of cases in ones' comparative generalizations in the social sciences, such as accounting for the ever present and non-constant external variables, have been thoroughly discussed in Chapter 6.

Second, functional analysis carries the researcher beyond the analysis of legal governmental institutions themselves in any given system. In asking what structure performs the given functions, the paradigm leaves open the possibility that functions vital to the political system may be performed by structures external to what is commonly thought of as the formal government proper. For example, the study of the socialization function leads one to analyze a nation's educational system. By including a greater number of potentially relevant variables in the analysis, any explanations derived from the analysis will be, to that extent, relatively more complete.

Third, function may be argued to conceptualize a process rather than a state of affairs. It also conceptualizes a form of relationship between certain structures and an analytical system, namely, the contribution of those structures to the persistence of the system. In suggesting a type of relationship, functional analysis appeared to hold the promise of greater explanatory potential than the previous emphasis on institutional description, a promise which, we have seen, was not fulfilled due to the tautological nature of the postulated relationships.

CONCLUSIONS

Despite the substantial popularity of the structural-functional paradigm, it is difficult to name any political phenomena that have been explained (in the scientific sense of the word used in this book) through the use of the paradigm and that could not have been explained without the use of the paradigm. In other words, functional analysis has failed to increase our explanatory power. Functionalism has, in itself, not led to the development of scientific generalizations (statements about *relationships* between classes of operationally defined phenomena) for a variety of reasons. Perhaps the most important of these reasons is the fact that the universal functionalist paradigm is not a formalized paradigm. Rather, it consists of lists of concepts which are usually not themselves defined in operational terms. This tendency to define key concepts, such as the functional (or structural) requisites of society, in rather general, non-operational terms constitutes a second reason for the lack of explanatory power in functional analysis. The circularity of the argument constitutes the third reason.

On the other hand, functionalism has proven to possess a descriptive value in that it provides for the description of many more relevant phenomena than did the traditional legal, institutional analysis. It provides a framework for indications that a number of variables, which were formerly dismissed as belonging to other social sciences, have relevance for the political systems. For example, structures such as the educational system or the family can now be shown to have political relevance through their role in the performance of the socialization function.

Therefore, the discussion of the limitations on the explanatory potential of functional analysis is not intended to constitute a total denial that functionalism has made any contribution to the discipline. Certainly, the functionalists have made a major contribution in helping to lead the discipline away from traditional legalistic studies. It must be concluded that functionalism is not likely to lead to a general theory of politics or even to significant explanatory generalizations. Yet, the contribution of the major functionalists, men like Almond, Apter, and, to a lesser extent, the other members of the Comparative Politics Committee of the S.S.R.C.,[38] goes beyond the success of the functional paradigm. This will become more apparent when political development is discussed in Chapter 12.

---

[38] The S.S.R.C. refers to the Social Science Research Council, a nongovernmental foundation that has been a major funding agency for research in the social sciences. The Comparative Politics Committee, a subdivision of that foundation, has sponsored periodic seminars on the theoretic aspects of comparative politics. Some of the most prestigious names in the field have participated in these seminars. The political development series of Princeton University Press is one of the major published outputs of these seminars. It is perhaps not too much to suggest that the work of the Comparative Politics Committee was one of the major influences on the discipline throughout the 1960s.

Political Culture:
A Link between Micro
Analysis and
Macro Analysis

Most approaches in political science are not actually formalized constructs like the models discussed in Chapter 7. Rather, they consist of concepts, made up of clusters of variables, that are applicable to a variety of social or political contexts. These concepts mainly serve the function of providing criteria for selecting data from a variety of political contexts and for assigning standardized meaning to such data. This standardized meaning permits cross-cultural comparisons. The intention, of course, is that such data will fall into patterns that can be related to political phenomena or events that we find interesting and important. The relationships cannot be deduced from such a nonformalized approach itself.

The very lack of formalization means that the approach, being a set of concepts, does not specify relationships. The concepts and approaches discussed in this chapter focus on individuals rather than systems as basic units of analysis. Such an individualistic approach is referred to as *micro analysis,* as opposed to the term *macro analysis,* which refers to taking social groups or systems as the basic unit of analysis. Micro analysis is reductionist in the sense discussed in Chapter 1; macro analysis is holistic.

One concept that has both micro and macro implications is the concept of political culture, a concept which has gained widespread popularity in recent years and which appears to contain variables of significant explanatory potential. These micro and macro attributes of a single concept are explained below.

Obviously, the content of any concept is a matter of definition, as pointed out in the first chapter. The precise set of variables included in a concept thus varies from author to author. Nevertheless, it may be justifiably asserted that there is a great deal of common content among the various definitions of the concept of political culture. Thus, it seems useful to begin this discussion with an attempt to specify those variables that that concept appears to contain in a generic sense.[1] It should then be possible to proceed to note major differences in the meaning assigned to the concept by prominent scholars who have seen fit to use it or discuss it.

Basically, *political culture* is perhaps a more modern (in the sense of being more systematically and precisely defined) and more politically oriented version of that old and rather imprecise concept *national character* that can be traced back at least to the writings of Montesquieu.[2] In the most general sense, political culture and/or national character (the terms may, at this point, be used synonymously)[3] refers to modal patterns of orientations toward specified political objects.

Modal is an important term here. It is the adjectival form of the statistical concept of mode, a measure of central tendency—specifically, the most frequently occurring type, the most typical. Thus, to attribute a certain characteristic to a society's character or culture is not to imply that all members of that society share that characteristic. Such an assertion simply means that a substantial majority of the members possess the attribute in question. For example, the assertion that the British are "a deferential people" is not meant to imply that there are no Britishers with strong egalitarian sympathies. Actually, modality connotes a strong tendency statement. There is some disagreement in the literature as to whether modal character types can be found for a given social system. It may be that the internal diversity of societies is such that it is necessary to speak of a nation's political cultures in the plural form. The distribution of political orientations may be multimodal in a given society rather than unimodal. This is an empirical question which can be resolved by appropriate research.[4]

---

[1] The term variable is defined in Chapter 1, p. 9. The word concept refers to an ideal comprised of a set or complex of related variables. Scientific variables are defined in terms of observable indicators; thus, concepts, variables, and indicators may be thought of as related in that order of descending generality.

[2] C. L. Montesquieu, *Esprit des Lois,* Books 1 and 4. See also Alexis de Toqueville, *Democracy in America* (New York: Vintage Books, 1955), Vol. 2, and James Bryce, *Modern Democracies,* 2 vols. (New York: Macmillan Co., 1921).

[3] National character is used as others use the concept of political culture in Alex Inkles, "National Character" in Roy Macrides and Bernard Brown, *Comparative Politics, Notes and Readings,* 3d ed. (Homewood, Ill.: The Dorsey Press, 1968), pp. 36–44.

[4] Alex Inkles and Daniel Levinson, "National Character" in Gardner Lindzey (ed.), *Handbook on Social Psychology* (Cambridge, Mass.: Addison Wesley, 1954), p. 982. See also Gabriel Almond and Sidney Verba, *The Civic Culture* (Princeton: Princeton University Press, 1963), p. 52.

It is the postulation of modal characteristics for a whole system that gives political culture its macro implications. Yet, insofar as the concept refers to individual dispositions, it is micro-analytical. The concept of modality combines the micro data into macro cultural characteristics on an additive basis. In this way, political culture offers one potential linkage between the heretofore separate micro and macro levels of analysis.

It is on the question of those variables included in the concept of orientations that scholars begin to differ with respect to details. Sidney Verba defines political culture as "the system of empirical beliefs, expressive symbols and values which define the situation in which political action takes place."[5] Gabriel Almond derives his definition of political culture from the action theory of Talcott Parsons, discussed above.[6] The components of orientations toward politics on which Almond suggests we focus consist of cognitive orientations, affective orientations, and evaluative orientations. Cognition, a term frequently used in the literature on political culture, simply means knowledge and information. It should be noted that knowledge is not identical in meaning to information. The latter terms refers to raw facts, questions such as the name of the current prime minister. Knowledge, on the other hand, includes understanding of how the facts interact and relate to one another. The answer to a question such as How does cabinet government operate? would constitute knowledge. Affective orientations refer to feelings of belonging or of alienation and rejection. Parsons refers to this variable as *cathectic* orientations. Evaluative orientation appears to be self-explanatory. It refers to the assignment of priorities to political objects or goals.

Samuel Beer conceptualizes political culture as that aspect of a society's general culture "concerned with *how* government ought to be conducted and *what* it should try to do" (his emphasis).[7] The more specific components of political culture for Beer consist of political values, subdivided into conceptions of authority and of national purpose, belief systems, and emotional attitudes and symbols. Conceptions of authority are attitudes about what the rules of the political game *ought* to be. As such, it is in what Almond and Parsons would call the evaluative dimension. This component of political culture would include the distinction between deference to authority as found in Great Britain or the converse attitude, egalitarianism and suspicion of authority, as found in the United States. While conceptions of authority

---

[5] Sidney Verba, "Comparative Political Culture," in Lucien Pye and Sidney Verba (ed.), *Political Culture and Political Development* (Princeton: Princeton University Press, 1965), p. 513.

[6] Talcott Parsons and Edward Shils (ed.), *Toward a General Theory of Action* (New York: Harper Torchbooks), p. 59. See also Gabriel Almond and G. Bingham Powell, *Comparative Politics, A Developmental Approach* (Boston: Little, Brown & Co., 1966), p. 50.

[7] Samuel Beer, "The Analysis of Political Systems," in Beer and Adam Ulam (ed.), *Patterns of Government* (New York: Random House, 1962), p. 32.

are procedural, conceptions of purpose are substantive. That is, while the former is concerned with the rules by which decisions are made and decision makers are chosen, the latter is concerned with the content of decisions. The idea of "manifest destiny" in 19th century America exemplified a conception of national purpose. It involves attitudes about what the goals of the political system ought to be.

While conceptions of authority and purpose involve attitudes about what ought to be, belief systems consist of perceptions of what is. The crucial question for the purposes of explanation is not the validity of the perceptions, it is the content of the perceptions themselves. People act on what they believe is true, not on some objective truth of which they may not be aware. Beliefs are not unrelated to attitudes. If people believe that the economic market is in fact self-regulating, their attitude toward the proper role of government in the economy will be one of hostility to political authority. This relationship should hold regardless of whether there is any objective validity to the belief. The effect of theological beliefs on politics is widely recognized. The Puritan beliefs in the nature of sin, damnation, and the nature of man have had a major impact on political output in the United States. The persistent American attempts to legislate morality constitute an example of the influence of this pattern of beliefs on American public policy.

What Beer means by his final component of political culture, emotional attitudes and expressive symbols, is not unrelated to the Parsonian concept of *cathexis*. Events, such as the French and Mexican Revolutions, or institutions, such as the British monarchy, acquire meaning to people which transcends the objective impact such phenomena have on their nation's decision-making process. Such symbolic phenomena become objects with which *ordinary* citizens can identify despite a diversity of views or preferences on day-to-day issues. In this way, such symbolic phenomena can perform the function of integrating the diverse elements of a heterogeneous society. This is usually, in the terminology of Merton, a *latent function* of such phenomena, as shown in the preceding chapter.

The foregoing highly incomplete survey of some of the various specifications of the concept of political culture should serve to indicate that, despite variations in details, there is also widespread consensus on the content of the concept. There is general agreement that the concept contains the variable of deferential or suspicious attitudes toward authority. This seems to be a function of broader attitudes toward one's fellow man, namely, an attitude of general trust or lack thereof. Consensus also exists on the relevance of attitudes about the proper goals or purposes of the political system. Such attitudes, conceptions of what ought to be, are clearly related to beliefs, conceptions of the way things are.

Attitudes about one's proper role in the political system are also relevant. These attitudes are concerned with such questions as the extent to which the average person ought to participate in politics. This is actually another dimension of attitudes toward authority. The extent to which tolerance is prevalent constitutes another relevant attitudinal variable. This may be conceptualized as the *intensity* of partisanship. The nature of a society's belief systems is relevant from the point of view of the extent to which belief is a weltanshauung-type ideology is pervasive among the decision makers and intellectuals of the society. This type of ideology refers to a closed, comprehensive, logically consistent set of ideas which can subsume all conceivable social issues or questions. In short, it may be relevant to ask whether a society approaches its problems and issues from an ideological or pragmatic perspective.[8] Ideologically oriented societies tend to engage themselves in a quest for certainty and essential "truth" at the expense of viable, if tentative, resolutions to temporary issues.

The powerful influence of an orthodox institutional church may be taken as one manifestation of an ideological propensity in a society. A religion tends to ideologism, of course, only insofar as it propounds a closed, comprehensive belief system as ultimate truth, a trait true of specific religions only to varying degrees. Such orthodox religious institutions judge social and political policies in terms of their compatibility with a belief system rather than in terms of their practical consequences for human welfare on earth. It is this propensity that leads scholars like Almond to equate modernity in a political culture with secularity.[9]

It scarcely seems necessary to point out that organized religion itself does not constitute the only antithesis of secularism in the sense in which that term is used in the literature on political culture and political development. Various ideologies, some of which may even claim to be profoundly anti-religious, may take on all the attributes of the religious dogmas they profess to despise, save possibly overt obeisance to a transcendental deity. Marxism-Leninism perhaps constitutes the most significant example of such a "secular religion" in the modern world.

It has even been argued in the 20th century that so-called secular societies have merely substituted an ideology of pragmatism[10] or an ideology

---

[8] Without further specification of their definitions, these concepts are not necessarily mutually exclusive; some countries, such as China, may find it pragmatic to remain ideological.

[9] Gabriel Almond and G. Bingham Powell, op. cit., pp. 51–58. Cf. also Seymour Lipset, *Political Man* (New York: Doubleday Anchor Books, 1966), p. 72n for the suggestion that Catholicism, presumably the epitome of a dogmatic faith, is incompatible with the open society that must form the basis of any viable democracy. The singling out of Catholicism as if it were the only dogmatic faith is the least of the criticisms that can be levied at this simplistic proposition. Nevertheless, it does point out a logical inconsistency between religion in the general sense and the cultural characteristics requisite for a viable industrial democracy. The specific impact of any given set of religious institutions or belief systems on the state of any political system can, in principle, be made an empirical question subject to inquiry.

of scientism[11] for the traditional weltanshauung ideologies. If this is meant to imply that the philosophy of science and pragmatism are simply closed ideologies resting on faith, the proposition is manifestly false by definition. Both of these related modern styles of thought are justified in terms of observable results rather than on faith; hence, they constitute open rather than closed thought systems.

In addition to their content, belief systems may be examined with respect to the proportion and sectors of a society's population that actually hold them[12] and with respect to the intensity with which they are held.

The nature of a society's beliefs and the intensity with which they are held clearly relate to the tolerance variable discussed above. Weltanshauung belief systems that are intensely held do not encourage toleration of political differences. Such toleration might be expected to be found to a greater extent in a political arena which emphasizes conflicts of interests rather than in one that is characterized by philosophical conflicts. The former type of political conflict would seem to be amenable to resolution through compromise as opposed to total victory of one side. When conflicts are defined in terms of moral philosophy, concessions to the opposition tend to take on connotations of amoral cooperation with evil or error. This assertion negates the whole area of political theory.

Investigation of what Parsons called the cathectic mode of orientation could yield data that are relevant for the explanation of the extent of national integration in a political system. Research into the emotional aspects of political orientations leads one to an inquiry into the objects of primary identification. Feelings of belonging, called affect, are generally attached to symbols representing a less concrete metaphysical entity, such as nationhood. Phenomena may take on a significant symbolic meaning that transcends their actual role in the operation of the political system in which they exist, as exemplified by a flag, Uncle Sam, the British monarchy, or national anthems. Such symbols can serve to unify a population despite wide-ranging disagreements on substantive issues. It is therefore useful to inquire into the extent to which the symbolic objects of emotional identification (affect) are uniform in a political system. For example, the bitter debate over the adoption of a new flag in Canada in 1964 may be taken as an indication of the deep-seated cultural regionalism that exists with respect to the French Canadian problem. The non-French leadership favored a flag incorporating the Union Jack pattern, symbolizing their identification with

---

[10] James Cristolph, "Consensus and Cleavage in British Political Ideology," *American Political Science Review,* Vol. 59, No. 3 (September 1965), pp. 629–42, especially p. 631.

[11] Peter Merkl, *Modern Comparative Politics* (New York: Holt, Rinehart & Winston, 1970), pp. 196–97.

[12] Ibid., pp. 199–200.

Canada's Commonwealth connection. The French Canadians, on the other hand, favored the fleur-de-lis, symbolizing their primary identification with ancien régime France. A compromise was finally reached on a maple leaf pattern. Thus, it is important to know whether primary indentification is with the symbols of political subsystems—indicating regionalism—or with the symbols of the political system as a whole—indicating a cohesive political system.

Other questions also relate to the objects of political orientation. For example, objects of national pride may be the general culture or social system, on the one hand, or the particular structure and pattern of the nation's political institutions, on the other.[13] While these alternative orientations are not necessarily mutually exclusive, Almond and Verba have shown that some peoples, notably the Italians, exhibit significantly more pride in their general culture than in their political institutions. One could logically expect the level of diffuse support, to use Easton's terminology, for a regime in such a system to be significantly lower. Easton suggests that when support for a regime is tied to its satisfactory output rather than to the regime itself, the legitimacy of the regime is much more fragile. It is virtually impossible for a regime to consistently satisfy the bulk of its constituents in terms of specific output over a long period of time. Sooner or later events beyond the regime's control, such as an externally caused economic depression, will produce a political crisis. Regimes with larger measures of diffuse support should be able to withstand such a crisis. The Almond and Verba data, insofar as they show a tendency for support for the political institutions to be significantly higher in the most stable of their five sampled nations, tend to corroborate this expectation.

The variable of political cognition, the distribution of knowledge and information in a political system, is not unrelated to another variable suggested in Almond and Verba's civic culture study, a sense of civil competence. This variable basically consists of the extent to which people perceive that they are capable of effectively participating in public affairs. Clearly, such a sense of competence should be directly related to the amount of political cognition that objectively exists or to the perception of such cognition. The more people feel that they know about public affairs, the greater the sense of competence we would expect them to have. It is important to remember, however, that a person's *perception* of the extent of

---

[13] This variable is one of many dealt with in what is probably the most significant empirical study of comparative political culture to date, *The Civic Culture,* op. cit. This study, consisting of an extensive cross-national survey in five more or less democratic nations, is discussed at length below. Despite the methodological criticisms of this study, discussed below, cross-national survey research of this type holds great promise for comparative analysis. A number of additional surveys are presently in progress, some of which are identified below. However, the costs of such a project are nearly prohibitive. The costs of the Almond and Verba study exceeded a quarter of a million dollars.

his political knowledge may be more important for explaining other political variables than the actual extent of his knowledge.

If political culture is defined as model orientations toward political objectives, then this concept would not logically encompass an array of sociological, economic, geographical, and demographic variables that often are discussed as part of a given nation's political culture. The economic and demographic categories include aggregate data variables such as are included in the Banks and Textor and the Russett data banks.[14] Specifically, such variables as literacy rates, amount of urbanization and industrialization, per capita income, and the extent to which a communications network has been developed are reciprocally related to the variables that comprise the concept of political culture as discussed above. However, such variables do not in themselves constitute mental orientations. The same could be said for sociological variables, such as the nature of the social stratification system and the degree of social mobility, the proliferation of nongovernmental organizations, and the prevalent type of family structure and interaction. While such variables do not constitute orientations toward political objects per se, they can certainly be determinants of such orientations or can be determined by such orientations.

SURVEY RESEARCH

Much of the work on political culture to date has consisted of armchair impressions based upon unsystematic observations of the country in question. Walter Bagehot's assertion that the British are "a deferential people,"[15] made way back in the mid-19th century, corroborates or reinforces the visceral impression of most observers of British society then and to this day. Yet, it does not seem unfair to inquire as to the nature of the evidence he offers for such an assertion. The most obvious method for the collection of empirical data on attitudes, beliefs, and emotions is survey research.[16] Yet, as previously hinted, the practical problems that face a scholar contemplating a cross-national survey project are formidable indeed.

---

[14] Arthur Banks and Robert Textor, *A Cross Polity Survey* (Cambridge, Mass.: M.I.T. Press, 1963). Bruce Russet, et al. *World Handbook of Social and Political Indicators* (New Haven: Yale University Press, 1964).

[15] Walter Bagehot, *The English Constitution* (New York: Doubleday and Co. Dolphin Books [1872] n.d.), p. 13. Bagehot's book remains a classic description of the British system and, noteworthy enough, remains to large extent applicable to modern Britain.

[16] A lengthy, detailed discussion of the methodological and procedural problems and obstacles encountered when undertaking cross-national survey research is Frederick Frey, "Cross-Cultural Research in Political Science," in Robert Holt and John E. Turner, *The Methodology of Comparative Research* (New York: The Free Press, 1970), pp. 173–294. A useful introduction to the methodology and procedures of survey research in political science in general is Charles Backstrom and Gerald Hursh, *Survey Research* (Evanston, Ill.: Northwestern University Press, 1963).

The past several decades have seen enormous progress in knowledge about how to obtain reliable and valid results from sample surveys. We have come a long way from the abortive *Literary Digest* poll of 1936 which, on the basis of a telephone survey of a quarter of a million respondents, predicted that Landon would beat Franklin Roosevelt in the Presidential election by a landslide. Now, nearly any schoolchild familiar with the facts could tell you in retrospect that the limitation of the sample to telephone subscribers, when the effects of the depression were still being felt, systematically eliminated those low income people to whom FDR most clearly appealed. The fact that this was not obvious to the *Literary Digest* is an indication of our progress in survey research since 1936.

Knowledge of survey research has increased in several areas. As the foregoing example indicates, we now know a great deal about scientific sampling. A sample represents a larger group from which the sample is drawn. This larger group is of such a size as to be impractical to observe directly. The facts one gathers from the sample are assumed to apply proportionally to the larger group. The larger group about which one generalizes from a sample is called a population or universe.

Unlike the perpetrators of the *Literary Digest* fiasco, we now realize that the extent to which the data drawn from a sample applies to its universe is not a function of the size of the sample. Rather, it is a function of the extent to which the sample is representative of the universe from which it is drawn. That is to say, the sample should be a microcosm of the universe with respect to those variables of the universe relevant to the study at hand. To reverse Plato's verbal imagery, the sample should be the universe "writ small." For example, if the study is investigating political attitudes of a population, the sample should represent the population with respect to those attributes of the population that one would expect to have some effect on such attitudes. Thus, the sample should be representative of the population with respect to such variables as occupation, level of education, or religious affiliation, but it would not be necessary to make the sample representative of the population with respect to hair color or entertainment preferences. A representative sample is one that is stratified in the same way as the population with respect to relevant variables. For example, suppose religion were a relevant variable. In that case, if the population consists of 70 percent Protestants, 20 percent Catholics, and 10 percent others, the sample should contain the same percentages of these denominations or at least approximate these percentages as closely as is practical.

A sample that is representative of a population that contains relevant differentiations is known as a *stratified sample*. A random sample is desired for a population that contains no relevant differentiations. The term *random sample* refers to a sample chosen in such a way that each unit in the population has an equal chance of being included in the sample. A stratified sample should be randomly selected *within each strata*. Obviously, the more relevant differentiations that exist in the universe, the larger a sample will have to be in order to remain representative. This is a result of having more categories to account for in the sample.

The problems involved in drawing representative samples in cross-cultural survey research are enormous. A detailed description of these difficulties is beyond the scope of this volume. A few of them can only be suggested to give the reader some comprehension of the size of the problem. The necessary data, such as census lists, are either unavailable or unreliable in many countries, especially in the non-Western world.[17] The significance of the rates of nonresponse may be culturally determined, thereby prejudicing the comparability of the results.[18] The distribution of characteristics in each population does not always have comparable meaning and significance in different cultures. The design of comparable samples thus requires extensive knowledge of each culture to be studied. This knowledge is required in advance of the sampling; yet, the validity of such knowledge may depend on sample surveys. Thus, to a certain extent, the comparability of samples in cross-national research depends to a large extent on a set of visceral a priori assumptions about the meaning and significance of a variety of characteristics in each cultural context. An obvious example of this point is the fact that the significance of socio-economic class status is, to a large extent, a function of the extent of class consciousness in a society. However, the extent of such class consciousness can only be determined through survey research. Finally, the indicators used in operationalizing the criteria for a stratified sample (the indicators of socio-economic class, for example) may be culturally relative. The status assigned to a university professor in an anti-intellectual and highly egalitarian culture may not correspond to the status assigned the same profession in a deferential culture. Even the significance of marital status may depend on the dominant religion of a country.[19]

The construction of questionnaires also presents a number of problems. Any survey researcher must resolve such questions as the choice between open ended (essay type) and highly structured (multiple choice) questions. Problems also present themselves when trying to inquire into controversial or socially disapproved orientations. To illustrate with an absurd example, when inquiring into the extent of some form of racial or religious intolerance, one would not ask of the respondent, "Are you a bigot?" Inasmuch as most intolerant individuals do not so regard themselves ("some of my best friends are ————"), much more subtlety is required.

For example, when inquiring into the political tolerance dimension of their famous five-nation survey, the Almond and Verba team asked the following questions: "Suppose a son or daughter of yours was getting

---

[17] Daniel Lerner (ed.), "Attitude Research in Modernizing Areas: Special Issue," *Public Opinion Quarterly,* Vol. 22, No. 9 (Winter 1958–59), pp. 568–75.

[18] Frey, op. cit., p. 232.

[19] Richard L. Merritt, *Systematic Approaches to Comparative Politics* (Chicago: Rand McNally, 1970), p. 152.

married. How would you feel if he or she married a supporter of (asked of all parties listed in each country) party? Would you be pleased, would you be displeased or would it make no difference?"[20] They further asked respondents to characterize members of parties other than their own in their country. Choices were provided ranging from "intelligent people" through "ignorant and misguided" and all the way to "betrayers of freedom and the country's welfare."[21] These latter choices could be regarded by respondents as objective judgments about others rather than evidence of their own intolerance.

Similarly, when inquiring into the extent of anti-Semitism, the authors of *The Authoritarian Personality* had to allow their respondents to indirectly classify themselves as anti-Semitic. Some typical statements with which respondents were asked to indicate levels of agreement or disagreement are as follows: "To end prejudice against Jews, the first step is for the Jews to try sincerely to get rid of the harmful and irritating faults." "Jewish leaders should encourage Jews to be more inconspicuous, to keep out of the professions and activities already overcrowded with Jews and to keep out of the public notice."[22] There are several things to note about the foregoing statements. First of all, they do not require a conscious admission of overt hostility toward Jews. The respondent may agree with them thinking he is genuinely concerned with alleviating anti-Semitism. When such attitudes as intolerance go against the national creed, they are often repressed below the level of consciousness. Therefore, they can best be elicited by questions regarding the respondent's feelings about the objects of his prejudices, feelings which can be given in the guise of objective judgments. The results of such questions are more likely to be reliable than those of questions about the respondent's perception of the extent of his own prejudices.

THE FIVE NATION STUDY

In the final analysis, the utility of an approach must be judged by the propositions that it generates. The body of literature that utilizes the concept of political culture to explain differences among political systems has grown at a substantial rate in the past decade. Perhaps the most famous of such studies is *The Five Nation Study,* a survey of political orientations of approximately one thousand respondents in each of the following nations: the United States, Great Britain, the Federal Republic of Germany,

---

[20] Gabriel Almond and Sidney Verba (principal investigators), *The Five Nation Study* (Ann Arbor, Michigan: The Inter-University Consortium for Political Research, 1968), p. 61. This is the printout of the questions and raw data that formed the basis for *The Civic Culture,* op. cit.

[21] Ibid., pp. 64–65.

[22] I. W. Adorno, et al., *The Authoritarian Personality* (New York: Norton & Co., 1969), p. 70.

Italy, and Mexico. The principal investigators, Gabriel Almond and Sidney Verba, published a summary and interpretation of the findings of this project entitled *The Civic Culture*. The five nations were selected as representative of democratic political systems at varying degrees of success and potential success. Success may be conceived of as the processing of the issues facing a political system or in terms of the stability of the system. Britain and the United States both epitomize stable and effective democracy; nevertheless, they differ in important cultural and structural characteristics. Prussia, Germany's political ancestry, exemplified stable and effective government that successfully repressed any democratic attributes in their political culture. Italy exemplifies an unsuccessful attempt to adopt democratic institutions to a preindustrial society. Mexico supposedly exemplifies, to the extent any one nation can, non-Western democracies.[23]

The investigators collected data on the following dimensions: patterns of cognition or knowledge, feelings or cathexis, types of partisanship, a sense of one's proper role in the political system, a sense of political competence, the organizational structure of the society, and personal data about the respondents. Each dimension, of course, includes several variables. Under the cognitive dimension, for example, they not only inquired into the extent that knowledge and information about politics exists among the populations; they also inquired into the awareness of the impact of government on the respondents and into the extent to which the respondents held opinions about politics. The cathectic dimension (having to do with feelings) involved, in addition to the amount of pride in the systems, the different objects of pride. As we have seen with respect to the Eastonian distinction between the kinds of support, people may orient themselves to or take pride in their society, their culture, political symbols, the existing pattern and structure of political institutions, or the output of the government (that is, specific policies or the maintenance of economic prosperity). Space does not permit a fully complete listing of all variables considered.

The investigators were attempting to establish a relationship between cultural patterns and system states (more specifically, the various manifestations of successful, stable democracy).[24] Even more concretely, they appear to suggest that a certain cultural pattern is more supportive of stable democracy than alternative patterns. This pattern they have labeled *the civic culture*. They attempt to show, both by logical argument and by empirical data, that this cultural pattern differs in important respects from the widely accepted but mythological model of the culture of a successful democracy, a culture dominated by a rational, activist, or involved citizenry. Like Lipset's article on the requisites of democracy, discussed above, the authors are not entirely clear as to whether the civic culture is a necessary or a sufficient condition for a successful democracy or both. They do not specify

---

[23] Almond and Verba, op. cit., pp. 35–39.
[24] Ibid., pp. 473ff. and pp. 74–75.

the extent to which a nation can deviate from these culture patterns and still maintain a stable democracy. In other words, unless the parameters of the civic culture are specified at some precise tolerance level, one cannot in principle disprove the assertion that such a culture is either a necessary or sufficient determinant of stable democracy.

This is not meant to imply that the authors of *The Civic Culture* failed to establish a rather clear relationship between measurable cultural variables and successful, stable democracy in the small sample of countries surveyed. Clearly, their findings do suggest such a relationship, a relationship that can be further justified on logical grounds. For example, Italy may be said to have the most unstable of the five democracies. This is reflected in the greatest degree of political alienation. This alienation is indicated in the pattern of responses to a variety of questions. The Italians were exceeded only by the Mexicans in absence of an awareness of the present impact of government on their lives and in the lack of information about politics. Italian respondents were the lowest among the five nations with respect to a sense of an obligation to participate in public affairs and with respect to those who would seek cooperation with fellow citizens to influence an "unjust regulation." Moreover, Italians show a far sharper polarization between the political left and right than do the Americans, British, and Germans,[25] and somewhat more than the Mexicans. Italians show by far the lowest amount of pride in their political institutions and the lowest amount of trust in (and political interaction with) their fellow citizens.[26]

It is not difficult to see how these cultural patterns might be *expected* to contribute to political instability on logical grounds. For example, the polarization of Italian partisanship, in part a reflection of the lack of trust in one's fellow man, and (in Professor Spiro's terms) an ideological political style should be expected to impede the compromises necessary to resolve the real issues of a society peacefully.[27] A lack of diffuse support for the political institutions in a political system places greater pressure on that system to maintain a satisfactory level of performance or output. For example, output failure in the United States and Great Britain in the form of the great depression did not result in anywhere near the extent of political extremism and opposition to the regime as it did in Germany. This contributed to the fact that the former two regimes survived the crisis while

---

25 Ibid., p. 90.

26 These data are also supported by Edward Banfield, *The Moral Basis of a Backward Society* (Glencoe, Ill.: The Free Press, 1958), pp. 83–101, and Joseph LaPalombara, "Italy: Fragmentation, Isolation and Alienation," Lucien Pye and Sidney Verba (eds.), *Political Culture and Political Development* (Princeton: Princeton University Press, 1966), pp. 282–329.

27 Robert Alford has persuasively argued that a politics of interests is a much more effective way of processing the *real* issues of a society than a politics based on ideology. From this he infers that a political system is better off with parties based upon socioeconomic class. See his *Party and Society* (Chicago: Random House, 1963), p. 339.

the latter did not. Finally, a belief in the competence or the capacity of the common man to act to protect his interest and a belief in the probability that he will so act is necessary to maintain elite responsiveness, beliefs which were present to the greatest extent in the United States and Great Britain and to a progressively less extent in Germany, Mexico, and Italy. As the authors put it, the ruler's "freedom to act is limited by the fact that there *will* be pounding on the door if he does not act in ways that are responsive." (Italic their's.)[28]

On the other hand, Almond and Verba have shown that this belief in the rational activist model does not correspond to actual behavior, that in actuality politics is of very little importance in the life of the average citizen. Thus, while the perception of citizen activity and influence maintain the necessary limits on the elite's discretion so as to keep them responsive, the actual lower level of citizen activity and influence permit the necessary level of discretion to allow the elites to govern. It is axiomatic that unless the power to resolve the issues arising out of real public problems exists somewhere in a political system, the resulting unresolved issues will create a level of discontent that can undermine the minimal level of legitimacy a system requires for survival or stability.[29]

In the light of the foregoing, it seems perfectly reasonable to infer that there is a connection between the cultural pattern revealed in Almond and Verba's study and stable, successful democracy (although this latter concept is never precisely defined in this study). This inference derives support from other inquiries into the social and cultural bases of democracy. However, other such literature on culture has been largely confined to intuitive impressions rather than extensive, carefully drawn surveys.[30] The role of providing hard data which largely corroborated and in some aspects forced the modification of long and widely held conjectures about those cultural patterns most supportive of stable democracy should in itself qualify the study as a landmark contribution to the discipline.

Unfortunately, the sample of nations surveyed was necessarily small, a necessity resulting from the enormous resources in time and money that survey research requires.[31] However, it is dangerous to infer conclusions about the relationship between cultural patterns and system states from only five nations. Clearly, a wider application of the questionnaire would be useful.[32]

---

[28] Almond and Verba, op. cit., p. 352.

[29] This was a basic thesis of the input-output model of Easton and Deutsch discussed above.

[30] For example, see Alex Inkles, "National Character and Modern Political Systems," in Francis Hsu (ed.), *Psychological Anthropology: Approaches to Culture and Personality* (Homewood: The Dorsey Press, 1961), pp. 172–202.

[31] This project took a team of investigators, with the collaboration of five professional polling organizations, three years to complete at a cost of approximately a quarter of a million dollars.

[32] They demonstrate their awareness of this point. Almond and Verba, op. cit., p. 74.

The comparability of the samples may be questioned to some extent. In actuality, convenience played some role in selecting the samples. The Mexican sample, for instance, was largely confined to urban areas due to the inaccessibility of the isolated rural villages in that country. Since Banfield suggests a distinct cultural difference between northern and southern Italy, it would be useful to know the geographical distribution of that nation's sample.

The cross-national comparability of the totals for each variable in some cases may be said to be compromised by the fact that the samples of the several nations were not standardized with respect to certain relevant variables. It is clear, for instance, that certain of the outcomes will be affected by the educational or income level of the respondents. This is demonstrated by the fact that the authors tried to account for sample differences by breaking down national totals by various levels of these individual characteristics. Thus, some of the observed differences in response patterns between the nations may be attributed to differences in such things as educational opportunities. This is not the same thing as saying the response patterns are a function of some deep-seated cultural predispositions. The authors, by breaking down certain responses by such variables as educational level, income level, and perceived class status, indicate their awareness of this point.[33]

However, the size of the differences between the "civic culture" nations and the less successful democracies were of such a size that these differences could not solely be accounted for by such individual characteristics. When differences between nations in these individual characteristics are subtracted from differences in cultural variables, significant cultural differences remain.

In other words, some of the observed variation must, in the terminology of Przeworski, be attributed to system-level variables rather than to within-system-level variables.[34] As explained in Chapter 6, one of the main tasks of comparative analysis is to distinguish in this way between variation in variables that can be attributed to the properties of individuals and groups within political systems and variations that must be attributed to properties of whole political systems. One attributes such variation to systems themselves when observed relationships between individual or group-level properties do not hold true consistently across different systems.

The rate of nonresponse was not uniform and this could affect the comparability of the results. It ranged from 17 percent in the United States to 41 percent in, surprisingly enough, the United Kingdom. The significance of refusals and unavailable subjects could vary from culture to culture; yet, the effect of this variable (response rate) on the results was not considered.

---

[33] Ibid., chap. 13.

[34] Adam Przeworski and Henry Teune, *The Logic of Comparative Social Inquiry* (New York: John Wiley & Sons, 1970) chaps. 2 and 3.

Although the measuring instrument was pretested around Princeton, New Jersey, in the five nations studied, and in Sweden, we are not informed that these included any inquiry into the reliability and validity of the measuring instrument. We might assume such tests were included but it would be useful to know the results. The *reliability* of a questionnaire refers to the consistency of responses that it elicits. Otherwise put, reliability is a measure of the extent to which the response to any one item on the questionnaire affords one a basis for predicting the responses to the other items on the questionnaire. Operationally, it may be defined as a ratio between total responses and inconsistent responses (1-inconsistent responses/total responses). Reliability can be taken as an indicator of whether any given dimension is being measured. For example, if one is trying to measure alienation and many of the same respondents who answer one question in a way that is supposed to indicate alienation also answer another question in a way that ostensibly indicates the converse of alienation, affect, one might reasonably conclude from the inconsistency of the responses that those two questions do not measure the same thing as previously assumed. Thus, a high level of consistency of responses on a set of questions indicates that these questions do measure some common dimensions.[35]

Reliability does not tell you that this common dimension is the one intended. The question of whether the questionnaire measures the dimension that it is supposed to measure is referred to as the *validity* of the questionnaire. For example, it will be recalled from Chapter 1 that McCloskey devised a scale that was supposed to measure the concept of conservatism. He asked graduate students unaware of the project what they would call a person who agreed with the statements on the questionnaire. When they all answered conservative or some logical equivalents, he assumed that the test was valid, that it really measured conservatism. We will note below that validity is the criterion for one of the major criticisms of the F scale in *The Authoritarian Personality*. There is a serious question as to whether the scale measures authoritarianism in general. It may measure a particular type of authoritarianism, facism, or it may measure a tendency for persons of low status to agree with what the high-status interviewer says.

An error in validity may be referred to as a *constant error* in that such errors, being based on incorrect assumptions about the relationship between the measuring instrument and the essential quality being measured, do not vary from item to item. Such errors result from the inescapable fact that measures of dispositional characteristics are indirect. It is not possible to

---

[35] Even if the questions do measure a common dimension, perfect consistency is not to be expected because of the human element. Such unavoidable chance occurrences as the misreading of items on the measuring instrument will lead to some chance variation. An excellent discussion of reliability and such "variable errors" may be found in G. C. Helmsteader, *Principles of Psychological Measurement* (New York: Appleton-Century-Crofts, 1964), pp. 37–38 and chap. 3.

observe the state of the nerve endings in a subject's brain. Therefore, one must make certain assumptions about how these mental dispositions will manifest themselves in a pattern of responses to certain questions. Such assumptions may, of course, be mistaken.

Validity is a difficult criterion to test. A common means of testing the validity of a measurement is to observe the extent that the results of the measurement are correlated with some variable that is independent of the test but is logically related to the essential characteristic the test is supposed to measure. For example, it would be interesting to note the extent to which those who score high on the conservatism scale tend to support right-wing political parties. In the case of *The Five Nation Study,* however, it is often not clear what precisely defined behavior patterns would be an expected result of the dispositional qualities that are the object of inquiry. Just exactly how should we expect an alienated person or an intense partisan to act that would distinguish people who possess such orientations from those who do not?

The reliability and validity of questionnaires has not been adequately dealt with in many such measuring instruments designed for use exclusively in the United States, not to mention the more difficult problem of question- naires designed for cross-cultural application.[36] The need for such cross- culturally valid and reliable instruments is one of the most pressing prior- ities of cross-national research. Such valid and reliable questionnaires can best be obtained by the process of repeated application and revision of the questionnaire in as wide a variety of cultural, political, and economic con- texts as practical. Such a process often entails an expenditure of money and time that proves to be prohibitive.

Almond and Verba clearly indicate their awareness of the problems which are inherent in any cross-national survey research project.[37] Problems of the cultural relativism of meaning, of the comparability of samples and of the characteristics used as criteria to stratify samples, as well as the problem of unique events in one of the nations (such as a national election or a political crisis) typify the difficulties inherent in cross-national re- search. Such problems could raise serious doubts about the equivalence of the results. The problem of the cultural relativism of meaning applies to the framing of the questionnaire, to its translation into the several languages used, and to the interpretation of the results of the survey.

These problems differ in degree from problems of national surveys. Of course, these problems assume greater importance in *cross*-national survey work as the extent of the cultural differences increases. A study among members of the older Commonwealth would raise such problems to a far less extent than would a study of the United States and Nigeria.

---

[36] See John P. Johnson, Jerrold G. Rusk, and Kendra P. Head, *Measures of Political Attitudes* (Ann Arbor, Mich.: I.S.R., 1968).

[37] Almond and Verba, op. cit., pp. 57–67.

Of course, the important question is not whether the authors were aware of these problems but rather of what was done to mitigate the effect of these problems. The authors tried to cope with the problem of equivalence of meaning in the framing of the questionnaire in the several languages in the following manner. Bilingual people translated the questions from English into the appropriate language. Other bilinguals, unfamiliar with the original English version, translated the questions back to English. This process was repeated a number of times.[38] Such a process only solves the linguistic problem.

Despite such efforts, several problems of cross-cultural equivalence remain. Some of these, such as the comparability of the samples, have already been discussed. Despite the fact that the authors dismiss the effect of unique events on the responses as unimportant,[39] the distinct possibility of such effects remains, especially with respect to such variables as the level of political awareness, interest, and participation.

Although one can admire the imagination and creativity demonstrated by the authors in drawing their conclusions, conclusions that appear to be supported by the data, one should bear in mind the fact that the inferences of the authors do not *necessarily* follow from the data nor are their generalizations the only possible way to account for the data obtained in the study. These methodological inelegancies detract from an otherwise landmark study. Although it seems undeniable that the authors have demonstrated the strong probability that some cultural patterns are more supportive of stable democracy than others, one might wish that the authors had been in a position to cope with the problems inherent in cross-national survey research more effectively.

A work that is among the first in its field of endeavor (in this case, cross-national survey research) always appears to be somewhat more subject to criticism than later efforts that have the opportunity to learn from the imperfections of the earlier works. There are, at present, several cross-cultural survey projects in progress.[40] One can hope that subsequent survey projects will reveal progress in the methodological sophistication of the invaluable cross-national survey technique.

POLITICAL CULTURE AND POLITICAL DEVELOPMENT

Not all studies utilizing the concept of political culture are based on the technique of extensive and rigorous surveys of carefully drawn samples.

---

[38] Ibid., pp. 60–61n.

[39] Ibid., pp. 59–60n. There were impending elections in the U.S.A. and Britain at the time of interviewing, while an election had occurred in Mexico just prior to the interviewing. There was a crisis over fishing rights between Mexico and Guatamala at that time.

[40] For example, Phillip Jacob and Henry Teune are surveying local officials in Poland, Yugoslavia, India, and the United States. Sidney Verba is engaged in directing an attitudinal survey in Brazil, Nigeria, and India.

Some work appears to be the result of an unsystematically acquired familiarity with the political system in question, supported by an unspecified number of rather unstructured interviews. Lucien Pye's landmark study of the effect of the Burmese culture on nation building in that country falls into that category.[41] This is not intended to deprecate the potential value of such a study, particularly when the subject matter being researched is still in the exploratory stage. The potential contribution of such efforts rely much more heavily on the fertile and creative imaginations of their authors. However, the generalizations offered by such imaginative research ought to be treated as tentative hypotheses to guide further rigorous empirical inquiry rather than as relatively established conclusions. Thus, it is of the utmost importance that the propositions offered by such research be framed in such a way that they are potentially falsifiable.

Pye's study attempts to demonstrate that Burma's difficulties in nation building may be, at least partially, due to certain personality characteristics that are widely found both among Burmese elites and the Burmese masses. More specifically, Pye relies on the psychological theorizing of Erik Erikson, who modifies the Freudian theories of sexual repression as the basic human motivating force with a concept of ego identity, to suggest that leaders must have succeeded in their own quest for identity in order to transmit to the people a collective sense of identity.[42] The Burmese leaders have not solved their identity crisis, due to patterns of Burmese child rearing and the particular nature of the Burmese colonial experience. The imposition of selected forms of modernity by the British upon the deep-seated traditionalism of the Burmese culture are alleged to have caused what Riggs called *formalism*.[43] That is, the formal structures of a modern political system exist, but the roles of these structures are not filled by their Burmese incumbents in the way for which the structures were intended by their Western creators. This formalism, this non-Western way in which essentially Western roles are viewed and filled by their Burmese incumbents, is traced by Pye to certain characteristics of the Burmese culture, that is, modal Burmese personality patterns. For example, Burmese "political parties operate on the basis that the opposition exists only to be crushed and whichever party gets into power sets about this task as systematically as it can."[44] Yet, the operation of a competitive party system requires an acceptance of

---

[41] Lucien Pye, *Politics, Personality and Nation Building: Burma's Search for Identity* (New Haven: Yale University Press, 1962).

[42] See Ibid., p. 52n., for an acknowledgement of this reliance on Erikson.

[43] Fred Riggs, *Administration in Developing Countries, The Theory of the Prismatic Society* (Boston: Houghton-Mifflin Co., 1964). The concept of formalism and the question of whether formalism, used in this sense, is unique to non-Western political systems will be discussed at some length in Chapter 12 with respect to the problem of political development.

[44] Pye, op. cit., p. 141, quoted from a Rangoon Newspaper, *The Nation* (August 31, 1958).

the ligitimacy of political opposition. This lack of tolerance is traced by Pye to the unpredictable emotional basis of the Burmese mother's relationship to her child and, second, to the manner in which the acculturation process appears to have threatened the modernizing Burman's sense of identity.[45] The former phenomenon refers to the alleged tendency of Burmese mothers to vacillate between extreme warmth and cold disinterest in her attitudes toward her child, attitudes apparently unrelated to the child's behavior and hence beyond his control. This is said to lead to a more diffuse expectation of aggressive and unpredictable behavior on the part of the generalized other. This results in turn in a lack of that trust in one's fellow man that is necessary for the viable operation of a competitive political system. In a later chapter, Pye, relying on several case studies of individual politicians, attempts to show that the Burmese politicians have a confused conception of the role of a politician in a democratic society, a conception that seems to be "grossly inappropriate for the workaday processes of a democratic system."[46] The Burmese conception of the politician's role, derived from their socialization processes and the colonial experience with its inadequate training of political leaders, is an idealized one epitomized by charismatic leaders such as Julius Caesar, Lenin, or Abraham Lincoln. They consider it a failure or demeaning to have to work out compromises on day-to-day issues on the basis of competing demands which is, of course, precisely what responsible politicians do.

Pye's basic thesis appears to be that a lack of a sense of personal identity on the part of the political leaders and a lack of a sense of collective identity (*system affect* in the lexicon of Almond and Verba) on the part of the masses of any political system impedes the political development (used here interchangeably with *nation building*) of that system. Although Pye is suitably cautious about generalizing from the Burmese experience alone, he seems to further suggest that there are characteristics inherent in the non-Western political process that make such identity crises more probable in such transitional political systems than in the Western industrialized systems.

It is this attempt to relate an implied modality of personality characteristics to macro-level outcomes that distinguishes Pye from the personality theorists discussed in the following chapter. This putative connection between micro and macro data constitutes the creative contribution of such works as the one presently described. Clearly, such heuristic linkages between the macro and micro levels of analysis is necessary if political psychology is to have major explanatory relevance.

Professor Pye is much more of an imaginative and creative theorist (in the speculative sense of that term) than a critical positivist in his methodo-

---

45 Ibid., p. 138.
46 Ibid., p. 248.

logical orientation. Consequently, he does not demonstrate a concern for the development of concepts that are precisely enough defined so as to be susceptible of being operationalized, let alone a concern for the specification of precise empirical indicators for such concepts. The result is that the evidence adduced to support his assertions takes on the character of illustrations rather than proof (even in the negative sense of failure to falsify). For example, there is no attempt to consider the extent to which the politicians and administrators interviewed are representative of the universe to which they refer.

In addition, Pye assertively constructs causal explanations for tendencies he ascribes to the Burmese. (It should be noted that he never specifies the extent of these tendencies or offers any systematic evidence for their existence. How many cases constitute such a tendency?) However, it is often the case that Pye's "explanations" are only one of several possible ways of accounting for the observed tendencies. An example of such an explanation is the assertion, quoted above, of a causal relationship between the Burmese lack of interpersonal trust, on the one hand, and the inconsistent feelings of Burmese mothers toward their offspring and the Burmese identity crisis, on the other.

It follows from the discussion of scientific explanation in Chapter 2 that in order for Pye's thesis to explain the relative success or lack thereof in nation building in any given system, a precise operational definition would have to be provided for successful nation building (or political development), and a precise set of observable indicators would have to be specified for the realization of ego identity or its converse concept, identity crisis. As Chapter 12 below clearly indicates, there remains a great deal of dissensus within the discipline as to the variables included in the concept of political development, not to mention precise indicators. This in itself would not necessarily be a serious objection if Pye had specified a set of precise empirical indicators for successful nation building for the purposes of this study. One cannot justifiably accuse Pye of failure in this regard for it cannot be said that he seriously tried to operationalize the concept of nation building.

Pye does suggest a rather simplistic dichotomous classification of political systems into Western and non-Western. In the first place, however, the construction of a model of the non-Western political process, a static concept, is not equivalent to a definition of political development, which is a dynamic concept. In the second place, Pye's variables are not defined in terms of empirical indicators. It is not clear that some of them are capable of being so defined. Pye's model of the non-Western political process will be referred to in more detail with regard to the discussion of political development in Chapter 12.

Thus, while Pye is saying that certain characteristics of the Burmese culture impede the process of nation building, it is not possible to know what the state of Burmese political system would be if those cultural characteristics were not present. What different set or observations would we encounter if we went to another non-Western system with different cultural characteristics? Moreover, in the absence of a more precise set of indicators for such concepts as identity crisis, it is impossible to state conclusively that the cultural characteristics in question are not present.

The significance of the foregoing critique is that the book neither explains any set of observations that constitute a system state nor enables one to predict such a pattern of observations about system states from empirical data about the culture. Explanation is used here in the sense, discussed in Chapter 2, of answering the question of why one particular set of observations is encountered rather than any other possible observations. Explanation in this sense requires empirically refutable propositions, a commodity not supplied by Pye's study of Burma.

This is not to disparge the ingenuity involved in advancing the suggestion that the character of political development in any given country is to a considerable extent a function of cultural variables in that country or to deny that Pye has amassed a certain amount of data to support his hypothesis of such a relationship. Nevertheless, the suggestion of interesting but untestable relationships between imprecisely defined concepts does not contribute to the goal of explanation unless such concepts can be operationalized. The presentation of supporting data does not in itself constitute empirical testing. The acknowledged contribution of Pye in suggesting that a link between personality and nation building exists and, in a general sense, what the nature of that relationship is must be distinguished from the direct explanatory power of this one particular study.

This book by Pye typifies tendencies among the pioneers on the Comparative Politics Committee of the Social Science Research Council. These pioneers made an undeniable landmark contribution in pointing out the inadequacies of the traditional modes of analysis and in introducing three major methodological improvements in the discipline of comparative politics. These improvements consist of the attempt to be genuinely comparative, to generalize on a cross-national basis; the attempt to analyze a greater variety of political systems; and the attempt to introduce a greater variety of relevant variables into their analyses. It has already been shown how such steps are necessary for the goal of building a science of politics. The book under consideration exemplifies these praiseworthy tendencies. It considers a non-Western system, it attempts to generalize beyond Burma to a class of political systems, and, perhaps most significantly, it was a pioneer in the consideration of cultural variables, variables heretofore excluded from traditional analyses. Such cultural variables, being a significant determinant of many political phenomena, are essential for sound political explanation. Yet, like his colleagues on the Social Science Research Council, Pye's epistemological style does not strictly conform to the critical positivism that characterize the modern science these scholars seem to regard as their ideal.

POLITICAL SOCIALIZATION

The increased attention to political culture has led to the study of how the political culture is disseminated. *Political socialization* is simply the name given to this process of disseminating a political culture. It is the study of how individuals acquire their political predispositions.

Dissemination can refer to the transmission of the unaltered political culture from one generation to the next, to the alteration of the culture in the process of transmitting it either between generations or within a generation, and, finally, to the creation of a political culture where one had not, up to that point, existed.[47] This last manifestation of disseminating a political culture would primarily refer to the attempt to create a new political entity where an integrated cultural base for such a political entity was lacking. The imposition of the nation state of Nigeria onto the fragmented tribal social base of what once was the Gold Coast of Africa constitutes a typical example of the way in which the creation of a new nation state can give rise to the necessity of creating a new national political culture to support it. The attempt to make the political culture of the Federal Republic of Germany more hospitable to the democratic institutions that the Allies imposed on it constitutes an example of the attempt to change or alter the culture.[48]

The literature on socialization may conveniently be divided into three main groupings: the agents of socialization, the extent to which discontinuities exist in the socialization process, and the way in which political orientations are acquired. They will be discussed briefly in this order.

Among the major objects of the study of political socialization are its agents, the means by which the dissemination of a culture is effected. This concern is with how the society performs the function of teaching the political orientations (rather than a concern for how such orientations are learned). This is not unrelated to the Parsonian function of pattern maintenance discussed in Chapter 7 above. Peter Merkl suggests that this pattern maintenance aspect of the socialization process may be dysfunctional for the viability of the system if the existing patterns into which succeeding generations are socialized are inadequate to handle the new challenges that such succeeding generations must often face.[49]

---

47 Richard E. Dawson and Kenneth Prewitt, *Political Socialization* (Boston: Little, Brown & Co., 1969), pp. 27–36. David Easton and Jack Dennis narrow the meaning of the term to the transmission of "political orientations . . . from generation to generation," the first of the three ways listed in which a culture may be disseminated. See Easton and Dennis, "The Child's Image of Government" in Roberta S. Sigel (ed.), *Learning About Politics* (New York: Random House; 1970), p. 31.

48 See Sidney Verba, "Germany, The Remaking of a Political Culture," in Pye and Verba, op. cit., pp. 130–70.

Considerable attention is given in the literature to the relative importance of the various agents of socialization: the family, the peer group, the system of formal education, and primary and secondary groups. It is widely asserted, for example, that the family is the most important factor in determining the basic political dispositions of most individuals. The empirical evidence for this consists of a high statistical association between the dispositions of individuals and the corresponding dispositions of their respective parents. The logical support for this consists of the evidence, widely accepted among psychologists and documented by political scientists, that basic loyalties and attachments are formed at an early age, loyalties that are generally maintained with amazing tenacity.[50] Inasmuch as the family dominates the attention and fulfills the essential needs of the child in these early years, its predominant influence on the formation of the child's political orientations may be quite justifiably inferred.

Influence, like causation, cannot be observed or measured directly. However, James Davies, for example, suggests that the positive appraisal of political authority on the part of most young American children is a function of the benevolent, nonauthoritarian behavior of most American fathers.[51] There is no way to test this generalization as stated, despite the fact that it "makes sense" on a logical level. Clearly, the relative, if not the absolute, strength of the influence of the family on political orientations could most easily be determined if the direction of the family influence (assuming that this could be unambiguously determined) were contradicted by the direction of other socializing agents. In other words, if the school, peer groups, etc., could objectively be said to act to impart a different set of orientations than those taught by the family, the strength of family influence relative to such other agents of socialization could in principle be assessed. Such a situation would constitute a discontinuity in the socialization process, a phenomenon discussed below.

Similarly, Hyman suggests that the technique of comparing the expected value of the correlation between parental and offspring orientations, if no influence existed, with the observed value would afford a basis for the inference of influence if the influence of other agents could be estimated. It is usually impossible to estimate that influence of other agents, however.[52]

---

49 Merkl, op. cit., p. 102.

50 See, for instance, J. Piaget and Anne Marie Weil, "The Development in Children of the Idea of the Homeland and of Relations with Other Countries," in Roberta S. Sigel (ed.) *Learning About Politics* (New York: Random House, 1970), pp. 18–30, and Easton and Dennis, loc. cit. See also David Easton and Robert D. Hess, "The Child's Political World," *Midwest Journal of Political Science,* Vol. 6 (August 1962), pp. 229–46 for the finding that the process of politicization begins around the age of three.

51 James R. Davies, "The Family's Role in Political Socialization," in Sigel, op. cit., p. 112.

52 Herbert H. Hyman, *Political Socialization* (New York: The Free Press, 1969), p. 52. When first issued in 1954 this study constituted the first systematic treatise of political socialization; hence, it has attained the status of something of a standard in the field.

Occasionally, the effect of certain socializing agents on the political process or on the social system appears to be obvious from a thorough examination of the operation of that agent. It seems clear, for instance, that the British educational system acts as a powerful force for the perpetuation of the relatively rigid socio-economic, class-based social stratification system. In the British educational system, all pupils at the age of 11 or 12 are given a battery of tests similar to our intelligence tests. Those who pass, about 20 percent, go to the state-supported "grammar" schools or, if they are wealthy, to the private boarding schools known paradoxically as "public schools" for university preparatory training. All those who fail the *11-plus exams* or who cannot afford the high costs of the public schools are channeled into trade school preparation in the secondary modern schools. Not only is it widely recognized that the students of the secondary modern schools have failed, but these pupils, by virtue of being barred from any plausible shot at university training, are denied any reasonable chance to enter the nation's elite.[53]

Learning theory offers a good deal of evidence that the kind of verbal and symbol manipulation skills required for success on the 11-plus exams is, to a large extent, transmitted from the family environment in the preschool years. When one is denied the environment best suited for the acquisition of these skills by birth, an environment largely confined to middle- and upper-class households, it may not be possible to catch up by age 11. Catching up later, however, is too late. It is an empirical fact that there is an exceedingly high contingency relationship between passing the exam and socio-economic class. Clearly, the inference that this mechanism for "tracking" students in the British educational system is a force for the perpetuation of the existing stratification system appears to be a justifiable one.

Another example of literature which infers the effect of a socializing agent from its operation or its teaching is the substantial body of literature which focuses on the effect of institutional religion. The emphasis here is to examine the relationship between the precepts or ideology taught by the church and the inferred behavioral consequences of such teaching. Of course, the classical literature in this regard is the Tawney-Weber thesis about the connection between the Protestant ethic and the rise of capitalism.[54] More recently, there has been attention given to the socializing role of the Catholic Church in Europe with its propensity to attempt to organize the life of its adherents on an inclusive basis. This means that the Church

---

[53] See Richard Rose, *Politics in England* (Boston: Little, Brown & Co., 1964), pp. 68–69, for a discussion of this point.

[54] R. H. Tawney, *Religion and the Rise of Capitalism* (New York: Harcourt, Brace and Co., 1936). See also Max Weber, "The Protestant Sects and the Spirit of Capitalism," in H. H. Gerth and C. Wright Mills (eds.), *From Max Weber: Essays in Sociology* (New York: Oxford Galaxy Books, 1958), pp. 302–23.

attempts to organize, not only the religious aspect of the lives of its adherents, but as many other aspects as possible. Thus, a French or Belgian Catholic may belong to a Catholic labor union, attend a Catholic school, belong to Catholic lodges, women's clubs, etc. Clearly, any institution which controls the lives of its adherents to this extent may be expected to have a powerful effect on their political and social orientations. Jesse R. Pitts, for example, infers that the formalism of the French political culture (the concern with rigid hierarchy and precise and exhaustive rules governing all activity) is a product of the "doctrinal hierarchical" tendencies in French Catholicism.[55] It should be stressed again, however, that the assertion of an influence of any socializing agent on specified behavioral outcomes is a causal *inference*. The discussion of causation in Chapter 2 attempted to demonstrate that causation and, hence, influence must be logically inferred on the basis of an observed contingency relationship and never *necessarily* follows from the data.

Another major variable which is frequently dealt with by the literature on the concept of socialization is the extent to which discontinuities exist in the socialization process. That is, the social and political orientations which are disseminated to a society at one time or place may be inconsistent with the corresponding orientations disseminated to that same society at another time and place. The phenomenon of discontinuity in the socialization process may be manifested in several ways. For one thing, some agents of socialization may act to inculcate social or political orientations inconsistent with the orientations inculcated by other agents. For example, if highly deferential or submissive authority patterns were taught in the predominant family patterns of a society while more egalitarian relationships were inculcated by the secondary associations of that society, this would exemplify one type of discontinuity. Similarly, discontinuity may be said to exist if the orientations or authority patterns taught by various socializing agents of a political system are not congruent with the orientations expected or presumed by the institutional arrangements of the whole political system. This type of discontinuity would be best exemplified by an attempt to impose a highly egalitarian set of political institutions on a culture in which deferential or submissive authority patterns are predominantly taught. This type of discontinuity provides the basis for Eckstein's "Theory of Stable Democracy,"[56] which suggests that such stability is a function of the congruence of authority patterns between the political institutions and the political culture. If, as in Weimar Germany, the political institutions are

---

[55] Jesse R. Pitts, "Change in Bourgeoise France," in Stanley Hoffman, et al., *In Search of France* (New York: Harper Torchbooks, 1965), pp. 238–39.

[56] Harry Eckstein, "A Theory of Stable Democracy," Research Monograph No. 10, Center for International Studies, Princeton University, 1961, reprinted as an appendix to Eckstein, *Division and Cohesion in Democracy* (Princeton: Princeton University Press, 1966), pp. 225–87.

highly egalitarian,[57] while the families, schools, etc., teach obedience, subordination, orderliness, and diligence,[58] the individual is forced to shift his conception of his role when he moves from a social sphere to the political sphere. The necessity of shifting from a role orientation of submission in one's social and professional life to one of assertive egalitarianism based upon a sense of personal competence in one's political life can produce a serious strain arising out of the incompatibility of these role orientations. Eckstein suggests that such incongruencies lie at the root of the nonviability of such systems.[59]

The so-called generation gap in the United States is a current manifestation of another recurrent problem in socialization discontinuities. The social and political circumstances under which one reaches political maturity can have a persisting impact on one's political orientations. A case in point would be the surprise of a number of over-40 liberals who discover the fact that many young leftists consider World War II to be "ancient history" or "irrelevant." Thus, the elders who came of age at the time of Hitler's holocaust are used to regarding the Jews as underdogs while their offspring, coming of age in the face of successive Israeli victories, consider the Jews to be imperialistic oppressors. Often the distinctions between the orientations of different generations are on less specific but much more basic issues. Merkl has shown that the prewar and postwar generations in Germany differ fundamentally on the issue of love for the fatherland and commitment to ideological causes,[60] a difference arising out of the prewar euphoric optimism conditioned by the failure of Weimar and the promises of Hitler, on the one hand, and the postwar disillusionment conditioned by their nation's crushing defeat, on the other.

Discontinuities may exist between classes. Bourgeois parents may conceivably impart a pattern of orientations quite different from the orientations imparted by working-class parents. Where questions of socialization along socio-economic class lines are concerned, the influence of one's occupational surroundings becomes important. Frequently, for instance, the contacts made while working in West European factories can lead to an increasing involvement in socialist political activities. Similarly, the rare offspring of British working-class parents who overcome all the obstacles

[57] The lack of discretionary authority in any executive role, together with the exaggerated impact of the weakest groups in the political spectrum, was encouraged by the highly proportional electoral system. There was no elite in the Weimar system that could take positive action that was opposed by any significant group that was affected by such action. It was in this sense that the Weimar republic is called egalitarian.

[58] Lewis G. Edinger, *Politics in Germany* (Boston: Little, Brown & Co., 1968), p. 132.

[59] Eckstein, op. cit., pp. 237–39, suggests an important modification of his thesis. The necessity of role congruence becomes greater as the agent involved is closer to the government itself in terms of generality (as with large secondary groups) and less as the agent in question is closer to the individual (as with the family).

[60] Merkl, op. cit., pp. 109–10.

and gain admission to the higher civil service tend to take on the esprit de corps and the political orientations of their professional peers of upper-middle and aristocratic class origins.

A third major focus of the literature on political socialization is how political orientations are acquired. The first object of the socialization literature, the agents of socialization, looks at the process from the point of view of how political orientations are taught. Here the concern is with how they are learned. There is a body of research, for instance, dealing with the nature of the political orientations acquired by children at various defined stages of their development.[61] It can readily be seen from a cursory glance at this literature that most of it is based upon data drawn exclusively from the United States. While there is no logical reason to believe that the basic principles discovered or supported by this research would not apply to most industrial democracies, the wider application of these principles has, by and large, yet to be empirically demonstrated. Moreover, there are reasons to suspect that learning patterns in non-Western or authoritarian systems might differ from Western nations in some respects. Yet, data on the acquisition of political orientations in such systems is both woefully lacking and difficult to obtain.

The research in this area suggests that stable political loyalties are acquired at a young age. Easton and Hess suggest that attachment to the basic political community takes place in the preschool years, and attachment to political parties occurs early in the elementary school period.[62] The attachments formed at these early stages in a child's development are diffuse attachments to labels. That is, they are devoid of any issue content. Children identify with a political party but they cannot tell you why.[63] The early attachments tend to be too personal, immediate, and concrete. The distinction between country and head of state is not clearly made. The ability to make such distinctions and to conceptualize issues begins to develop in the adolescent period.

Clearly, such data can be accurately obtained by appropriate questionnaires administered to carefully drawn samples of children. The question of the utility of such data can only be answered by efforts to relate it to other data (or empirical concepts) to explain and predict relevant political events.

---

[61] It is impossible to adequately summarize this literature. A few illustrative examples might include Easton and Dennis, loc. cit.; Mary Goodman, "Emergent Citizenship: A Study of Relevant Values in Four Year Olds," in Sigel, op. cit., pp. 15–17; Robert D. Hess and Judith Torney, *The Development of Political Attitudes in Children* (Chicago: Aldine Publishing Co., 1967); Fred I. Greenstein, "The Benevolent Leader: Children's Images of Political Authority," *The American Political Science Review,* Vol. 54, (December 1960), pp. 934–43; and Pye, op. cit.

[62] David Easton and Robert D. Hess, "The Child's Political World," *Midwest Journal of Political Science,* VI, No. 2 (May, 1962), pp. 238–45. See also Paiget and Weil, op. cit.

[63] Hyman, op. cit., p. 35.

It seems that research in the area of political socialization is still in its infancy. There is very little attempt to suggest how various patterns of socialization can be used to explain differences in the states of political systems. The literature rather consists largely of a number of rather discrete studies. There have been relatively few attempts to synthesize the data, let alone to theorize about the concept.[64] Clearly, this is the direction that research in the field of socialization must soon take if it is to have relevance to the goals of comparative political analysis.

CONCLUSIONS

While the attempt to characterize whole political systems on the basis of the mental dispositions of their inhabitants is not a new activity in comparative analysis, the attempt to support such assertions about cultural characteristics with systematically collected empirical data is a post–World War II phenomenon. Despite the almost prohibitive costs and staggering practical problems of establishing equivalence in cross-cultural survey research, the amount and sophistication of this form of activity seems to be increasing. The initial findings suggest that there is reason for optimism about the prospects of eventually relating such cultural characteristics to systemic or macro characteristics in testable empirical generalizations. The extent to which a whole system may be characterized on the basis of accumulated individual dispositional traits appears to be subject to measurement. The concept of modality provides a conceptual basis for assigning individual characteristics to a whole system. The problems of the measurement of individual dispositional characteristics are explored in more detail in the following chapter.

---

[64] Dawson and Prewitt, op. cit., make the most systematic attempt at a synthesis of the field of socialization.

Micro Analysis—Political Psychology

While political culture and political socialization refer to modal characteristics of whole systems and, in this sense, have macro-analytical as well as micro-analytical implications, political psychology is strictly micro-analytical. Political psychology refers to data and generalizations about individuals. Thus, political psychology does not refer to an attempt to characterize whole systems on the basis of the personality characteristics, nor does it imply explanations of macro-level political outcomes using these personality characteristics as explicans (premises). It is this attempt to relate micro-analytical data to macro or whole-system outcomes that distinguishes work in political culture, such as the work of Pye and of Almond and Verba, described in the previous chapter, from political psychology.

Political psychology does not necessarily imply an inquiry into the extent to which any given personality types or dispositional characteristics are widespread or modal in any given system. It would seem to follow, therefore, that the conclusions of political psychology are incapable of explaining system states or other macro-level outcomes unless such conclusions about individual dispositions are accumulated into propositions about system-level, modal cultural characteristics. Yet, sound research in political psychology should be able to provide a basis upon which propositions about political culture can be constructed.

Related to the concept of culture, as commonly used in comparative political analysis, is the concept of personality type as developed by the prominent social psychologists. Such research in the field of social psychology has been based on relatively sound empirical methods as will be shown below; consequently, it appears to offer some promise of a contribution to political explanation.

Some aspects of psychology in general and social psychology in particular appear to be more promising for explanation in political science than other aspects. One must distinguish the general personality theorists, who try to posit the basic human motivations and their causes, from that aspect of social psychology that has concerned itself with documenting and measuring personality types. A *personality type* may be defined as a complex of interrelated and mutually reinforcing attitudes and beliefs. In this sense, personality type is a concept referring to individuals that consists of many of the same variables as the concept of culture. Thus, modal personality types are one of the major components of the concept of political culture.

PERSONALITY THEORISTS

The former aspect of psychology, concerned with basic human motivations and their causes, is very poorly developed by the standards of scientific methodology. For this reason, indiscriminant borrowing of such "theory" by political science is unlikely to contribute to the goal of building a science of politics. The preceding chapter has already provided an example of this danger in Lucien Pye's heavy reliance on the theories of Erik H. Erikson in *Politics, Personality and Nation Building.*

This aspect of psychology will henceforth be referred to as *personality theory.* The aspect of psychology concerned with empirically documenting and describing complexes of socially relevant attitudes and beliefs will be called *social psychology.* For the sake of clarity, this somewhat artificial distinction will be rigidly adhered to despite the fact that some personality theorists are sometimes also called social psychologists.[1]

The personality theorists—Freudians, neo-Freudians, field theorists, Gestalt psychologists, etc.—do produce bodies of data which support their theory. It should be clear to anyone that has read the discussions of testability in Chapter 3 that there is a distinction between presenting illustrative facts and rigorously testing a theory.

This distinction is based upon two points. The first point is that it is one thing to say a theory can account for a set of facts, and it is quite another thing to say that no other theory, logically incompatible with the first, can also account for those facts. The personality theorists succeed with respect to the former task and fail with respect to the latter. The very proliferation of competing and incompatible personality theories is evidence of this. The second point is that the presentation of data to support a theory does not constitute a test of that theory unless it can be demonstrated that such data is representative of all the data and potential data to which the theory

---

[1] For example, see Calvin S. Hall and Gardner Lindzey, *Theories of Personality,* 2d ed. (New York: John Wiley & Sons, 1970), chap. 4. Hall and Lindzey so label Adler, Fromm, Horney, and Sullivan because the basic human motivations which they posit are said to be socially determined. Their work is as speculative as that of Freud, however. Incidentally, the Hall and Lindzey volume provides an excellent introductory survey of personality for the nonspecialist.

refers. Thus, the researcher or theorist must make a genuine effort to account for all relevant data or a representative sample of it, rather than to seek out data that supports the theory in question.

It would be impossible for the personality theorists to systematically account for relevant data because their concepts are so imprecisely defined that it is not possible to specify the universe of data to which these theories refer. In other words, it is not possible to specify all of the precise behavioral consequences that can be deduced from these vaguely articulated theories. To put the matter in an oversimplified form, a different set of observable consequences does not necessarily follow from Freudian theory, which is based upon the axiom that repressed sexual desire is at the root of human behavior, than those consequences that *must* logically follow from the Adlerian theory, which posits that the basic human motivation is primarily derived from social urges.[2] Adler, familiar with the same evidence available to Freud, could produce a theory of personality totally incompatible with Freud's, a theory in which consciousness becomes the center of the personality structure (as opposed to the Freudian assumption that behavior is primarily the product of unconscious urges) and a theory in which the concept of *the creative self* replaces sexual satisfaction as the basic human drive.

Much the same could be said about the incompatibility of most of the other so-called personality theories. It is beyond the scope of this volume to undertake a systematic survey of such theories.[3] It is only necessary to make the point that, due to the absence of empirical referents to their concepts, such theories are of little use to political scientists trying to produce scientific explanations of observable political phenomena. One cannot, of course, dismiss thinkers such as Freud, Adler, Erikson, Horney, and Sullivan as totally irrelevant. For example, they called attention to phenomena, such as the role of the subconscious and irrational determinants of human behavior, which, given the possibility of more empirically adequate conceptualization, may have important heuristic or suggestive value for future research.

MEASURING PERSONALITY TYPES AND PERSONALITY THEORY—SOME DISTINCTIONS

The aforementioned body of psychological literature discusses personality in terms of an inquiry into the basic causes of human behavior. It has

---

[2] This refers to the writings of Alfred Adler, especially *The Practice and Theory of Individual Psychology* (New York: Harcourt, Brace & World, 1927).

[3] A discussion, adequate for the purposes of most political scientists, of the content of most personality theory and its shortcomings from the point of view of scientific methodology may be found in Eugene Meehan, *Contemporary Political Thought, A Critical Study* (Homewood, Ill.: The Dorsey Press, 1967), chap. 4.

been shown that whether these theorists posit these basic drives as internally determined (Freud, Jung, etc.), socially determined (Adler, Horney, etc.), or a combination of both (Erikson, Fromm), there has been a basic failure to specify what have been called rules of correspondence, that is, the rules that specify the relationship between the concepts utilized in their causal generalizations and raw observable data.

On the other hand, a body of psychological literature exists that attempts to delineate personality types in terms of precise indicators. As contrasted with the aforementioned body of psychological literature, this literature is essentially descriptive rather than causal in its purpose. The writings of Harold Lasswell attempting to analyze a power-wielding personality type would fall in between these two types of social psychological research. Lasswell suggests that there is a personality type that both enjoys and is skilled at using power. He further suggests, with illustrative evidence, that such a personality type is caused by a severe blow to the ego. Power is thus a compensation for low estimates of the self. However, the *deprivation must not be too severe* so as to overwhelm the individual. This qualification becomes a hypothesis-saving device. After all, how overwhelming, in terms of observable indicators is "too overwhelming"? Clearly, Lasswell's attempt to posit the causes of a power-wielding personality is interesting but speculative and his propositions untestable.[4]

The problem of specifying behavioral indicators for basic human predispositions is an enormous one, a problem the descriptive typologies are able to avoid. The problem is essentially this. The basic human drives are concepts that are utilized to explain behavior. If behavior also constitutes the indicators for the existence of such drives, a great danger of a tautology exists. Fred Greenstein claims that such generalizations only become tautological when the behavior used to define the personality characteristics is the same behavior that the concept of personality is used to explain.[5] Actually, what we are left with in such a situation is a pattern of association between two different patterns of behavior, and the concept of personality that constitutes the theoretical explicans rests on a very tenuous inference, an inference upon which reasonable and equally expert scholars in the discipline widely disagree. Except for the contribution, such as it is, of the concept of personality to the meaning of the behavioral explicans, it might be argued that the concept of personality is superfluous to an empirical relationship between two patterns of behavior. Thus, it appears that

---

[4] See especially Harold Lasswell, *Power and Personality* (New York: The Viking Press, 1948), pp. 37–58. Cf. Lasswell, *Psychopathology and Politics* (Chicago: University of Chicago Press, 1930). Lasswell is an important figure in political psychology at least by virtue of the fact that he was a pioneer in this field.

[5] See Fred Greenstein, *Personality and Politics* (Chicago: Markham Publishing Co., 1969), p. 65. Greenstein is here referring to the psychological analysis of single political actors. It is to such political research that the personality theories discussed above would be most relevant.

the major value of the concept of personality is that it is one way to logically account for the consistency with which types of attitudes recur in some people over a variety of subject matters or ideological areas.[6]

The source of this problem is that assertions about basic human motivations require an enormous leap of inference from observable data. Personality types are usually defined in terms of complexes of attitudes that tend to occur together. Until one attempts to explain the causes of such attitudes, the relationship between concept and indicator does not rely upon such highly tenuous inference. These attitudinal complexes, which can be empirically measured by the use of questionnaires, become the explicans, the vehicle for explanation, rather than the explicandum, the phenomenon to be explained.

In other words, the utility of generalizations about the relationship between complexes of attitudes and political behavior does not depend on satisfactory explanations of the causes of such attitudinal predispositions. Inasmuch as the state of psychology as a discipline does not now (nor will in the foreseeable future) permit scientifically adequate explanation, empirical research into the state of attitudinal predispositions appears to have greater utility for the goal of scientific explanation than speculative inquiry into the basic causes of such human predispositions.

MEASURING AUTHORITARIANISM AND DOGMATISM

It seems clear that the publication of *The Authoritarian Personality* in 1950 was a landmark event not only in terms of the relevance of that particular work for comparative political analysis but also in terms of its impact on other attempts to test and measure complexes of attitudinal predispositions.

The importance of the authoritarian personality study for comparative research transcends the particular phenomenon of authoritarianism. In a methodological sense, it was important in pointing the way to inquiry into other personality types or attitudinal syndromes, syndromes whose presence in some threshold proportion of the population of a system may be shown to be related to some specified states of that system. The methodological problems of measuring personality types or attitudinal syndromes can best be discussed with reference to a particular study. The particular study chosen for illustrative purposes, landmark as it is, is now dated. It is merely one of numerous attitudinal syndromes subject to similar inquiry. One of the great advantages, for illustrative purposes, of the study examined here is that it displays many of the methodological shortcomings that such studies are prone to manifest. It is only natural that it should be

---

[6] T. W. Adorno, et al., *The Authoritarian Personality* (New York: The Norton Library, 1969), p. 56.

expected to do so in light of the fact that it attempted to plow new theoretical ground. Innovative studies usually are more subject to criticism with the benefit of hindsight.

The underlying logic of such research is that attitudes on relatively specific questions are not autonomous from one another. Rather, there is thought to be some unspecified essential quality in certain attitudes that causes them to occur together. It is the fact of this joint occurrence that constitutes an empirical question rather than essential qualities of the attitudes that lead one logically to expect such joint occurrence. Thus, assertions about the essential logical relationship between such attitudes are inferences that are based upon and reinforce confidence in empirical findings of a high rate of joint occurrence.

The original intent of the authors of *The Authoritarian Personality* was to conduct an inquiry into anti-Semitism. However, the results, such as certain logical inconsistencies among specific attitudes of the anti-Semites, indicated that anti-Semitism was one manifestation of a broader pattern of conceptual trends:

stereotypy; rigid adherence to middle class values, the tendency to regard one's own group as morally pure in contrast to the immoral outgroup; opposition to and exaggeration of prying and sensuality; extreme concern with dominance and power . . . ; fear of moral contamination; fear of being overwhelmed and victimized; the desire to erect social barriers in order to separate one group from another and to maintain the dominance of one's own group.[7]

Since such trends, if present, should manifest themselves in subject matters other than Jew and Jewishness, "in ways of thinking about people and life generally," the scope of the inquiry logically broadened to include some of these other subject matter areas. In other words, the authors have hypothesized that these psychological predispositions manifested themselves in general ethnocentrism (a hostile frame of mind toward alien or out groups generally) and in a predisposition to respond favorably to the ideologies of political and economic conservatism, on the one hand, and authoritarianism, on the other.[8]

Political-economic conservatism, anti-Semitism, ethnocentrism, and authoritarianism are conceptualized as attitudinal syndromes or complexes. An *attitude* may be thought of as a mental predisposition to respond in a certain way to certain stimuli or issues. An *attitudinal syndrome* refers to

---

[7] Adorno, op. cit., p. 100.

[8] Throughout the book the authors use the terms authoritarianism and fascism interchangeably. The work is subsequently criticized, as we shall see, on the ground that these are not equivalent terms. Fascism implies a particular type of authoritarianism, right-wing authoritarianism, which may differ in important respects from left-wing authoritarianism. See Roger Brown, *Social Psychology* (New York: The Free Press, 1965), pp. 486–87.

a cluster of attitudes that tend to occur together to such an extent that knowledge of a person's attitude on one question would afford a basis for the prediction of that person's attitude on other related questions, with a probability substantially above chance of being correct. In the words of the authors, each of these syndromes may be thought of as "a relatively organized, relative stable *system* of opinions, values and attitudes."[9] (Emphasis mine.) Beliefs, of course, are not synonymous with attitudes. The former is a conception of what *is* true; the latter is a conception of what *ought* to be true. However, they are integrally part of the same syndrome since attitudes follow from beliefs. If you believe that Jews *are* inherently different, it follows that they *ought* to be treated as such. The ability to unambiguously classify people on the basis of an empirically defined attitudinal syndrome would constitute a clear contribution to a scientific enterprise. Since scientific generalizations relate classes of data to one another, classification constitutes a necessary first step to scientific explanation.

Since anti-Semitism is incompatible with the American creed, an attempt was made to frame the items of the anti-Semitic scale in such a way as "to express subtle hostility without seeming to offend the democratic values which most prejudiced people feel they must maintain."[10] Obviously, one would not crudely ask people if they hate Jews; the principles of the American creed which most Americans superficially espouse would cause most anti-Semites to deny such raw bigotry even to themselves. However, if such statements are framed as "objective facts," one could accept such statements without consciously abandoning one's pseudodemocratic façade (for example, "I'm not prejudiced but it's true that Jews are _____").

As with all of the scales in this study, the range of possible responses for each item was from $+3$ (indicating strong agreement) to -3 (indicating strong disagreement). To avoid negative scores, seven points were assigned to a $+3$ response, six for a $+2$, and so on. The scale was framed in such a way that an anti-Semitic predisposition should result in a positive response on each item. While the authors argue that this permits greater discrimination (in separating prejudiced from nonprejudiced respondents) and the expression of subtle, covert anti-Semitism, this way of constructing the scale has provided the basis for one of the most telling criticisms of the study, a criticism that applies to three of the four scales used.[11] The criticism is that some people are simply predisposed to accept or express agreement with any plausible statement they see in print. This criticism, known as the *response-set* criticism, argues that such people would tend to score high on the scale even if they were not anti-Semitic.

---

[9] Adorno, op. cit., p. 58.

[10] Ibid., p. 59.

[11] See the concise discussion of this problem and summary of the mass of confused literature on the topic in Roger Brown, op. cit., pp. 510–14.

Studies have indicated that the response-set phenomenon does exist and must account for some measure of the agreement with the scales. Nevertheless, once the probable effect of "yea-saying" (as determined by specific tests of the response-set phenomenon) has been subtracted from the scores on each of the four scales and the correlations between them, considerable evidence of the existence of definable personality syndromes remains. The remaining or discounted levels of reliability would still be far too high to have conceivably occurred by chance.[12] As the authors point out, the questionnaire results are corroborated in Part II of the book by relatively unstructured interviews that are unaffected by the response-set phenomenon. The reliability of the total anti-Semitic (A-S) scale was .92,[13] a figure which meets rigorous statistical standards. Combined with high correlations of .74 to .85 between the subscales, the results indicate that one may speak of anti-Semitism as a "general frame of mind" with confidence.[14] Thus, people who tended to view Jews pejoratively on one item had a distinct tendency to view them pejoratively on the other items of the scale despite the diverse content of the items and logical inconsistencies among them.

The ethnocentrism (E) scale was designed to measure a pejorative frame of reference to all outgroups. The expectation, of course, was that the E and A-S scales would strongly correlate with one another. The authors expected general ethnocentrism to have "a psychological affinity" with political and economic conservatism; therefore, a scale (P.E.C.) was constructed to measure this latter phenomenon. In short, it was hypothesized that ethnocentrism, anti-Semitism, political and economic conservatism, and a receptivity to political authoritarianism were all measurable manifestations of the same underlying personality characteristics. These attitudinal syndromes were viewed as responses to subconscious psychological (and, perhaps, by implication, pathological) needs.[15] The expectation that all of the scales would significantly correlate with one another logically followed from the hypothesis that each of these attitudinal syndromes reflected the same underlying personality type.

Of course, it must be recognized that while attitudinal syndromes can in principle can be measured with appropriate survey instruments, person-

---

[12] The P.E.C. scale is a partial exception in that its reliability was only .73 on the first version and .70 on the second. This is not high for the precise measurement of individual predispositions. The presence of anticonservative items counteracting the response set tendency may partially account for this lower score, or it may be true that Americans are simply less consistent or extreme in their political ideologies. See Ibid., pp. 158ff.

[13] The authors generally used a "split half reliability," which consists of the mean correlation between one half of the scale items with the other half. This is a rougher measure of reliability than the formula given above.

[14] Adorno, op. cit., pp. 74–75.

[15] Ibid., pp. 55–56 and p. 223. This implication of pathology indicates a distinct value orientation on the part of the authors.

ality, in the sense of a set of subconscious psychological needs and predispositions that caused these attitudinal syndromes, must be inferred. In
one of the most famous critiques of the study, Hyman and Sheatsley[16]
show at some length that such inferences do not *necessarily* follow from
the data. It seems useful to reiterate that it is insufficient to offer a theory
that can account for a set for data unless it can be demonstrated that no
other explanation of that data is available. The Freudian personality dynamics, such as projection, displacement, etc., that are hypothesized and
occasionally asserted as explaining the data presented do not *necessarily*
follow from them. Thus, the authors of *The Authoritarian Personality* may
be said to have crossed "a methodological boundary"[17] in the sense that
they move from the relatively sound empirical measurement of manifest
attitudinal syndromes to the highly tenuous inference of underlying Freudian personality dynamics characteristic of clinical psychology.

The authors faced a problem in the construction of the P.E.C. scale in
framing items whose conservative content transcended the issues of that
point in history. It is not obvious that they succeeded. For example, it is not
entirely clear that the anti–labor union sentiments forming the basis of several items would not be shared by some individuals with a leftist orientation today. In addition, many conservatives are more sympathetic to
government intervention in the economy today than they were in 1950. The
difficulty in isolating the content manifestations of broad cognitive predispositions from more specific issues was never quite overcome.[18]

The fourth scale is the famous F scale (F for fascism) which purports
to measure antidemocratic potential, a propensity to be receptive to antidemocratic appeals. The F scale contained no anti-authoritarian items;
consequently, it is subject to the response-set critique.

The F scale had a split-half reliability of .74 on the first version and .90
for the final version.[19] Thus, it is defensible to infer that there was some

---

[16] Herbert Hyman and Paul Sheatsley, " 'The Authoritarian Personality,' A Methodological Critique," in Richard Christie and Marie Jahoda (eds.), *Studies in the
Scope and Method of the Authoritarian Personality* (Glencoe, Ill.: The Free Press,
1954), pp. 96ff.

[17] Brown, op. cit., pp. 481 and 490.

[18] Milton Rokeach, *The Open and Closed Mind* (New York: Basic Books, 1960).
See the discussion below of Rokeach's attempt to transcend political content while
measuring "personality" traits.

[19] Each scale underwent several revisions and consolidations. The best items were
retained according to the following criterion: the mean score for each item on the
part of those who scored in the lowest quartile for the scale as a whole was subtracted
from the corresponding mean score of those in the highest quartile, yielding a score
for each item called its discriminatory power (D.P.). This score provided an indication of that item's success in distinguishing those who score high on the scale from
those who score low and, thus, assuming the validity of the scale as a whole, this
score indicated whether that item was good at measuring whatever dimension the
scale was designed to measure. Of course, such subsequent revisions tended to improve the reliability of the scales.

underlying unifying element for the diverse group of items. In short, the results give support to the proposition that this heterogeneous set of specific attitudes constitutes an attitudinal syndrome. The conclusion that some dimension has been measured is not equivalent to identifying that dimension; thus, the internal consistency of the scale does not constitute evidence that it measures general authoritarianism.

The question is not only whether each scale measures some definable dimension but also (1) Does each scale measure the dimension it purports to measure? and (2) Are the dimensions measured by each of these scales manifestations of the same underlying personality type? The former is a question of validity which, as previously indicated, is difficult to substantiate. A partial indication of the latter question may be found in the extent to which the scales intercorrelate with one another.

With regard to this latter question, a positive and significant correlation was found between the F scale and the other three scales. The term *significant* is used here in the statistical sense meaning that a correlation of that magnitude would not occur by chance more frequently than a given number of times (five or fewer) per hundred; thus, the *null* hypothesis of no essential relationship between the scales would be based on a very remote probability.

It may be suggested that part of the high correlation between the F and E scales or between the F and P.E.C. scales may be due to an overlap in ideas if not in precise wording. Otherwise put, some of the items in the F scale may be expressing essentially the same idea as some items in the E scale or P.E.C. scale with a different wording. For example, Hyman and Sheatsley point out that an item in the first version of the P.E.C. scale, "young people sometimes get rebellious ideas, but as they grow up they ought to get over them and settle down," has a counterpart in the F scale, "obedience and respect for authority are the most important virtues children should learn."[20] To the extent that such a content overlap exists, a positive correlation is built into the study.

While such direct overlap seems to be exaggerated in the Hyman and Sheatsley critique, it seems clear that since the authors were trying to measure the very mental dispositions that directly result in ethnocentrism and anti-Semitism (for example, predisposition toward stereotypy; uncritical attitudes toward the ingroup, etc.), one would logically expect a high correlation between the E and the F scales. The authors felt obliged to point with pride to the less than perfect correlation between the E and F scale as evidence that the two scales do not measure precisely the same thing.[21] Despite the foregoing qualifications, it must be concluded that the levels of correlations are strong enough to justify the inference that ethnocentrism, political and economic conservatism, and "authoritarianism" (or

---

[20] Hyman and Sheatsley, op. cit., pp. 73–74.
[21] Adorno, op. cit., p. 264.

whatever the F scale measures) are in large part all manifestations of the same type of personality system. One should keep in mind here a distinction between an inference that can account for the data at hand and a conclusion that necessarily follows from the data. The hypothesis of an integrating personality system would fall in the former category.

The main attempt to validate the results consisted of relatively unstructured interviews and thematic apperception tests (T.A.T.) with a selection of extreme high scorers and extreme low scorers on the scales. (The T.A.T. consists of showing a picture to the subjects and asking them to write a story about it. The story is then coded for indicators of mental dispositions.) While the interview and T.A.T. results generally corroborated the results of the scale, it is not obvious that the interviews provided an adequate validation of the results. In the first place, the interviewers were aware of the subjects' scores. It is entirely possible that an interviewer, armed with considerable discretion in the selection and framing of questions, might have set out to corroborate the test results of which he or she was already aware, thus distorting the results with systematic bias.[22] In the second place, it seems that the problem of content overlap, discussed above with respect to the intercorrelations between the scales, applies here. This means that much of the same sense content of the structured scale was reintroduced in the interview under slightly different wording. Validation requires that the dimension in question be measured by indicators which are entirely independent from the measuring instrument being validated.

Although, as already pointed out, validation is a difficult problem at best, validation by behavior seems to suggest itself here. It would be interesting to know, for instance, the extent to which people who score high on the F scale join or support political parties that are generally regarded as authoritarian. Some fragmentary evidence exists in this regard. T. S. Cohn and H. Carsch[23] administered a translation of the F scale to 140 workers in a German cosmetics factory and found the highest mean score recorded for a group to the date, 5.26 as opposed to the high of 4.73 in the original study. However, it is not clear that German equals former Nazi. Moreover, the subjects were all working-class, who tended to score higher than middle-class subjects, while the Berkeley study was administered primarily to middle-class subjects. It has been found, moreover, that communists score significantly lower than facists.[24]

All of this raises a serious question about the validity of the F scale as a measure of general authoritarianism. There seems to be considerable justi-

---

[22] Hyman and Sheatsley, op. cit., pp. 80–81.

[23] T. S. Cohn and H. Carsch, "Administration of the F Scale to a Sample of Germans," *Journal of Abnormal and Social Psychology,* Vol. 49 (1954), p. 471.

[24] Thelma Coulter, *An Experimental and Statistical Study of the Relationship of Prejudice and Certain Personality Variables* (unpublished Ph.D. dissertation, University of London, 1953), cited in Brown, op. cit., p. 527–28. Rokeach found English communists scored the lowest of five political groups. See Milton Rokeach, op. cit., p. 115.

fication for the suspicion that the scale rather measures right-wing authoritarianism, namely fascism, while the scale is not a good indicator of left-wing authoritarianism,[25] such as the position of communists or American New Left militants. It has been suggested that the lower correlation of the F scale with the P.E.C. scale is due to the failure of the latter scale to distinguish conservatives and radical-right reactionaries.[26]

The essence of the criticism is that a conception of the political spectrum as a unidimensional continuum moving from left to right is a gross over-simplification. While the extreme-right fascists differ from the extreme-left communists in many respects (such as attitudes toward private property), they also resemble one another in important respects (such as the suppression of civil liberties). Thus, the political spectrum is multidimensional.[27] It is interesting to note that one of the important sets of attitudes that has been asserted as distinguishing the authoritarian right from the authoritarian left, namely, the humanitarian façade of the latter as opposed to the pervasive and official ethnocentrism—especially anti-Semitism—of the former no longer provides such a clear distinction. The radical left in all countries has recently embraced anti-Semitism with increasing boldness. Seymour Lipset presents evidence for this increasingly clear trend in his essay, "The Socialism of Fools."[28] Other left-leaning authoritarian movements in the past have been similarly anti-Semitic. Witness the Populists in the United States. It may be that the radical-left authoritarian is not as distinct from the radical-right authoritarian as some critics of *The Authoritarian Personality* imply. Shils, in fact, shows many similarities between the left and right authoritarians in order to demonstrate that the radical left can be distinguished from democratic liberals. In short, the simplistic equation that right wing on the political spectrum equals authoritarian while left wing equals nonauthoritarian is clearly untenable. Yet, the point is that it may be that right and left authoritarianism are more similar in political content than at first supposed. If this is true, a measure of general authoritarianism in terms of social and political content may not be as impossible as critics of the F scale imply.

DOGMATISM AS A POLITICALLY NEUTRAL CONCEPT

Criticism of the F scale has provided a major catalyst to an important study by Milton Rokeach, *The Open and Closed Mind,* which attempts to

---

[25] See the essay by Edward Shils, "Authoritarianism: 'Right' and 'Left,' " in Christie and Jahoda, op. cit., pp. 24–29.

[26] Morris Janowitz and Dwaine Marvick, "Authoritarianism and Political Behavior," in Neil Smelser and William Smelser, *Personality and Social Systems* (New York: John Wiley & Sons, 1963), p. 455.

[27] Shils, op. cit., pp. 27ff.

[28] Seymour M. Lipset, "The Socialism of Fools," *New York Times Magazine,* January 3, 1971, p. 6ff.

devise a way of measuring a mental predisposition to dogmatism and rigidity autonomous from political ideology on the left-right continuum "so that bigots of the left, center, and right all achieve a similar score on the same scale."[29] In calling the principal scale he used to measure general authoritarianism the *dogmatism scale,* Rokeach was identifying authoritarianism as a cognitive style. He felt that the F scale erred in defining authoritarianism in terms of political and social content. Thus, Rokeach's high scorers will be distinguished from his low scorers by the way in which they solve problems that require a receptivity to new information rather than by a set of substantive attitudes.[30]

Rokeach's dogmatism scale purports to measure the extent to which a person's belief system is open or closed. System is used in the sense defined in Chapter 4; thus, a *belief system* is a set of interacting and logically related beliefs. The openness of a belief system refers to the capacity of the system to assimilate and utilize new information.

The logic of this scale depends on a distinction between the belief system and the *disbelief system.* The latter is not a mere residue of that which is not in the belief system. To reject beliefs is not the same thing as simply not believing in them in a passive sense. Thus, Rokeach's scale contains the following subdivisions or dimensions: overemphasis of differences between the belief and disbelief systems; the identification of items that cannot logically be assimilated by the belief system as irrelevant; the tolerance of contradictions within the belief system; the increased perception of similiarity among disbelief systems; a perception of human isolation in a hostile world; a tendency to accept or reject ideas on the basis of what authority espouses them rather than on their merits; a belief in the importance of causes; a basic intolerance toward renegades and disbelievers; and a tendency to selectively avoid other events or facts inconsistent with one's belief system.[31] Rokeach suggests that dogmatism, referring to a "closed configuration of beliefs," may be distinguished from rigidity, referring to difficulty in overcoming any single belief.

A companion scale was the opinionation scale used to measure general intolerance. The specific assumption underlying this scale is that when an intolerant person rejects a belief or belief system, he also rejects those people who accept such beliefs. Since it was not possible to construct a set of items for the scale free from political and social content, Rokeach constructed a left opinionation scale and a right opinionation scale. The idea is that an opinionated person will receive a greater total opinionation score

---

[29] Rokeach, op. cit., p. 9.

[30] In fact, one of the primary methods of validation is to correlate results on his dogmation and rigidity scales with success in solving a hypothetical imaginary puzzle that is totally autonomous from real-world issues. See "The Doodlebug Problem," Part 3 in Rokeach, op. cit., pp. 171–224.

[31] Ibid., pp. 73–79.

than a non-opinionated one, irrespective of the subject's political or social preferences, if each subject responds to both scales.

It appears from an examination of the content of the scales concerned that whatever Rokeach is measuring is somewhat closer to what the E scale in the Berkeley study measured than to whatever the F scale measured. Rokeach's scale corresponds to the F scale about to the extent that the E scale and the F scale overlap. This observation, if valid, would render Rokeach's conception of dogmatism similar to Brown's suggestion that general authoritarianism may be best conceived in terms of "the kind of information that will induce (a person) to change his attitudes. The authoritarian will reverse his evaluations on the simple say-so of an authority figure."[32] Thus, Brown's authoritarian is closed-minded in the sense that his beliefs are not altered by new information. This is basically the same point Rokeach appears to be trying to make with respect to his distinction between ideological structure and ideological content. Thus, an authoritarian is identified by his resistance to new ideas and information except when decreed by an authority figure (ideological structure). Yet, various authoritarians, such as fascists and communists, may differ with respect to the content of their beliefs.[33] Thus, ideological structure refers to a cognitive process which is dynamic while ideological content is static.

In addition to validation of his scale through the testing of hypotheses about expected differences between high and low scorers, an example of which was referred to in footnote 19, Rokeach used two sets of intuitive judgments as a means of validation. Teachers and peers of the subjects were requested to evaluate the subjects as more less dogmatic. The judgment by faculty members did not corroborate the dogmatism scale findings (nor, for that matter, the F scale results), possibly due to the probability that submissive tendencies in high scorers cause them to conceal their dogmatism from authority figures like teachers. Selection by peers did corroborate the findings, however.[34]

Sampling procedures in the Berkeley study were based primarily on considerations of convenience. No serious attempt was made to draw a sample that was representative of the general population. The sample specifically consisted of white, Christian subjects. The education and intelligence for the sample was as a whole above the national average. The researchers acquired their subjects through the use of captive audiences in college classrooms and through organizations. The authors recognize the nonrepresentative nature of their sample. Their defense consists, first, in the disclaimer that they were less interested in generalizing about larger popula-

---

[32] Brown, op. cit., pp. 542–43.
[33] Rokeach, op. cit., pp. 127–29.
[34] Ibid., pp. 103–4.

tions than in the intensive study of groups possessing characteristics deemed crucial to the problem and, second, in the claim that they were less interested in questions of the intensity with which attitudes were held than with the relationships among attitudes.[35] While it is fairly clear that the intensity with which the attitudes in question are held should be affected by sampling considerations,[36] it is less clear that the nature of the relationship between such attitudes are a function of the representative nature of the sample.

Yet, Hyman and Sheatsley take issue with these claims. They cite some evidence that it is possible for the degree of cognitive organization (relating attitudes to one another) to vary from one group to another.[37] They admit, however, that sampling considerations do not justify a denial that there is a considerable relationship between the attitudes in question. Their point is that sampling considerations affect the strength of such relationships,[38] a point that Adorno and his associates readily admit. Hyman and Sheatsley also concede that Adorno and his associates duly qualify their generalizations for the most part. Their claim appears to be that the Berkeley study authors are not forceful enough in stressing the qualifications to their generalizations.

It appears that while one must grant that, other things (like considerations of time, money, etc.) being equal, it would have been preferable for Adorno and his associates to construct a sample more representative of the general population, it cannot be said that the nature of the sample used casts serious doubt on the basic conclusions of the study. The evidence that several intercorrelated attitudinal syndromes have been measured remains intact. Issue may only be taken with the stated strength of such relationships.

AUTHORITARIANISM AS A PERSONALITY TYPE

The foregoing survey does not pretend to be a thorough survey of the extensive, often contradictory literature on authoritarianism.[39] Nor should it be supposed that authoritarianism constitutes the only dimension along which attempts have been made to construct personality types potentially relevant to comparative analysis. Certainly, for example, the characteriza-

---

[35] Significant differences in the strength of F scale scores among important social and economic groupings in society are reported in Janowitz and Marvick, loc. cit.

[36] Adorno, op. cit., pp. 18–21 and p. 288.

[37] Hyman and Sheatsley, op. cit., p. 58.

[38] Ibid., p. 60.

[39] For a somewhat dated but to the point complete bibliography of this literature, see Richard Christie and Peggy Cook, "A Guide to the Published Literature Relating to the Authoritarian Personality Through 1956," *The Journal of Psychology,* Vol. 45 (April 1958), pp. 171–99.

tion of the achieving personality by McClelland is a landmark study of utmost relevance to the literature on political development and will be considered more fully under that heading.[40] However, the large volume of literature on authoritarianism as a personality type renders this particular personality syndrome a convenient and important illustrative example of this type of research.

After all of the criticisms of the Berkeley study have been taken into account, what remains of the "authoritarian personality"? Clearly, it appears that the authors of the Berkeley study have described some personality dimension with the F scale. The question of whether this dimension should be labeled authoritarianism, fascism, or something else is separate from the question of whether some personality syndrome has been measured. Even after making allowances for the argument that the response-set problem adds to the magnitude of reliability scores, the obtained score for reliability is of such a magnitude as to provide solid evidence that the beliefs and attitudes which make up the items in the F scale are connected in some essential way. The frequency of joint occurrence of these attitudes is too high to make the null hypothesis plausible (that there is no relationship between the items and that such joint occurrence as is observed is due to chance). Moreover, the high correlation between the F scale and the E and A-S scales constitutes sound evidence that these latter scales are part of the same syndrome.

The fact that the avowed communists do not get consistently high scores on the F scale is evidence that the scale is a better indicator of fascism than of general authoritarianism. Rokeach's dogmatism and opinionation scales have been more successful in isolating some cognitive variables that fascists and communists share. Rokeach's scales appear to be more similar in content to Adorno's E scale than to his F scale. The research surveyed seems to suggest that it might be fruitful to conceptualize authoritarianism in terms of general authoritarianism combined with an exaggerated concern for power relationships. Thus, authoritarianism appears to be more of a cognitive style, a way of resolving issues, than a substantive set of beliefs.

Science, as repeatedly stated, is a generalizing activity. Although the ability of social scientists to isolate and measure attitudinal syndromes appears to be promising, the scientific utility of such an enterprise depends on whether such attitudinal syndromes can be utilized to explain relevant political behavior or empirically defined system states. The problem of constructing such explanations from micro-analytic data is the problem of reductionism discussed in Chapter 1. As a whole is more than the sum of

---

[40] David C. McClelland, *The Achieving Society* (New York: The Free Press, 1961).

its parts, the states of systems are not simply a function of the psychological predispositions of the individuals that comprise such systems. Yet, if micro-analytic data cannot provide a neat causal explanation of macro-level explicanda (facts to be explained), certainly such data do affect the relevant outcomes to some extent. Thus, the increased attention paid by political scientists to micro-analytic variables can only be a healthy trend.

Part III

Selected Applications

11

The Search for a
Theory of Parties

The preceding chapters in Part II were concerned with approaches to the study of politics, that is, with relatively standardized criteria for framing questions about political events. This and subsequent chapters, on the other hand, will concern themselves with the actual questions about given political systems. Thus, while still surveying literature from a methodological point of view, Part III will focus on literature that is concerned with explaining or describing events or states of specified political systems or with explaining or describing specified phenomena. The preceding Part focused rather on literature that suggested *means* of seeking the explanation or description of a variety of unspecified systems or phenomena.

It would be foolish to pretend that this distinction is clear and unambiguous. Certain pieces of literature could reasonably be classified as either analytic or substantive. For instance, Downs's *Economic Theory of Democracy,* discussed above as an example of analytic model building, could be just as justifiably discussed in the present chapter insofar as Downs derives explanations of relatively well defined categories of political party behavior from his model. Nevertheless, because a difference in emphasis or intent is apparent in the case of most literature, the distinction between analytic and substantive literature being suggested here remains a useful organizing principle in a survey of this type. Some important pieces of literature exist with a status that is so ambiguous with respect to this analytic-substantive classification that they ought to be mentioned under more than one heading.

A major criterion used in selecting the foci of substantive research is the extent to which a literature on that subject has developed. The subject of

211

political parties is outstanding in the field of comparative analysis in meeting this standard. The attention of political scientists has been directed to the study of parties for some time now, inasmuch as parties are manifestly relevant to the discipline. By contrast, the attention of political scientists to social, cultural, and psychological variables is, despite a few rare early exceptions, a relatively recent phenomenon. The institutionalization of the study of parties as a relevant enterprise for political scientists may be indicated by the fact that the study of parties, unlike other objects of the political scientists' attention, has been accorded a name, *stasiology*. The much larger quantity of literature on parties than on sociological or psychological variables is a function of the time that the former body of literature has had to cumulate. The quality of the party literature is, to be sure, a separate question from its quantity, a question with which this chapter will presently concern itself.

THE DIMENSIONS OF THE LITERATURE—AN OVERVIEW

The prospect for integrating the research and writings on political parties in the political systems of the world suffers from the disparate nature of the questions raised, the lack of comparable units of analysis, the lack of agreement on an appropriate conceptual framework, and a disturbing dissensus on the objects of a study of parties. These problems, which are not unrelated to one another, require further discussion and elaboration.

The problem of the units of analysis is basic. One aspect of this problem is the scope of the term *political party*. Because the role or function performed by the parties or party systems depends to such a large extent on the nature of the political systems in which they operate, these roles vary greatly from system to system. However, parties and party systems derive much of their meaning from the role they play in the political system in which they operate. Clearly, the parties in Western democracies, most of whose important functions center around and stem from the basic goal of rendering the political elites formally accountable to the masses they govern, are very different from totalitarian parties, whose functions center around a very different conception of authority and national purpose, a conception that holds a different purpose for government than that of serving the governed. Hence, how totalitarian parties succeed in their ostensible purposes is another question that will presently be examined. For now, the very different raison d'être of these two types of parties renders them logically different entities despite their shared label. For this reason, a question exists as to whether a single theoretic framework can encompass such distinct entities. It has been suggested by one authority on the subject of parties that the notion of a one-party system, let alone a totalitarian party, is a contradiction in terms; the concept of party presupposes a democratic system of elite accountability.[1] Thus, while democratic parties help the masses control the government, totalitarian parties are virtually synonymous with the government.[2] The question will be presently raised of whether more than one party is necessary for a party system to foster such accountability.[3]

The unit of analysis problem also extends to a question of whether one wishes to focus on parties as discrete entities or upon party systems. Basic to the study of party systems is their classification according to the number of parties. Depending upon whether one wishes to include single-party systems in the study of political parties, the common classification scheme is either in terms of one, two, and multi (meaning here three or more) party systems or just the last two classes. As will be presently shown, a case can be made for the position that the operation of two-party systems makes them a fundamentally different type of system than multiparty systems. In short, there is a far greater distinction to be made between two and three or more party systems than between three parties and any number greater than three. It will be shown, however, that the decision to label any given party system as a two-party system or a multiparty system is a decision often involving considerable discretion, a decision that depends upon the indicators one specifies for the definition of a two-party system.

The study of party systems focuses on patterns of interaction between parties in any given political system rather than upon the characteristics of individual parties as discrete entities. Among the possible foci of attention under this heading could be the manner in which the party system, irrespective of the program, doctrine, or structure of any particular party, has a responsiveness to public opinion inherent in its pattern of interaction. For example, Etzioni argues that despite the fact that all governing coalitions in Israel are dominated by the Mapai (Labor) party, the choice of that party's coalition partners is a function of the relative strength of all the other parties at the previous election.[4] If the strength of right-oriented parties is increased in the Knesset (Israeli parliament) relative to the strength of the left-oriented parties in a general election, the Mapai party will choose right-wing rather than left-wing parties as its junior coalition

---

[1] Sigmund Neumann, "Toward a Comparative Study of Political Parties," in Neumann (ed.), *Modern Political Parties* (Chicago: University of Chicago Press, 1956), p. 395.

[2] David Apter, "Introduction" to Part 5, Political Parties, in Harry Eckstein and David Apter (eds.), *Comparative Politics, A Reader* (New York: The Free Press, 1963), p. 328.

[3] See Leon Epstein, *Political Parties in Western Democracies* (New York: Praeger, 1967), pp. 47–55, for a concise statement that one party can foster such accountability.

[4] Amitai Etzioni, "Alternative Ways to Democracy: The Example of Israel," *Political Science Quarterly*, Vol. 74, No. 2 (June 1959), pp. 196–214.

partners. More importantly, the policy output of such a coalition would shift to the right in response to the shift in public opinion as measured by the electoral process.

Thus, if democracy is defined in terms of elite responsiveness to shifts in public opinion, such responsiveness may be effected in two different ways. On the one hand, there is the classical Anglo-American style of democracy. This system relies on competitive alternation between two parties offering alternative policy positions. This competition increases the likelihood that public policy will reflect the shifting distribution of power and interests in those societies. On the other hand, a single dominant party may maintain its dominance by shifting its own policy orientations in line with the shifting currents of opinion and influence in its society. Thus, while the Anglo-American systems effect responsive policy shifts between parties, a dominant party system effects responsive policy shifts within the single party. The Israeli dominant party situation, described by Etzioni, to some extent resembles the way elite responsiveness has been to some extent institutionalized in Sweden, Norway, India, and, until the recent Social Democratic government, the Federal Republic of Germany, not to mention the several single-party states in Africa described by Ruth Schachter.[5] This elite responsiveness does not appear to be so much a function a whether more than one party is likely to control the government as it is a function of whether political opposition is legitimate, even if ineffective with regard to winning elections. For the very existence of a potential alternative apparently induces the dominant party to be somewhat responsive in order to maintain its dominance.

Individual parties may be studied along several dimensions to varying degrees autonomously from the context of the system in which they operate. One such dimension is with respect to party ideology and party program. As a matter of fact, scholars have frequently addressed themselves to this very distinction between parties which promote a weltanschauung (complete, closed, comprehensive ideology) and parties which promote concrete, although often rationally inconsistent, policies on the basis of expediency and interest. It has been suggested in several quarters that this distinction is becoming progressively less useful.[6] This controversy has important implications that will be explored below.

Of course, aside from the basic distinction between ideology and a plat-

---

[5] Ruth Schachter, "Single-Party Systems in West Africa," *The American Political Science Review,* Vol. 55, No. 2 (June 1961), pp. 294–307.

[6] For example, Neumann, op. cit., pp. 400–401. This question is related to the end-of-ideology controversy cited above and mentioned again below. Peter Merkl has suggested that the labeling of a party as ideological or pragmatic is to a large extent a function of the compatibility of the party's position with the position of the observer. The more one agrees with the policy positions of a party, the more pragmatic such positions appear. Peter Merkl, *Modern Comparative Politics* (New York: Holt, Rinehart and Winston, 1970), p. 275.

form in interests, the actual content of a party's platform or principle may become an object of study. For example, most texts on British government and politics will discuss ways in which the principles of the Conservative, Labour, and Liberal parties differ from one another. Related to the foregoing are important questions with respect to the goals of parties: specifically, Do the parties want to simply control the government for the sake of power and for the rewards of power itself? Do the parties want to achieve certain policy goals? or Do the parties seek to destroy the system in which they operate? Some parties may see themselves as spokesmen for certain interests; other parties may be willing to support whatever interests it seems expedient to support in the light of a goal of vote maximization; finally, the extremist party may seek to define everyone's interests in terms of some ideological goals.

Naturally, the classification of any given party in one or the other of these categories is a decision that involves a certain amount of subjective discretion. The British Labour party, for example, is ostensibly the parliamentary arm of the trade union movement, the designated political representative of the interests of organized labor. Yet, as Prime Minister Harold Wilson's 1969 austerity program indicated, the Labour party will occasionally take steps opposed by organized labor which appear necessary to acquire the level of middle-class support the Labour party needs to stay in office.

The American parties and Canadian parties, on the other hand, are generally thought of as epitomizing parties of expediency, parties that will take any position or appeal to any interests that can contribute to the goal of aggregating the support of a majority of a diverse electorate. Yet, it can be shown that the respective major parties in each of these two nations differ from one another both with respect to broad orientations of policy and principle and with respect to a relatively stable clientele to which each of the parties appeals.

Another dimension along which parties may be individually studied is that of party organization. Among the most basic questions with which the early literature on parties concerned itself is the extent of internal party democracy that occurs in any given party or is logically possible in parties in general. This involves not only the question of the centralization and decentralization of decision-making processes but a specification of the structural mechanisms by which party leadership can control the party rank and file and by which the party rank and file can hold the party leadership to some extent accountable to them. For example, it has been argued that control of nominations is a crucial mechanism by which party discipline is maintained in British Commonwealth and some Continental parliamentary parties.[7] On the other hand, the regular election of the leadership of the

---

[7] David Truman, "Federalism and the Party System" in Arthur MacMahon (ed.), *Federalism Mature and Emergent* (New York: Columbia University Press, 1955), pp. 118–19.

British Labour party and the 1922 Committee in the British Conservative party have been cited as structural mechanisms designed to render party elites accountable to party rank and file. A further question is whether such structural mechanisms are effective instruments for the achievement of their intended purpose. Indications are, for example, that the election of the leadership of the British Labour party by the parliamentary party rank and file is a procedural formality; the victory of the incumbent is a foregone conclusion.

The concern with structural mechanisms leads to attempts to classify parties by structural type. This, in fact, is the thrust of the first half of one of the landmark pieces of literature in the comparative study of parties, Maurice Duverger's *Political Parties.*[8]

Finally, the functional approach discussed in Chapter 8 has implicitly or explicitly played a major role in the literature on political parties for some time, particularly with respect to much of the early literature on the American party system. This concern with the functions of parties far antedated the discovery by political scientists of functional analysis as a relatively systematic paradigm in the forms discussed in Chapter 8. As early as 1913, for example, A. Lawrence Lowell suggested that political parties in democratic nations perform a "brokerage function."[9] That is, the party is conceived of as an instrument for the translation, transmission, and mediation of amorphous and conflicting demands of the masses and groups in society into public policy. When one goes to a stockbroker, one generally has a set of goals in mind and a conception of the resources he can risk to achieve his goals. However, he lacks the understanding of the market needed to translate his goals into concrete decisions about how much of what kinds of securities to buy, an understanding supplied by the stockbroker. Similarly, the public lacks the knowledge and information about the political process needed to translate perceived interests and demands into concrete legislative proposals. Since parties function as intermediaries in the translation of demands to decisions in the political arena while brokers function as intermediaries in the translation of goals to decisions in the market, the broker analogy seemed appropriate. Clearly, the putative designation of a brokerage function as generic to political parties means that one is in effect limiting the term party to entities which function in democratic systems.

ELECTORAL SYSTEMS AND PARTY SYSTEMS

As implied above, the literature on party systems has, to a considerable extent, concerned itself with the number of parties, especially with the

---

[8] Maurice Duverger, *Political Parties,* trans. Barbara and Robert North (New York: John Wiley & Sons Science Editions, 1963).

[9] A. Lawrence Lowell, *Public Opinion and Popular Government* (New York: Longmans, Green and Co., 1913), pp. 61ff.

causes of two or multiparty systems and with the effect of each type of system on political stability. At one point in time, something of a vigorous debate flourished over whether the electoral system of a nation can be singled out as a principal determinant of the number of parties and, hence, the presence or lack of political stability in a nation.

The F. A. Hermans proposition, cited in Part I, constitutes the clearest and most extreme statement of a simple causal relationship between electoral systems and the number of parties. He then similarly asserts a linear causal relationship between the number of parties and the stability, and even the very viability, of a parliamentary democracy. Simply stated, any of the commonly used forms of proportional representation cause a multiparty system which, in turn, causes political instability in a parliamentary democracy. When the extent of such instability reaches some unspecified level, the political process becomes immobilized and unable, in Almondian terminology, to convert demands into outputs. The resulting unrelieved stress on the system is likely to bring about the replacement of that system with one that is able to act.

It may be that there is a certain psychological comfort in the belief that the type of electoral system can be a sufficient cause of the success of failure of democratic government. After all, electoral systems are relatively susceptible to conscious change while complex social, cultural, or historical factors are not. Therefore, to the extent that electoral systems are the cause of the presence or lack of political stability in democratic systems, social engineering becomes much more feasible and man has greater control of his destiny.

The relationship between proportional representation and multiparty systems appears to withstand prima facie scrutiny on a logical level. Proportional representation is actually a generic term applied to a variety of specific electoral systems.[10] Proportionality is a continuous variable, a goal which specific types of electoral systems may approach to an infinitely divisible number of degrees. That goal is for the percentage of seats each party acquires in the legislature to approximate the percentage of votes that party receives in the general election. Thus, a party that receives

---

[10] Among the more commonly used forms of proportional representation are the single-member district majority system with runoffs of the French Third Republic; the list voting of the Fourth Republic; the Hare system of the single transferable vote with multimember constituencies based upon the Droop quotient; and the D'Hondt or highest average system, also based on list voting and the quota system, with a national remainder pool as in Weimar Germany. Those constitute just a few of the many varieties of proportional representation discussed in W. J. M. McKenzie, *Free Elections* (London: Allen & Union Ltd., 1958). One advocate of proportional representation points out that the term refers to a "principle" rather than to any specific type of electoral system, "the principle that the views of the electors should be represented in the elected body in the proportion to the extent to which they are held in the electorate." J. F. S. Ross, *Elections and Electors* (London: Eyre & Spottiswoode, 1955), p. 160.

about ten percent of the total vote should be alloted about 20 seats in a 200-seat legislature.

All of a great variety of election systems have a considerable proportional effect except one, the type of electoral system commonly used in Anglo-American democracies. The Anglo-American system is commonly referred to as the single-member-district system with plurality vote or, more conveniently, the plurality system. In this system, as the name implies, the single candidate in each district with the most votes—irrespective of whether or not he receives a majority of votes—wins the election. There is no reward for coming in second or for being close; therefore, an unequal distribution of voting preferences will not be of much benefit to third, fourth, etc., strongest parties. Only rarely will they be first.

In addition, the tendency among supporters of weak parties to not waste their votes on candidates unlikely to win further prejudices the plurality system against the electoral success of minority parties. Thus, it is easy to see how proportional systems tend to maximize the representation of minor parties while the plurality system works to minimize such representation.[11] Yet, it is one thing to point out that the imperatives of proportional representation encourage multiparty systems and that the imperatives of the plurality system encourage a two-party arrangement, while it is quite another thing to assert a single causal relationship between electoral system and party system.

On an empirical level, the putative causal relationships between electoral system and party system, on one level, and between the party system and stability, on another level, begin to run into difficulty. It is true that many examples can be presented to support the contention of Hermans and, in fact, he does present such data. Weimar Germany, prewar Italy, and Third and Fourth Republic France constitute classic examples of the political stalemate, instability, and political breakdown in multiparty parliamentary democracy with proportional representation. Yet, it is also true that other multiparty parliamentary democracies, unaccounted for by Hermans, do exist with great political stability. The Scandinavian democracies stand out in this respect. In these countries, one party, the Social Democrats in Sweden, the Labor party in Norway, and the Social Democratic party in Denmark, dominated their respective governments for more than ten consecutive years.[12] Switzerland, Belgium, and the Netherlands

---

[11] The votes cast for all but the winning candidate in a district in a plurality system do not have any effect on the composition of the legislature. It matters not if a man loses his district by one vote or a million votes. Hence, votes for losers are in a sense wasted. The imperatives of proportionality work to overcome this wasting effect so as to produce some impact for every few votes and hence every shade of opinion. The Weimar system, by placing votes over and above the quota for a party in a national pool for redistribution, wasted very few votes.

[12] The Social Democrats have been in power in Sweden continuously since 1932. The Norwegian Labor party came to power in 1927 and remained there continuously except for a 28-day interval in 1963. A socialist-liberal coalition governed Denmark

have also combined multiparty parliamentary democracy with relatively stable government.

Moreover, it is not clear that proportional representation necessarily leads to an increase in the number of parties. The number of parties has remained stable and at a manageable number of five since the introduction of proportionality in Sweden. By comparison, Canada has had four to five significant national parties utilizing the Anglo-American voting system. In late 19th century Belgium a two-party system flourished despite the availability of a second ballot. The claim that the second ballot was rarely used raises the question Why not? The answer may lie in the general assessment, attempted below, of the effect of electoral systems on the number of parties.

The claim that the plurality system can cause a two-party arrangement appears at first glance to be somewhat more defensible depending, of course, on how narrowly one defines a two-party system. If one simply counts the number of parties that put up candidates for national office, even the classic two-party states, the United States and the United Kingdom, become multiparty systems. In order to construct useful distinctions among existing political systems, it is necessary to distinguish major and minor parties. But this is difficult to do in an unambiguous fashion. Leslie Lipson would classify a system as two-party under the following conditions: "(1) Not more than two parties at any given time have a genuine chance to gain power. (2) One of these is able to win the requisite majority and stay in office without help from a third party. (3) Over a number of decades two parties alternate in power."[13] Aside from a certain ambiguity in such indicators as "a genuine chance" and "a number of decades," a practical difficulty arises with this definition. This definition would exclude a nation such as Australia, whose party system operates with the effect of a two-party system in that two stable political forces compete for and alternate in power, Labour and antilabour. The antilabour forces have not only undergone several name changes but have, since World War II, consisted of a stable coalition between two structurally distinct parties. The smallest of the three parties, the Country party, is farther to the ideological right than its permanent ally, the Liberal party. Therefore, there is very little chance of the Country party aligning itself with the left-oriented Labour party. In this way, the Country party relinquished its potential as an autonomous balance-of-power force. Much the same argument could be made with respect to the Federal Republic of Germany, where the country is often governed by a coalition of a dominant minority party and a weak ally (the Free Democrats). Yet, the political struggle can be said to consist

from 1929 to 1940. Since the war, there has been an alternation of power at two or three-year intervals between Social Democratic and moderate Liberal Conservative administrations.

[13] Leslie Lipson, "The Two Party System in Great Britain," *The American Political Science Review,* Vol. 47, No. 2 (June 1953), pp. 337–58.

of the alternation of two basic political forces, the Christian Democrats and the Social Democrats.

It does appear that when two stable political forces alternate in control of a parliamentary government, the party system operates more like the British two-party variety. The very stability of such a recurring coalition causes that coalition to act in the system with the effect of a single party. The autonomy of the component parties to such a coalition is compromised. The point of the foregoing is that reasonable men can and do disagree as to whether a given system is a two-party system.

If one defines a two-party system in the broad sense suggested above, few deviant cases suggest themselves to the proposition that the plurality system is invariably associated with the two-party system.[14] Maurice Duverger, in his classic book *Political Parties,* suggests that the four exceptions can be explained away.[15] Canada's struggle for control of the executive is limited to two parties. Australia's exception is explained as the result of a slight modification in the plurality nature of their electoral system, preferential voting. However, since Australia's three parties function as two, it is questionable whether Australia is, in fact, a deviant case. This leaves pre-1920 Denmark and pre-1911 Sweden. In both Sweden and Denmark, the multiparty arrangement was at the national level, while generally only two parties would compete in each individual constituency.

In short, the crucial factor is not how many parties have significant representation in the national legislature. Rather, the distribution of party support is crucial. If the parties rely on a localized or geographically defined basis of electoral support, it is possible to have several parties operating in a nation while having only two seriously competing in any given district.[16] What Duverger has, in fact, said is that the plurality system exerts great pressure on the perceived diversities of a political system to aggregate into a two-party alignment. He does not exclude the possibility that under certain relatively rare circumstances these pressures may be resisted and that multiparty systems could exist with a plurality election system. What is lacking for the formulation of a law of the universal nomological variety is a precise specification of those rare circumstances under which the imperatives of a plurality election system are resisted by a party system. Wildavsky, in his well known methodological critique of Duverger's work, has argued that the problem lies in the fact that Duverger has limited his analysis to institutional variables (party systems,

---

14 Duverger, op. cit., p. 217.

15 Ibid., pp. 220–26.

16 Duverger does not specify the conditions under which local two-party competition becomes national two-party competition. It is suggested here that the geographical distribution of electoral support may be crucial. Cf. Aaron Wildavsky, "A Methodological Critique of Duverger's Political Parties," *Journal of Politics,* Vol. 21, No. 2 (May 1959), p. 307.

electoral systems, and party structure), while other important variables may be highly relevant to the outcomes he wishes to explain.[17]

Accordingly, Leslie Lipson has argued that the two-party system in Great Britain is not a function of specific procedural institutions. Rather the system is a consequence of broader social and economic tendencies that cannot be consciously engineered.[18]

Historically, Lipson argues, reinforcing socioeconomic and religious cleavages tended to bifurcate into dichotomous alternatives. Thus, rather than causing the two-party alignment, the plurality electoral system reflects a tendency toward a dichotomous cleavage that already existed in British society. A question of temporal sequence is relevant for the inference of causation; it does not make sense to say x causes y unless x comes before y in point of time. Lipson's point is that a dichotomous alignment on issues (for example, Cavaliers versus Roundheads, monarch versus aristocracy, aristocracy versus middle class, Anglicans versus dissenters) was already well established in Great Britain before the electoral system was institutionalized.

It is therefore questionable whether the imposition of a plurality system on a political system containing more than two segmental and intensely felt cleavages would necessarily result in a two-party system. It seems that the degree of compromise necessary to aggregate the diverse interests of a nation into two parties is a function of social, cultural, and historical circumstances. If there exist minority interests that are so intensely felt that they demand minority representation, interests that are discriminated against by a plurality system, then it is possible that either the electoral system or the political system will undergo substantial changes in response to the stress generated by such repressed demands. Denmark, which switched to proportional representation in 1920, may be a case in point. Or, as with the case of Canada, the plurality system may simply fail to prevent the existence of substantial third and fourth parties.[19] Thus, while it can be said that the plurality system strongly discourages more than two parties, it appears that such an electoral system is only adopted or maintained in societies willing and able to support a two-party system. The electoral system should not be thought of as some ultimate first cause of political outcomes. After all, a political system does have the option of what election system to adopt, and that choice must be accounted for in any relatively complete explanation of the number of parties.

---

[17] Wildavsky op. cit., pp. 308–9.

[18] Epstein, op. cit., pp. 60–61, and Lipson, loc. cit.

[19] For contrasting analysis of how these cultural, ethnic, and economic minorities achieve representation in Canada's aggregative party system, see Steven Muller, "Federalism and the Party System in Canada," in Aaron Wildavsky (ed.), *American Federalism in Perspective* (Boston: Little, Brown & Co., 1967), pp. 144–62, and Lawrence Mayer, "Federalism and Party Behavior in Australia and Canada," *Western Political Quarterly,* Vol. 23, No. 4 (December 1970), pp. 795–807.

It is even more doubtful that proportional representation can cause an increase in the number of parties. The number of parties remained stable in Scandinavia upon the adoption of proportional representation. As a matter of fact, the situation in Norway and Sweden is approaching a pattern of a conflict between two stable political forces under a multiparty façade. One might even say that the operation of their party system is closer to the modified one-party dominant arrangements one finds in Israel, Africa, and India than to the multiparty systems of pre-Gaullist France and Weimar Germany.

Eckstein reports the existence of strongly felt segmental cleavages in Norway, cleavages which are so resistant to aggregation that the one party that sought a wide and diverse audience is one of the weakest parties.[20] It is hard to see how any electoral system could in itself force these cleavages to aggregate into two ideological amorphous parties. Similarly, the ideological, religious, and socioeconomic cleavages that form the basis of the French multiparty system far antedated the adoption of the election systems of the Third or Fourth Republics.

It therefore seems reasonable to infer that proportional representation will permit and even encourage the existing cleavages in a society to be expressed in the party system. But it will not lead to the formation of more cleavages than already exist.[21] The degree to which a society is fragmented along cultural, socioeconomic, religious, etc., lines is a function of factors other than the electoral system. A proportional system will faithfully reflect the existing cleavages, while a plurality system will encourage a greater aggregation of existing cleavages.

It should be pointed out that the term *encourage* is more qualified than the term *cause*. Since the precise nature of the qualifications is not spelled out, the above proposition is inherently untestable. Unless one can either say that a given electoral system, by itself, is a sufficient and necessary precondition for a given party system or state the precise circumstances under which the electoral system becomes such a necessary and sufficient precondition, one must conclude that a precise scientific proposition on the effect of electoral systems on the number of parties has thus far eluded us, despite all of the literature on the topic.

The impact of electoral systems on political stability may be viewed as a separate although related question. It has been pointed out by Hermans that proportionality tends to radicalize parties. Because under a plurality system a party must aggregate a diverse body of followers to achieve any

---

[20] Harry Eckstein, *Division and Cohesion in Democracy* (Princeton: Princeton University Press, 1966), chap. 3, especially p. 56.

[21] Cf. Ferdinand Hermans, *Democracy or Anarchy* (Notre Dame, Ind.: The Review of Politics, University of Notre Dame, 1938), p. 15, who says "P.R. facilitates—and thereby creates—a multiplication of parties." My point is that "facilitates" should not be equated with "creates."

electoral success, the party must moderate its platforms to appeal to this wider audience. However, under the proportional system a party is not faced with this necessity. On the contrary, such a party is encouraged to emphasize the small differences between it and those parties ideologically adjacent to it. This reasoning is suggested by Anthony Downs, who attributes this tendency to the fact that since parties cannot move ideologically past one another nor attract votes from an adjacent party on one side without losing just as many votes to the party on the other side, their rational self-interests lie in more completely mobilizing their own faithful but narrow group of adherents.[22] In other words, since parties in a proportional system are not forced to aggregate diverse points of view, they can keep their ideology pure.

The proposition that proportionality makes stability more difficult to maintain[23] is based to a large extent upon the assumption that this electoral system results in a proliferation of the number of parties such that no one party can obtain a majority. Stable parliamentary government clearly requires the support of a stable majority in the lower house of the legislature inasmuch as the cabinet only continues to govern at the sufferance of such a majority. Such a majority must be sufficiently disciplined to insulate the prime minister or premier and his cabinet (hereafter referred to as the government) from accountability to the shifting day-to-day currents of public opinion, thus affording them the discretion inherent in the function of governing. A single party holding a majority of seats in the legislature seems much more capable than a coalition of relatively autonomous parties of insuring that the support on which the government relies remains stable and reliable from issue to issue.

However, when one examines the Scandinavian democracies, one realizes that neither proportionality nor a multiparty system precludes the possibility that a single party may, in fact, obtain a legislative majority. The Social Democratic party in Sweden and the Labor party in Norway have obtained such majorities on several occasions. There appears to be some relationship between multiparty systems in which the government was either composed of one party that had obtained a legislative majority or

---

[22] Anthony Downs, *An Economic Theory of Democracy* (New York: Harper & Row, 1957), pp. 126–27.

[23] This proposition reflects the position of A. J. Milnor, *Elections and Political Stability* (Boston: Little, Brown & Co., 1969), pp. 185ff. Cf. Hermans, op. cit., who more directly asserts a causal relationship Milnor's position is sufficiently interspersed with qualifiers to be immune from empirical challenge. For example, he says, "In periods of significant social change [this phrase itself being an ambiguous qualification on the conclusion—what constitutes such a period?] proportional representation *may* fail the social system by not providing a stable coalition powerful enough to weather the social challenge." (p. 186) But, under what conditions, defined in terms of observable indicators, will proportional representation fail the social system, and under what conditions will it fail the political system? Until these conditions are spelled out, *any* outcome is consistent with Milnor's statement as quoted here.

was dominated by a party that had obtained a near majority and political stability. Obviously, in such a case, the logic of a two-party system would apply. The principal exceptions to this generalization appear to be the stable coalitions between two parties of relatively equal strength, the so-called grand coalitions in West Germany and Austria.[24] It appears reasonable to tentatively infer that compromises among large numbers of parties of relatively weak but relatively equal strength will be more unstable than coalitions among fewer strong parties or coalitions dominated by one party.[25] This is a long way from stating with Hermans that proportional representation inexorably creates instability.

The foregoing has been concerned with a body of literature that implicitly or explicitly advocated the plurality system over the proportional system. This advocacy was based upon a normative preference for stability and a conception of democracy as a system that converts inputs into policy, policy that is relatively responsive to public opinion. Another body of literature has engaged in an equally vigorous advocacy of proportional representation. This latter group of writers based their advocacy of proportionality upon a normative conception of fairness and justice and a conception of democracy defined in terms of the accuracy of the representation of interests in the national decision-making process. The advocates of proportional representation are concerned that the plurality system, by allowing a single party to obtain a majority and govern, effectively disfranchises all who did not support that majority party. Otherwise put, the all-or-nothing results of plurality elections is unfair in that it distorts the distribution of opinion in society with respect to the institutionalized influence of those opinions on the national decision-making process. Every significant body of opinion should thus have effective representation in that decision-making process. While it is not explicitly carried this far, the argumentum ad absurdum of this logic is that each significant body of opinion should have veto power over national policy relevant to their perceived interests,

---

[24] A coalition between the Christian Democrats (C.D.U./C.S.U.) and Social Democrats (S.P.D.), representing about 80 to 90 percent of the German electorate, ruled Germany from late 1966 until 1969. A coalition of the Austrian People's party (O.V.A.) and the Socialists (S.P.O.), representing 83 to 89 percent of the Austrian electorate, has governed that nation since 1947. At other times since 1947, West Germany has exemplified the stability of a single dominant party in a governing coalition. Other examples around, such as the P.S.C. of Belgium.

[25] In accounting for system states at the macro level, rarely does the state of comparative analysis permit the formulation of generalizations to which exceptions cannot be found. One can only try to account for such exceptions as precisely as possible. Exceptions do exist to the proposition that nations governed by coalitions of numerous small parties, no one of which is clearly dominant, will tend to be unstable. Switzerland is a case in point. The weakness of such multiparty cabinets manifests itself in disagreements over how to process divisive issues. It may be tentatively suggested that such smaller nations have relatively fewer such issues to process, and it is for this reason that they survive with the luxury of less efficient political institutions.

the Calhoun conception of the concurrent majority. This is tantamount to an insistence upon unanimity.

This advocacy of proportionality is based upon the assumption that democracy is solely a function of the accuracy with which the composition of the legislature mirrors the distribution of opinion in the electorate, rather than upon the equally defensible conception of democracy as a function of the extent to which the policy output of a government is responsive to public opinion. These two standards of how democratic a system is must be distinguished. The second, responsiveness in policy output, does not necessarily follow from the first, accuracy of representation. In actuality, the accuracy of representation virtually precludes such institutionalized responsiveness.

The reason for this last statement lies in the function of an electoral system and of parties which underlies this polemic between the advocates and critics of proportionality. One leading advocate of proportionality suggests that this system "is better adapted . . . to producing an image of the feelings of the nation, *the first of our aims which an electoral system should fulfill.*" (Emphasis mine.)[26] Another leading polemicist against plurality in effect dismisses the entire aggregating function of parties, the function of consolidating enough similar opinions to produce a majority, thus enabling someone to govern. He dismisses this as a valid function when he suggests that elections should not resolve political issues because electors "lack the knowledge or experience necessary for this purpose."[27] However, if issues are not resolved by the electoral process, there is no imperative for the resolution of issues (that is, public policy) to reflect public opinion. Elections are, after all, the only institutionalized process by which public opinion can influence the political decision-making process. For example, in France during the Third and Fourth Republics, governments were formed in a bargaining process among the multifarious parliamentary groups after the election and, in fact, numerous times between elections. The composition of the governments and their policies that constituted the outcome of these bargaining sessions bore no necessary relationship to the distribution of party strength in the French legislature. Often, the electorally strongest parties were excluded by a coalition of weaker groups. Thus, for the advocate of proportionality the policy decision-making process does not necessarily have to reflect the outcome of the electoral process.[28]

It should be obvious by now that no objective resolution exists to the debate between the advocates of the two systems of election. Each position is based upon assumptions about the nature of democracy and values that

[26] Enid Lakeman and James Lambert, *Voting in Democracies* (London: Farber & Farber, Ltd., 1955), p. 149.

[27] Ross, op. cit., p. 47.

[28] Milnor, op. cit., p. 87. Cf. also his discussion of will versus good as objects of the democratic process, pp. 15–17.

are imcompatible with the other position; thus, the two sides are in effect arguing past one another. If one assumes with Lakeman and Lambert that the primary purpose of a democratic election system is to mirror the opinions of the electorate in the legislature, then some form of proportionality is the logical choice. On the other hand, if one assumes that an electoral system ought to maximize responsiveness of public policy output to shifts in public opinion and thus strengthen lines of accountability between the political decision makers and the electorate, the plurality system appears to be a logical choice. Representativeness, accountability, stability, and responsiveness are values whose consequences may in principle be empirically determined. However, since values cannot be scientifically justified, much of the literature on the impact of electoral systems on party systems takes on the character of a polemic rather than scientific inquiry.

TRENDS IN PROGRAM AND IDEOLOGY

The basic distinction between programmatic parties and parties of expediency or interests constitutes a typology of ideal types or paradigms rather than a useful typology of existing parties. The labeling of a party as a manifestation of one or the other of these types involves a judgment of emphasis or tendency. Obviously, no party of principle can afford to be totally oblivious to considerations of expediency if it expects to be viable. Similarly, no party of expediency is totally devoid of principle.

Ideology may be viewed in two senses. In a broad sense, it can refer to a system of separate but related attitudes, values, and principles. In the narrow and more traditional sense, it refers to a comprehensive, consistent, and closed system of ideas and beliefs.[29] It is to this more complete latter system that the German designation weltanschauung is applied. In its narrow sense, an ideology can generate answers to all questions. In this narrow usage, the term ideology has taken on pejorative connotations. However, used in the broader sense, ideology can be a useful and even necessary device. By obviating the burden on the voter of acquiring information needed to rationally choose between the parties on an issue-by-issue basis, party ideology serves the function of a "cost saving device." That is, it provides some basis for the choice between political alternatives, with a tolerable expenditure of resources. As Downs points out, information is not free and can only be acquired through some expenditure of time,

---

[29] This distinction is made in James B. Cristolph, "Consensus and Cleavage in British Political Ideology," *American Political Science Review,* Vol. 59, No. 3 (September 1965), p. 629ff; Karl Mannheim, *Ideology and Utopia* (New York: Harcourt, Brace & World Harvest Books, 1936), pp. 55ff; and Joseph LaPalombara, "The Decline of Ideology: A Dissent and Interpretation," *The American Political Science Review,* Vol. 60, No. 1 (March 1966), p. 7. Actually, ideology has been variously defined in the literature. Robert Lane, *Political Ideology* (New York: The Free Press, 1962) pp. 13–16, lists a number of such definitions.

effort, etc.[30] Ideologies in the broader sense of the term abet rational choice on the part of the electorate in that they afford a modicum of consistency in party policy and platform, thus making party behavior to some extent predictable.

Principled parties thrive best in multiparty situations, where success can be based upon appeal to a fixed and ideologically homogeneous clientele. Parties in two-party systems, on the other hand, are forced to aggregate a more diverse clientele because political success consists of winning a plurality of the total vote (or a majority of the seats in the legislature.)[31]

A body of literature has developed in recent years suggesting that ideology has become progressively less useful in predicting party behavior. The decline-of-ideology thesis, as applied to political parties, suggests that parties of principle are either becoming or being replaced by parties of expediency. This position, identified most notably with Otto Kirkheimer,[32] is based upon the narrow conception of ideology. The basic proposition is that there has been a progressive resolution of the basic economic controversies of the 19th century, a resolution based upon compromises between the polar extremes of revolutionary socialism and the concept of the self-regulating market. Therefore, the ideologies based upon and reflecting such 19th-century issues are increasingly irrelevant to 20th-century problems and issues. The consequence of this increased lack of relevancy has been a transformation of European parties from parties of principle, with an appeal to a fixed clientele, to parties of expediency, appealing to the broadest possible clientele. This latter variety of parties has been designated as a "catch-all people's party" by Kirkheimer.

This trend is most clearly reflected in the increased bourgeois orientation of what heretofore were socialist or at least labor-based parties.[33] Such parties have increasingly taken a more or less Keynesian economic stance in order to not alienate potential middle-class support. However, in adopting their immediate policy proposals to the need to attract proponents of the existing economic order, socialist parties have been paradoxically loathe to explicitly repudiate their ideological baggage of chiliastic millenarianism. (This refers to the idea that *the* revolution will be followed by a millennium in which all social problems will have been solved. The revolution in this ideological context becomes an ultimate goal rather than a

---

[30] This concept of ideology as a cost saving device is drawn from Downs, op. cit., pp. 198–99.

[31] Downs, op. cit., pp. 126–27, explains the logic of this generalization.

[32] Otto Kirkheimer, "The Transformation of Western European Party Systems," in Joseph LaPalombara and Myron Weiner (eds.), *Political Parties and Political Development* (Princeton: Princeton University Press, 1966), pp. 184–200. Cf. also "The Wanning of Opposition in Parliamentary Regimes," *Social Research,* Vol. 24, No. 2 (Summer 1957), pp. 127–56.

[33] See Robert C. Tucker, "The Deradicalization of Marxist Movements," *The American Political Science Review,* Vol. 61, No. 2 (June 1967), pp. 343–59.

means of reaching other goals, such as improving the material welfare of the blue-collar worker.)

Such eschatological revolutionary ideology proved inappropriate for solving specific social and economic problems of the society because it explicitly rejected that society as a whole. Consequently, socialist parties, when forced to come to grips with the problems of existing society, lacked a theoretical basis for deriving such solutions.[34] Of course, the irrelevance of revolutionary socialism as a guide to problem solving in a mature industrial economy became increasingly manifest as parties relying on working-class support came to power and had to cope with the responsibility of governing an entire society. As Robert Tucker points out, such parties acquire a vested interest in the viability of the existing order. Consequently, there was an increasing discrepancy between the ideological baggage of such labor-based parties and the policies with which they governed (or on which they stood for election).[35]

A classic example of these tendencies may be seen in the case of the Social Democratic party of Germany (S.P.D.). The original Marxist party, apparently sensing a chance to acquire genuine power within the context of the existing political system, allowed the reformist wing of the party, led by Ferdinand Lassalle, to prevail over the revolutionary Eisenacher faction of the party at the party's genesis. The result, much to the dismay of Marx and other socialist purists, was the distinctly reformist Gotha program of 1875.[36] Nevertheless, the party remains deeply split between revolutionary and reformist wings. The repressive antisocialist policies of Bismark rendered the S.P.D. much more receptive to orthodox Marxism,[37] resulting in what Schorske calls "the Erfurt Synthesis" of 1891. This platform was divided into two parts: first, a statement of ultimate objectives, especially the overthrow of the capitalist order, and, second, a statement of immediate aims which could be attained prior to this overthrow, aims revolving around an amelioration of the working and living conditions of the German worker. Since such improvements, as Marx well recognized, would weaken the revolutionary fervor of the workers, the two parts of the program were basically incompatible with one another. This schizophrenic bifurcation of the party program into a philosophical program based upon either revolutionary or democratic socialism and an action program of im-

---

[34] Daniel Bell, *The End of Ideology* (New York: The Free Press, 1961), p. 278.
[35] Tucker, op. cit., p. 350.
[36] Karl Marx, *Critique of the Gotha Program* (New York: International Publishers, 1935), p. 14. Cf. Carl E. Schorske, *German Social Democracy, 1905–1917, The Development of the Great Schism* (New York: John Wiley & Sons Science Editions, 1955). Schorske's book is the standard account of early German social democracy.
[37] This is the thesis of Guenther Roth, *The Social Democrats in Imperial Germany, A Study in Working Class Isolation and National Integration* (Touowa, N.J.: The Bedminster Press, 1963), Part 3 and *passim*.

mediate pragmatic policy proposals, usually designed to improve the lot of the working class within the existing system, is a concrete manifestation of the growing discrepency between socialist ideology and governing policies, as commented upon by Tucker. This bifurcated program was also adopted by the Australian Labour party beginning in 1902. The difference is that its ideological baggage was democratic rather than revolutionary socialism. The schism in the S.P.D. came to a head when the party found itself in power, with the responsibility of conducting or disposing of Germany's role in World War I. At this point, the slogan "to this system, no man and no penny" was easily replaced by the slogan "In the hour of danger we shall not leave the fatherland in the lurch."[38]

In the post–World War II era, the S.P.D., faced with a fixed minority clientele in the context of an emerging two-party alignment, again chose to abandon the socialist ideology that limited the party's appeal. The practical necessity of attracting non-working-class support if they did not want to remain in permanent opposition resulted in the S.P.D.'s adoption of the 1959 Bad Bodesburg Program, which stated, among other things, that "Private ownership of the means of production can claim protection by society just as long as it does not hinder the establishment of social justice."[39] This virtual abandonment of the party's long-standing socialist objective did not come about without resistance from the orthodox socialists in the party organization.

This tenacious resistance to the alteration of a party doctrine that apparently had condemned the party to permanent opposition status may be attributed to what Kirkheimer refers to as "the expressive function of the party,"[40] that is, the formulation and expression of opinions held by a significant portion of the electorate as opposed to the more mundane function of the processing of issues arising out of practical problems faced by a society. The expressive function of an ideology may involve providing an emotional outlet for the adherents of that ideology.

One generalization to be drawn from the experience of socialist parties, such as the S.P.D., the Australian and British Labour parties, and the Austrian Socialist party, appears to be that socialist doctrine tends to be modified or abandoned to the extent that the party in question either obtains, or perceives a realistic opportunity to obtain, the power and responsibility of government. Even the Italian Communist party (P.C.I.), reports LaPalombara, has undergone significant ideological transformations in the 60's in an effort to attract middle-class votes,[41] an effort perhaps not un-

---

[38] Schorske, op. cit., p. 285.

[39] *Basic Program of the Social Democratic Party* (adopted November 13–15, 1959 at Bad Godesberg), p. 11.

[40] Kirkheimer, op. cit., p. 189.

[41] Joseph LaPalombara, "The Decline of Ideology: A Dissent and an Interpretation," *The American Political Science Review* Vol. 60, No. 1 (March 1966), p. 10.

related to the possibility that, as the second strongest Italian party, it perceived a possibility of success in the existing political process. The abandonment of revolutionary or socialist ideology may be indicated by statements in party platforms or by party leaders according legitimacy to private ownership or market economics. This is a problem of content analysis and is clearly a researchable question.

The validity of the decline-of-ideology thesis with respect to parties is basically a function of one's definition of the concept of ideology. La Palombara's critique of the decline-of-ideology literature is based upon a broad definition of the term, similar to the broad definition discussed above.[42] The point is that there is little, if any, visible disagreement on the facts. LaPalombara (as suggested above with respect to his analysis of the P.C.I.) and Lipset would apparently agree that rather than espouse revolutionary Marxism, European labor-based parties are tending toward the espousal of incremental reforms of the existing economic situation. Since these newer positions still involve sets of principles, if not closed, comprehensive weltanschauunger, LaPalombara characterizes the transformation as ideological change. Lipset, on the other hand, conceives of ideology in the more narrow sense of the term. He specifically accepts the proposition that a commitment to pragmatism can itself be a principle that can be construed as ideological in the broad sense of the term.[43] His argument, therefore, is that political conflict is no longer carried on in terms of the traditional weltanschauugen of either revolutionary socialism or social democracy versus pure free-enterprise capitalism or rigid proclericalism versus rigid secularism to the extent that it was before World Warr II.

To illustrate, economic principles of parties of the left and parties of the right have converged in support of a mixed economy that is neither socialistic nor capitalistic. The British Conservative party has accepted the welfare state. The Swedish Social Democrats have opted for advanced welfare rather than state ownership, a policy opposed in degree rather than in principle by the nonsocialist opposition parties. This is not to deny that parties still espouse and even vigorously debate principles. But the total, comprehensive thought systems have been replaced by more loosely structured sets of principles held with less certitude and intensity. Lipset suggests that the result should be a reduction in the intensity of political conflict and an increased respect for the rights of minorities.[44]

The intensity of conflict is said to be a researchable variable. It is alleged to be related to the degree of tolerance of opposition.[45] These are vari-

---

[42] Ibid., p. 7 and passim.

[43] S. M. Lipset, "The Changing Class Structure and Contemporary European Politics," *Daedalus,* Vol. 93 (1964), p. 296.

[44] S. M. Lipset, "Some Further Comments on the 'End of Ideology'," *American Political Science Review,* Vol. 60, No. 1 (March 1966), p. 17.

[45] Ibid.

ables that appear to play a major role in the literature on the requisites of a stable democracy.[46] Yet, it is difficult to see what indicators may be posited for the intensity of political conflict other than overt expressions of one's tolerance (or lack thereof) of the opposition. Unless these two variables can be defined autonomously from one another, any suggested relationship between them becomes tautological. This does not detract from the logic of the suggestion that one is less likely to tolerate deviance from intensely held positions than from casually held ones. However, empirical verification of the suggestion depends on the specification of indicators.

The intensity-of-conflict and tolerance variables appear to bear some relationship to the variable of political stability, particularly in the case of multiparty coalitions. Insofar as total, comprehensive ideologies become equated with truth and certainty, the resulting increase in the intensity of conflict may impede the processes of political compromise on which the effective resolution of issues in heterogeneous societies appears to depend.[47] It is not logical to compromise with that which one is sure is fundamental error.

Kirkheimer's catch-all parties operate on the basis of principles derived from perceived interests rather than principles based upon conceptions of truths and moral absolutes. Such parties can more effectively aggregate interests to the level of manageability that enables issues to be resolved through the electoral process.[48] To the extent that parties and party systems stand on total ideologies, interests must be aggregated and issues resolved in the legislature after the election. To the extent that the responsive capacity of a government depends on the connection between elite and masses provided by the electoral process, parties of expediency appear to be potentially more functional for such responsiveness than parties of total ideology.

Writers such as Spiro attempt to show these relationships between ideology and stability and between ideology and responsive capacity with respect to specific nations. LaPalombara and Weiner suggest a relationship between the ideological-pragmatic dimension and political change.[49] This

---

[46] For example, Gabriel Almond and Sidney Verba, *The Civil Culture* (Princeton: Princeton University Press, 1963).

[47] See Herbert J. Spiro, *Government by Constitution* (New York: Random House, 1959) chap. 14, pp. 196–210, for a stimulating discussion of the dysfunctional effect of ideologism on the processing of issues.

[48] See Robert Alford, *Party and Society* (Chicago: Random House, 1963), p. 339, for the argument that parties based on interests are more functional for issue resolution than parties based upon "values." Using a measure of class voting, Alford has measured differences among the Anglo-American democracies with respect to this variable. Class voting is said to lead to interest-oriented rather than value-oriented politics. Class voting also ostensibly promotes national rather than regional-oriented politics.

[49] Joseph LaPalombara and Myron Weiner, "The Origin and Development of Political Parties," in LaPalombara & Weiner, *Political Parties and Political Development* (Princeton: Princeton University Press, 1965), pp. 35–37.

FIGURE 11–1

HEGEMONIC TURNOVER

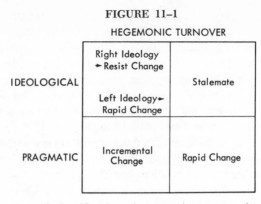

depends on a second classification: hegemonic systems, in which one party dominates power over an extended period of time, and turnover systems, which involve relatively frequently alternation of dominating elites. These variables may be cross-classified as illustrated in Figure 11-1.

When hegemonic parties are ideological, the amount of change depends on the content of the ideology. Ideological parties of the right tend to be static while ideological parties of the left may bring out very rapid and fundamental change. Pragmatic parties will move more rapidly in turnover situations and incrementally in hegemonic situations.

Such generalizations lack significant predictive power for real-world situations because the cross-classification matrix from which they are derived fails to establish nonambiguous boundaries between the categories in each dimension. For example, how long must one party be in control or dominate coalitions to be classified as hegemonic rather than turnover? Why was the New Deal–Fair Deal situation in the United States called hegemonic by the authors while the Canadian situation was classified as turnover despite equally long periods of control by the Liberal party? The criteria for such decisions are far from clear. In addition, the testing of such relationships depends on the more precise specification of the indicators by which we differentiate ideological from pragmatic orientations.

THE ORIGIN AND STRUCTURE OF PARTIES

Much of the literature on parties is concerned with the classification of individual parties along structural or organizational lines. The type of party structure is often hypothesized to be a partial function of the forces which gave rise to the party. Therefore, these variables are discussed together.

One of the most fundamental structural variables is the distinction between mass-membership parties, cadre parties, and devotee parties.[50] This

---

[50] Duverger, op. cit., pp. 63ff.

distinction is based upon the concept of party membership. Party members have more formalized connections to the parties to which they adhere than the mere act of voting for the party's candidates at periodic elections. Often, this takes the form of actually paying dues and attending party meetings. Mass parties are those in which the adherents to the party become formal members. Cadre parties are those in which the adherents to the party merely support the party through the act of voting for its candidates. Devotee parties constitute a type of party in which membership is more open than cadre parties but less open than mass parties. For example, the percentage of the population that forms the membership of many communist and fascist parties has been higher than the percentage of the population that is active in American parties. Yet, that percentage of the population that actually holds membership in that country's communist party is still quite small, generally less than ten percent. The distinction between mass, cadre, and devotee parties, admits Duverger, who suggests it, is not always clear in practice. The question is precisely what activities distinguish a member from a supporter.

Mass-membership parties tend to be those that originated as the political arm of a social or economic mass movement. Thus, they tend to be parties which are created outside the principal legislative body of their political system. Such externally created parties may be distinguished from internally created parties. The latter are generally regarded as creations of members of the legislature in response to the need to secure mass support generated by an expanded suffrage.[51] The origin of internal parties in Great Britain, however, may be traced to factions that existed in British politics and even in Parliament prior to the development of the election of members of Parliament. Those who argue that parties grew up in response to the development of the suffrage simply would define the concept of party to exclude such factions. Nevertheless, some continuity does exist between such parliamentary factions and the cadre parties.

Such internal parties, being entities created to promote the electoral success of the parliamentary group that created them rather than to achieve programmatic goals, tend to be less ideological than externally created parties.[52] Cadre parties preceded the formation of mass parties in point of time because mass membership only became technically feasible when two conditions were fulfilled: one, when universal suffrage gave the masses political influence, a condition that was not fulfilled until well into the 19th century in the Western industrial democracies and even later elsewhere; and, second, when the level of technology permitted the development of a national communication network adequate for the integration of the

---

[51] Epstein, op. cit., p. 19.
[52] Duverger, op. cit., pp. 65–66.

masses into the political process, also a 19th and in some places 20th-century development. Thus, the British Liberal and Conservative parties developed constituency organizations in response to a franchise (right to vote) that, although expanded, was still based on a property qualification. The introduction of universal suffrage was followed by the rise of mass parties throughout the Western world.

There seems to be a rather clear relationship between party organization and party ideology. Mass-membership parties have originated as the political arm of a mass social or economic movement with a rather definite set of goals. Often, such goals have been derived from a more or less closed and complete ideology. Marxist parties dominate this category. The Nazi party could also be so categorized. In such cases, the goals usually consist of tearing down the existing order. In other words, such parties arose out of a mass movement based upon a widespread sense of alienation from the system. Accordingly, a party based upon such a mass movement begins in effect with a mandate to destroy the system. Thus, because they have not developed a vested interest in the system, such parties are perceived of as a threat by the older cadre parties.[53] Intolerance, a lack of legitimacy for the opposition, and an inability to resolve political issues through compromise will characterize the political style of systems in which such revolutionary mass parties acquire significant strength. Such systems will become more volatile or immobilized and somewhat less viable over time.

Clearly, not all mass parties are revolutionary. The ideology or goals that give rise to the mass movement may be quite compatible with the existing political and economic system; such goals may arise rather from the perception of interests that were inadequately represented by existing political alignments. Parties based upon trade-union movements would epitomize such parties. The difficulty is that it is not always entirely clear whether a given party is a revolutionary socialist or a trade-union party. The discrepancy between party rhetoric and party ideology discussed above contributes to this confusion. The French S.F.I.O. (French Section of the Workers' International) and the German Social Democrats beautifully illustrate this ideological ambiguity. The goals of a trade-union-oriented party, the improvement of the material welfare of the laborer, can be quite incompatible with revolutionary socialism. Collective bargaining, the raison d'être of trade unions, presumes a capitalistic economic system. It cannot exist in a classless society. Thus, parties that waver between these two ideological positions will be subject to deep-seated schisms.

Insofar as the mass movements represent economic interests inimical to the economic interests of the existing political alignments, a milder threat may still be perceived, and some initial political repression can occur and, in fact, has occurred. Nevertheless, eventually the integration of trade-

---

[53] LaPalombara & Weiner, op. cit., pp. 10–11.

union parties into the political process formerly dominated by middle and upper-class parties has occurred wherever trade-union parties have developed.

Epstein points out that the labor-based parties are the most frequent type to have mass memberships and, in fact, all such labor-based parties are mass parties.[54] The logic in this is that a party arising outside of and challenging the existence of the economic order could not depend on funding from the wealthy capitalists whose interests were being challenged, nor could such a party depend upon patronage for an organizational base. In other words, such working-class parties had to derive their strength from numbers rather than privilege or quality of membership.

In cases where the party originates as a national independence movement in a colony, a mass organization and a relatively specific ideological foundation also generally result.[55] Three factors seem to largely account for this relationship. In the first place, such parties have often acquired rigorous organizational skills and habits while compelled to operate more or less covertly against a colonial regime that refused to accept the legitimacy of the independence movement. In the second place, such parties usually so dominate the nationalist movement that once the colonial authority has been removed, the nationalist parties frequently identify themselves as coterminous with the state. In the third place, one of the major issues facing many newly independent regimes is Pye's "crisis of integration."[56] The dominant nationalist party in such a regime frequently per ceives its primary function as the engineering of national integration through the mobilization and control of the masses.[57] The ideological content of such nationalist hegemonic parties is often a more or less comprehensive and consistent combination of socialism and anticolonialism in the spirit of Lenin's writings on imperialism.

Mass parties generally have a commitment to rank-and-file democracy as part of their ideological baggage. Inasmuch as the party leadership's reason for being is to transform the goals and aims of a mass movement into public policy, it is only logical that those leaders should be formally accountable to that movement. The members of the legislature or the government belonging to such a party exist in theory to give political effect to the demands of the mass movement they putatively represent.

---

[54] Epstein, op. cit., p. 130.

[55] Rupert Emerson, "Parties and National Integration in Africa," in LaPalombara and Weiner, op. cit., p. 274. Examples of such parties include Sekou Touré's *Parti Démocratique de Guinée* in Guinea; The North Vietnamese Worker's party that grew out of the *Vietnam Doc Lap Dong Minh Hoi;* Nkrumah's Convention People's party in Ghana; Houphouet's *Parti Démocratique de la Côte d'Ivoire* on the Ivory Coast; and the Burmese Anti-fascism People's Freedom League.

[56] Lucien Pye, *Aspects of Political Development* (Boston: Little, Brown & Co., 1966), pp. 65–66.

[57] Cf. David Apter, *The Politics of Modernization* (Chicago: University of Chicago Press, 1965), p. 191 and pp. 197–99.

It is possible, however, to distinguish, normative of commitment to rank-and-file democracy, the structural forms of rank-and-file democracy (such as the periodic election of party leaders) and the actual extent to which party leaders are subject to rank-and-file control. The extent to which the commitment in principle leads to the structural forms and the extent to which the structural forms reflect genuine accountability appear to be researchable questions. Accordingly, a literature on this topic has developed with respect to Western parties.

The classic generalization in this respect comes to us from an Italian sociologist writing shortly after the turn of the century. Robert Michels's "Iron Law of Oligarchy," while applicable to large organizations in general, was derived from a study of the Social Democratic Party of Germany.[58] Michels's thesis is that while parties of the left must accept internal party democracy as a norm and even usually go through the motions of adhering to that norm in form, in practice the leadership of any large organization is inherently oligarchical. That is, any large organization is led by a relatively small number of individuals who, despite democratic forms, cannot be in any meaningful sense accountable to the rank-and-file membership.[59]

Michels's iron law is principally developed by means of a logical argument buttressed by selected illustrative examples. His premise is the necessity of organization for any large social movement.[60] The need for organization stems from its alleged efficiency. This is consistent with the writings of another early 20th-century sociologist, Max Weber, discussed in Chapter 7. It was seen there that the efficiency of large organizations is based upon the specialization and competence of the occupants of each role. Thus, every complex organization acquires leadership roles to which the occupants must devote full attention in order to acquire the requisite competence. Michels takes a Rousseauian view of the world in suggesting that "a mass that delegates its sovereignty [authority] . . . abdicates its sovereign functions."[61] Michels appears to be suggesting that when a group delegates discretionary authority to a leader or leaders, it loses control of decision making for the group. This amounts to a denial of the possibility of a representative function. The leaders, by virtue of their specialized roles, acquire esoteric information and knowledge not shared by those whom they rule. This renders the leaders not subject to effective control by the masses. Finally, by virtue of their full-time roles not shared by the rank and file of the organization, leaders acquire a perspective and a set of interests

---

[58] Robert Michels, *Political Parties,* trans. Eden & Cedar Paul (New York: Dover Publications, 1959) especially part 6, Chap. 2.

[59] Gaetano Mosca, *The Ruling Class* (New York: McGraw-Hill, 1939), p. 50 and passim.

[60] Michels, op. cit., p. 21–23.

[61] Ibid., pp. 36–37.

not necessarily coterminous with the interests of their rank and file. This is partly a result of the fact that such leaders are more knowledgeable, economically better off, and have a greater stake in the organization itself. Thus, the organization, created as a means, becomes an end in itself, an "entity . . . not necessarily identifiable with the totality of its members and still less so with the class to which these belong."[62] It seems doubtful, for example, that a great American union leader, such as the late Walter Reuther, had as much in common intellectually, culturally, or in terms of economic interest with his workers as he did with management. Picture Reuther in blue overalls on an automobile assembly line.

Such an iron law as represented by the writings of such scholars as Michels and Mosca constitutes an effort to look behind the procedural forms of organization to gain insight into the "real" power structure of parties. More recent inquiry into the power structure of parties has tended to reveal that the leader-follower relationship is more complex than the simplistic iron law would seem to indicate.

McKenzie's monumental study of British parties[63] concluded that the Labour party leaders are not as subject to rank-and-file control as their egalitarian ideological baggage seems to require and their procedural mechanisms seem to provide. McKenzie similarly finds that the leaders of the Conservative party are not as oligarchical and free from backbench influence as one might expect from the theoretical basis of that party. The annual election of the leadership of the parliamentary Labour party that the party rules require does not render the Labour leader's tenure less secure than that of the Conservative party leader, who was (until the recent election of Ted Heath) not elected. Despite the formal requirement of annual reelection, no Labour leader has had to stand opposed for reelection since 1922.[64] Moreover, Tory leaders have been driven from their post by backbench revolts on more than one occasion.[65]

The contribution of the book is the suggestion that the distribution of power in a political party is not so much a function of the party's ideological orientation as it is a function of the imperatives of the political structure in which the party operates.[66] On the other hand, the imperatives of cabinet government demand a higher degree of centralization despite the Labour party's egalitarian philosophy, which demands a decentralized power structure. On the other hand, the system demands that the views of

---

[62] Ibid., p. 389.

[63] Robert T. McKenzie, *British Political Parties* (New York: St. Martin's Press, 1963). A summary of the thesis and conclusions of the book may be found in McKenzie, "Power in British Parties," *British Journal of Sociology,* Vol. 6, No. 2 (June 1955), pp. 123–32.

[64] McKenzie, *British Political Parties,* op. cit., p. 299.

[65] Ibid., chap. 3.

[66] Ibid., p. 635ff.

organized supporters outside Parliament and the views of backbenchers in Parliament be taken into greater account than the literature on the Conservative party suggests is the case with that party.

In McKenzie's analysis, constitutional structure takes on the character of an independent variable or explicans, and the power structure of political parties becomes the dependent variable or explanandum. Party ideology becomes irrelevant to the explanation of the party power structure. McKenzie confines his analysis to the British system, and it would be inaccurate to attribute to him any attempt to generalize beyond his British data. However, we have seen that unless the scope of propositions extends beyond the data on which they are based, such propositions lack explanatory or predictive power.[67] Therefore, any assessment of the scientific value of McKenzie's study must necessarily lead to an inquiry into the extent that his propositions apply to other party systems. This is so despite the fact that McKenzie is never clear as to whether only the British cabinet system provides organizational imperatives of adequate strength to shape the structure of its parties or whether any constitutional structure can shape internal party structure.

Thus, McKenzie's basic proposition seems to be that the leader-follower relationship in political parties is exclusively or primarily (McKenzie is not clear on this point) a function of that country's constitutional order. If this proposition were generally applicable, all the parties in a given constitutional order would maintain approximately the same balance between oligarchy and internal democracy. Clearly, this is not the case. It is undeniable that there is a certain trend toward similarity in a number of respects among parties of the Western world.[68] Nevertheless, important differences between parties within a given country appear to persist. Western communist parties constitute the most obvious example. It follows that some variable other than the nation's constitutional structure must in some circumstances at least exert a significant influence on the distribution of power within parties. It seems reasonable to infer from the above that the impact of party ideology on the distribution of power in parties has diminished; however, it has not disappeared to the exent that McKenzie seems to suggest. Indeed, Samuel Beer implies that McKenzie has overstated the structural similarity of parties even in the British case. Beer takes the Labour party's theoretical and structural egalitarianism much more seriously and infers much more rank-and-file control than does McKenzie.[69]

---

[67] See Chapter 3, pp. 33–47.

[68] Kirkheimer, "The Transformation of Western European Party Systems," op. cit., p. 190.

[69] Samuel Beer, *British Politics in the Collectivist Age* (New York: Alfred A. Knopf, 1965), pp. 156–63 and pp. 371–72. Beer's book constitutes the most recent of the highly respected "standards" on the British party system. Beer's analysis also

Richard Rose further reveals the complexities of the leader-follower relationship in British parties. It is Rose who suggests the source of the disagreement between McKenzie and Beer.[70] McKenzie relies on the retention of office as virtually his sole index of the power and autonomy of the party leader. Beer and Rose are interested in the reciprocal influence between party leader and party rank and file with respect to party programs. As Rose so clearly points out, both in the article cited here and in his larger study of the British political system,[71] the policy proposals of the British cabinet are not framed with complete disregard of the will of the backbenchers of the governing party. The maintenance of cohesion on legislative roll-call votes is not only a function of the formal institutional threats of party discipline, it is also rendered possible by a process of formal and informal consultation between party leader and backbencher in the formulation of policy. Indeed, McKenzie himself discusses such formal institutions for interchange between party leadership and party rank and file as the Tories' "1922 Committee." Thus, differences between leader and party rank and file are resolved before confidence issues come to a vote, and party leaders often do adjust their legislative program to meet the parliamentary party halfway.

These studies constitute major manifestations of the fact that the British party system is one of the most thoroughly described subjects in all of political science. The scientific value of such descriptions is a function of the extent to which they suggest relationships that are applicable to some defined class of other political systems. McKenzie suggests that the power structure of British parties is a product of cabinet government. Rose is less clear in postulating such generalizations beyond the fact that the problem is complex. Presumably, institutional factors interact with cultural factors, such as British pragmatism, bargaining style, and authority patterns, to produce the observed result. Thus, while Rose's sophisticated analysis provides an understanding of the British process in the nonscientific sense of the term,[72] it does not explain the state of affairs in the scientific sense of an explanation with predictive power. The thrust of these studies remains essentially descriptive despite the fact that they go beyond formal, legal variables. The value of descriptive studies drawn from Great Britain is

---

encompasses British political style and the role of groups in Britain; hence, it is broader in the number of variables it encompasses than the McKenzie study. The latter pretty well confines itself to party organization and power structure.

[70] Richard Rose, "Complexities of Party Leadership," *Parliamentary Affairs,* Vol. 16, No. 3 (Summer 1963), pp. 257–73.

[71] Richard Rose, *Politics in England* (Boston: Little, Brown & Co., 1964), pp. 220 and 143.

[72] See my discussion of explanatory appeal on pp. 44–46. This imparts an understanding best described by Weber's concept, *verstehen.* The observer experiences a psychic satisfaction that his explanation accounts for the events in question. However, his explanation does not increase his predictive power.

circumscribed by the limited use of cabinet government as a constitutional form in other countries insofar as the outcomes in question are wholly or partially attributable to that constitutional form. In other words, insofar as the power structure of British parties is a product of cabinet government, the description of that power structure is of little relevance for nations outside the older Commonwealth that do not share this constitutional form.

Duverger presents a classificatory schema that extends well beyond the cadre-mass-devotee breakdown discussed above. The first half of his attempt to construct a theory of parties may be argued to consist of a number of classifications, essentially of Western party systems, along a number of structural dimensions. Cultural, historical, geographical, or other sociological variables that shape party variables are largely ignored, as pointed out earlier.[73] The distinctions made by Duverger, such as that between direct and indirect membership or between weak and strong articulation, are significant only insofar as they are precise and insofar as countries grouped in one such category can be related to other significant outcomes in an empirical generalization. Duverger sometimes attempts to "explain" these variables. For example, he suggests several variables that probably have played a part in the adoption of the indirect form.[74] Aside from the obvious criticisms of such a highly qualified and imprecise explanation, Duverger never makes a convincing case that the distinction is worth making let alone explaining. He fails to show how such characteristics can be related to other phenomena in such a way as to account for the other phenomena.

THE FUNCTIONAL APPROACH TO THE STUDY OF PARTIES

The fact that institutions bearing the common name of parties play diverse roles in different political or social settings renders the functional approach a useful tool for the organization of data about parties. In this approach, issues such as the metaphysical question of whether parties in single-party systems are "really" parties are moot questions. The approach presumes that the institution known as political parties is not confined to the functions performed in any given political context. Rather, the approach poses the question of how the functions performed by parties in one context differ from the functions performed by parties in other contexts.

One difficulty is that parties are sometimes defined in terms of the functions they perform in democratic systems. Thus, because the institutions in authoritarian political systems do not perform the functions that demo-

---

[73] There are some exceptions; for example, he suggests that national temperament has also influenced the choice between a direct or indirect structure. Duverger, op. cit., p. 14.

[74] Ibid., pp. 13–16. He duly qualifies his putative causal relations as "a basic tendency" rather than "a sociological law."

cratic parties perform, they are not justified in calling themselves parties. This is essentially a semantic argument. It is one thing to note that the functions of democratic parties differ in some respects from the functions of authoritarian parties. It is another question to ask if there are *any* functions that *all* of the institutions calling themselves political parties share. If the answer to this latter question is affirmative, it is possible to make a case for assigning a common name to all of these institutions.

The literature on party functions varies with respect to the specificity with which functions are listed. At a high level of generality parties are said to organize opinion and, in so doing, provide a link between the elites and the masses.[75]

Almond suggests that in open and industrialized societies, parties and bureaucracies are the major specialized structures performing the functions of interest articulation and interest aggregation, functions that are putatively performed in all political systems.[76] These two functional requisites may present conflicting imperatives, however; to the extent that the aggregation function is performed by a given structure, interest articulation by that same structure is compromised. The precise balance in the role of parties with respect to these two functions may be determined to a significant extent by the presence or absence of a well-developed system of secondary associations in that society. In cases where interest groups exist to transmit with great specificity the demands arising out of the differences of interests in any complex, heterogeneous society, parties are thereby freed in a sense to consolidate these demands and present policy positions at a much higher level of generality. The situation is characteristic of the most highly developed Western democracies, such as the United States, Britain, the Scandinavian countries, and, increasingly since World War II, the Federal Republic of Germany. In a situation like that of France, where a Rousseauian ideology deprecates the legitimacy of interest groups, parties act to fill the void in the articulation of specific or unaggregated interests.

Thus, the absence of other means of articulating specific interests or positions of principle may account for the fragmentation of the party system as much as the electoral system variable discussed above. Of course, this only applies to an open and complex system in which the masses are mobilized and politicized to the extent that a variety of interests is perceived by the masses with some threshold level of intensity. In this way, Almond's assumption that the articulation function must be performed, at least in certain types of systems, logically can give rise to the concept of a func-

---

[75] For example, David Apter, *The Politics of Modernization* (Chicago: University of Chicago Press, 1965), p. 181.

[76] Gabriel Almond and G. Bingham Powell, *Comparative Politics, A Developmental Approach* (Boston: Little, Brown & Co., 1966), pp. 100–101. See Chapter 8, p. 147, for a discussion of these functions.

tional vacuum. That is, if the structures that normally perform a function for one reason or another fail to do so, other structures will develop in such a way as to fill the void.

This is not to say that the interest-group structure that causes the party system in a given system is a simple one-to-one relationship. For example, this hypothesis of the relationship between parties and groups is complicated by the fact that a two-party alignment was clearly established in Britain before the development of interest groups in the modern sense of the term. In fact, it was before the perception of distinguishable corporate interests brought on by the industrial revolution. However, such a group structure did develop in response to these perceived interests. It is arguable that this group structure made it easier for the existing dichotomous party alignment to withstand the pressures for fragmentation to which other, Continental party systems succumbed. For example, the British Labour party is clearly more than a mere spokesman for the trade-union movement. This higher level of aggregation, which at times leads the party leadership to oppose the perceived interests of organized labor, permits the Labour party to appeal to sufficient non-working-class support to win a majority of seats in the House of Commons. The austerity program of Harold Wilson constitutes one example of a Labour Prime Minister vigorously opposed by organized labor. The "Premier's Plan" of the Australian Labour party's Prime Minister Scullin to deal with the Great Depression by orthodox financial means constitutes another such example. The articulation of working-class interests, partly neglected by the Labour party, is carried out through the trade-union movement.

The functional vacuum created by the failure of parties to perform the aggregation function is filled by governmental institutions so as to make the demands manageable with respect to number and variety. In such cases, the aggregated policy alternatives upon which decision makers act are not formulated through the party system; hence, such systems have a diminished responsive capacity. Coalition formation in the Chamber of Deputies of the fourth French republic illustrates this type of situation.

Other functions commonly associated with parties in a democratic system include the selection and recruitment of candidates for office, the control of the executive, the formulation and communication to the masses of relatively clear and meaningful alternatives of public policy, the integration and politicization of the masses into the political system, the control and management of conflict and, hence, the peaceful resolution of issues. It would be difficult if not impossible for any individual to formulate a list of such functions that all would accept as complete. The content of such a list depends on how one chooses to define the functions. Functions are, after all, concepts, not empirical facts. Therefore, one could always conceptualize some function that he could argue was not subsumed by any given list.

Obviously, the relative importance of such functions depends on the political and social context in question. Rupert Emerson, for example, points out that the fact that most African states achieved independence with a lower level of integration than most Western states renders the integration function for African parties "more difficult and more necessary" than in any other part of the world.[77] In hegemonic systems (one party dominance), where a party becomes virtually coterminous with the state itself, the control function is deemphasized.

The functional approach to parties shares the strengths and weaknesses of functionalism in general. The functional approach to stasiology [the study of political parties] enjoys the descriptive advantage of being able to subsume a very heterogeneous body of data under common, comparable units of analysis. This approach suffers, however, from the explanatory weaknesses of functionalism discussed in Chapter 8.

In applying functionalism to the study of parties, the inquiry is directed to the consequences of parties or party system characteristics[78] on the political system in which they operate. The parties or party systems in this mode of analysis may be conceived of as relatively independent variables, givens, if you will, that have an impact on the system.[79] The question posed is, What is the nature of that impact? not Why do parties or party systems possess varying sets of characteristics in different contexts? The problem of why functions are performed differently in one system or type of system than in another is resolved on the basis of need. This is the same problem of a tautological argument discussed in Chapter 8. This tendency is illustrated by the Emerson example cited just above. African parties em-

---

[77] Rupert Emerson, "Parties and National Integration in Africa," in LaPalombara & Weiner, op. cit., p. 267. Cf. Ruth Schacter, "Single Party Systems in West Africa," *The American Political Science Review,* Vol. 55, No. 2 (June 1961), pp. 294–307, for the argument that the performance of the integration and politicization function by single parties in West Africa enhances the movement of these regimes toward democracy.

[78] These characteristics may involve the presence of parties, the nature of parties or party systems, or the behavior of parties. Howard Scarrow, *Comparative Political Analysis* (New York: Harper & Row, 1969), p. 81.

[79] The contrast between this analysis and that of Scarrow should be noted. Scarrow draws a distinction between functional and causal analysis on the basis of whether parties act willfully or not (Ibid., pp. 85ff). It is difficult to extract the necessity of this distinction from the logic of functionalism. Scarrow points out the inferential aspect of drawing causal conclusions from correlation data. It is difficult to see, however, how the problem of inference can be avoided. Clearly correlation and contingency data can, as he argues, lead to spurious correlations (p. 95). That is precisely why *logical* processes must be relied upon as an additional check on the validity of conclusions based upon such data. A temporal sequence can serve as additional evidence but cannot, as he implies (p. 94), demonstrate the necessity of a causal relationship. My analysis, on the other hand, simply makes the point that the performance of functions cannot account for system states. The distinction between willful action and behavior "as part of an ongoing system" is not relevant to the issue of whether a scientific explanation has been formulated.

phasize the integration function because their societies are less integrated. This is another illustration of the functional vacuum concept implicit in the logic of the paradigm. Functionalism does not in this argument account for either the nature of West African party systems or for the extent to which West African political systems are integrated because both the party characteristics and the system states are used here to account for each other. The need is to find explicans to account for the differences in functional performance among parties and party systems other than the characteristics of the political systems that such functional performances are themselves used to explain.

PARTY COHESION AND ROLL-CALL ANALYSIS

The analysis of legislative roll-call votes is a convenient object of empirical research simply because this is an easily obtainable and quantitative body of data. Its quantitative characteristic renders roll-call analysis susceptible of great precision and mathematical manipulation. All Western countries publish an official record of their legislative debates and votes corresponding to our *Congressional Record*. Such documents are readily available in most university libraries.

Yet, despite the apparent advantages of roll-call analysis, the focus of inquiry on roll calls has been almost exclusively confined to the United States. One reason for this parochialism is the prevalence of parliamentary systems more or less approaching the British cabinet form in those nations where reliable data is most readily available. The imperatives of this political form generate great pressures for the maintenance of party cohesion. The pressures are the result of the need for an aggregating institution that can mobilize a stable majority in the legislature and, thus, insulate the cabinet from the day-to-day shifting currents of opinion in the legislature to which the cabinet is formally accountable. Without succumbing to the temptation of adopting the functional orientation just criticized and arguing that the need is sufficient to account for the fact of cohesion, one can argue that the need creates the pressures. Some party systems respond to these pressures by becoming cohesive, others do not. The factors that underly this differential response to the pressures for cohesion are apparently exceedingly complex.

The important point here is that many parliamentary democracies have responded to the imperatives of this political form with cohesive parties. This is the prevailing fact of life in the United Kingdom and the older Commonwealth, and to a lesser extent in the Scandinavian democracies, the Federal Republic of Germany, and the Benelux democracies. Since issues are resolved before the roll calls are taken and all members of the legislature almost invariably vote their party line, it seems that the analysis of roll-call votes is unlikely to yield any new information. One knows before looking how each legislator will vote and how the votes will cluster, irrespective of the issue at stake.

The fact that in some nations, such as Italy, important roll calls are kept secret presents another difficulty for the analysis of roll-call votes. As one moves to the study of the non-Western political process, data on roll-call voting tends to be either absent or less reliable.

Despite these persuasive arguments, some scholars are suggesting that roll-call analysis in parliamentary democracies with disciplined parties can yield useful data.[80] In the first place, there are some indications that the level of cohesion in some of these nations, the United Kingdom excepted, is not as nearly perfect as once assumed.[81] There is often considerable lee-way between the level of cohesion necessary for the survival of the government, as required by the imperatives of cabinet government, and the near perfect cohesion generally assumed, leeway for individual legislators to occasionally respond to individual conscience or constituency pressures and vote against their party whip. In the second place, it is possible that individual legislators may respond to a conflict between individual conscience or constituency pressure and their party whip by simply abstaining. Both of these possibilities constitute useful subjects for empirical inquiry.

Mathematical indices of cohesion are available to measure this variable. The standard index appears to be the Rice Index. However, the Rice Index is based solely upon those actually casting a vote. There are other indices whose magnitude is affected by the level of abstention, the absolute index and the index offered by Rasmussen.[82]

The difficulty here is the absence of any empirical foundation for the inference that the observed level of abstention is wholly or partially due to conflicting pressure on the legislator between conscience or constituency, on the one hand, and party whip, on the other, rather than due to illness, laziness, or some other such "natural cause."

CONCLUSION—THE ELUSIVE GOAL OF THEORY

The title of this chapter suggests that an attempt to integrate a set of empirical generalizations and observed facts about parties into a theoretic construct from which precise expectations about party behavior, party structure, or party system states may be deduced has characterized a significant portion of the literature on parties. The failure to achieve such

---

[80] For example, Jorgen Rasmussen, "The Measurement of Cohesion in Tightly Disciplined Parliamentary Parties" (unpublished paper: Vanderbilt University Research Council, 1968).

[81] For example, Lawrence C. Mayer, "Federalism and Party Behavior in Australia and Canada," *The Western Political Quarterly,* Vol. XXIII (December 1970), pp. 795–807.

[82] See Lee F. Anderson, Meredith Watts, and Allen Wilcox, *Legislative Roll-Call Analysis* (Evanston, Ill.: Northwestern University Press, 1966), pp. 32–36, and Rasmussen, op. cit.

theoretical coherence, despite the abundance of research on parties, is made manifest from the foregoing survey.

The reasons for this failure may best be summarized with reference to a notable attempt to pull together knowledge and data on one aspect of party research—the role of political oppositions in Western democracies.[83] This appears on first glance to be a manageable and well-defined focus of inquiry. However, substantial complications manifest themselves upon closer inquiry. In the first place, the difficulties involved in the specification of the outcomes to be explained have not been overcome. Since the contributing authors followed no coherent conceptual framework, it is difficult to discover patterns in the heterogeneous body of data presented. This difficulty is a consequence of the very lack of precision in the meaning of the word *patterns,* although the phrase *patterns of opposition* is used throughout the integrative chapters in this book. Dahl has taken a first step toward generalizing about the data in listing six variables, applicable to the variety of systems under consideration, for comparative purposes.[84] Thus, by posing a common set of questions, it is in principle possible to gather data from the variety of political systems susceptible of being integrated in generalizations.

Some of the variables are not exclusively opposition characteristics but party system characteristics. It is apparent from reading the various country studies in the book that it is often impossible to separate political opposition as a focus for inquiry from the entire party system or, for that matter, from the entire political system or even the entire social system. For example, Dahl finds a tendency toward the decline of what he calls structural opposition or what Kirkheimer calls "opposition of principle."[85] It is difficult, however, to separate this opposition tendency from the general transformation of European parties into catch-all parties. Furthermore, all of this may be a manifestation of a general secularization or de-ideologization of Western social systems.

Relationships among the six variables are suggested by Dahl. For example, competitiveness is said to be a function of the concentration variable. (Competitiveness is used by Dahl to refer to a zero-sum relationship, in the game theory sense discussed in Chapter 7, re the political utilities at stake.) In this case, the relationship takes on tautological aspects. A two-party system must be competitive by its definition (two more-or-less alternating political forces that, together, monopolize control of the executive). Such a relationship thus fails to account for significant outcomes.

---

[83] Robert Dahl (ed.), *Political Oppositions in Western Democracies* (New Haven: Yale University Press, 1966).

[84] Ibid., p. 332. The variables are organizational cohesion, competitiveness, distinctiveness, goals and strategies of opposition, and site of encounter between opposition and government.

[85] Kirkheimer, "The Waning of Opposition in Parliamentary Regimes," op. cit.

Much the same could be said for the putative relationship between cohesiveness, competitiveness, and distinctiveness. In a strictly competitive two-party system, the opposition is bound to be distinct from the government. This is inherent in Dahl's definition of competitive.

However, an effort is made by Dahl to isolate a set of autonomously defined variables that can, in fact, account for differences in the configurations among the aforementioned six variables.[86] The enormous variety of variables and the elusiveness of precise indicators for them underly the difficulty scholars have had in satisfactorily explaining any party variables.

This point is illustrated where Dahl, perhaps unwisely, ventures briefly into the quagmire of the electoral system–party system polemic discussed above. Like the others, in recognizing the importance of the constitutional and structural variable, he is unable to assess its impact relative to other variables, primarily of a sociological and economic nature. This difficulty is due, in no small part, to the inability to operationalize and measure any relevant variables.

The *extent of polarization* is a case in point. The necessity of accounting for the impact of such variables on relevant structural outcomes in a more precise and empirical fashion underscores the importance of micro-analytic research. In this way, it may be argued that pioneering studies in political culture, such as the Almond and Verba study, or in political psychology contribute more to the scientific explanation of party variables than all of the studies that try to focus on parties per se.

It thus begins to appear that attempts to build a theory of selected aspects of a political system run aground on the shoals of the very interrelatedness of the elements of the system. Dahl and his associates clearly recognized the futility of trying to explain party variables in isolation from micro-analytic variables. This recognition is made manifest by the very fact that they raised and discussed so many of the latter variables, albeit in an impressionistic way.

The major lesson that appears to emerge from this survey of the literature on political parties is that any theory of parties or party systems constructed without precise reference to the other elements of the political system cannot yield generalizations with satisfactory explanatory and predictive power. It very nearly appears that any satisfactory theory of parties would have to be a theory of the political systems of which parties are so integrally a part. The prospects for such general theory, we have seen, are not promising. The search for a theory of parties may, therefore, have created another vicious circle.

---

[86] Dahl, op. cit., pp. 348ff.

The Elusive Concept
of Political Development

12

The methodological and conceptual reorientation in the field of comparative politics, described and analyzed throughout the present volume, has occurred simultaneously with the discovery of a new geographical focus for the field.[1] The attention devoted to the study of the non-Western areas, chiefly located in Asia, Africa, and Latin America, has not only complemented the study of the traditional geographical areas, chiefly North America, Europe, and the older Commonwealth, but has at times threatened to overshadow the study of the traditional geographical concerns.

This joint occurrence of the methodological and geographical reorientation is not coincidental. The nature of the new subject matter presented conceptual difficulties and raised questions that could not be adequately handled by the traditional concepts and methods.[2] The traditional units of analysis, legal institutions and constitutional structure, were inapplicable to primitive nonindustrialized societies in which such institutions and structures were so much less visible, so much more intermittent (coming into being only in response to a clear and present need), and so different from what we are used to as to appear nearly nonexistent.[3] One cannot develop generalizations about parliaments, for example, and apply them to political systems in which the most complex political institutions consist of single individuals who perform all of the political functions of their system. More commonly, institutional comparison is further complicated by the

---

[1] Dankwart A. Rostow, "New Horizons for Comparative Politics," *World Politics,* Vol. 9, No. 4 (July 1957), pp. 530–47.

[2] Gabriel A. Almond, "A Functional Approach to Comparative Politics," in Almond and James Coleman (eds.), *The Politics of the Developing Areas* (Princeton: Princeton University Press, 1960), pp. 3–4.

[3] Ibid., p. 12.

fact that structures that bear the same names as structures in Western political systems do not perform corresponding functions. The supreme representative assembly in a non-Western system may not perform a deliberative function as such assemblies do in the Anglo-American democracies. It is thus not difficult to see how the search for the common properties of political systems, both Western and non-Western, and for universally applicable units of analysis could lead non-Western specialists to espouse functional analysis as a way out of this dilemma.[4]

Despite the methodological difficulties inherent in functional analysis, discussed at length in Chapter 8, this methodological and conceptual reorientation of comparative politics could not but help to make scholars aware of new variables and unaccounted-for outcomes; thus, the inadequacy of our traditional explanations of political phenomena became painfully apparent to many. The search for new units of analysis, which led scholars away from legal institutions and constitutional structures, led to a sociological perspective introducing a Pandora's box of variables from that discipline as relevant to political analysis. In addition to revealing the inadequacy of traditional explanations, the wealth of newly relevant sociological variables has made the criterion of simplicity, discussed in Chapter 4, virtually impossible to adhere to.

TOWARD A SPECIFICATION OF SYSTEM STATES—
DICHOTOMOUS TYPOLOGIES

Accurate, generalized description is a prerequisite to scientific explanation. The development of generally applicable concepts is essential to give meaning to the inchoate variety of observed data. Without such organization and interpretation of the data to be described, it will prove impossible to subsume such data in scientific generalizations.

The objects of description are of two types: system states and processes. The former is static and the latter dynamic. The focus of the static phenomena in question involves a distinction between Western and non-Western political systems. The dynamic process in question is variously called political development, modernization, or other more specific labels, such as industrialization. While it is far from clear whether the various terms refer to the same process or to different aspects of the same process, they often tend to be used interchangeably. In any event, the process in question implies a movement from one state of the political system to another state. Thus, it would seem that the specification of the two system states at the polar ends of the continuum would be a logical starting point in the effort to specify the essential characteristics of the process of moving

---

[4] Ibid., pp. 9–26, and Almond, "A Developmental Approach to Political Systems," *World Politics,* Vol. 17, No. 2 (January 1965), pp. 183–244.

from one state toward the other. In other words, if development consists of the process of moving from one place to another, it would be relevant to first ask, From where to where?

Although the several attempts to typologize political systems into Western and non-Western categories have been occasionally referred to as models, they are actually ideal types in the Weberian sense discussed in Chapter 7. That is, they are not intended to describe any real-world political systems (or societies) as such, nor do they possess any structural isomorphism (correspondence) to real symptoms. Rather, they are non-formalized sets of characteristics that epitomize tendencies. Observable political systems resemble these types to greater or lesser extents, but no observable political system will correspond to the ideal type with respect to all characteristics. Thus, there is no purely traditional system, utterly lacking in any attribute of modernity. Conversely, there is no purely modern system.

The typologies of societies into Western and non-Western systems are generated in part from the Parsonian pattern variables discussed in Chapter 7. These pattern variables consist of five dichotomous variables based upon alternative orientations toward social roles. Ostensibly, these pattern variables provide a conceptual framework for the description of alternative sets of norms and role expectations, one set corresponding to non-Western societies and the other set predominating in Western societies.[5] The universalistic-particularistic, achievement-ascriptive, and functionally specific–functionally diffuse dichotomies are particularly relevant to the typologies referred to here, with the former alternatives of each pair characterizing Western systems and the other alternatives found predominantly in non-Western systems.[6]

Three efforts to typologize political systems into the Western–non-Western dichotomy are noteworthy for the attention they have received and because they typify such efforts: Pye's "The Non-Western Political Process," Riggs's "Agraria and Industria," and Sutton's "Social Theory and Comparative Politics."[7]

Of course, in all typologies certain simplifications are involved. In seeking to categorize a group of political systems on the basis of the similarities

---

[5] See Francis X. Sutton, "Social Theory and Comparative Politics," paper presented to the Committee in Comparative Politics of the Social Science Research Council, Princeton, N.J., June, 1955. Reprinted in Harry Eckstein and David Apter, *Comparative Politics, A Reader* (New York: The Free Press, 1963), pp. 67–81, especially p. 69.

[6] Almond, *The Politics of the Developing Areas,* op. cit., pp. 22–23.

[7] Sutton, op. cit., p. 71. Fred W. Riggs, "Agraria and Industria," in William J. Siffen (ed.), *Toward the Comparative Study of Administration* (Bloomington, Ind.: Indiana University Press, 1959), pp. 28ff and passim. Lucien W. Pye, "The Non-Western Political Process," *The Journal of Politics,* Vol. 20, No. 3 (August 1958), pp. 468–86. Cf. the earlier article by George M. Kahan, Guy Pauker, and Lucien Pye, "Comparative Politics of Non-Western Countries," *The American Political Science Review,* Vol. 49, No. 4 (December 1955), pp. 1022–41.

among them, one necessarily overlooks the differences among them. These typologies are based upon an unstated assumption that the characteristics that non-Western political systems have in common can be stated at a useful level of specificity, a level that would permit the specification of precise empirical indicators for the characteristics in question.[8] If the richness of the differences among the so-called non-Western political systems is such that only the vaguest and most general common characteristics can be attributed to them, then the non-Western political process is not a useful concept. In other words, the essential question is, Does the group of political systems referred to by the concept in question differ in significant and precisely defined ways from other (Western) political systems? Obviously, if the only attributes non-Western systems could be said to share were characteristics shared by all political systems (or at least by many systems commonly thought of as Western), the non-Western concept would have failed to generate useful distinctions among the universe of political systems.

The variables that underlie these typologies may be conveniently grouped into four broad categories: cultural variables, sociological variables, political variables, and economic variables.[9] The earlier typology by Sutton, based upon five sets of dichotomous alternatives, consists of variables at a higher level of generality than Pye's later typology, which consists of 18 dichotomous variables. In this sense, Sutton's typology is cruder than Pye's, whose subcategories of each variable are more precisely specified.

The Parsonian *pattern variables* referred to above constitute examples of cultural variables, as would a tendency of non-Western political parties to espouse weltanschauung ideologies. The prevalence of a charismatic, as opposed to a legal-rational, basis for political legitimacy is another putative cultural characteristic of non-Western societies. Deferential, rather than egalitarian, attitudes toward authority are ostensibly another cultural characteristic of non-Western political systems.

Sociological variables may also be called structural or institutional variables insofar as these latter terms refer to a recurring pattern of behavior and interaction. Variables such as the degree of upward and downward mobility in the social stratification system would fall under this heading. The distinction between a mass or pluralistic society, referred to earlier, would be another example of a sociological variable. The extent of the "generation gap" might be still another. One of the most important and

---

[8] This assumption is posited as an empirical fact in Kahan, et. al., op. cit., p. 1022. Cf. pp. 16–19 above.

[9] These categories provide a basis for organizing putatively distinguishing characteristics of non-Western political systems for preliminary descriptive purposes. However, it is not always clear which category best subsumes a given variable. This is due in part to the imprecision with which the variables are stated and due also to the lack of precise criteria for inclusion in one or the other categories.

frequently mentioned variables is the one referred to by sociologists as functional specificity or role differentiation or what may simply be called the degree of specialization or division of labor with respect to social roles.

Political variables are another type of structural variable dealing with patterns of legitimate authority and the relationship between such authority and the society that the authority governs. The bases of political legitimacy exemplify such a variable. Non-Western systems are ostensibly characterized by charismatic or sacred bases of legitimacy, while Western political systems are ostensibly characterized by legal and rational bases of legitimacy. Charisma refers to the personal qualities that inhere in a leader and generate among his followers enthusiastic loyalties to him personally. Latin American caudillos epitomize charismatic leaders as did such leaders of national independence movements as Sukarno, Touré, Ho Chi Minh, or Nkrumah. However, many Western leaders, such as de Gaulle and Churchill, also generated a substantial personal following. Sacred authority might be exemplified by such institutions as divine-right monarchies. Also related to this political variable is the distinction between diffuse loyalty (to political authority regardless of what it does) and loyalty contingent upon policy output. The latter is supposedly more characteristic of modernity than the former.

The expressive, as opposed to the problem-solving, orientation of the political process is also mentioned as a relevant political variable. This appears to be an alternative manner of phrasing Herbert Spiro's distinction between ideological, pragmatic, and purposive interest oriented political styles. Yet, it must be recalled that Spiro found a substantial degree of ideologism among political systems widely accepted as Western, France, for example.

Economic variables largely refer to the indicators of the transition from an essentially agrarian to an industrialized economy. Included here are variables such as gross national product, per capita income, percentage of the working force in secondary rather than primary occupations, capital accumulation, and the distinctions between a barter or a money economy. Some scholars use economic indicators for political modernity while others do not. It is becoming increasingly apparent, however, that useful distinctions can be made between economic and political modernization. Whether it is possible to have one without the other is to some extent a matter of how these two concepts are defined. A body of research makes it apparent, however, that political and economic development are far from unrelated, as will be shown below.

Substantial problems appear to present themselves with respect to such simple dichotomous classifications.[10] In the first place, a great number of potentially significant variables are obscured by grouping such a wide

---

[10] Pye demonstrates that he is clearly aware of the methodological limitations of his dichotomous classification. See Pye, *Politics, Personality and Nation Building* (New Haven: Yale University Press, 1962), pp. 37–38.

variety of political systems under a common heading like non-Western. Gideon Sjoberg's distinction between *folk* and *feudal* societies may be one case in point.[11] There are clearly substantial political differences between those nations, such as the Philippines or Malaya, that may be classified as democratic (in the sense of permitting competitive elections) and highly authoritarian systems, such as Touré's Guinea or Nkrumah's Ghana, in which political opposition is not legitimate. To simply attribute to non-Western systems characteristics such as the lack of social integration or lack of differentiation between social and political spheres of activity (*boundary maintenance* in Eastonian terms) distorts the fact that non-Western systems differ greatly in the degree to which such characteristics are manifested.

In the second place, it is not clear that the non-Western political systems will always possess the attributes that ostensibly distinguish them to a greater extent than political systems widely accepted as Western. The presence of charismatic leadership in Western societies has already been cited. The lack of national integration is another putatively non-Western attribute that clearly applies to many Western systems. The system alienation of the French Canadians is a classic example of this point.

Alfred Diamant, in making similar comments on Pye's article, suggests that an implied continuum with the ideal types at its polar ends would be preferable to Pye's rigid dichotomy.[12] This criticism misses the point. Pye recognizes that actual non-Western systems will only resemble his ideal type to greater or lesser but always imperfect extents. The point is that it is not obvious that some of the new nations of Asia, Africa, Latin America, or the Middle East would be closer to the non-Western end of Diamant's continuum than some established European or Anglo-American democracies. This difficulty stems from two sources. One is the extent to which the established democracies possess the putatively non-Western attributes. Second, the attributes are, for the most part, so imprecisely stated or defined that it is impossible to specify the extent to which they are or are not possessed by any given political system.

Almond's early recognition that all political systems possess both attributes of traditionality and attributes of modernity suggests the more sophisticated attempts to construct static paradigms of those new nations undergoing more rapid change than the established democracies.[13] Such paradigms are based upon the impact of the attributes of modernity on the attributes of traditionality within the same society and the resulting interaction and accommodation of the elements of such a mixed culture. They are

---

[11] Gideon Sjoberg, "Folk and Feudal Societies," *American Journal of Sociology,* Vol. 58, No. 3 (November 1952), pp. 231–39.

[12] Alfred A. Diamant, "Is There a Non-Western Political Process? Comments on Lucien Pye's 'The Non-Western Political Process,'" *Journal of Politics,* Vol. 21, No. 1 (February 1959), pp. 123–27.

[13] Almond, *The Politics of the Developing Areas,* op. cit., p. 24.

essentially static insofar as they still describe a state of a system rather than a process.

TOWARD A CHARACTERIZATION OF THE MIXED OR TRANSITIONAL SYSTEM—RIGGS AND APTER

Riggs's *prismatic society* constitutes one of the most elaborate and best known examples of a paradigm of the mixed or transitional system.[14] The term *prismatic* is based upon Riggs's conceptualization of political development as a movement from functional diffuseness (few structures performing numerous poorly defined functions) to functional specificity (many structures performing specialized functions). In short, modernity is characterized by specialization and division of labor. Traditional systems are referred to as fused in that functions are fused in a few structures, and modern societies are called diffracted because the functions are distributed among specialized structures. Using the analogy of diffracting a beam of light, Riggs likens that stage of the process in which the catalysts for modernization are felt to a prism that diffracts a light beam. Hence, transitional societies are called prismatic societies. The term connotes a system that is neither traditional nor modern. The term transitional refers to a process, an ineluctability of movement toward modernity. Since Riggs denies the inevitability of such progress, he prefers the neologism prismatic.

Riggs's paradigm is intended to represent that class of political systems that has taken on many of the attributes of modernity while retaining many attributes of traditionalism. Such a system is characterized by institutions that do not precisely resemble either the corresponding institutions in modern societies or the corresponding institutions in traditional societies. Since Riggs believes he has characterized phenomena that are in significant respects distinct from any previously described phenomena, he has coined a new vocabulary—a new set of names for the newly described institutions of the prismatic system. Thus, a bureau in a prismatic society cannot be called by names such as department or ministry for these connote the modern institution. Words such as bailiwick or court connote traditional institutions. Thus, Riggs redefines the Spanish word for room, *sala,* for his purposes.[15] Prismatic groups are not the kinship or status groups of traditional society, nor are they the functionally specific, formally organized groups that typify modern systems. Thus, Riggs combines the words clique and sect for the neologism *clect* in order to describe this allegedly distinct institution.[16] Riggs's predisposition toward the use of neologisms becomes a predominant characteristic of the book and reaches a point where Riggs's

---

[14] Fred W. Riggs, *Administration in Developing Countries, The Theory of the Prismatic Society* (Boston: Houghton-Mifflin Co., 1964), p. 268. It is impossible to adequately summarize this extremely complex model in the space of a few pages.

[15] Ibid., p. 268.

[16] Ibid., pp. 169–71.

meaning becomes obscured to all but the most careful reader. (It helps to keep a running dictionary of previously defined terms to avoid flipping back through the pages in order to translate a given sentence.) Consider the following sentence written in classic "Riggsian":

We have seen how the inefficiency of the sala is reinforced by the price indeterminancy of the bazaar-canteen, by pariah entrepreneurship and intrusive access to the elite, by the agglomeration of values, by strategic spending and strategic learning as instruments of elite recruitment, by poly-communalism and poly-normativism, by double talk, blocked through puts, bifocalism and equivocacy, by the dependency syndrome, inference complex and the formalism effect.[17]

The value of new words may outweigh the loss in readability that accompanies their use if the new words actually symbolize new and useful concepts. There is nothing inherently scientific, scholarly, or profound in being incomprehensible. In some cases, as with the concept of a transitional society, Riggs's critique of traditional concepts appears well taken. In other instances, Professor Riggs appears to be substituting his own colorful language for well-understood terms and phrases. For example, his *poly-communalism* apparently refers simply to a lack of cultural integration.[18] It is not clear how the creation of a new vocabulary for its own sake contributes to the building of a body of scientific knowledge.

It should be noted that, as with Pye's model, many of the characteristics suggested by Riggs as unique to prismatic societies may be found in Western systems. The United States and Canada both have pockets of poly-communalism. Two of the more important characteristics attributed to prismatic societies by Riggs are formalism and the heavy weight of bureaucratic power. Formalism refers to a state of affairs in which institutions do not operate in the way for which they are intended. The second characteristic refers to the tendency for the administrative sector of the government to exercise a political role. Both of these characteristics may be applied to Western systems. The decline of legislatures in parliamentary democracy may illustrate one type of formalism found in Western nations. The imposition of federal institutions on a relatively homogeneous society may constitute another example. The political role of the bureaucracy applies to industrial nations par excellence. This is related to the decline of legislatures. Only the bureaucratic sector possesses the expertise necessary to govern many aspects of a technological society. Bureaucracy plays an even greater role in Western nations characterized by political instability. In such systems, bureaucracy fills a void created by the failure of political institutions.[19] Thus, without denying the suggestive richness

---

[17] Ibid., p. 284.

[18] Ibid., pp. 157–60.

[19] See Alfred Diamant, "The French Administrative System, The Republic Passes but the Administration Remains," in William J. Siffin, op. cit., pp. 782–218, and Michel Crozier, *The Bureaucratic Phenomenon* (Chicago: University of Chicago Press, 1964).

of the concepts themselves, one should exercise caution in characterizing such phenomena as peculiarly non-Western.

Apter has also contributed a typology of a transitional system based upon normative and structural variables. Specifically, Apter suggests a four-celled typology based upon two criteria: the degree of hierarchy and the type of values.[20] The former variable is dichotomized into pyramidal and hierarchical authority. The *hierarchical* authority form consists of a rigid centralization of power. The *pyramidal* apparently involves prescribed rights and responsibilities and, thus, a degree of autonomy for each level.[21] The values may be *consumatory* (sacred and ultimate) or *instrumental* (secular). Apter focuses on two ideal types: a *secular-libertarian system,* based upon instrumental values and a pyramidal structure, and a *sacred-collectivity system,* based upon consumatory values and a hierarchical structure.

Apter indicates a recognition of the limitations of pure ideal type analysis by suggesting a typology of actual systems. These types constitute departures from the "pure" types described above. Thus, the secular-libertarian model is most closely approximated in the observable world by that class of systems known as *reconciliation systems,* and the sacred-collectivity model is most closely approximated in the observable world by what Apter calls *mobilization systems.*[22]

Apter attempts to demonstrate that, given certain prevalent values (instrumental or consumatory) in a society, either the mobilization system or the reconciliation system epitomizes a set of political system characteristics most efficient for achieving that set of values. Consumatory values imply dissatisfaction with the status quo. Hence, a mobilization system with its hierarchical authority patterns can effectively mobilize the resources of society to achieve rapid socioeconomic change and to withstand the pressures created by the social dislocations inherent in the process of rapid industrialization. As the resources of such a society are increasingly diverted from consumption to capital, the advantages of an authoritarian system over a responsive system become apparent. Thus, for Apter, the advantages of the mobilization system are greatest in the early stages of modernization when the needs to forgo present consumption and satisfaction of demands are greatest. The advantages of such a system are limited

---

[20] David E. Apter, *The Politics of Modernization* (Chicago: University of Chicago Press, 1965), pp. 22ff.

[21] Ibid., pp. 92–93. Apter later introduces a third authority form, segmental. This describes a system composed of segments or lineages that ultimately have complete autonomy; hence, the importance of this form is confined to international systems composed of sovereign states.

[22] Ibid., chaps. 10 & 11. See also Apter's briefer exposition of the same models in his "Political Systems and Developmental Change," in Robert Holt and John Turner (eds.), *The Methodology of Comparative Research* (New York: The Free Press, 1970), pp. 160–63.

because authoritarian systems restrict the input of information; consequently, the choices available to them are limited.

Apter's paradigms, based upon empirical rather than normative criteria,
possess the scientific utility of any otherwise sound empirical classification.
Apter has constructed a class of actual systems which performs the function of organizing and giving meaning to an amorphous and otherwise
disparate group of political systems. If it is possible to logically derive a set
of expectations about outcomes from this class of systems, the paradigm
would have some explanatory utility. For example, if one could say that because of certain characteristics that mobilization systems share, all such
systems will also do, have, or be thus and so, one would have the essence
of a scientific generalization. (This is provided, of course, that the concepts
used are empirically defined.) Apter seems to be successful in establishing
logical relationships between his mobilization system or his reconciliation
system, on the one hand, and specified stages in the industrialization
process, on the other.

Thus, one is led to expect certain political formats, given certain economic situations and certain normative goals. In this sense, certain political
patterns can be accounted for. The relationship between information and
coercion is a case in point. High coercion is associated with low information. At an early stage of the industrialization process, the need is for action rather than information; hence, the mobilization system with its high
degree of coercion is most efficient. In the latter stages, information is
needed to cope with the increased complexity of an industrial society.
Therefore, at this stage of economic development, it is to be expected that
mobilization systems will be supplanted by reconciliation systems.

The danger is that in operating at such a macro level of analysis, Apter's
paradigm may generate explanatory appeal rather than explanatory
power.[23] That is, he may produce explanations that logically account for
loosely defined phenomena but fail to increase the ability to predict precisely defined outcomes. The movement from explanatory appeal to explanatory (read: predictive) power depends on the specification of precise
indicators. Macro concepts like a higher or lower degree of coercion, despite their rich suggestiveness on a logical level, seem difficult to operationalize.

Apter has combined a set of elements—normative, structural, and behavioral—and has suggested how they are related. Were these relationships posited in a precise and rigorous fashion, Apter's paradigm would be
a model in the sense that the latter term was used in Chapters 4 and 7. One
could wish that Riggs and Apter had been able to specify more precise
empirical indicators for their concepts. Nevertheless, the attempt to construct paradigms of how a variety of social, political, economic, and ideo-

---

[23] See the discussion of these two concepts on pp. 44–45.

logical phenomena actually interact seems to hold greater promise of contributing toward explanation than the specification of normative ideal types. To suggest that the characteristics of Western industrial political systems constitute the standards for calling a political system "developed" is ethnocentric. Such an argument precludes the possibility that the new nations of Africa, Asia, the Near East, and Latin America might develop along lines distinctly different from the patterns of development that the Western nations experienced.

POLITICAL DEVELOPMENT AS A DYNAMIC PROCESS

The foregoing discussion has been limited to paradigms of particular states or political systems. Although, as will be presently shown, the characteristics of such paradigms are to some extent a function of particular conceptions of the process of development, the paradigms themselves were essentially descriptive. That is, they described particular *states* of political systems rather than *processes* of change. Clearly, an explanation of political development or political change must be preceded by an adequate conceptualization of that process. Otherwise put, political development must be described before it can be explained.

Two tendencies characterize much of the early groping for a conceptualization of political development: historicism and ethnocentrism. *Historicism* is used here in the sense that Karl Popper has used the term to refer to the kind of determinism that characterized the writings of Marx, Hegel, Spengler, and Toynbee. It refers to an assumption that "the forces of history" move in an inexorable and in a unidirectional manner. Thus, the process of change moves societies inevitably in a single direction (unilinearly), often along a single dimension, beyond the capacity or will of mankind to alter either the nature or direction of change. Only the rate of the process may be affected by the will of mankind. With regard to the problem of development, this tendency takes the form of assuming that development proceeds always toward the Western model, never away from it.

Ethnocentrism implies a tendency to regard that which is characteristic of, and often peculiar to, one's own social system as a universally applicable normative standard. Specifically, ethnocentrism refers here to a tendency to assume that Western industrial democracies constitute a model (in the normative or Weberian sense) of what the new nations *want* to become, *ought* to become, and/or necessarily *will* become. The want, ought, and will of this position are often not easily distinguishable.

To some extent, these tendencies may be a product of the enormous influence of systematic sociology on early behaviorally oriented political scientists. In particular, the writings of Max Weber were influential on such pioneers in the political development field as Gabriel Almond.[24] For Weber, social change is characterized by a progressive *rationalization,* a process that is manifested in an implicitly inexorable and unilinear movement from traditional or charismatic bases of legitimizing authority to the rational-legal authority type.[25] It is further manifested in forms of economic organization[26] and in the conduct of life in general.[27] Rationalization, for Weber, is not unrelated to our concept of efficiency in the sense of rationally relating means to ends. Thus, legal-rational authority is justified because it fulfills certain standards of competence (achievement rather than ascription) or more closely represents the perceived interests of the governed, while charismatic authority is justified in terms of personal qualities of the leader that bear no necessary relationship to his performance in office. Rationalization is also related to secularization, the demythologizing of life in general.

This influence can also be seen in the pattern variables of the sociologist Talcott Parsons referred to in Chapter 7. It can also be seen in the writings of still another sociologist, F. X. Sutton, who offers a highly ethnocentric model of modernity.[28] Sutton relies on such characteristics as universalistic, specific, and achievement norms, high social mobility, an egalitarian class system, etc. Such a paradigm of modernity would seem to preclude the possibility of any authoritarian political system being classified as modern.

A similarly ethnocentric conceptualization of the process of development may be found in the writings of Lucien Pye, who conceptualizes development around the broadening basis of popular participation in public affairs.[29] Pye argues that at a certain stage in the development, elements of the traditional culture must be reconciled with elements of the modern culture. (This appears to be another way of stating Almond's concept of *cultural dualism.*) In any event, such a reconciliation "requires a more intimate relation between the government and the masses. . . . It is at this point that the basic functions of representative government become critical. . . ."[30]

---

[24] Almond, *The Politics of the Developing Areas,* op. cit.

[25] Max Weber, *The Theory of Social and Economic Organization,* ed. Talcott Parsons (New York: The Free Press, 1947), p. 328. See H. Gerth and C. Wright Mills, "Introduction," in Gerth and Mills (eds.), *From Max Weber: Essays in Sociology* (New York: Oxford Galaxy, 1958), pp. 51–55.

[26] Weber, op. cit., pp. 158ff. Weber regarded the capitalistic market system as more rational than the precapitalistic economic system it displaced.

[27] Weber, "The Social Psychology of the World's Religions" in Gerth & Mills, op. cit., p. 270.

[28] Sutton, op. cit., p. 71.

[29] Lucien Pye, *Aspects of Political Development* (Boston: Little, Brown & Co., 1966), pp. 39–40 and pp. 78ff.

[30] Ibid., p. 80.

In addition, only under conditions of representative government are the processes for the articulation of interests well developed. The consequence of a failure to develop representative institutions is "an avoidance of the demands of problem solving in terms of real issues."[31] Perhaps the case of Indonesia's Sukarno focusing on the artificial issue of neo-imperialism with regard to West Irian while his nation suffered the unattended woes of runaway inflation and a serious lack of national integration might exemplify what Pye is trying to convey. Had Sukarno been forced to reconcile articulated demands, he might have attended to these "real" problems.

One difficulty with this argument is that it ignores the possibility that the mobilization and politicization of the masses may constitute a functional equivalent of democracy in the sense of governmental responsiveness to demands generated outside the government. The process of instilling new values, attitudes, and cognitive dispositions in the masses that Pye suggests to be a requisite for the modernizing society bears no necessary relationship to representative government. Indeed, this is one function that Apter suggests can be more aptly performed by his mobilization system. While it may be granted that modernization implies greater politicization of the masses, such politicization may come from above (through, perhaps, the use of Apter's *political religions*) and does not necessarily imply representative democracy. In short, care must be taken not to confuse mobilization of the masses with elite responsiveness.

Indeed, it has been cogently argued by Samuel Huntington that improvement of the channels for the articulation of interests and demands is dysfunctional for political development. The increase of demands places a stress on inadequately developed political institutions and results not in political development but political decay.[32] Such stress is generated by two factors: the newly opened channels for transmission of demands and the so-called revolution of rising expectations that greatly accelerates the rate at which new demands are generated. Huntington thus conceptualizes political development as *institutionalization*.

Institutionalization is the process by which organizations and procedures acquire value and stability. The level of institutionalization of any political system can be defined by the adaptability, complexity, autonomy of its organizations and procedures.[33]

Unlike many other writers on the subject of political development, Huntington has drawn a clear distinction between *political* development and other forms of modernization, such as industrialization. Huntington's conception of development is not unlike that of Alfred Diamant. For Diamant,

---

[31] Ibid., p. 83.
[32] Samuel P. Huntington, "Political Development and Political Decay," *World Politics,* Vol. 17, No. 2 (April 1965), pp. 386–430.
[33] Ibid, p. 394.

A political system is said to be developing when there is an increase in its ability to sustain successfully and continuously new types of social goals and the creation of new types of organizations. For political development to continue over time a differentiated and centralized polity must come into being which must be able to command resources from and power over more spheres and regions of the society.[34]

Both scholars, among others, focus the concept of political modernity around the *capacity* of the system's *institutions* to *adapt* to the stress generated by changes in the quality and quantity of demands.[35] The concept of institution is to be understood in the sociological sense of a persistent and recurring pattern of behavior and interaction. Thus, institutionalization means the establishment of the strength of such patterns so that they become viable and persistent in the face of pressures for their breakdown.

The advantage of distinguishing political development from industrialization or economic development is that it becomes possible to speak of the occurrence of one without the other and to analyze the relationship between the two phenomena. Further, the conceptualization of political development in this fashion is, unlike the conceptualization of Professor Pye, flexible enough to accommodate a wide variety of constitutional forms. When the concept of political development implies some form of elite accountability and responsiveness, political systems such as Nazi Germany and Stalinist Russia are placed in the same category as systems such as Uganda and Mauritania. While there are no logical barriers to such a conceptualization, a class of systems containing such a wide range of obvious differences would not be very useful from a practical standpoint. Too many relevant distinctions would be ignored for such a categorization to yield much explanatory and predictive power. Thus, it seems useful to conceptualize political democratization as a separate dimension from political development. This would yield a four-fold rather than a two-fold classification with the power to make somewhat more subtle discriminations among political systems. Thus, the conceptualization of development in terms of systems' capacities avoids the ethnocentrism of defining development

---

[34] Alfred Diamant, "Political Development: Approaches to Theory and Strategy," in John D. Montgomery and William J. Siffin (eds.), *Approaches to Development, Politics, Administration and Change* (New York: McGraw-Hill Book Co., 1966), pp. 25–26.

[35] Cf. the later formulations of Gabriel Almond, who also conceptualized development in terms of systemic "capabilities." "A Developmental Approach to Political Systems," *World Politics*, Vol. 17, No. 2, p. 195ff, and Almond and G. Bingham Powell, *Comparative Politics, A Developmental Approach* (Boston: Little, Brown & Co., 1966), chap. 8. Cf. also S. N. Eisenstadt, "Bureaucracy and Political Development," in Joseph LaPalombara (ed.), *Bureaucracy and Political Development* (Princeton: Princeton University Press, 1963), pp. 98–99, who defines political development as a "potential capacity to sustain continuously changing new types of political demands and organizations. . . ."

(clearly an implicitly value-laden term) in terms of one's own state of affairs or some particular system state that one prefers.

If scientific explanation and prediction are serious goals of the study of political development, the flexibility of the institutionalization and systemic capacity conceptualization of development is not in itself sufficient to guarantee the utility of this concept for those purposes. It is also necessary to be concerned with the specification of observable indicators for the concept. What concrete actions or measurable phenomena indicate the increase or decrease in the level of institutionalization or provide a criteria for determining the extent of institutionalization in one system relative to another system? Is it possible to objectively resolve the question of whether the capacities of one system exceed the capacities of another system, or, if so, by how much?

Professor Huntington, more aware of the requirements of an empirically oriented discipline than some of his colleagues, does try to suggest several such indicators. One indicator for the concept of adaptability is the age of the institutions and the extent to which a system's institutions have withstood the crisis of leadership succession. There is an element of tautology here, however. The capacity of institutions to withstand stress over time is explained at least in part by their adaptability. Yet, their adaptability is known by the fact that they have lasted. Clearly, the adaptability of institutions needs to be operationally defined in terms of some observable phenomena that are not connected with that which the concept of adaptability is adduced to explain, the viability of the institutions. Huntington suggests that his second criterion of institutionalization, the complexity-simplicity dimension, may be indicated by the number of organizational subunits and the extent to which they are functionally distinct. While more precise criteria may be needed for making such judgments in certain practical instances, there is no logical reason in principle why the number and functional specificity cannot be ascertainable. The autonomy and integrity of political systems, Huntington's third dimension, presents somewhat more difficult problems for the goal of operationalism. Here again, observable indicators do not clearly suggest themselves. Huntington suggests the distinctiveness of an institution's norms and values; however, the concept of distinctiveness itself does not seem to provide a precise and objective standard for making judgments. His final dimension, disunity-coherence, is defined in terms of the ratio of contested succession to leadership to total succession, the cumulative or cross-cutting nature of cleavages, and the amount of alienation as determined by survey research. These appear to be manageable indicators.

Whatever quibbles one may choose to make about the indicators suggested for the concept of institutionalization, Professor Huntington is almost unique among his colleagues, especially those who operate on this macro level, for his concern for the need to operationalize his major concepts.

Another structurally flexible and, in principle, empirically manageable conceptualization of the modernization process is that of Apter, who conceptualizes the process as the increasing proliferation of modernizing roles.[36] Assuming that such roles can be precisely defined and identified, the presence of such roles becomes essentially a quantitative variable.

The proliferation of such roles is not unrelated to another putative attribute of political development, an attribute that appears in one form or another in many, if not most, essays on the subject. This attribute is structural differentiation and functional specificity. This means that in modern political systems there are more structures and each structure is more specialized. Each specialized structure has a smaller number of specific functions to perform. In simpler, less modern political systems (the two tend to be equated), there are fewer institutions or structures and these few structures perform a wide variety of poorly defined roles. Thus, as political systems become more modern, there is a tendency to attempt to separate political, administrative, judicial, and religious functions into separate structures (with varying degrees of success). In primitive societies all these functions may become indistinct and performed by a single institution such as the Eskimo shaman (or the Platonic philosopher king?). This is what Huntington meant by institutional complexity and what Riggs meant by diffraction. Such structural-functional complexity has less of an ethnocentric connotation than Almond's first formulation of the development process. Here, Almond strongly implies that modernization is a function of how effectively seven specified functions are performed, a position that Almond apparently abandons in his later formulation.[37]

Almond's later formulation also disavows an assumption of unilinearity in the development process that had been seen by many as implicit in his earlier formulation.[38] The recognition that change may occur in more than one direction is one of the merits of Huntington's concept of political decay.

The assumption of inexorable movement toward the Western model, somehow reminiscent of the idea of inevitable progress in the writings of French rationalists like Condorcet, is also brought into question by Riggs's model of the prismatic society. The heavy weight of bureaucratic power, meaning the political role of the administrative sector, results in a tendency toward stagnation at that point in the development process rather than further development. The imperatives of bureaucratic organizational

---

[36] Apter "Political Systems and Developmental Change," op. cit., p. 157, and *The Politics of Modernization,* op. cit., p. 45 and pp. 60ff.

[37] Cf. Almond, *The Politics of the Developing Areas,* op. cit., pp. 26ff, with Almond, "Political Systems and Political Change," *American Behavioral Scientist,* Vol. 6, No. 10 (June 1963), p. 8. In the latter work Almond is defining "political change" as "the acquisition of a new capability." We may assume political change is virtually coterminous with political development.

[38] Almond, "Political Systems and Political Change," op. cit., pp. 3–4.

forms result in status quo–oriented and noninnovative behavior patterns; consequently, one can expect a degree of stagnation in any political system that is heavily bureaucratized.[39] Bureaucratic forms, after all, evolve in response to a perceived need for efficiency in relating means to predetermined goals or ends, while development seems to imply the creative process of formulating new goals or values. This is not meant to imply the oversimplified suggestion that bureaucracies are unmitigatingly dysfunctional for political development. Non-Western bureaucracies, especially the military, often have a vested interest in Western technology, for instance, as clearly shown by Lucien Pye.[40] The point is that the bureaucratization of developing nations, the weakness of institutions to process the widening input of demands and other factors, casts serious doubt on the historicist assumption of inexorable, unilinear development.

The clear tendency among most students of the non-Western systems is to distinguish political development from economic development and political development (which perhaps implies a given direction) from political change (which may be toward whatever is meant by increased "development" or in the opposite direction). Political development is a concept which has proven difficult to operationalize. In order to avoid the ethnocentric tendency of equating it with some particular set of constitutional forms, political development has increasingly been conceptualized in terms of an increased capacity for processing issues and solving problems. In order to avoid the pitfalls of trying to specify indicators for the amorphous concept of political development, scholars sometimes restrict themselves to discussing economic development, which is much easier to operationalize. Variables such as gross national product, percent of the population living in urban areas or working in secondary rather than primary occupations, per capita consumption of electricity, and number of automobiles per capita can serve as measurable indicators of the degree to which a society has become industrialized.

SOCIAL MOBILIZATION—ONE ASPECT
OF POLITICAL DEVELOPMENT

It may be that political development is too broad a topic to be analyzed empirically. It may be that only aspects of the topic can be readily operationalized. If it is possible to develop empirical generalizations of a narrower scope, it may be possible to relate these narrower generalizations to one another at a later stage in the development of the discipline. What is

---

[39] This thesis is most eloquently stated with respect to France in Michael Crozier, *The Bureaucratic Phenomenon* (Chicago: University of Chicago Press, 1964).

[40] Lucien Pye, "Armies in the Process of Political Modernization," in J. J. Johnson (ed.), *The Role of the Military in Underdeveloped Countries* (Princeton: Princeton University Press, 1962), pp. 69–89.

being suggested here is that it may be more fruitful to analyze narrower parts of the broad concept of political development with a view to subsequently integrating the resultant generalizations.

A promising effort to conceptualize one aspect of the broad topic of political development is Karl Deutsch's work with the concept of social mobilization.[41] Deutsch begins with Edward Shils's two-stage conceptualization of the process of mobilization: "(1) the stage of uprooting or breaking away from old settings, habits and commitments and (2) the induction of the mobilized persons into some relatively stable new patterns of group membership, organization and commitment." Deutsch, however, moves beyond this level of generality and specifies constituent processes for the generalized process of mobilization and measurable indicators for each of the constituent processes. The various indicators correlate with one another (meaning here that when one changes the others tend to change in the same direction if not precisely at the same rate). This indicates that they do measure some common and existing dimension, that something which we call social mobilization exists in an essential sense.

Deutsch further notes the value in specifying levels of significance ("thresholds of significance") for his indicators of mobilization below which no significant disruptions in the traditional society will be observed. It should also be possible to specify threshold magnitudes for each indicator beyond which certain "side effects" are likely to be observed. Examples of Deutsch's indicators include shift to mass media audience (exposure to mass media), increase in voting participation, occupational shift out of agriculture, and income growth per capita. All of these indicators appear susceptible to measurement. Deutsch is primarily interested in changes in the magnitude of the indicators rather than in their absolute value. Thus Deutsch's measurement indicates a process rather than a state of affairs. An increase in social mobilization is likely to produce more significant consequences than a stable, although somewhat higher, level of mobilization.

It should be noted that social mobilization as conceptualized by Deutsch says little or nothing about the institutional structure of the political system. As such, it refers to only a part of what Huntington, Almond, Riggs, etc., meant by political development. However, an increase in social mobilization would lead one to expect consequences for the other aspects of a political system. Huntington indicated that mobilization is dysfunctional for the construction of a viable political system when not accompanied by a compensatory level of institutionalization. His prescription was to inhibit the mobilization process until a level of institutionalization developed adequate to handle the increased stress generated by the mobilization process. Deutsch, on the other hand, suggests that the other aspects of the development process,

---

[41] Karl Deutsch, "Social Mobilization and Political Development," *The American Political Science Review,* Vol. 55, No. 3 (September 1961), pp. 493–514.

such as an increased scope of governmental activity (and, by implication, increased governmental capabilities and increased institutionalization), are the result of pressures generated by the mobilization process, a process that may be impossible to stop or reverse anyhow. Deutsch and Huntington are at one on the position that mobilization generates an increase in human needs that must be coped with by social and political institutions. However, if Deutsch is correct in suggesting that repressing the mobilization process diminishes the capabilities of the political system, Huntington's prescription could lead to political difficulties.

The attractiveness of Deutsch's approach is that the formulation of *testable* propositions about the effects of mobilization on other aspects of the political and social systems becomes feasible by virtue of his use of precise indicators. The development of such propositions would perhaps resolve some of the speculative exercises such as exemplified by the preceding paragraph. The lack of ability to operationalize the concept of political development seriously diminishes that concept's explanatory utility.

EXPLAINING POLITICAL DEVELOPMENT

Beyond the preoccupation with the difficult task of conceptualizing political development, political scientists have only just begun to address themselves to the difficult task of explaining or accounting for differential rates and styles of development. Why does one new nation appear to develop a set of institutions that is relatively successful in resolving that nation's problem while other new nations appear unable to develop such institutions? Why does one nation move in a more responsive direction while another becomes increasingly authoritarian? The discipline has only recently begun to address itself to such questions.

Such attempts at explanation as have been made tend to be impressionistic rather than formulated according to rigorous methodological criteria. That is, they are characterized by broad, inadequately justified inferences of causation. Nevertheless, such explanatory attempts perform a useful function in giving direction and guidance in the search for causal variables. Pye's study of Burma, discussed in Chapter 9, provides a good example of such an impressionistic but useful study. Pye makes a persuasive case that cultural differences among societies and psychological predispositions among significant political actors can, to a significant extent, account for some of the developmental outcomes we wish to account for. The fact that he does so in a largely impressionistic or logical manner rather than by adhering to rigorous methodological standards does not detract from the fact that it is useful to have sound guidance as to what kinds of variables might be fruitfully conceptualized and operationalized in the search for explanations. That Professor Pye has been a pioneer in relating micro-analytic variables to developmental outcomes is in itself a significant contribution whatever the methodological shortcomings of his work. The importance of sound logic in giving direction to empirical research was stressed in Part I. As discussed above, Pye contributes suggestive insights into the identity crisis created in large part by the impact of Western values and norms and the psychological orientation and predispositions of native elites, insights developed in *Politics, Personality and Nation Building*.[42] Pye further suggests the relevance of *associational sentiments*—the psychological capacity to work cooperatively—as a determinant of the nature and direction of the development of a given political system.[43] He recognizes, however, that we lack the means of precisely specifying the nature or the magnitude of the impact of this variable on the developmental process.

This search for micro-analytic explanations of differences between systems in the rate and nature of the development process should be distinguished from Almond's infinitely simpler, almost Toynbeeish explanation. "*Development* results when the existing structure and culture of the political system is unable to cope with the problem that confronts it . . . ," says Almond. (Italics his.) Therefore, "Relating system challenges to system responses is the way to explanation and prediction in the field of political development."[44] This application of Toynbee's challenge-and-response thesis to the problem of political development fails to provide any explanatory or predictive power. First, the assumption that challenges are *necessarily* responded to has never been established and, in fact, is highly dubious. (This assumption is another manifestation of the "historicist" tendency that Almond seems to have difficulty avoiding.) Second, it is not clear that any objective criteria exist for measuring either the intensity of challenges or the adequacy of responses. Consequently, it is impossible to say that a challenge of this nature and intensity has occurred and, therefore, it can be predicted with such and such probability that some precisely defined response will follow.

One of the most ambitious attempts to explain any aspect of development in terms of psychological or micro-analytical variables is David C. McClelland's work on the achieving personality. McClelland appears to be committed to the methodological standards discussed in Part I and used

---

[42] Pye, *Politics, Personality and Nation Building,* op. cit., is discussed at greater length in Chapter 9.

[43] Pye, *Aspects of Political Development,* op. cit., p. 100.

[44] Almond and Powell, op. cit., pp. 34–37. Cf. Arnold J. Toynbee, *A Study of History,* abridged by D. C. Somervell (New York: Oxford University Press, 1947), pp. 48–163.

throughout this book. Consequently, he makes every effort to posit empirical indicators ("objective measure" in his words) of the concepts or "variables thought to be related."[45] McClelland avoids the pitfalls of trying to operationalize such concepts as political development by restricting his generalizations to economic development, for which precise indicators are readily available. Some difficulties exist in positing a generally applicable measure of even economic growth due to the great divergence in range of economic pursuits from one culture to another. McClelland's basic measure is real national income (income adjusted for the purchasing power of some standard unit of exchange—the American dollar at some defined point in time).[46] McClelland feels a need to complement this indicator by referring to another concept implicit in the idea of economic growth, the technological capacity to produce and utilize modern technological innovations. For this purpose, he uses production of electric power. This indicator is not as biased toward industrial (as opposed to agrarian) economies as are other possible indicators of technological growth (such as indices of manufacturing output). McClelland notes a potential problem in that absolute size of gains in the indicators are correlated with the initial absolute magnitudes of the indicators. In short, the more developed the economy is initially, the faster the economy can grow. McClelland's method is to discount the absolute gain in electric production by the predicted gain, a prediction obtained from the relationship between initial level of productivity and the gain in productivity over a fixed time period. Thus, a country which is high to begin with ought to gain faster than a country which is lower; therefore, the same absolute level of increase will indicate greater economic growth in the less developed country. The point here is to note the care with which McClelland has selected his indicators in the light of both measurability and their conceptual implications.

A more difficult problem is introduced in measuring the achievement motive. For current or modern societies, the primary technique is the use of the thematic apperception test (T.A.T) referred to in Chapter 10. This involves eliciting spontaneous stories about pictures shown to the subjects. The stories are then subjected to content analysis for achievement imagery. For instance, one picture shows a boy at a desk with a book opened in front of him. Low achievers write about a boy day dreaming and escaping problems. High achievers write about the boy meditating and trying to solve heavy intellectual problems.[47] This same method is used for content analysis of children's readers and folk tales for indications of achievement imagery. The procedures as outlined here are of course limited in their applica-

---

[45] David C. McClelland, *The Achieving Society* (New York: The Free Press, 1961), p. 21.

[46] Ibid., pp. 80–87. McClelland explores the advantages and disadvantages of his and alternative possible indicators in some detail, a discussion which should be examined in its entirety before his indicators can be properly evaluated.

[47] Ibid., p. 41.

tion to either present societies in which live subjects are available or societies that have left us a body of written literature.

McClelland tries to surmount even this limitation by applying his proposition to ancient or preliterate systems. For this purpose, he has devised a method of scoring for achievement imagery in nonverbal markings and designs ("doodles"). E. Aaronson has discovered that subjects who score high on the verbal achievement tests also tend to scribble in consistently characteristic ways. The *inference* was therefore made that such doodles, scribbling patterns, or design patterns constitute a valid indicator of high achievement motivation. The decorations on ancient pottery were scored for achievement-related design patterns providing a quantitative measure of achievement motivation in preliterate societies. It must be recalled that the validity of such a test was based upon an *inference* of an essential connection between the design patterns and the achievement motive. This inference was largely based on a contingent (associational) relationship between such designs and high scorers on the T.A.T. tests.

By careful training of the judges to interpret the cues in the stories, etc., as other judges have done, a high level of reliability (agreement on the achievement value of a given story by the several judges that score that story) can be achieved.[48] A strong element of subjectivity inevitably remains in such a measure since the training really amounts to learning to anticipate the judgments and reactions of one's fellow judges.[49] While what one is willing to call objective is partly a problem in semantics, it is possible to distinguish between learned agreement among judges and agreement that is a result of lack of room for human interpretation in the data.

The kinds of tests for validity that the measure has been subjected to in other studies constitute a topic beyond the scope of this book. The important point for our purpose is that McClelland found a strong positive covariance between achievement motivation scores and rates of economic growth. The temporal relationship between the two factors, moreover, was in each instance consistent with the inference of causation. It should be noted that the demonstrated relationship between the achievement motive and economic development might logically be expected to apply to the effect of motivation on political development insofar as it is possible to come to grips with the latter concept.

It is not possible to do justice to so complex a book in this short summary. McClelland explicitly recognizes that any single variable explanation of so complex a phenomenon as economic growth is necessarily an oversimplification.[50] Despite this, it seems reasonable to conclude that

---

[48] Roger Brown, *Social Psychology* (New York: The Free Press, 1965), p. 437.
[49] Brown argues that objectivity is simply agreement.

McClelland and his associates have made a major contribution to the study of political and economic development by empirically demonstrating the relevance of such psychological variables.

NATIONALISM, COLONIALISM, AND COMMUNISM

The study of the non-Western world has been characterized by a recurring theme, namely, an inquiry into the nature or direction of change. This has taken a variety of concrete manifestations. One of these is a concern with the viability of the new nations to survive as autonomous states. Another is a concern for the prospects that the new nations will evolve toward democratic forms of institutions. A third is a concern for the susceptibility of newly emergent nations to communist influence or domination, a concern reflecting America's cold war posture. These concerns are not unrelated.

The viability of the new states has been thought to bear some relationship to colonial policies and practices. Specifically, it is suggested that colonial policies that encourage the growth of native institutions during the colonial period afford the new nation an increased ability to govern itself after independence. In this light much has been made of Furnivall's distinction between *direct* and *indirect* forms of colonial rule.[51] The latter form refers to the use of native elites to apply the policies of the mother country. It also implies a certain degree of discretion and autonomy for native elites with respect to matters primarily local. Under systems of direct rule, on the other hand, all but the most menial jobs in the colony, and virtually all positions of any responsibility, were filled by Europeans.

First, this distinction is difficult to make clearly and precisely in practice. Second, it is not obvious that indirect rule leads to post-independence political success. While the intransigence of the Dutch in their bloody effort to retain control of the East Indies may in part account for that nation's political woes, post-independence Indonesia hardly constitutes a model of political success (in the sense of resolving basic issues). It may be, as Pye suggests, that indirect rule did not provide the Indonesians clear perceptions of their own proper political roles.[52]

Clearly, the characteristics of any new independent state result from such a complex of factors that it is difficult to assess the precise impact of any given colonial practice.

The assessment of the prospects for democracy in the new nations has,

---

[50] McClelland, op. cit., p. 159.

[51] J. G. Furnivall, *Colonial Policy and Practice* (New York: New York University Press, 1956). This is a comparison of Dutch policy in Indonesia (indirect) and British policy in Burma (direct) with much sympathy for the former. It was first published in 1928.

[52] Lucien Pye, "The Politics of Southeast Asia," in Almond and Coleman, op. cit., p. 93.

to a significant extent, taken the form of a logical judgment of the efficiency of democratic forms for the goals of development. For instance, Apter suggests that the spread of modernizing roles gives rise to a new scientific elite, an elite that has a vested interest in the reduction of coercion and the spread of information.[53] These imperatives imply an open society.

As shown above, Pye argues that a closer relationship between the elites and the masses is essential for the long-term success of a nation state. Pye assumes that stability is, to a large extent, a function of the capacities of a political system to adapt to the changing needs and demands of its people.[54]

The point has already been made several times in this book that one cannot explain the existence of phenomena or states of affairs on the basis of need. To say that scientific elites require an open society begs the question of why some political systems will respond to this imperative and others will not. The drive for power may be, to a large extent, a nonrational psychological need; hence, authoritarian rulers of newly successful nationalist movements cannot be expected to voluntarily relinquish their own authority in response to allegedly rational requirements of their political systems.

Explanations of the success of communism in obtaining a substantial influence in newly emergent nations often involve analyses of how the Leninist interpretations of Marxism, especially those aspects of Leninism incorporating J. A. Hobson's theory of imperialism, are logically complementary to the ideology of nationalism.[55] Lenin adapted Marxism, an ideology of the Western industrialized nations, to the peasant society of 1917 Russia by emphasizing the leading role of the intellectual and the party. Through these two mechanisms, revolutionary consciousness may be externally imposed by elites rather than depending on the spontaneous evolution of such revolutionary consciousness, an evolutionary process stemming from the imperatives of industrial democracy.

Lenin attributes to the phenomenon of Western imperialism the failure of capitalism to collapse according to Marx's predictions. By exploiting the colonies, the mother countries can siphon off the surplus value that was supposed to result in ever more frequent financial crises. The Western workers, prosperous from such exploitation, lose their revolutionary consciousness. Thus, the way to bring about the downfall of Western capitalism is to support non-Western peasants in the struggle for national independence. The class struggle now becomes a struggle between east and west.

It is important to recognize that the arguments summarized here are on a logical level. What has been established is the logical compatibility of

---

[53] Apter, *The Politics of Modernization*, op. cit., pp. 434–50, especially p. 444.

[54] Pye, *Aspects of Political Development*, op. cit., pp. 74–78.

[55] For example, J. A. Brimmel, *Communism in South East Asia* (New York: Oxford University Press, 1957) especially the introduction, and John A. Kautsky, "An Essay on the Politics of Development," in Kautsky (ed.), *Political Change in Underdeveloped Countries* (New York: John Wiley & Sons, 1962), especially pp. 62–89.

two ideological systems, nationalism and communism. The inference that nationalist movements are likely, in fact, to be infiltrated by communists depends upon the premise that alliances are made to a large extent on the basis of ideological compatibility. The validity of this assumption was a question that concerned Rokeach, discussed above.[56] It should be noted that this explanation does not account for differences among nationalist movements with respect to their susceptibility to communist infiltration.

SUMMARY AND CONCLUSIONS

The discovery of the non-Western areas by political scientists has clearly led to a reorientation in the field of comparative politics. This has been most noticeable in the realm of conceptualization, due to the inappropriateness of the traditional concepts for those new areas of interest. This chapter attempted to distinguish the attempt to conceptualize the non-Western system states, a static concept, from the attempt to conceptualize the process of changing from traditional systems to something else, a dynamic concept.

It may be fairly concluded from our examination of the ways that the concept of political development has been treated that the concept may be too broad and all-inclusive to permit easy operationalization. More promising are the efforts to specify indicators of aspects of political development (such as industrialization or social mobilization). The relationship between such aspects of development is clearly a subject that invites much further inquiry.

---

[56] Milton Rokeach, *The Open and Closed Mind* (New York: Basic Books, 1960), p. 328.

Concluding Remarks 13

The foregoing survey describes a field in a state of flux and ferment. A comparison of the present *methodological survey* with books used for courses in comparative politics just a few years ago would reveal that the criteria for what constitutes appropriate subject-matter foci for students of comparative politics have been significantly altered. A number of trends in the literature of the discipline may be discerned.

In the first place, it is possible to note significant changes in the conceptualization of the discipline. There appears to be a significant tendency to utilize nonindigenous concepts from such sister social sciences as sociology, cultural anthropology, and social psychology. Such sociological, cultural, and psychological concepts have not only complemented but have tended to supplant those foci of description and inquiry for traditionally oriented specialists in comparative politics. Prior to the impact of the behavioral revolution, comparative political analysis was largely concerned with the description of the legal and structural aspects of foreign political systems. Scholars confined themselves to a concern with constitutions, legislatures, executives, and bureaucracies, especially in Great Britain, Germany (The Federal Republic since World War II), and France.

In the second place, it is possible to discern changes in the goals of comparative analysis. Traditionally, comparative politics was devoted to description either of legal relationships among present institutions or of the historical development of the legal, institutional structure of the state. Because the discipline did not aspire to explanatory purposes, comparison was not emphasized. Rather the emphasis was on a country-by-country *configurative* approach. The idea here is that each state is unique and it requires as much time and energy as one scholar can muster to get the feel of that unique cultural, social, etc., context. Thus, scholars were encouraged to become experts in one nation, or at least in one geographical area, in order to be able to empathize with the particular and unique configuration of the many social, political, cultural, historical, religious, etc., variables that make that country the way it is. Traditionalists did seek understanding of the various manifestations that given political systems took. However, they apparently thought of understanding in the sense of Weber's *verstehen,* in the sense of explanatory appeal rather than explanatory power as these terms have been used in this book. They appeared to seek intuitive understanding that relevant and interesting characteristics of nation states have been accounted for.

It is, or course, dangerous to characterize and label all of the work that went on in the comparative field before the behavioral revolution came to prominence in the discipline. Some classical works made a genuine effort to be comparative, to avoid a country-by-country approach, and to note patterns of similarities and differences. Among the most noteworthy examples of such efforts are James Bryce's *Modern Democracies,* Karl Friedrich's *Constitutional Government and Democracy* and C. Herman Finer's *The Theory and Practice of Modern Government.*[1] Yet, such books, while possessing selected attributes of modernity, are still not fully modern. Bryce, for example, still tends to consider his countries one at a time. Finer does not devote substantial and systematic attention to social, cultural, and psychological determinants of institutional forms. Friedrich, while perhaps the most modern in spirit among these three, still does not attempt to develop precisely testable generalizations about politics. Friedrich's criterion for the validity of his propositions might be more aptly described as common sense.

In the third place, one might note major changes in method and technique. Most notable in this regard is a commitment to the increasing reliance on rigorous quantitative techniques. Whereas, in the past, the most prestigious practitioners of the art of comparative political analysis were distinguished by the elegance of their language, the extent of their erudition, and the suggestive richness of their insights, today's practitioners of the art tend to be distinguished not only by their mastery of an esoteric scientific and/or sociological jargon but also, to an increasing extent, by a demonstrated capacity to understand and apply the methodological standards and advanced quantitative techniques of modern empirical science.

What all these trends boil down to is an increasing commitment on the part of the practitioners of comparative political analysis to the goals and methodology of natural science. These goals consist of scientific explanation and prediction. The commitment of modern comparative politics to the methodology of modern science is one of the basic themes of this volume. It has been argued that comparative politics, among the subfields of political science, is in a particularly advantageous position with respect to scientific methodology. Only comparative politics, among the subfields of political science, does not imply the artificial exclusion of variables or cases

---

[1] James Bryce, *Modern Democracies* (New York: Macmillan Co., 1921); Karl Friedrich, *Constitutional Government and Democracy* (Boston: Blaisdell Publishing Co., 1950); and C. Herman Finer, *The Theory and Practice of Modern Government,* rev. William B. Guthrie (New York: The Dial Press, 1934).

relevant for explanatory purposes. The scientific utility of the comparative method has been discussed at some length in Chapter 6.

GENERALITY AND EMPIRICISM

A second recurring theme in this survey of the literature is the dilemma generated by two conflicting imperatives of scientific epistemology: the requirement of precision and the requirement of generality. We have seen how generality is indispensable for accounting for the greatest variety of nonconstant variables that are relevant to the outcomes we wish to explain or predict. To the extent that a research design opts for general applicability, the concepts involved become abstracted from specific contexts. It thus becomes increasingly difficult to define such concepts in terms of concrete, observable patterns of behavior. The meaning of such observable behavior patterns is usually inexorably tied to the contexts in which they are found. The concept of demand is applicable to a wide variety of political systems, for example, but when this concept is defined in terms of particular activities (such as lobbying by formal interests groups or letter writing to legislators), the concept becomes identified with the particular institutional contexts in which such activities can take place. Even such seemingly straightforward data as voting turnout must be interpreted in the light of the culturally determined sense of an obligation to participate.

Because comparative analysis is particularly well-suited to meeting the requirement of general applicability in its research designs, the literature of this field has tended to opt for this criterion at the expense of empirical precision. Comparative politics has been much more heavily influenced by the Parsonian school of macro sociology than by the methodological imperatives of logical positivism. In this sense, comparative political analysis has generally stood in contrast to the kind of rigorously defined empirical studies carried on by the University of Michigan–based consortium in the field of American government. Fortunately, from the point of view that has been developed in this book, a number of exceptions to the above generalization have been appearing in the literature on comparative politics. The consortium is increasingly interested in non-American data, and the Institute for Social Research, in which the consortium is located, is now deeply involved in comparative work. The development of cross-national aggregate data banks mentioned in Chapter 1 constitutes another such promising trend.[2] Some of the work by the Feierabends or by Gurr and Ruttenberg on cross-national studies of civil violence evidence a propensity to

---

[2] Especially Arthur Banks and Robert Textor, *A Cross Polity Survey* (Cambridge, Mass.: M.I.T. Press, 1963) and Bruce Russett, et al., *World Handbook of Social and Political Indicators* (New Haven: Yale University Press, 1964). A number of such data sources are noted and discussed in Richard Meritt, *Systematic Approaches to Comparative Politics* (Chicago: Rand McNally & Co., 1970). See also R. H. Retzlaff, "The Use of Aggregate Data in Comparative Political Analysis," *Journal of Politics,* Vol. 27, No. 4 (November 1965), pp. 797–817.

postulate empirical indicators.[3] Seymour Lipset has contributed several cross-national studies that make use of empirical indicators.[4] Richard Merritt and Stein Rokkan have edited a volume containing several papers based upon cross-national quantitative data.[5] Peter Merkl is engaged in research on attitudes of German and Italian political elites.[6] This list is only meant to be illustrative. There are too many fine empirical studies to make it exhaustive.

There are a number of problem areas that lend themselves more readily to quantitative research than other areas. Obviously, voting studies in the comparative as well as in the American field lend themselves readily to comparative analysis. The same applies to roll-call voting studies. Reliable election data is readily available for most Western industrial democracies. Alford's study of class voting in Anglo-American democracies typifies an increasing proliferation of studies utilizing election or voting data.[7] Although the ability to quantify test scores would suggest micro-analytic studies in the field of political psychology as likely candidates for rigorous quantitative research, we have seen that much of the comparative work in this field is impressionistic. This may be due to the expense and technical problems involved in administering a structured questionnaire to a systematically drawn sample. Despite promising beginnings, much work remains to be done with respect to cross-national survey research.

It seems reasonable to conclude from this survey of the literature in comparative politics that such empirical studies as do exist in the field have manifested some tendency to be designed with considerations of convenience rather than theoretic relevance. It is difficult to find examples of empirical research that may reasonably be said to constitute examples of what was called in Chapter 6 *paradigm articulation*. That is, empirical research in comparative politics does not appear to contribute empirical content to the theoretic structures that have been developed in that field. This is due in no small part to the lack of susceptibility of the major theoretic structures to the assignment of empirical content. We have seen how political

---

[3] Ivo K. and Rosalind Feierabend and Betty Nesvold, "Social Change and Political Violence: Cross National Patterns," in Hugh Graham and Ted Gurr (eds.), *Violence in America, Historical and Comparative Perspectives* (New York: Bantam Books, 1969) and Gurr, "A Causal Model of Civil Strife: A Comparative Analysis Using New Indices," *The American Political Science Review*, Vol. 62, No. 4 (December 1968), pp. 1104–24.

[4] Especially Lipset, "Some Social Requisites of Democracy," *The American Political Science Review*, Vol. 53, No. 1 (March 1959), pp. 69–105, and *Political Man* (New York: Doubleday Anchor Books, 1960).

[5] Richard Merritt and Stein Rokkan (eds.), *Comparing Nations: The Use of Quantitative Data in Cross National Research* (New Haven: Yale University Press, 1966).

[6] Peter Merkl, "Ideological Attitudes of West German and Italian Socialists and Christian Democrats" (unpublished paper prepared for delivery to the 1971 meeting of the Western Political Science Association, April 8–10, Albuquerque, New Mexico).

[7] Robert Alford, *Party and Society* (Chicago: Rand McNally & Co., 1963).

scientists, committed to the sociological traditions of systems analysis and functionalism, engaged in theoretic exercises that may be characterized as neo-scholastic exercises in pure logic. Little or no thought was given to the empirical import of major concepts. Some may choose to place the blame for this upon an insufficient effort to specify indicators for existing theoretic concepts rather than placing it upon a tendency to choose data and construct research designs on the basis of convenience. Be that as it may, the problem posed by Eckstein in the early 1960s still remains a fundamental problem of the discipline, the continued separation of theory and research.[8]

It appears that the efforts at theory building that are most promising from the point of view of scientific explanation are those that are limited in scope to a manageable universe of data. Theoretic constructs intended to refer to whole political systems (such as the works of Easton or Parsons) have had precious little success in specifying precise, observable indicators for their key concepts. Efforts to deal with more tightly defined universes of data (such as Downs's effort to relate democratic party systems, ideologies, and voting behavior) appear to hold greater explanatory potential than efforts to deal with undissected political or social systems as basic units of analysis. Of course, such less ambitious research designs weaken their conclusions by the deliberate omission of numerous relevant variables.

The imperatives of empiricism have resulted in a greater attention to middle-range theorizing, in which the advantages of including the maximum number of potentially relevant variables have been compromised in the name of empirical manageability. This trend is manifested in two ways. First, scholars tend to confine their analyses to a defined class of political systems. For example, the field of comparative politics is characterized by a distinct tendency among its scholars to compartmentalize themselves as students of industrial democracies, authoritarian systems of the communist bloc, or non-Western, developing systems. This tendency has survived the postwar interest in becoming more broadly comparative.

Second, there are a number of subfields of comparative politics that take as their focus selected aspects of the political system under consideration. For example, one growing field is the study of comparative administration. There are even students of comparative law. Political elites and political recruitment are increasingly studied on a comparative basis. This partial listing could be greatly extended. Yet, when scientific explanation and prediction become the goals of inquiry, it becomes difficult to restrict the objects of study to selected aspects of a political system. Since, as the systemic concept implies, the various elements of a political system are so interdependent, it becomes difficult in practice to explain any aspect of a political system in isolation from other aspects.

With respect to the study of comparative administration, this inability

---

[8] Harry Eckstein, "A Perspective on Comparative Politics, Past and Present," in Eckstein and David Apter (eds.), *Comparative Politics, A Reader* (New York: The Free Press, 1963), p. 9.

to separate the putative focus of inquiry from other aspects of the political systems in question has been manifested in several ways. While it is one thing to describe or even classify the various patterns of administrative organization (as, for instance, "classical" bureaucracies), any effort to explain such patterns must relate them to other aspects of the political system. Crozier, for example, brilliantly relates French administrative patterns to the French political culture.[9] Riggs's analysis of the role of administration in developing countries encompasses not only cultural factors but also economic factors and the character of the other political institutions.[10] These other factors are what is known as *the ecology of administration.* Thus, while it is useful to focus upon one aspect of given political systems as explicanda, no aspect of a political system can be fruitfully studied in isolation from other elements of the same system. The explicans of any chosen focus of inquiry generally consist of complex combinations of a variety of system characteristics.

THE COMPLEMENTARY ROLE OF
TRADITIONAL FOCI OF INQUIRY

It is possible to detect a tendency to overcompensate for the former emphasis on the legal institutions of Western industrial democracies by virtually abandoning a concern for these structures. At the onset of the behavioral revolution, and to this day at some of the more provincial and less prestigious schools, one could encounter the deplorable spectacle of ostensible students of comparative politics utterly incapable of applying (and only dimly aware of) the social and cultural variables and quantitative techniques that have become the workaday tools of the more sophisticated practitioners of the art of comparative analysis. Now, however, it is possible to encounter the equally deplorable spectacle of students of comparative politics, skilled in quantitative techniques and data processing, adroit at discussing the most esoteric sociological or anthropological concepts, yet amazingly ignorant of the basic constitutional structure of the major types of political systems. If it is true that the elements of political systems interact with one another, traditional objects of study, such as constitutional form, are as important for the construction of explanations of political phenomena as more contemporary objects of study, such as sociological or cultural variables. Thus, while it is one thing to say that electoral systems do not constitute a necessary or complete explicans for political stability, it is probably equally erroneous in the other direction to argue that electoral systems are irrelevant to the stability of a political system. If the

---

[9] Michel Crozier, *The Bureaucratic Phenomenon* (Chicago: The University of Chicago Press, 1964), especially part 4.

[10] Fred Riggs, *Administration in Developing Countries: The Theory of the Prismatic Society* (Boston: Houghton-Mifflin Co., 1964).

power of dissolution does not explain a propensity to curb potential legislative omnipotence in a parliamentary system with cabinet vigor, dissolution may constitute the institutional means of giving effect to such a propensity, whatever its deep-seated cause. The existence of the power of dissolution may even be viewed as one indirect indicator of a deep-seated cultural inclination to counterbalance potential legislative dominance with executive strength. Continued attention to the traditional foci of comparative politics is, therefore, complementary to inquiry into the impact of more recently discovered variables and entirely consistent with the purposes of scientific inquiry.

RESEARCH STRATEGY FOR A PRE-THEORETIC DISCIPLINE

Throughout this book I have tried to stress the advantages of integrating observable data with the construction of political theory. The survey of existing attempts at theory building has revealed that political science is at what might be called a pre-theoretic stage of development. Most of the existing theoretical work has been concerned with establishing logical relationships between nonempirically defined concepts or imprecisely defined classes of phenomena.

It will be recalled that scientific generalizations consist of empirically falsifiable statements about the relationships between autonomously defined *classes* of phenomena. Such classes need to satisfy Carl Hempel's two principles of concept formation; they should have theoretic import and empirical import.[11] The lack of testability of most generalizations in the discipline is a function of the lack of empirical import for most of the concepts or classes used in the construction of such generalizations.

Students of comparative politics have, we have seen, been working with rubrics such as developing area, pragmatic culture, totalitarianism, competitive or semicompetitive party system, and mobilization system, just to name a few of the labels under which they try to group given political systems or bodies of political data. It has been shown that such labels often possess theoretic import. That is, they can be integrated into existing theoretic systems on a logical level. Yet, these labels do not refer to a precisely defined class of observable phenomena. It is not manifestly clear whether or not a given political system fits under one label or another. This is what is meant by empirical import.

It appears that the difficulties students of comparative politics have had in generating explanations of phenomena in which they are interested are inevitable, given the fact that there has been a tendency to try to move the discipline into the theoretic stage of development without first having re-

---

[11] Carl Hempel, "Fundamentals of Concept Formation in Empirical Science," in Otto Neurath, Rudolf Carnap, and Charles Morris (eds.), *International Encyclopedia of Unified Science* (Chicago: University of Chicago Press, 1952) No. 7, pp. 39–50.

solved the problems of the pre-theoretic stage. They have tried to relate classes of phenomena to one another without first having established the precise criteria for the assignment of observable phenomena to one class or another. Consequently, they have produced a plethora of generalizations that are incapable of being tested in terms of observable data. Such generalizations, lacking any precisely defined empirical implications, are scarcely of more explanatory utility than the impressionistic insights of the now discredited traditionalists.

THE FUTURE OF SCIENTIFIC COMPARATIVE POLITICS

It follows from the above discussion that there exists a great need for the development of classificatory schemes in which relevant observable data can be unambiguously grouped and given theoretical meaning. A further need exists for the formation of concepts that can give useful meaning to political data and that have precise empirical content. Such concepts need to have cross-cultural applicability; however, the applicability of such concepts should only be as wide as is consistent with their remaining tied to precisely defined empirical indicators. It might be said that the imperatives of the scientific method require the practitioners of comparative political analysis to tread a perpetual tightrope between the conflicting goals of generality and operationalism.

If comparative politics is ever to succeed in producing a body of scientific generalizations, it must divorce itself from its fascination with general theory. Theoretic systems must undergo a constant process of testing and revision if they are to be of any relevance for the purposes of explaining and predicting real-world phenomena. This implies keeping the scope of our inquiry (the variety of systems and variables upon which we focus) within the bounds of empirical manageability. We have seen that attempts to construct theoretic models of unrestricted applicability have resulted in a level of abstraction devoid of empirical content. It is not necessary to foreclose the possibility of developing empirical generalizations applicable to a variety of very different types of whole political systems at some future point in the discipline. It does appear prudent and potentially more fruitful, however, at this stage in the development of the study of comparative politics, to restrict the construction of concepts and typologies to a level of generality at which it is presently possible to retain some empirical content.

It perhaps needs to be clarified at this point that the foregoing is not meant to imply that empirically oriented conceptualization and classification together constitute the only fruitful or acceptable form of political inquiry at this stage of the discipline's development. On the contrary, this book has suggested at several points that inquiry on a logical, or even on a speculative, level is not only a useful but even a necessary activity in building a body of political knowledge. What is being suggested is that it is dangerous to build upon such logically or speculatively derived generalizations without first establishing the empirical validity of such generalizations and revising them accordingly. Logical inquiry must be followed by the specification of rules of correspondence between the concepts involved and the observable world. Throughout this book, I have tried to suggest that logical, speculative, and empirical inquiry are not mutually exclusive but rather ought to complement one another.

Thus, a critical need in comparative politics is for the legally and structurally oriented traditionalists, the computer-oriented data collectors, and the logically oriented system builders to reestablish lines of communication with one another in order that each mode of inquiry can benefit from what other modes have to offer.

Glossary

Glossary

The literature on the philosophy of science and the literature of modern comparative politics are filled with terms and concepts unfamiliar to the student lacking a background in these fields. In many cases, it is difficult to find a familiar equivalent for such words without resorting to awkward phrases. For this reason and for the reason that students of comparative politics will encounter such words sooner or later, it was decided to cope with the jargon of the field rather than to try to avoid it. It is hoped that this glossary will ameliorate the pain inflicted on the student by the introduction of new words. Words in the glossary are defined in the way that they are used in this book. These definitions are framed, to the best of the author's ability, to correspond to the definitions of the words that are most commonly accepted by authorities in the fields in question.

Affect—a feeling of belonging, a positive emotive or cathectic orientation toward something. The converse of alienation.

Attribute—a characteristic of a variable that is not defined in quantitative terms.

Axiom—a proposition that is assumed to be true. A given or postulate. Such propositions are never testable.

Bias—inaccuracies in empirical inquiry attributable to human predispositions or perceptual distortions. Hence, they do not occur according to the laws of probability and, unlike random error, inaccuracies due to bias do not tend to cancel one another out in the long run.

Boundary—the analytical criteria that distinguish elements included in an analytic system from elements not included in the system or from the system's environment.

Calculus—a system of symbolic notations from which nonempirical conclusions can be deductively derived.

Cathexis (adjective: cathectic)—a dimension of sociological variables referring to socially relevant feelings on the emotive level.

Cause—a relationship between two phenomena such that one is an effective agent in bringing the other about. If one phenomenon is such an effective agent in bringing about an event or state of affairs only when complemented by another phenomenon, it is said that the former phenomenon is a partial cause of such an event.

Cognition—knowledge and information.

Concept—an idea which can give meaning to patterns of action or other phenomena. A construct of the mind. An operationalized or empirical concept assigns meaning to the raw observed activity that constitutes its definition.

Constant—a concept that does not vary either its magnitude, if defined in quantitative terms, or its attributes, if not defined in quantitative terms.

Contingency—a measure of association. Association refers to the extent to which two phenomena occur or appear together.

Correlation—a measure of the extent that change in the magnitude of one quantitative variable is proportional to change in the magnitude of some other variable. Two correlated variables will change at proportional rates.

Data (singular: datum)—facts; information.

Deduction—a form of logical reasoning proceeding from a general proposition to a less general proposition or fact such that if the more general proposition is true, the less general proposition or fact must be true.

Deterministic—a type of proposition such that if one fact appears another *must* follow. Deductive inferences are usually thought of as deterministic in that the specific fact or law deductively derived must necessarily be true. Some argue that such deductive inferences may also be probabilistic.

Dispositional—a type of trait or characteristic that consists of a mental or psychological inclination to react in a given way to a specified class of stimuli.

Empirical—referring directly or indirectly to sensory perception for justification. Such perception usually consists of observation; however, it does not seem useful to exclude by definition the possibility of a blind person proceeding empirically.

Equivalence—a goal of cross-cultural research. The aim is to have the concepts or variables utilized in the study interpreted in such a way as to transcend the unique contexts of the cultures under consideration so that the meaning of concepts and the impact of variables will not be a function of the several unique cultural contexts under consideration.

Error—mistakes or inaccuracies in empirical inquiry that are due to human error and not attributable to bias; hence, they fall randomly according to the laws of probability. Accordingly, the extent of error can be statistically estimated. Errors tend to cancel one another out in the long run.

Essence—the core reality of a thing. This may be used to imply that such a reality exists in the realm of ideas beyond the observed properties of the thing. A transcendental reality.

Explanation—The explanation of a fact consists of integrating that fact in a general proposition that logically accounts for the fact's existence; the explanation of a law consists in the subsumption of that law (or proposition) in a more general law or proposition that accounts for the validity of the law to be explained. Explanations answer the question *why*. Why did this occur rather than any other possibility? The answer consists of the necessary and sufficient conditions to bring out the fact or relationship to be explained.

Explanatory appeal—the extent to which a law or theory can engender subjective satisfaction that an event has been understood.

Explanatory power—the ability of a theory or law to increase the probability of predicting an event over chance.

Explicandum (explanandum) (plural: explicanda)—the phenomenon to be explained.

Explicans (explanans)—the premise, phenomenon, concept, or proposition that accounts for a phenomenon to be explained.

Fallacy—an error in logic. An inference which fails to satisfy the criteria of logic.

Formalize—When used with reference to a set of elements or phenomena (a theoretic construct), this means to specify the logical relationships between such elements. Formalization distinguishes systems, models, and theories from concepts or other approaches which merely consist of lists of variables unrelated to one another.

Function—consequence. To say x is a function of y means x is a consequence of y. In structural functional analysis, function refers to activities which are necessary for the maintenance of the system or which at least have consequences which are relevant for the performance of the system.

Generalization—a statement of a pattern of similarities or regularities among a specified set of phenomena which differ in other respects. A generlization states how a set of phenomena that share one characteristic also share at least one other characteristic.

Historicism—the philosophic school that holds that events are determined by impersonal (and usually cyclical) forces of history beyond the will or power of man to alter them.

Hypothesis—a generalization which may logically be true but which has not thus far been tested.

Ideology—two senses: (1) a closed, comprehensive system of thought from which one can deduce answers to most questions relevant to the subject matter focus of the ideology; (2) any set of more or less related principles (see weltanschauung).

Incomplete explanation—a specification of some but not all of the necessary conditions to bring about the phenomena to be explained. Completeness becomes a matter of degree depending on what fraction of the causal variables are specified.

Indicator (referent)—an intersubjectively observable phenomenon or set of actions that constitutes a definitional equivalent for a concept. In some cases, a set of several such phenomena or actions collectively constitutes the definitional equivalent for a concept. The presence of one or more observable indicators may constitute intersubjective clues for the presence of or absence of a concept.

Induction—a logical process of inferring a generalization from a pattern of specific observations.

Inference—the process of reaching a conclusion that can *logically* account for known empirical data but does not *necessarily* follow from such data (as the inference of causation). In statistics, inference refers to the process of estimating unknown population characteristics (parameters) from known sample characteristics (statistics).

Isomorphic—similar (isomorphism = similarity).

Institution—a recurring pattern of activity and interaction. May be used synonymously with structure.

Intuition—a means of arriving at conclusions by nonlogical mental processes alone, without reference to observable or other sensory phenomena and without reference to the cannons of logical inference. Insight.

Law—a statement of a universal and invariable relationship. A deterministic rather than probabilistic generalization.

Macro analysis—inquiry that focuses on social groups as the unit of analysis. Often implicitly refers to inquiry that focuses on the society or whole political system as the unit of analysis.

Method—a way of proceeding in inquiry consisting of a set of techniques, such as quantitative or qualitative methods.

Methodology—the study of methods, the description and justification of methods.

Micro analysis—inquiry that focuses on individuals as the basic unit of analysis.

Modal (mode, modality)—An indication of central tendency, it refers to the most typical, the most frequently occurring type.

Model—A scientific model consists of a set of logically related elements—a system—that is structurally similar to some aspect of reality. It is selected from the reality it represents according to some criteria of relevance and its elements lack precisely defined empirical content.

Neologism—a coined or new word.

Objective rationality—the selection of the most efficient means to reach given ends, regardless of the perceptions, knowledge, or belief system of the observer. (See perceptual rationality.)

Operational definition—a definition or concept that consists of a specification of the concrete observable phenomena or raw activity that serve as unambiguous indicators of the presence or absence of that concept. An operationalized concept is a mental construct that assigns meaning to the raw observed activities that constitute its definition.

Paradigm—used in this book to refer to all constructs, at various levels of formalization, that have an instrumental value in the comparison, selection, and organization of data. Thus, paradigm would include models, conceptual frameworks, and approaches. The word is sometimes used elsewhere in the sense of Weber's ideal type, that is, the classic or typical example of a class of phenomena.

Parameter—a characteristic of a population or universe.

Perceptual rationality—the selection of the most efficient means to reach given ends, given the knowledge, information, and belief system of the observer. Distinguished from objective rationality, which does not account for possible biases and misinformation of the observer.

Politicization—recruitment of the masses into the political process.

Population (**universe**)—Used interchangeably, these words refer to the totality from which a sample is drawn and to which propositions derived from the sample refer. One never knows the characteristics of a universe; they must be inferred from knowledge of the sample.

Probabilistic—an adjective referring to statements which, rather than affirming or predicting the necessary occurrence of a specific event at a specific time, merely relate the precise chances that such an event will occur. This is done in terms of the percentage frequency such an event will occur in an infinite number of repetitions of a given set of circumstances.

Random sample—a sample in which each item in the universe has an equal probability of being included in the sample.

Recruitment—the process of selecting and training political elites.

Referent—see indicator.

Relationship—the manner in which two phenomena (concepts or variables) are connected. It may take on a number of dimensions. Relationships may be symmetrical, meaning each element in the relationship affects the other variable in the same manner in which the other element affects it. In short, it means a two-way relationship. Asymmetrical relationships are one-way. An asymmetrical relationship may be causal. Other forms of relationship along this dimension are associational (two elements occur together) and correlational (two elements covary).

Reliability—Referring to tests, questionnaires, etc., it is a measure of the extent to which the items on the scale are internally consistent so that the response on one item will afford a basis for predicting responses on other items with an accuracy significantly above chance.

Significance (**statistical**)—the probability that a quantitative result as high as the one obtained in a statistical manipulation could have occurred by chance if there were no intrinsic relationship between the variables. It is expressed in terms of how often a result of this magnitude would occur by chance (probability laws based upon the bell-shaped normal curve) given an infinite number of samples to be tested.

Socialization—the process of disseminating cultural variables among members of a society. It may involve transmitting such variables from one generation to the next, changing the culture, or creating a new culture.

Spurious relationship—a finding of a high measure of covariation or a high rate of association between two elements which is based upon mere chance rather than on some attribute inherent in the elements themselves. A spurious relationship may be thought of as the direct opposite (or negation) of a causal relationship.

Statistics—There are two basic branches of this set of quantitative techniques. *Descriptive statistics* is a set of quantitative techniques dealing with the aggregation, organization, and summarization of masses of data so large as to be otherwise unmanageable. *Inductive statistics* is a means of precisely specifying the probability of error in generalizing about an unknown universe of data from a sample. It is based on probability theory.

Stratified sample—a sample that is broken down by characteristics that are relevant to the focus of inquiry in proportion to the extent such characteristics are thought to exist in the universe.

Structure—an institution; a stable pattern of interactions.

System—a set of related elements and the interactions among them which are distinguished from those elements not in the system by unambiguous, analytical boundaries.

Tautology—something which is true by definition. A circular argument.

Taxonomy—a classification scheme.

Theory—a system of logically related, empirically testable propositions. A theory in this sense deductively generates some precisely defined expectations of observable outcomes.

Threshold—Used in connection with variables that have a putative impact on some outcome in question, the term refers to the minimal magnitude of that variable that will produce the impact. It logically is limited to quantitative variables but has been frequently used with respect to qualitative variables.

Unilinear—a type of progression from a single point to another single point in a single direction. Usually implies a developmental progression (as from primitive to advanced).

Universe—see population.

Validity—A valid measure is one that measures the phenomena it purports to measure. A valid proposition is one that is consistent with the observable data insofar as we are able to determine them.

Variable—a concept that can manifest itself in more than one quantitative magnitude or qualitative type or attribute. A *dependent variable* is a variable whose magnitude or attributes depend on the magnitude or attributes of at least one other variable. An *independent variable* is a variable whose magnitude or type is completely autonomous from other variables. A *quantitative variable* is a variable to which numerical values can be assigned (for example, age and weight). All other variables are designated as qualitative. Qualitative variables can only be subdivided into types.

Weltanschauung (plural: weltanschauungen)—a barely translatable but commonly used German term. It basically implies a closed, comprehensive ideological system that gives its adherents a perspective for the interpretation of nearly all socially relevant experience (see ideology).

Bibliographic Notes

Bibliographic Notes

Part I, Epistemology

The basic, most comprehensive work in the classical or orthodox tradition of the philosophy of science is Ernest Nagel, *The Structure of Science* (New York: Harcourt, Brace & World, 1961). Also in this more orthodox tradition is Carl G. Hempel. His brief *Philosophy of Natural Science* (Englewood Cliffs, N.J.: Prentice-Hall, 1966) is a very readable and excellent introduction to the topic. A somewhat more specialized and advanced but often cited work is his "Fundamentals of Concept Formation in Empirical Science" in Otto Neurath, Rudolf Carnap, and Charles Morris, eds., *International Encyclopedia of Unified Science,* Vol. 2, No. 7 (Chicago: University of Chicago Press, 1952). Several of his essays are collected in *Aspects of Scientific Explanation and Other Essays in the Philosophy of Science* (New York: The Free Press, 1965). Karl Popper, *The Logic of Scientific Discovery* (New York: Basic Books, 1959) is an excellent analysis of the nature of scientific propositions, especially with regard to their falsifiability, and of the nature of scientific theory. Beginners find the later chapters difficult, however. Also excellent but challenging to beginners is Alfred J. Ayer, *Language, Truth and Logic* (New York: Dover Publications, 1952). Ayer is particularly useful in differentiating scientific statements from other kinds of statements. Less formal and addressed to beginners or laymen is Stephen Toulmin, *The Philosophy of Science, An Introduction* (New York: Harper Torchbooks, 1960). Toulmin's book is not designed to provide a comprehensive grasp of scientific epistemology and should be supplemented with a more comprehensive, structured treatment. Also provocative and readable but not designed as a comprehensive treatment is James Conant, *On Understanding Science* (New York: New American Library Mentor Books, 1958). R. B. Braithewaite, *Scientific Explanation* is also less formal but aimed primarily at advanced students. Thomas Kuhn, *The Structure of Scientific Revolutions* (Chicago: University of Chicago Press, 1962) develops a provocative thesis on the resistance of scientific theory to the incorporation of new discoveries.

The most comprehensive and best treatment of the philosophy of science as applied to social and behavioral sciences is Abraham Kaplan, *The Conduct of Inquiry* (San Francisco: Chandler Publishing Company, 1964). Robert Dubin, *Theory Building* (New York: The Free Press, 1969) is also useful in that it is more readable, if less formal, than Kaplan. Dubin's failure to distinguish models and theory is troublesome. Richard Rudner, *The Philosophy of Social Science* (Englewood Cliffs, N.J.: Prentice-Hall, 1966) is useful for advanced students, but undergraduates find Rudner difficult to follow despite his brevity.

Several books in the Dorsey series are addressed specifically to epistemology for political scientists. Eugene Meehan, *The Theory and Method of Political Analysis* (Homewood, Ill.: The Dorsey Press, 1965) and Alan Isaaks, *The Scope and Methods of Political Science* (Homewood, Ill.: The Dorsey Press, 1969) are more readable than Kaplan and, being directed specifically at political inquiry, are very useful for beginning political scientists. Less useful from the standpoint of poor organization is Fred Frohock, *The Nature of Political Inquiry* (Homewood, Ill.: The Dorsey Press, 1967). George Graham, *Methodological Foundations for Political Analysis* (Waltham, Mass.: Xerox Publishing Co., 1971) is an excellent introduction to this topic. Meehan, *Contemporary Political Thought* (Homewood, Ill.: The Dorsey Press, 1967) effectively combines a discussion of epistemology with a critique of major approaches. His recent *The Foundations of Political Analysis, Empirical and Normative* (Homewood, Ill.: The Dorsey Press, 1971) contrasts these two forms of inquiry.

Among the best readers in the field of the philosophy of science are May Brodbeck and Herbert Feigel, eds., *Readings in the Philosophy of Science* (New York: Appleton-Century-Crofts, 1953), May Brodbeck, ed., *Readings in the Philosophy of Social Science* (New York: The Macmillan Co., 1968), Llewellyn Gross, ed., *Symposium on Sociological Theory* (New York: Harper & Row, 1959) and Ernest Nagel and Richard Brandt, eds., *Meaning and Knowledge, Systematic Readings in Epistemology* (New York: Harcourt, Brace & World, 1965).

Chapter 6

A good discussion of the logic of comparison may be found in Robert T. Holt and John Turner, eds., *The Methodology of Comparative Research* (New York: The Free Press, 1970), Chapter 1. A good general discussion of major approaches in the discipline may be found in Chapter 2. The remainder of the book consists of more specialized essays. The best source is Adam Przeworski and Henry Teune, *The Logic of Comparative Social Inquiry* (New York: John Wiley Interscience, 1970), especially Part 1. Part 2 deals with the problems of equivalence and measurement of micro-level research. Both books are aimed at a fairly advanced level. A highly useful essay is Sidney Verba's essay review, "Some Dilemmas in Comparative Research," *World Politics*, Vol. XX, No. 1 (October 1967), pp. 111–27, especially with regard to the dilemma focused upon in this volume, the conflicting imperatives of general applicability and empirical import for paradigms. Arthur Kalleberg, "The Logic of Comparison: A Methodological Note for the Comparative Study of Political Systems," *World Politics,* Vol. XIX, No. 1 (January 1966), pp. 69–82, has a misleading title. It primarily focuses upon classification and typologies with respect to their role in establishing comparable classes of data. Howard Scarrow, *Comparative Political Analysis, An Introduction* (New York: Harper & Row, 1969) discusses a number of methodological problems of comparative political inquiry but does not explicitly address himself to the logic of comparative analysis. Michael Haas, "Comparative Analysis," *The Western Political Quarterly,* Vol. XV, No. 2 (June 1962), pp. 292–304, is primarily addressed to such methodological problems of cross-national research as equivalence and inference.

Chapter 7

The best overall discussion of the nature and use of models in the social sciences is found in Abraham Kaplan, *The Conduct of Inquiry,* (San Francisco: Chandler Publishing Co., 1964), Chapter 7. Eugene Meehan, *Contemporary Political Thought* (Homewood, Ill.: The Dorsey Press, 1967), Chapters 3 and 5 discusses several of the models and quasi models critiqued in this book. The essential writings of Max Weber are collected in two volumes: Max Weber, *The Theory of Social and Economic Organization,* edited by Talcott Parsons (New York: The Free Press, 1964) and H. H. Gerth and C. Wright Mills, eds., *From Max Weber: Essays in Sociology* (New York: Oxford University Press, 1946). Both books contain introductory overviews of Weber's work.

David Easton's thoughts on systems analysis are contained in a trilogy of books: *The Political System* (New York: Alfred A. Knopf, 1953), *A Framework for Political Analysis* (Englewood Cliffs, N.J.: Prentice-Hall, 1965), and *A Systems Analysis of Political Life* (New York: John Wiley & Sons, 1968). The essentials of the first two volumes are effectively summarized in the third. His article, "An Approach to the Analysis of Political Systems," *World Politics,* Vol. IX, No. 3 (April 1957), pp. 383–400, gives a highly simplified overview of his paradigm. Oran Young, *Systems of Political Science* (Englewood Cliffs, N.J.: Prentice-Hall, 1968) presents a basic overview of systems analysis in political science. Young is more impressed with systems analysis than the present author and makes a number of assertive statements about systems analysis that are subject to debate. Talcott Parsons's writings are too voluminous to list here. The best single statement of his action theory is found in Parsons and Edward Shils, eds., *Toward a General Theory of Action* (New York: Harper Torchbooks, 1951), Parts 1 and 2, especially, pp. 3–29 and pp. 47–110. His writings on systems analysis appear in Parsons, et al., *Working Papers in the Theory of Action* (New York: The Free Press, 1953) especially Chapters 3 and 5; Parsons, "On the Concept of Political Power," *Proceedings of the American Philosophical Society,* Vol. CVII, No. 2 (June 1960), pp. 260–62; and Parsons and Neil Smelser, *Economy and Society* (New York: The Free Press of Glencoe, 1956). A very sympathetic summary of the contribution of Parsons to political analysis is William C. Mitchell, *Sociological Analysis and Politics* (Englewood Cliffs, N.J.: Prentice-Hall, 1967). For a briefer but much more critical analysis of the Parsonian contribution, see Meehan, *Contemporary Political Thought,* op. cit., pp. 121–158. Meehan's comments are probably the most readable introduction to this complex thinker for the neophyte scholar. A worthwhile book of critical essays on Parsons plus a rejoinder by Parsons is Max Black, ed., *The Social Theories of Talcott Parsons* (Englewood Cliffs, N.J.: Prentice-Hall, 1961).

A brief summary of several models and quasi models discussed here is found in Robert Golembiewski, et al., *A Methodological Primer for Political Scientists* (Chicago: Rand McNally, 1969), pp. 241–51.

In addition to the *Nerves of Government* (New York: The Free Press, 1953), readers interested in Karl Deutsch's cybernetic paradigm should consult his *Nationalism and Social Communication* (Cambridge, Mass.: M.I.T. Press, 1953). Deutsch's thinking on cybernetics has been heavily influenced by the writings of Norbert Weiner. These should be consulted by serious and advanced students of cybernetic research. Weiner's key works are *Cybernetics,* 2d. ed. (New York: John Wiley & Sons, 1961) and *The Human Use of Human Beings* (Boston: Houghton-Mifflin Co., 1950). Y. W. Lee, *Statistical Theory of Communication* (New York: John Wiley & Sons, 1960) and W. Ross Ashby, *An Introduction to Cybernetics* (New York: John Wiley & Sons, 1956) are also useful. However, Deutsch remains virtually alone in trying to relate cybernetics to the study of politics. Beginners might find two pieces in James C. Charlesworth, ed., *Contemporary Political Analysis* (New York: The Free Press, 1967) a more readable introduction to cybernetics and politics: Robert C. North, "The Analytical Prospects of Communication Theory," and Deutsch, "Communications and Decision Making Systems," at pp. 273–316. The latter is a brief summary of *The Nerves of Government.*

The best introduction to game theory is Martin Shubik, ed., *Readings in Game Theory and Political Behavior* (Garden City, N.Y.: Doubleday Short Studies in Political Science, 1954). Advanced students should consult the classic work, John Von Neumann and Oscar Morgenstern, *Theory of Games and Economic Behavior* (Princeton: Princeton University Press, 1944). Non–mathematically oriented students may find it hard to follow, however. Other introductions are R. D. Luce and Howard Raiffa, *Games and Decisions: Introduction and Critical Survey* (New York: John Wiley & Sons, 1957) and Richard C. Snyder, "Game Theory and the Analysis of Political Behavior," in Nelson Polsby, et al., eds., *Politics and Social Life* (Boston: Houghton-Mifflin Co., 1963), pp. 130–45. Also useful for introductory purposes is Anatol Rapoport, *Two Person Game Theory: The Essential Ideas* (Ann Arbor: University of Michigan Press, 1966). Among the attempts to apply game theory, or some modification of it, to political phenomena (other than those efforts discussed in this book) are Thomas Schelling, *The Strategy of Conflict* (New York: Oxford Galaxy, 1963), Kenneth Arrow, *Social Choice and Individual Values* (New York: John Wiley & Sons, 1951) and Kenneth Boulding, *Conflict and Defense, A General Theory* (New York: Harper & Row, 1962). The major contribution of the Arrow book is "the voters' paradox" which is adequately summarized in Hayward Alker, *Mathematics and Politics* (New York: The Macmillan Co., 1965), pp. 143–46. Alker's Chapter 7 is another good introduction to game theory.

Chapter 8

The classic statement of functional analysis in comparative politics is Gabriel Almond's introduction to Almond and James Coleman, eds., *The Politics of the Developing Areas* (Princeton: Princeton University Press, 1960), pp. 1–63. Revised formulations of Almond's paradigm may be found in Almond, "A Developmental Approach to Political Systems," *World Politics,* Vol. XVIL, No. 2 (January 1965), pp. 183–214, and in Almond and G. Bingham Powell, *Comparative Politics: A Developmental Approach* (Boston: Little, Brown & Co., 1966). The various Almondian formulations are arranged in chronological order in a single volume: Almond, *Political Development* (Boston: Little, Brown & Co., 1970).

David Apter's use of structural functional analysis is presented most clearly in Apter, *The Politics of Modernization* (Chicago: University of Chicago Press, 1965), Chapter 7, and in Apter, "A Comparative Method for the Study of Politics," *The American Journal of Sociology,* Vol. LXIV, No. 3 (November 1958), pp. 221–37. Another presentation of a functional paradigm for comparative analysis is Robert T. Holt, "A Proposed Structural-Functional Framework," in Charlesworth (New York: The Free Press, 1967), pp. 86–107.

Political scientists working with functionalism have been heavily influenced by the sociologist Marion Levy, *The Structure of Society* (Princeton: Princeton University Press, 1952). Roots of functionalism may also be found in cultural anthropology, for example, A. Radcliffe-Brown, *Structure and Function in a Primitive Society* (New York: The Free Press, 1956) and Radcliffe-Brown, "On the Concept of Function in Social Science" *American Anthropologist,* Vol. XXXVII, No. 3 (July–September 1935), pp. 394–402. Other sociological contributions to functional analysis include F. Y. Sutton, "Social Theory and Comparative Politics," in Harry Eckstein and David Apter, *Comparative Politics, A Reader,* (New York: The Free Press, 1963), pp. 67–81, and D. F. Aberle, et al., "The Functional Prerequisites of Society," *Ethics,* Vol. LX, No. 2 (January 1950), pp. 100–11. The writings of Parsons, cited above, have also contributed to the development of functionalism in political science. The basic work of Robert K. Merton is *Social Theory and Social Structure,* rev. ed. (New York: The Free Press, 1957). Most of the crucial parts of *Social Theory and Social Structure* plus other essays are reprinted in Merton, *On Theoretical Sociology* (New York: The Free Press, 1967).

The best critiques of functional analysis are Carl G. Hempel, "The Logic of Functional Analysis" in Lewellyn Gross, ed., *Symposium or Sociological Theory,* op. cit., pp. 271–307, and in Brodbech, ed., *Readings in the Philosophy of the Social Science,* op. cit., pp. 179–210; William Flanagan and Edwin Fogelman, "Functional Analysis" in Charlesworth, op. cit., pp. 72–85; A. James Gregor, "Political Science and the Uses of Functional Analysis," *The American Political Science Review,* Vol. LXII, No. 2 (June 1968), pp. 425–539; and Alexander J. Groth, "Structural Functionalism and Political Development; Three Problems," *Western Political Quarterly,* Vol. XXIII, No. 3 (September 1970), pp. 485–500.

On social stratification, see William Kornhouser, *The Politics of Mass Society* (New York: The Free Press, 1959) for one of the best-known analyses of the effect of the social structure on politics. Joseph Gusfield, "Mass Society and Extremist Politics," *American Sociological Review,* Vol. XXVII, No. 1 (February 1962), pp. 19–30, critiques Kornhouser's thesis that mass (non-stratified) society is conducive to the rise of political extremism.

Chapter 9

An excellent introductory discussion of the variables included in the concept of political culture and of the importance of the concept for a science of politics may be found in Sidney Verba's concluding chapter to Lucien Pye and Verba, eds., *Political Culture and Political Development* (Princeton: Princeton University Press, 1965). Pye's introduction and several of the country studies are also worthwhile, especially Verba's essay on Germany and Joseph LaPalombara's essay on Italy. Another good introductory discussion of the concept and its components may be found in Samuel Beer's introduction to Beer and Adam Ulam, eds., *Patterns of Government,* 2d. ed. (New York: Random House, 1962), pp. 32–45. The various country studies in the Little, Brown & Co. comparative politics series each contain discussions of that country's political culture and political socialization—for example, Richard Rose, *Politics in England* (1964), Henry Ehrman, *Politics in France,* 2d ed. (1971), Jean Grossholtz, *Politics in the Philippines* (1964), and Leonard Fein, *Politics in Israel* (1967). Gabriel Almond and Sidney Verba, *The Civic Culture* (Princeton: Princeton University Press, 1963) is a must despite certain methodological shortcomings discussed in my Chapter 9. An abridged version, with much of the discussion of methodological considerations omitted but with the substantive material largely intact, is published by Little, Brown & Co. in paperback. The questions and the responses, broken down by country, may be obtained from the Inter-University Consortium for Political Research (Ann Arbor: University of Michigan) in computer printout form. The data decks are also available for reprocessing as are all the data at the consortium.

While the British culture possibly has been subjected to excessive analysis, James Cristolph, "Consensus and Cleavage in British Political Ideology," *The American Political Science Review,* Vol. LIX, No. 3 (September 1965), pp. 629–43, is particularly worthwhile and provocative. While it does not refer specifically to any particular country, Charles E. Lindblom, "The Science of Muddling Through," *Public Administration Review,* Vol. 29, No. 2 (Spring 1959), pp. 79–88, describes the same cultural propensities. This excellent argument for incrementalism is also found, though less blantantly so, in Robert Dahl and Charles Lindholm, *Politics, Economics and Welfare* (New York: Harper & Row, 1953). Students interested in the French political culture should consult Stanley Hoffman, et al., *In Search of France* (Cambridge, Mass.: Harvard University Press, 1963), especially the introductory essay by Hoffman, pp. 1–117. Michel Crozier, *The Bureaucratic Phenomenon* (Chicago: University of Chicago Press, 1964) is a brilliant study of how the French bureaucratic patterns reflect the French political culture. See especially Part 4. Robert Lane, *Political Ideology* (New York: The Free Press,

1962) is an important inquiry into the attitudes held by Americans. There may be some question as to whether his sample is approximately representative of the common man, as alleged, however. See also Lane, *Political Thinking and Political Consciousness* (Chicago: Markham Publishing Co., 1969) for in-depth self-analyses by 24 college students. Aspects of the Italian culture are provocatively explored by Edward Banfield, *The Moral Basis of a Backward Society* (Glencoe, Ill.: The Free Press, 1958). A rebuttal to Banfield's interpretation is Alessandro Pizzorno, "A Moral Familism and Historical Marginality," in Mattei Dogan and Richard Rose, eds., *European Politics: A Reader* (Boston: Little, Brown & Co., 1971), pp. 87–98.

Clifford Geertz has a critical review of Pye's Burma study. Geertz takes issue with Pye's conceptualization of culture as limited to psychological dispositions alone. See Geertz, "A Study of National Character," *Economic Development and Cultural Change*, Vol, XII, No. 2 (January 1964), pp. 205–9.

Insofar as the concept of national character overlaps the concept of political culture, see *National Character in the Perspective of the Social Sciences,* Annals of the American Academy of Political and Social Science (March 1967). See also Alex Inkles and Daniel Levinson, "National Character: The Study of Modal Personality and Socio Cultural Systems," in G. Lindzev, ed., *Handbook of Social Psychology,* Vol. II (Cambridge, Mass.: Addison Wesley, 1954), pp. 977–1020, and Alex Inkles, "National Character and Modern Political Systems," in Francis Hsu, ed., *Psychological Anthropology: Approaches to Culture and Personality* (Homewood, Ill.: The Dorsey Press, 1961), pp. 172–202. Hadley Cantril has done several studies on cross-national dispositional patterns. Among them are *Patterns of Human Concern* (New Brunswick, N.J.: Rutgers University Press, 1965) and *The Politics of Dispair* (New York: Basic Books, 1958).

The best introductory overview of literature on political socialization is Richard Dawson and Kenneth Prewitt, *Political Socialization* (Boston: Little, Brown & Co., 1969). Herbert Hyman, *Political Socialization* (New York: The Free Press, 1959) is usually cited because it was one of the first in the field, but it is now dated and somewhat superficial. It is impossible to summarize the literature consisting of the growing number of studies in this field. Many important articles are collected in Roberta S. Sigel, ed., *Learning About Politics, A Reader in Political Socialization* (New York: Random House, 1970). Robert Hess and Judith Torney, *The Development of Political Attitudes in Children* (Chicago: Aldine Publishing Co., 1967) is a good study of this area with respect to American children.

Chapter 10

The best overview of micro analysis for beginners is Fred T. Greenstein, *Personality and Politics* (Chicago: Markham Publishing Co., 1969). A comprehensive bibliography of the field is Greenstein and Michael Lerner, eds., *A Source Book for the Study of Personality and Politics* (Chicago: Markham Publishing Co., 1971). The best summary of the existing theories of personality is Calvin Hall and Gardiner Lindzey, *Theories of Personality,* 2d ed. (New York: John Wiley & Sons, 1970). An excellent source of important Journal articles is Neil J. and William T. Smelser, eds., *Personality and Social Systems* (New York: John Wiley & Sons, 1963). The major works of Erik Erikson, whose theories form premises for several pieces of micro research—among them, Lucien Pye, *Politics, Personality and Nation Building* (New Haven: Yale University Press, 1962)—are *Childhood and Society* (New York: Norton, 1950); *Young Man Luther* (New York: Norton, 1958); and *Identity and the Life Cycle* (New York: International Universities Press, 1959). For Freud, the complete primary source is James Strachey, ed., *The Standard Edition of the Complete Psychological Works* (London: Hogarth Press, 1953). Calvin Hall, *A Primer of Freudian Psychology* (Cleveland: World Publishing Co., 1954) is a useful introduction to Freud's theories.

The most famous and most well done psychoanalysis of an individual political actor is Alexander and Juliette George, *Woodrow Wilson and Colonel House: A Personality Study* (New York: John Day, 1956). Bernard Brodie, "A Psychoanalytic Interpretation of Woodrow Wilson," *World Politics,* Vol. 9, No. 3. (April 1957), pp. 413–22, discusses the George and George study.

A pioneer in the field of political psychology is Harold Lasswell. His major works in this field are *Power and Personality* (New York: Norton, 1948) and *Psychopathology and Politics* (New York: Vilting Press, 1960). The latter was first published in 1930. See also his *World Politics and Personal Insecurity* (New York: McGraw-Hill Book Co., 1935). Lasswell was interested in the description of character types. His interest in the "democratic character" appears in Harold Lasswell, *Political Writings* (New York: The Free Press, 1951), which also includes his *Psychopathology and Politics* & *Who Gets What, When, How* (Glencoe, Ill.: The Free Press, 1936).

Erich Fromm, *Escape from Freedom* (New York: Holt, Rinehart & Winston, 1941) is a classic attempt to construct an explanation of macro-level events from psychoanalytic premises. It should be read as an example of gross overgeneralization and extensive inference from inadequate and mostly impressionistic data.

The work of Robert Lane, mentioned with respect to the literature on political culture, is also clearly relevant to political psychology, especially his *Political Thinking and Political Consciousness* (Chicago: Markham Publishing Co., 1969).

The beginning student of personality types will find an excellent critical overview of the literature on authoritarianism in Roger Brown, *Social Psychology* (New York: The Free Press, 1965), Chapter 10. Of course, T. W. Adorno, et al., *The Authoritarian Personality* (New York: The Norton Library, 1960) is a must for students interested in this field of study. The best critiques of this landmark study are found in Richard Christie and Marie Johoda, eds., *Studies in the Scope and Method of the Authoritarian Personality* (Glencoe, Ill.: The Free Press, 1954). Especially useful in this volume are Edward Shils, "Authoritarianism, 'Right' and 'Left'," for the argument that Adorno and his associates confuse fascism with general authoritarianism, and Herbert Hyman and Paul Sheatsley, "The Authoritarian Personality, A Methodological Critique." The latter, the best methodological critique of the study, perhaps constitutes an example of critical overkill, however. Milton Rokeach, *The Open and Closed Mind* (New York: Basic Books, 1960) is a careful, systematic attempt to measure a propensity toward dogmatism and opinionation autonomously from the substantive political, social, or economic issues. Thus, Rokeach attempts to satisfy some of the weaknesses of the authoritarian personality study pointed out by Shils's cirtique. See also Richard Christie and Peggy Cook, "Guide to the Published Literature Relating to the Authoritarian Personality Through 1956," *The Journal of Psychology,* Vol. LXV (April 1958), pp. 171–99. An interesting study of social and behavioral characteristics of high scorers on the California F Scale is Morris Janowitz and Dwaine Marvick, "Authoritarianism and Political Behavior" in Smelser and Smelser, op. cit.

Another personality type is David McClelland, *The Achieving Personality* (New York: The Free Press, 1961), a careful and systematic attempt to establish an empirical association between economic development and modal psychological predispositions.

There are a large number of cross-cultural studies of politically relevant psychological variables to be found in the *Journal of Social Psychology* (J.S.P.). Some examples of this body of literature are listed below. A. J. Rabin, "A Comparison of American and Israeli Children by means of a Sentence Completion Technique," *J.S.P.,* Vol. 49., No. 1 (February 1959), pp. 3–12, involves some relevant variables, such as fear, trust, guilt. Lufty N. Diab, "Authoritarianism and Prejudice in Near Eastern Students Attending American Universities," *J.S.P.,* Vol. 50, No. 2 (November 1959), pp. 175–89, relates the California F scale to traditional family ideologies. Diab finds these ideologies only relate to anti-Jewish prejudice and not to other Arab groups. Carol Martin and Robert C. Nichols, "Personality and Religious Belief," *J.S.P.,* Vol. 56, No. 1 (February 1962), pp. 3–8, relates religious belief to authoritarianism. They find a lower (but still significant) correlation than in C. W. Gregory, "The Orthodoxy of the Authoritarian Personality," *J.S.P.,* Vol. 45, No. 2, (May 1957), pp. 217–32. William Ectchardt and Norman Alcock, "Ideology and Conformity in War-Peace Attitudes," *J.S.P.,* Vol. 81, No. 1 (June 1970), pp. 105–16, applies Tomkins ideo-affective resonance theory of a connection between ideological beliefs and such human feelings as compassion to a Canadian sample. See also H. H. Anderson and G. L. Anderson, "Cultural Reactions to Conflict: A Study of Adolescent Children in Seven Countries," in G. M. Gilbert, ed., *Psychological Approaches to Intergroup and International Understanding* (Austin: University of Texas Press, 1956).

Chapter 11

It is impossible to present a comprehensive summary of this vast topic. Good overviews of the dimensions of the literature are Sigmund Neumann, "Toward a Comparative Study of Political Parties," in Neumann, ed., *Modern Political Parties* (Chicago: University of Chicago Press, 1956); David Apter, "Introduction" to Part V in Harry Eckstein and David Apter, ed., *Comparative Politics, A Reader* (New York: The Free Press, 1963); and Neil McDonald, *The Study of Political Parties* (New York: Random House, 1955), Chapter 2. Avery Leiserson, *Parties and Politics* (New York: Alfred A. Knopf, 1958) also provides an overview of the field from a comparative perspective.

Maurice Duverger, *Political Parties,* translated by Barbara and Robert

North (New York: Wiley Science Editions, 1963) is a comprehensive, comparative attempt to typologize parties on the basis of numerous structural variables and to relate the number of parties to electoral systems. Comprehensive and full of suggestive insights, this book is a must for any student of parties. For a more forceful, polemical, and unqualified argument that the proportional electoral systems cause a proliferation of parties and cabinet instability in parliamentary regimes, see Ferdinand A. Hermans, *Europe Under Democracy or Anarchy* (South Bend: University of Notre Dame Press, 1940) or his earlier *Democracy or Anarchy* (South Bend: The Review of Politics, University of Notre Dame Press, 1938). Although this position in its most extreme form has been effectively rebutted in several places, it is incredibly still argued by A. J. Milner, *Elections and Political Stability* (Boston: Little, Brown & Co., 1969). The most effective critique of the election-system-causes-party-system proposition is Aaron Wildavsky, "A Methodological Critique of Duverger's Political Parties," *Journal of Politics,* Vol. XXI, No. 2 (May 1959), pp. 303–18. Proportional representation also has its polemical advocates. Among the best known are Enid Lakeman and James Lambert, *Voting in Democracies* (London: Farber and Farber Ltd., 1955), and J. F. S. Ross, *Elections and Electors* (London: Eyre and Spottiswoode, 1955).

Joseph LaPalombara and Myron Weiner, eds., *Political Parties and Political Development* (Princeton: Princeton University Press, 1966) is an important collection of analytical and substantive articles. Leon Epstein, *Political Parties in Western Democracies* (New York: Praeger, 1967) is a useful and well-known survey with a comparative perspective but limited to traditional structural and logical variables. Neumann, op. cit., contains a collection of country-by-country descriptions of party systems. It is often cited but now somewhat dated. Seymour Lipset and Stein Rokkan, eds., *Party Systems and Voter Alignments* (New York: The Free Press, 1967) contains a more modern set of essays. Robert Dahl, ed., *Political Oppositions in Western Democracies* (New Haven: Yale University Press, 1966) assembles analyses of the dynamics of a number of Western party systems by experts on the respective countries, including some relatively neglected smaller European democracies. Robert McKenzie, *British Political Parties,* rev. ed. (New York: Praeger, 1963) and Samuel Beer, *British Politics in the Collectivist Age* (New York: Alfred A. Knopf, 1965) are studies of the ideology and internal organization of British parties. Beer's book is also noteworthy for his introductory discussion of the historical evolution of aspects of the British political styles. Harry Eckstein, *Division and Cohesion in Democracy; A Study of Norway* (Princeton: Princeton University Press, 1966) contains a good discussion of the Norwegian party system. Louis Overacker, *The Australian Party System* (New Haven: Yale University Press, 1952) and James Jupp, *Australian Party Politics* (Melbourne: Melbourne University Press, 1964) are the two best-known studies of that country's political parties. The best book on Italian parties is Samuel Barnes, *Party Democracy: Politics in an Italian Socialist Federation* (New Haven: Yale University Press, 1967). James Coleman and Carl Rosberg, *Political Parties and National Integration in Tropical Africa* (Berkeley: University of California Press, 1964) is a useful introduction to parties in that area.

Among important and well-known studies of individual political parties are Seymour Lipset, *Agrarian Socialism* (Berkeley: University of California Press, 1950), a study of Canada's C.C.F., and Douglas Chalmers, *The Social Democratic Party of Germany, From Working Class Movement to Modern Political Party* (New Haven: Yale University Press, 1964), the most up-to-date study of that fascinating party.

Among the important articles dealing with ideological trends in European parties are Otto Kirkheimer, "The Transformation of Western European Party Systems," in LaPalombara and Weiner, op. cit., pp. 184–200; Kirkheimer, "The Waning of Opposition in Parliamentary Regimes," *Social Research,* Vol. XXIV, No. 2 (Summer 1957), pp. 127–56; and Robert Tucker, "The Deradicalization of Marxist Regimes," *The American Political Science Review,* Vol. LXI, No. 2 (June 1957), pp. 343–59. The end-of-ideology dialogue is found in Seymour Lipset, *Political Man* (New York: Doubleday Anchor Books, 1960), "The End of Ideology," pp. 439–56; Daniel Bell, *The End of Ideology* (New York: The Free Press, 1961); Joseph LaPalombara, "The End of Ideology: A Dissent and Interpretation," *American Political Science Review,* Vol. LX, No. 1 (March 1966), pp. 5–16; Seymour Lipset, "Some Further Comments on the End of Ideology," *The American Political Science Review,* Vol. LX, No. 1 (March 1966), pp. 17–18; and Lipset, "The Changing Class Structure and European Politics," *Daedalus,* Vol. 93 (1964). A classic in the discussion of ideology is Karl Mannheim, *Ideology and Utopia* (New York: Harcourt, Brace & World, 1963). It is not for beginners, however.

Robert Alford, *Party and Society* (Chicago: Rand McNally, 1963) is a rigorous study of the extent of socioeconomic class-based voting in Anglo-American democracies. Ruth Schacter, "Single-Party Systems in West Africa," *The American Political Science Review,* Vol. LV, No. 2 (June 1961), pp. 294–307, argues that such single party systems may actually contribute toward the eventual development of a democratic political process. Amitai Etzioni, "Alternative Ways to Democracy: The Example of Israel," *Political Science Quarterly,* Vol. LXXIV, No. 2 (June 1959), pp. 196–214, shows how the Israeli party system has a built in responsiveness to public opinion despite one-party dominance. David Truman, "Federalism and the Party System" in Arthur MacMahon, ed., *Federalism Mature and Emergent* (Garden City, New York: Doubleday & Co., 1955), pp. 115–36, is a good nonrigorous overview to the problems of party behavior in federal systems, especially with respect to Anglo-American democracies. Howard A. Scarrow, "The Function of Political Parties: A Critique of the Literature and the Approach," *Journal of Politics,* Vol. XXIX, No. 4 (November 1967), pp. 770–90, is a provocative critique of that approach to the study of parties. Samuel P. Huntington, "Social and Institutional Dynamics of One Party Systems" in Samuel Huntington & Barrington H. Moore, *Authoritarian Politics in Modern Society* (New York: Basic Books, 1960), pp. 3–47, is one of the best discussions of such systems. Huntington is one of the most lucid writers in the discipline.

Anthony Downs, *An Economic Theory of Democracy* (New York: Harper & Row, 1957) is the closest thing available to a theory of parties in democratic systems. It is a must for students of parties.

Chapter 12

Gabriel Almond and James Coleman, eds., *The Politics of the Developing Areas* (Princeton: Princeton University Press, 1960) contains, in addition to Almond's now classic functional paradigm, still one of the best overall analyses of each of the non-Western areas by an expert in that area. Almond's theoretical writings on the topic are collected and arranged chronologically in *Political Development* (Boston: Little, Brown & Co., 1970). The most recent of Almond's conceptualization and theorizing on this subject is fully set forth in Almond and G. Bingham Powell, *Comparative Politics: A Developmental Approach* (Boston: Little, Brown & Co., 1966). The best known static, dichotomous typology of political systems into developed and underdeveloped categories is Lucien Pye, "The Non-Western Political Process," *Journal of Politics,* Vol. XX, No. 3 (August 1958), pp. 468–86. Other such typologies are George Kahin, Guy Paukes, and Lucien Pye, "Comparative Politics of Non-Western Countries," *The American Political Science Review,* Vol. XLIX, No. 4 (December 1955), pp. 1022–41, and Fred Riggs, "Agraria and Industria," in William J. Siffen, ed., *Toward The Comparative Study of Public Administration* (Bloomington: University of Indiana Press, 1959), pp. 23–110. See Alfred Diamant, "Is There a Non-Western Political Process? Comments on Lucien Pye's The Non-Western Political Process," *Journal of Politics,* Vol. XXI (February 1959), pp. 123–27, for a critique of Pye. Gideon Sjoberg distinguishes two types of non-Western systems in "Folk and Feudal Societies," *American Journal of Sociology,* Vol. LVIII, No. 3 (November 1952), pp. 231–39.

Lucien Pye's ideas on the concept of political development are clearly presented in Pye, *Aspects of Political Development* (Boston: Little, Brown & Co., 1966). David Apter's ideas on the concept as well as on the process itself are brought together in *The Politics of Modernization* (Chicago: University of Chicago Press, 1965). Pye, *Politics, Personality and Nation Building* (New Haven: Yale University Press, 1962) attempts to relate putative psychoanalytic characteristics of significant Burmese political actors to patterns of Burmese political development, albeit in a more impressionistic than systematic fashion. For the stage theory, unilinear or historicist conceptions of development, see W. W. Rostow, *The Stages of Economic Growth* (London: Cambridge University Press, 1960) and Kenneth Organiski, *The Stages of Political Development* (New York: Alfred A. Knopf, 1965).

The two best-known works on transitional political systems are Fred Riggs, *Administration in Developing Countries: The Theory of the Prismatic Society* (Boston: Houghton-Mifflin Co., 1964) and David Apter, *The Politics of Modernization* (Chicago: University of Chicago Press, 1965). Apter's book is full of theoretic insights suggestive of logical relations between normative, structural, and behavioral variables. It is a must in the field. Riggs's book purports to treat how administrative and nonadministrative variables interact in the non-Western world. However, due to Riggs's proclivity for neologisms, the book not only makes for tedious reading but tends at times to degenerate into lists of definitions.

The most sophisticated conceptualization of political development may be Samuel Huntington, "Political Development and Political Decay," *World*

Politics, Vol. XVII, No. 2 (April 1965), pp. 386–430. Huntington's ideas on this expanded in a very perceptive and readable book, *Political Order in a Changing Society* (New Haven: Yale University Press, 1968). Other conceptions of development, free from the early pitfalls of ethnocentrism and unilinearity but difficult to operationalize, may be found in S. N. Eisenstadt, "Bureaucracy and Political Development," in Joseph LaPalombara, ed., *Bureaucracy and Political Development* (Princeton: Princeton University Press, 1963), pp. 96–119, and in Alfred Diamant, "Political Development: Approaches to Theory and Strategy," in John Montgomery and William Siffin, eds., *Approaches to Development, Politics, Administration and Change* (New York: McGraw-Hill Book Co., 1966), pp. 25–26. Princeton University Press has issued a whole series on the subject of political development, as follows: Lucien Pye, ed., *Communications and Political Development* (1963); Joseph LaPalombara, ed., *Bureaucracy and Political Development* (1963); Robert Ward and Dantewart Rustow, eds., *Political Modernization in Japan and Turkey* (1964); James Coleman, ed., *Education and Political Development* (1965); Sidney Verba and Lucien Pye, eds., *Political Culture and Political Development* (1965); and Joseph LaPalombara and Myron Weiner, eds., *Political Parties and Political Development* (1966). These are collections of articles by "name" scholars either of a "think piece" analytical nature or descriptive of the relevant process and institutions in one foreign country. They are not data oriented. The work by McClelland cited above is the best empirical attempt to explain industrialization. Karl Deutsch, "Social Mobilization and Political Development," *The American Political Science Review,* Vol. LV, No. 3 (September 1961), pp. 493–514, is the best attempt to specify indicators for one aspect of modernization.

J. J. Johnson, ed., *The Role of the Military in Underdeveloped Countries* (Princeton: Princeton University Press, 1962) is the best coverage of this problem. A classic study of patterns of colonialism is J. G. Furnivall, *Colonial Policy and Practice* (New York: New York University Press, 1956). Furnivall compares indirect rule in Indonesia with direct rule in Burma with much sympathy for the former. It was first published in 1928. The two best analyses of the interaction of nationalism and communism in the non-Western world are John A. Kautsky, "An Essay on the Politics of Development," in Kautsky, ed., *Political Change in Underdeveloped Countries* (New York: John Wiley & Sons, 1962), pp. 3–122, and J. A. Brimmel, *Communism in South East Asia* (New York: Oxford University Press, 1967). A. Doak Barnett, ed., *Communist Strategies in Asia* (New York: Praeger, 1959) provides a comparison of the Russian and Chinese revolutionary strategies and a good historical summary of the activity of communist parties and insurgents in various Asian countries. Rupert Emerson, *From Empire to Nation* (Cambridge, Mass.: Harvard University Press, 1960) is a well-known discussion of the development of nationalist movements.

General

When first published, Harry Eckstein and David Apter, eds., *Comparative Politics, A Reader* (New York: The Free Press, 1963) was the best reader in the field. Although it is now becoming somewhat dated, it still contains many valuable articles. Roy Macridis and Bernard Brown, *Comparative Politics, Notes and Readings* (Homewood, Ill.: The Dorsey Press, 1969) is the most up-to-date reader. However, the articles contained in it are abridged to a considerable extent. Roy Macridis, *The Study of Comparative Government of Politics* (New York: Random House, 1955) is useful as a general introduction to the field for beginning undergraduates. Peter Merhl, *Modern Comparative Politics* (New York: Holt, Rinehart and Winston, 1970) is an introductory survey of substantive problems in the field. For methodological considerations in the field, see Robert Holt and John Turner, eds., *The Methodology of Comparative Research* (New York: The Fress Press, 1970) or Adam Przeworski and Henry Teune, *The Logic of Comparative Social Inquiry* (New York: Wiley Interscience, 1970). Both books are aimed at a fairly advanced level. The former is a book of readings on a disparate variety of theoretic and mechanical issues of cross-national research. The latter is a more coherent discussion of the logic of comparison and problems of equivalence and measurement in cross-cultural research. Richard Merritt, *Systematic Approaches to Comparative Politics* (Chicago: Rand McNally, 1970) is the best survey and discussion of the use of aggregate and survey data in cross-national research. It is an excellent introductory source of what kinds of empirical data are available for cross-national comparison. Richard Merritt and Stein Rohkan, eds., *Comparing Nations: The Use of Quantitative Data in Cross-National Research* (New Haven: Yale University Press, 1966) is a significant collection of empirical studies and analytical articles.

Arthur Banks and Robert Textor, *A Cross Polity Survey* (Cambridge, Mass.: M.I.T. Press, 1963) and Bruce M. Russett, et al., *World Handbook of Social and Political Indicators* (New Haven: Yale University Press, 1964) are the best compilations of cross-national aggregate data.

Index

This book has been set in 10 and 9 point Times Roman, leaded 2 points. Part numbers and titles are in 24 point Univers Medium. Chapter numbers are in 30 point Venus Bold Extended and chapter titles are in 24 point Univers Medium. The size of the type page is 27 by 45½ picas.